REVIVAL AND REBELLION IN COLONIAL CENTRAL AFRICA

Revival and Rebellion in Colonial Central Africa

Karen E. Fields

HEINEMANN
Portsmouth, NH

Heinemann
A division of Reed Elsevier Inc.
361 Hanover Street
Portsmouth, NH 03801-3912
Offices and agents throughout the world

Library of Congress Cataloging-in-Publication Data
is on file at the Library of Congress

Editor: *Jean Hay*
Production: *J. B. Tranchemontagne*
Manufacturing: *Elizabeth Valway*
Cover design: *Melissa Inglis*

Printed in the United States of America on acid-free paper
00 99 98 97 DA 1 2 3 4 5 6 7 8 9

FOR MY PARENTS,
LILLIAN AND ROBERT FIELDS
AND FOR MY TEACHER,
EGON BITTNER

Any attempt to preach a purer religion must go along with attempts at social reform.

ARNOLD TOYNBEE

CONTENTS

ILLUSTRATIONS

(following page 176)

MAPS

(Reprinted from Robert I. Rotberg, *The Rise of Nationalism in Central Africa: The Making of Malawi and Zambia, 1873-1964*, Cambridge, Mass., Harvard University Press, 1965, courtesy of the press and the author.)

TABLES

PREFACE TO THE HEINEMANN EDITION

The very phrase "Apocalypse now!" rivets the imagination. This book about the African Watchtower movement began more than two decades ago, when my own imagination was riveted by stories of New Jerusalems defiantly built in twentieth-century colonies. Here were locales in which predictions that the world would soon end undid political order. Why, I asked, did religion in colonized societies have a political valence, so to speak, and the capacity to form explosive compounds? What mechanisms, at work under what conditions, produced the incongruous joining of my title: Revival and Rebellion? How did prophecy, talking in tongues, and revival preachers' catalogs of individual sin flow into strikes, boycotts, tax resistance, opposition amid two deadly wartime mobilizations—and, indeed, into explicit challenges to the jurisdiction of the state?

I thought of my project as historical and ethnographic. Close description at a double remove of space and time would help me pose general questions about the relationships between two dynamic claimants to the fundamental organization of collective life: religion and politics. Since, as seemed obvious then, millenarian religion was extinct as a political force in the West, the remoteness of my immediate subject went without saying. This was to be a book about an exotic kind of movement in the exotic institutional context of the colonial state. So I plunged into reading dusty British archives about spectacular preachers with resonant biblical names—for example, a certain Shadrach who led one of the many rebellions that exploded worldwide in the turbulent aftermath of World War I. One fact mitigated the dustiness, however. Charles Taze Russell, founder of the Watchtower Bible and Tract Society and inheritor of William Miller's Adventism, in the 1870s had begun the countdown toward Armageddon, predicted to begin in 1914. Old publications by Russell and his brethren showed me that Shadrach's preaching had not only an American lineage but also living American kin.

Still, the script of Shadrach's actual campaign against private sin and an oppressive state was an ancient artifact: intense preaching about the fateful choice between salvation and the doomed satanic world; converts' severing themselves from unconverted kin and from ungodly political allegiance; the community of new sisters and brothers becoming an obnoxious state

within a state; opposition that fulfills prophecy; prophecy that both pre-
dicts and provokes a final battle; the unsaved laying siege; the saved preparing to make the supreme sacrifice; the countdown. "Bring maxim guns!"
shouted the followers of Shadrach. "Talk will not move us." They did not
move until, after long deliberation, the state resorted to force. That script
seems antique still, but no longer remote. To evoke it today is to evoke
American names.

Back in the 1970s, however, Americans had not yet encountered news
about the preachers Jim Jones and David Koresh, or revisited Max Weber's
classical concept of "charisma" in its initial religious sense. We had not yet
been forced to ponder the dynamics by which such communities come to
threaten the jurisdiction of states, or to imagine how far-reaching the political repercussions of millenarian countdowns and final battles can be. Nor,
more importantly, had a shift in America's mainstream yet exposed to general notice other feathers of its religious life. Still largely unnoticed were
the political valences of the less extreme but deeply rooted American
revival traditions that nurtured Jones and Koresh, their followers, and
many thousands of others. But, noticed or not, those traditions had never
stopped inspiring ordinary preachers less reckless than those two men but
not necessarily of lesser conviction. In the 1990s, ordinary congregations
inspired by those same traditions are now extraordinarily visible. Old
voices of those enthusiastically building spiritual and moral New
Jerusalems in Africa have American echoes. Today it is commonplace to
witness the joining of congregational forms such as prophesying and talking in tongues to political purposes from tax protest to the legal re-empow-
erment of traditional family norms. Indeed, in a development that was
hardly thinkable two decades ago, mobilized congregations have succeeded in projecting the term "sin" onto the public surface of America's
political discourse.

Back then, it was easy to miss the political valences of those traditions.
Sociology was operating, by and large, with conceptual instruments that
missed or dismissed them. At the same time, America's public norms of
keeping church and state separate, in tandem with private norms against
mixing religion with "worldly" politics, supposed that what was to be pur-
posely kept separate was separate inherently. In any case, those valences
are hard to detect where congregational practice seeks to transform the
world by cultivating emotionally charged experiences of withdrawal from
it. But even then, I submit, the core vision of revival practice—that of a
transformed world emptied of sin and oppression—is politically electric,
able to create heat as well as light. Consider this: A British magistrate con-

trasted the singing and shouting of the Shadrach episode with the "harm-less Negro camp meetings" of the American South. Now recall that Martin Luther King and the Southern Christian Leadership Conference attacked the Jim Crow South's old-time politics by redeploying its old-time religion.

The axis of sociology's own real world turned at a great distance from the "Bible Belt" reality shared by King and his opponents in the 1950s and 1960s. Mainstream sociologists debated Weber's thesis that the intellectual essence of modernity is "rationalization," regarding its institutional essence in the public realm as secularization. The declining significance of religion seemed to follow. Moreover, conceptual dichotomies, such as rational/non-rational (or irrational) and instrumental/expressive, tended to shape in their own image our understanding of religion and politics as they exist on the ground. But in the real real world, what was religious was not necessarily non-instrumental, non-rational, or non-modern. I thought the SCLC's political-religious mobilization imposed limits on the evolutionary contentions and on the simplifying concepts attached to them. Besides, such notions easily led to the kind of circular argument that abounded in the literature on Africa's millenarian movements: Consequences predefined as non-rational, irrational, non-modern, or expressive had non-rational, irrational, non-modern, or expressive causes. More adequate conceptions seemed called for.

In *Revival and Rebellion* I explore the concept of rationality throughout, while pushing the instrumental/expressive dichotomy to its extremes. At one extreme, I focus on precisely the kind of emotional religiosity that would seem most apolitical because of its preoccupation with deliverance from worldly evil. But the stories show how this-worldly conflicts tend to flow naturally from the pursuit of other-worldly interests. They bear out Max Weber's contention that physically separate community is the logical culmination of practice that cultivates and here-and-now emotional experience of salvation. The possibilities for what happens next run the full range from official permission to official destruction—and from the grim, once-only millenarian countdown toward the Last Day to the fortifying and cathartic, but politically sublimated, weekly watch-night shout. We can say, then, that the inherent paradox of religious otherworldliness is the practical fact of its collective existence in this world. Salvation takes up space. And space for it is allocated differently by different political regimes.

Political power as organized by the colonial state had limited space for religiously motivated attempts at transformation. At my other extreme, then, are the unemotive, calculating, self-aware, and thoroughly pragmatic improvisations of a state built to perpetuate conquest. If an instrumental turn of mind characterizes states in general, even in democratic societies,

Revival and Rebellion reveals the colonial form of authoritarian state as hyper-instrumental and hyper-political. Even so, the inherent paradox of political this-worldliness is the appetite all states have for belief. Colonial officials tackled the problem of state power nakedly, as the problem of creating power without the constant use or threat of force. Universally, that means invoking legitimacy, a sanction for rule built, in Weber's terms, on matched inner dispositions: belief that it is one's right to command and belief that it is right and one's duty to obey. But because recent conquest entailed no direct access to legitimacy in that sense, officials proceeded not by organizing public consent but by coopting private constraint, as deployed through the cultural machineries of religiously legitimated power. To forestall the atrophy of inner controls so as to keep policing minimal, they worked to improvise state power in the ordered spaces of life. Congregations like Shadrach's claimed those spaces for the spirit.

Prepare now to meet him and his colleagues, their congregations, and their opponents. Consider them all, Africans and Britons, fellow travelers through the modern world of the twentieth century, meeting challenges and perplexities not so different or distant from ours as to contain no lessons for our own present. And since pragmatic British officials saw the inherent drawbacks of religious freedom, think of colonial struggles over the demarcation of religion from politics as particularly instructive. The presence of such struggles, not their absence, defines secular society in America today. Finally, as the second millennium ends, we will witness more shouts of "Apocalypse now!" and face the public quandaries they raise. American law enforcers will get to the point of finding out what dates for Apocalypse are being pronounced, where, by and to whom—just as the British opponents of Shadrach and his colleagues did. If any of them were alive to read the 31 December 1996 cover article in the National Review, "End of the World—Closer Than Ever Before," they would have a great deal to say.

—Karen E. Fields

ACKNOWLEDGMENTS

In writing this book I have incurred many debts: to James Ault, Barbara Fields, Gila Hayim, John Higginson, Wellington Nyangoni, and George Ross, for reading many versions of the manuscript; to Evan Harriman and the late Margaret Hazard, for typing and retyping through many drafts; to Sally Alexander and Sam Geza, for hospitality in London and Lusaka; to Stephanie Sjoman, for sharing with me her reading, as a Jehovah's Witness, of the Bible; to Kenneth John McCracken, Fergus Macpherson, Andrew Ross, and Jaap Van Velsen, for sharing with me their knowledge about missions; to Sholto J. Cross, Harry Langworthy, and Margaret Read for letting me read unpublished works of theirs; to Nancy Jay, for offering inspired insight into the nature of ritual; to Moussa Bagate, for unending encouragement; to Marilyn Aaron, Joyce Scardina, and Gerda Van Duin, for practical solutions to practical problems of writing a book; to the staffs of the National Archives of Zambia and the National Library of Scotland, for often knowing before I did what I had better look at; and to anonymous citizens of Zambia and the United Kingdom, for their many kindnesses, large and small, to an anonymous foreigner.

I am grateful to have received, from the Sachar International Center, Brandeis University, and from the Social Science Research Council, fellowships that have assisted my ongoing research about missionary enterprise.

REVIVAL AND REBELLION IN COLONIAL CENTRAL AFRICA

INTRODUCTION: THE NATIVE
WITH THE GOLD TEETH

O NE AUTUMN AFTERNOON in 1918, a Catholic priest of the Kayambi Mission was traveling along a wilderness path in the Isoka District of Zambia. He traveled with the band of African helpers that was usual for the time and place—people to carry baggage, to show the way and translate if need be, to assist in hunting and, generally, to keep the man of God company in the unceasing pastoral travel that was his duty to his flock. Sometimes missionaries arranged to be carried by their African helpers in shaded palanquins. But this particular missionary may well have walked; he belonged to the Society of Missionaries of the Venerable Geronimo, an order renowned for the hardihood of its brethren. The priest, a certain Father Tanguy, wore the long white cassock that set his order apart wherever they worked in Africa and that eventually gave the society its popular name, the White Fathers.

Besides wearing his white habit, Father Tanguy carried a hippopotamus-hide whip—a *cikoti*, in local parlance; or, possibly, one of the helpers carried the *cikoti* for him. Tanguy also carried a gun. Some thirty years after the imposition of colonial rule in Zambia, guns did little further service in aiding the propagation of the Gospel or the movement of the Gospel's spokesmen. Let us imagine, therefore, that the gun was to be used if the band was set upon by a lion, say, or in case the band decided to set upon some wilderness creature for supper, but not in the ordinary event against bellicose villagers. However, the close of 1918 was a season of extraordinary events. Both the gun and the whip figured in a serendipity of this particular journey.

Father Tanguy happened upon a man preaching excitedly in the wilderness. "Take care, God is great," cried the preacher. "Pray to God alone!" And then occurred something that may at first appear improbable. Tanguy took exception to these seemingly unexceptionable Christian injunctions. Calling them seditious, he had his foreman order the man to desist; but the man set loose a torrent

ls, which the priest could not understand. Tanguy
ɔ arrest the man. This task turned out to be harder
ɔan he had supposed, for while the inhabitants of
e failed to receive the priest or his purpose in the
ɔɪᴏn to which he was accustomed, they welcomed the
ɔacher, who quickly escaped into their rather noisy protection.
Five minutes later, the man began preaching again, whereupon
Tanguy raised his gun and fired a shot into the air. Immediately
a voice rose. "A gun has killed me!" And then rose many voices in
a general hubbub. Since the authorities of the village gave no help,
it was only with the aid of his African fellow travelers that Tanguy
managed to free the man from the villagers and make good the
arrest. When the group reached the nearest outpost of the district
administration, they found no one. Unable to hand the preacher
over from churchly to civil power, and unable to continue his journey with the preacher in custody, Tanguy had no choice but to
improvise. He gave his captive a stern warning and five lashes with
the *cikoti* and then released him.

Upon returning to Kayambi, Tanguy hurried to inform the local
justice of the peace about the incident. The preacher had not only
insisted upon God's majesty and upon the necessity of prayer to
him, but he had also been telling his flock, "Stop tree cutting, there
is something behind; you will die in nine days; you who are polygamists, leave your wives; leave your cattle." In the same statement before the JP, Tanguy recounted the angry speech he had
not understood at the time. It was so foul that the helpers had
evaded giving him a translation until their arrival back at their base.
Even then, he said, they translated reluctantly and perhaps incom-
pletely. That in itself gave cause for worry. Worse, the preacher
was not acting alone. A certain Shadrach Sinkala had baptized him
and others. These were dangerous men, Tanguy concluded, and
it was up to the authorities to stop them.[1]

What I have just recounted was a common sort of alarm that lit
and relit colonial Central Africa—the countries that are now Malawi, Zimbabwe, Zambia, and Zaire (and that formerly were the
colonies of Nyasaland, Southern Rhodesia, Northern Rhodesia,
and the Belgian Congo). These alarms, the revivals they reported,
and the rebellions the alarms signaled are the subject of this book.
They are queer alarms, in that they reveal twentieth-century men
bristling at threats of supernatural harm. And the queer alarms
signaled queer rebellions, in that whatever violence was envisaged
would be God's, not that of angry men and women. Tanguy re-

ported "sedition" and feared worse, but he could report no attempt by the villagers to turn the tables and "arrest" him, although they surely outnumbered the priest's traveling party. Thus Tanguy reacted neither to actual violence nor to the threat of it, but rather to a certain kind of talk with and about God. He was neither the first nor the last to do so.

The talk was the talk of the Watchtower movement, whose ideas percolated into remote African hinterlands from their place of origin in the United States. In Part 2 I shall describe this remarkable American export in greater detail. Here, suffice it to say that the late-nineteenth-century prophecies of a Pennsylvanian, Charles Taze Russell, gave rise to an African genus of revival that repeatedly undid the calm of colonial Malawi and Zambia, the societies with which this study is mainly concerned. As Watchtower revivals succeeded one another between 1907, when they first appeared in Malawi, and World War II, missionaries, settlers, colonial officials, customary rulers, and non-Watchtower Christians had to come to grips with Watchtower talk—its praying, its charismatic healing and "talking in the unknown tongue," above all, its prophesying that the world would end soon and, with it, colonial rule. There would be no more taxes, forced labor, confiscation of property, arrogant foreigners, false religion, and senseless laws. There would be peace and plenty in a millennial Kingdom of God on earth. For all this the Bible, and particularly the Book of Revelation, provided abundant authority.

Watchtower talk indicated moral regeneration as well. Although the wrongs of the colonial system would be righted by God in the final Consummation, Africans were to prepare for the day by purifying themselves and their communities of sin and immorality. In classic millenarian style, Watchtower preachers insisted that only those who had shown themselves obedient to God's commandments would survive the coming convulsion and inherit "a new heaven and a new earth." The faithful must accept Christianity, by undergoing baptism and agreeing to live by its rules. There must be no lying, cheating, killing, or stealing. There must be no covetousness, hatred, adultery, or idol worship. And the faithful must also renounce the practice of witchcraft. In these teachings, missionaries heard their own repeated literally, but with a charismatic intensity that disconcerted them. And they heard their own proclamation of God's ultimate triumph preached with an immediacy of which they could not approve. Their reaction was not pleasure in the evident success of their work but apprehension about its growth through the efforts of preachers independent of them. The promise of the millennium is a powerful political idea, and Christian establishments going back to the time of Saint Augustine have sought to denature it.

In Central Africa, movements combining the ambitions of moral regeneration and political revolution had far-reaching political consequences, even though they did not create large-scale political organizations to evict the colonizers and seize control of the colonial state. Secular militants, not millenarian believers in divine intervention, won this historic victory. But even though they preached that God would do the main work of revolution, Central African millenarians shook the colonial regime again and again. The fact that they succeeded in doing so is remarkable. Typically, millenarian belief does not prescribe revolutionary action.[2] Views of the "world turned upside down" may be quite radical and yet remain in the dream visions of a believer or group of believers. Or they may lend drama to esoteric cult rites insulated from society at large. Again, a revolutionary crusade against injustice without may be turned entirely against sin within. In many circumstances, the excitement of mass revival creates color without fireworks. But in Central Africa, millenarians generated a continuing threat to order. Part of my problem is to show that this was so and to uncover the reasons.

Five years after Father Tanguy sounded his alarm against prophesying in the Northern Province of what is now Zambia, new alarms began circulating in the central part of the country. One of those reporting was the Reverend Mr. Moffat, of the Scottish Free Church mission at Chitambo, who communicated his worries to the secretary for native affairs. "Dear Mr. Taggart," Moffat began,

> I am sure you know that I am not an alarmist and I have no desire to enter their ranks. At the same time I am sure that it is my duty to write and tell you of what I have seen and heard in connection with the Watchtower men who have started their propaganda in the district.

After describing an encounter with two of the preachers, in which he "showed them their folly," Moffat continued, "I did not feel much concerned after my talk with them and thought it would fizzle out."

Apparently, however, he did not immediately calculate how much men like the antagonist of Father Tanguy might accomplish behind the backs of missionaries and administrators, in villages away from direct observation by whites, and in the bush. Tanguy had met the preacher he arrested and flogged only because he happened to have been abroad in the wilderness. Moffat learned of other preachers because mission employees came to Chitambo to inform him. He in turn told them not of the "folly" in Watchtower prophecy but of its "seriousness."

> [I]n the morning . . . our senior teacher came to speak and said they were afraid this teaching was going to cause much trouble. . . . I took the opportunity to impress upon them the seriousness of this propaganda, and urged them to get a clear knowledge of the teaching . . . and to report to the Boma [administrative headquarters].

Nor were the morning reports of a besetting danger all. These worrisome prophesiers kept turning up.

> When I got back to the station I was met by two men from Chisengalumbwe's Village. They had come in to report that these two preachers . . . held very emotional services . . . the result being that nearly all the village, including the chief, has joined them.[3]

Although Tanguy did not say, we may speculate that the headman who did not come to his aid had been converted—that the Watchtower there, as at Chisengalumbwe's, had found the means to convert a ranking pagan; that it, too, had conquered its Clovis.

At approximately the same time that these mass conversions were occurring in cental Zambia, a worried African Christian farther south addressed a query to the magistrate at Mazabuka. He wished to know which preachings of a certain Shadrack were worthy of belief.

> Please am asking you shall this year 1924 the whole world finish? It says that God will start now to judge, is it so? Shadrack at Pemba . . . he is baptizing people, he also states that Jesus is on earth here. He is judging you Boma people and other missions. Free Church all of you there is a rock on your heads and you will be smashed up.[4]

I found no record of a reply. But although administrators found the prophecies unworthy of belief, they did not fail to take the prophesiers seriously. They carried on a great deal of correspondence, year after year, regarding the purveyors of Watchtower humbug, as some called it. The supernatural threat activated mundane police.

Each time a new wave of millenarian excitement broke over some locality, the man on the spot tracked the preachers as best he could, often without investigative resources surpassing those of Tanguy or Moffat, and commonly with the help of men like them, as well as that of loyal chiefs and headmen or troubled mission Christians. Not only did the man on the spot arrest and prosecute the prophesiers whenever he could catch them, but he shared with his colleagues what impressions he had formed as to the existence, or not, of a territory-wide, conspiratorial organization. Was the Watchtower merely a religious disguise in which anticolonial politics stalked the land? Although repeatedly answered in the negative, this question loomed throughout the 1920s and 1930s. The issue was reopened more than once.

As a matter of more immediately practical import, the man on the spot also had to take into account the fear of white settlers. Some of their fear reflected the humdrum reality of colonial economic life and labor, and some was stranger. What was stranger reflected an anxiety that is indigenous to the collective psychology of colonizing minorities. What was humdrum did not necessarily take a form that is familiar to Westerners of the twentieth century. In 1924-1925, workers animated by Watchtower prophecy of "a new heaven and a new earth" hurried to accept Watchtower baptism unto hope and the remission of sin. Many then hurried home, there to await the End in purity. Waiting instead of working, they in effect went on strike. Many farmers in the designated "European farming area" along the Zambian railway line loudly complained about the economic impact of baptism, and courts examined preachers charged with inciting the cessation of work.

For their part, the preachers vaunted the apotropaic qualities of the baptism they gave. When employees of the settler J. E. Stephenson delivered themselves from evil by undergoing baptism, Stephenson nastily remarked that they need not have delivered themselves from his employ as well. If they felt themselves foul, he continued, he would gladly invite them to use his neighbor's cattle-dipping tank, "for sure riddance of bugs, fleas, lice and ticks."[5] Whistling Dixie a bit: Stephenson also admitted the fear of being "murdered in bed" or "bearded in my barn" by people who had stolen away to be baptized. In the nature of things, given a colonial setting, when the economic danger of prophecy occupied the foreground, the political threat was rarely far behind. Since

Africans enjoyed no right to strike, whenever refusal to work seemed in any way collective or principled, it inevitably portended something more.

But the oddity of Watchtower revival and rebellion is that its adherents never attempted what the settlers feared most. Mass baptisms, emotional services, and apocalyptic prophecy were the core of Watchtower revival wherever it occurred. Whenever it occurred, the opponents of the Millennium watched apprehensively as preachers foretold Christ's return to earth and as the faithful flexed their political muscle by praying and by being baptized. An informer told Stephenson that he had overheard Watchtower adherents discussing ways of equitably dividing among themselves his orchard, farm, house, and other property in God's New Era. Stephenson conveyed this distressing news to the local administration. But although the informer had eavesdropped upon a private conversation, he reported no decision to take the path of violent rebellion. The Watchtower men apparently satisfied themselves with believing and propagating belief, placing their full reliance upon God's future work and, in the meantime, purifying their communities of sin.

In 1926, settlers learned the full story of a preacher calling himself the Son of God, who had used the rite of baptism in a witch-killing campaign (an episode to be recounted fully in Chapter 5). Although the victims were African villagers (and extensive investigation uncovered no evidence that white targets were ever considered), Stephenson called the incident "as near an approach to rebellion as will be without the actuality occurring."[6] And, characteristically, he continued to note in ominous terms that Africans were reluctant to work for him, even to assist in hunting, a preferred sort of employment.[7] To Stephenson, the Son of God was a dangerous rebel; those who explained the incident as simply an awful manifestation of "native superstition" deluded themselves. Naturally, it brought scant reassurance to many in Stephenson's position to be told that Watchtower adherents did not glow with the revolutionary's fervor in militant action, but instead, with the believer's hope of supernatural deliverance.

Settlers feared worse things than hope. Following World War I, the colonial administration had sold large tracts of land to white immigrants wishing to begin anew under the favorable conditions of cheap land and labor made cheap by fiat.[8] Africans began again, too—as the losers. Landownership in the areas designated "European farming areas" transformed the previously independent owners into squatters, rent payers, and hired hands subject to the will of persons who were making themselves virtual squires. From the vantage point of the "manor houses" on these lands, religious ceremonies in the surrounding bush conjured up the "native rising bogey," as one official said. The nocturnal ambience of many ceremonies served to underline the point. Not surprisingly, false alarms of a coming bloodbath and factual reports of amazing prophecy jostled one another in the offices of colonial police and administrators.

If the subject of this study is a series of strange alarms signaling an unfamiliar sort of rebellion, the subject is also the colonizers' impassioned and sometimes contradictory response to it. Perhaps the strangest alarms were the rumors about "America," who was to come and rescue the people. America would bring a mighty army at the end of the world—and in 1924, the End was said to be imminent. According to J. W. Hinds, a legal officer, the Afrikaner settlers along the line-of-rail bore main responsibility for fanning the rumor into white-hot panic. (Malcolm Moffat meant to dissociate himself from this group by proclaiming, "I am not an alarmist. . . .") As it spread through the little community of jumpy settlers, this story incarnated the God of Watchtower prophecy: America was made man, an African whose distinguishing mark was some man-made dentition. The following year, amid renewed excitement, Hinds had this to say about the incident:

> The Dutch raise yearly the native rising bogey. They talk a lot. In this way rumors are spread, fancies become fact, a refractory farm hand a rebel, and so on ad lib. Last year we had an example in the native with the gold teeth scare who thoroughly scared the whole sub-district. All this I know is extremely childish and silly, but the worst of it is the natives themselves know the white man's weakness and undoubtedly laugh at us.[9]

Hinds laid the blame for an undignified excitement at the doorstep of Boer immigrants, whose white skin did not quite raise them to the same category as their British counterparts. While declaring himself "personally not worried," he nevertheless pinpointed a psychological danger: the supposed nearness of America had made "the whole sub-district" feel in full blast the *frisson* that always chills settler conditions; the Africans lived near enough not only to see the settlers scurry for protection but also to see what protection they got. Even if Hinds was right to insist that there was nothing to fear but fear itself, and however roundly he condemned the alarmists' exaggerations, he could not and did not choose inaction. He proposed that a certain Kumwenda, an African detective, "might with advantage become a leading light in the movement."

While the star of America loomed on the horizon, colonial administrators and police followed it. In 1924, they had tracked America along the line-of-rail. In March of that year, during his trial for illegal preaching, Isaac Nyasulo had occasion to tell a court, "I don't know the colour of the people in America. I don't know a native called America, with gold in his teeth, I never heard of him." And J. B. Manda, arrested on similar charges, told his questioners, "I don't know a native called America."[10] Thereafter America's pursuers turned westward toward the Zambian and Zairian copperbelts. They were still on the lookout for him five years later, when they at last arrested two men, one of whom was suspected of being the fabulous America. Both told the police that the man sought was hundreds of miles away, in the south of the country. The America the police at last reached had every appearance of being an ordinary workman, quietly and respectably employed in the town of Livingstone, by the shores of the Zambezi.[11]

George Shepperson has suggested that the American origin of Watchtower prophecy and America's decisive role in World War I may have combined with two other elements to create this remarkable myth.[12] The first is a much-publicized tour in 1924 by the Ghanaian educator James K. Aggrey on behalf of the Phelps-Stokes Fund. His purpose was to survey the possibilities of black advancement in Africa through schooling along the lines suggested by experiments in the southern United States. The second is the possibility that workers spread garbled reports about the coming ships of Marcus Garvey's Black Star Line, as they traveled along the huge southern African circuit of migrant labor—the Lupa gold fields in Tanzania, the Rand gold mines in South Africa, the Wankie Colliery in Zimbabwe, the farms of Malawi's Shire Highlands and elsewhere, as well as countless other enterprises. Returning at intervals from such locations to the villages, the migrant laborer became a link between subsistence and cash economies, between remote hamlets and the capitalist world. These nodes of colonial enterprise also served as distribution points for exotic ideas and news of the world outside Africa. By the mid-1920s, the Watchtower Bible and Tract Society had been present in South Africa for some twenty years. (Certain notorious preachers, whom we will meet in Part 2, are known to have sojourned there and to have taught men they met in other centers of employment.) It would have been easy for workers passing through the bustle of Cape Town or Durban to learn of Garvey's exploits in America or Aggrey's travels in Africa, and then to report what they had learned, while journeying to other sites or homeward to distant villages. One part of the real passed directly into the social imagination: Garvey had a prominent gold tooth that glistened as he spoke.

It is difficult to translate these general truths into specific ones about "the native with the gold teeth." Fortunately, it is not crucial to our story to discover the origin of the America myth. Whatever its origin, a mythic vision of America's greatness was cultivated in Africa—as on other continents during this century—and it gave blacks and whites a luxuriant symbolic language in which to think about African liberation. The importance of this myth lies in its vivid representation of Watchtower prophecy as a phenomenon capable of engaging believers and unbelievers alike.

Although settlers' fears about the personified America died out, disconcerting rumors about the country came back to life periodically. As late as 1946, police on the Copperbelt found themselves investigating a new version: The Americans, victorious in war for a second time, were on the point of ousting the exhausted British. British officials, who could feel assured that such a calamity was impossible, nevertheless worried that such stories might undermine the confidence of black and white subjects in the majesty of their rulers. Thus the American stories, like the alarms of Tanguy, Moffat, and Stephenson, manifest the phenomenon to be examined here: the susceptibility of the regime's watchmen to Watchtower talk—or, to use Hinds' plain language, their "weakness" in the face of it. A common stereotype pictures colonial states in Africa as having held huge populations to the British Crown by virtue of superior force. Power grew out of the barrel of a gun, so to speak. But if we are to follow the vicissitudes of Watchtower revival and to appreciate what men meant when they feared it as rebellion, we must abandon this stereotype; the problem of rule was by no means so straightforward. We must abandon this stereotype because it provides no means of accounting for recurrent official anguish in the face of Watchtower talk or for the methods employed in the attempt to silence it.

Those whose job it was to silence Watchtower talk changed their minds about the nature and extent of the threat, sometimes thinking that preaching and praying were harmless manifestations of local superstition, sometimes seeing conspiracy and rebellion in them. On the face of things, it would appear that the regime need not have bothered itself greatly about periodic religious excitement in one sector or another of an unarmed African population, a population that was, moreover, so differentiated by village, tribe, and region that it could not possibly have mounted a territory-wide anticolonial campaign. Urging calm during the fireworks of 1925, J. Moffat Thompson made precisely this judgment of the Watchtower movement's potential as a "Pan-Africanist" force.[13] Men like Hinds and Thompson deemed the worries of settlers in particular localities overblown. For example, a penciled notation on Stephenson's letter about the scarcity of farm labor minimized Watchtower influence and said, "The mines [of the Copperbelt] offer greater attraction. The people are tired of being ruled by J.E.S. . . . [He] is no longer the 'squire.' "[14] Similarly, the men who responded to alarms that equated heresy with sedition often took a more relaxed view of events than did their brethren of the cloth.

But skepticism and the resolve to keep a cool head were only one side of the reality. The other side of it was that officials sought at first to stamp out the activities of Watchtower congregations— and failed. Thereafter, by means they invented as they went along, they struggled to eliminate what they considered the "political" aspect of the movement, while tolerating the "religious" one. The means they devised to enforce this distinction reveal what the common stereotype conceals about the nature of colonial law and order and are the basis of Part 1. However, they were by no means entirely successful, and officials could not make this distinction with certainty.

Justice P. J. Macdonnell, who tried scores of Watchtower adherents in 1919, insisted that colonial officials had no right to prosecute Africans for religious activity alone, but that they should bring the law's full weight down upon political agitators.

> Now one of two things. Either the movement is mischievous because its adherents break a positive law, in which case the adherents guilty must be proved so; or this movement does not lead to adherents breaking a positive law, in which case it is not mischievous and must be left alone.[15]

According to Macdonnell, who compared loud Watchtower services to equally loud but politically anodyne camp meetings in the American South, revival held no danger. It must be tolerated as a colorful sort of religious expression, so long as people merely prayed without causing any breach of the peace, and so long as religion was not politics in disguise. He went on to outline a legal and administrative strategy designed to effect this principle, the subject of Chapter 6. But, as those who tried to implement the strategy discovered, phrases such as "God is great"; "Those who are baptized are saved"; "Leave adultery and witchcraft"; or "Thy Kingdom come," could contain a mighty threat to colonial law and order. The Watchtower's God was the author of confusion where Macdonnell's distinction was concerned.

Since, to many writers, it has seemed important to distinguish between political and religious aspects of such movements, the God of twentieth-century millenarians has sown a curiously similar confusion in social scientists' interpretations. This confusion has engendered hot debate, partly because the historical record exports into scholarly accounts the questions urgently asked by contemporary observers, and partly for another reason, which I shall presently examine. In his essay on David Lazzaretti, the Messiah of Monte Amiata, Eric Hobsbawm argues that this "meaningless" debate inhibits our understanding of a millenarian episode that occurred last century in an Italian backwater. According to him, millenarians are properly regarded as revolutionaries—although of an "archaic" sort, for their characteristic trust in divine intervention does not immediately indicate, at least to the secular-minded observer, politically efficacious means. He writes:

> The extraordinary impracticality of millenarian movements has often led observers to deny not only that they are revolutionary but also that they are social. ... It is argued, for instance, by Sig. Barzellotti that the Lazzarettians were a purely religious movement. This is in any case an unwise statement to make. The kinds of community which produced millenarian heresies are not the ones in which clear distinctions between religious and secular things can easily be drawn.[16]

This pregnant idea, that millenarianism flourishes in particular "kinds of community," forms the basis of my study. I intend to describe such a community and to show that the resulting description leads us to question widely held assumptions about millenarian movements and about the regimes they attacked. But let us continue a step further with Hobsbawm's critique of a "meaningless" argument and the solution he proposes. Far from being purely religious, the Lazzarettians were "passionately interested" in politics. An exchange between the messiah and his people shows this:

What do you want of me? I bring you peace and compassion.
Is that what you want? (Response: Yes. Peace and compassion.)
Are you willing to pay no more taxes? (Response: Yes.) But
don't think it will be the Republic of 1849. It will be the republic
of Christ.[17]

Hobsbawm remarks in conclusion, "It is far from surprising that
the authorities of the Kingdom of Italy, as distinct from the Republic of God, regarded the Lazzarettians as a subversive movement."

Reasonable as this conclusion is, we cannot escape the malign
consequences of a banal dispute simply by agreeing that millenarianism contains elements of both religion and politics, or by adopt-
ing the common qualifier *politico-religious*. This dispute is the result
of fundamental confusion about the nature of the analytical problem, a confusion that has wreaked havoc not only with sensible
interpretation of historical events but also with proper historical
description. To make a brief preliminary sketch of this argument
comprehensible, I must examine the second reason that the God
of millenarians has tricked academics into battle over the wrong
terrain. Part of a sterile debate among scholars has arisen from
their subjects' own confusion, but the more important part has
arisen because the debate engages two well-defined points of view.
For brevity's sake, let us call the first *political* and the second *cultural*.[a]

The political approach emphasizes the link between millenarianism and the secular forms of social movement that have succeeded
it. According to this view, millenarianism represents an underde-
veloped mode in which the downtrodden express their discontent.
According to Hobsbawm, religious ideology provides a makeshift
to "prepolitical people who have not yet found a specific language

---

[a] My two categories somewhat oversimplify. They leave aside theological analysis,
as well as investigations of symbolism and the psychology of religious experience,
on the grounds that such inquiries are properly applied to a much larger class of
phenomena than the millenarianism with which this study is specifically concerned.
Two exemplary works that pursue such inquiries may be mentioned: Benetta Jules-
Rosette, *African Apostles: Ritual and Conversion in the Church of John Maranke*, Ithaca,
N.Y., 1975, explores the subjective experience of conversion into an African independent church; and David B. Barrett, *Schism and Renewal in Africa: An Analysis
of Six Thousand Contemporary Religious Movements*, Nairobi, 1968, correlates such
factors as date of Bible translation, size of church community, number of years'
mission activity, and other variables, in an attempt to arrive at a series of general-
izations about the timing and type of schisms to which African mission churches
are subject.

in which to express their aspirations about the world."[18] Further, this makeshift may be a necessary initial step. According to Peter Worsley, mission Christianity, from which the millenarianism of the colonized often borrowed, provides the organizational vehicle needed to transcend the limitations of traditional villages and to lay the basis for large-scale political action.[19] Worsley insists that adherents act rationally—however bizarre millenarian ideology may appear at first glance—but that the dissatisfaction and hope they temporarily embody in such beliefs will ultimately be given effective expression by secular trade unions and political parties. In other words, "expressive" behavior will be supplanted by an "instrumental" substitute. Underlining the significance of this progression, Sholto Cross writes of the Watchtower:

> Millennial movements provide a new revolutionary conscious-
> ness through a vision of the overthrow of civic authority, re-
> newed self-respect and pan-African content; it offers a new
> organization not based on kinship, ethnic loyalties, or custom-
> ary political leadership; and it promotes a mass expectation of
> independence . . . which is crucial to the constitutional bar-
> gaining of the nationalist elite.[20]

In sum, the political approach understands millenarianism in terms of an evolutionary sequence whose *telos* is a secular fight to seize state power. Therefore, despite its obvious political content, millenarianism only succeeds politically to the extent that it merges with and amplifies secular movements that have quite different ends in view. Awaiting Christ's Second Coming to establish his Kingdom on earth is not, after all, the same as mobilizing to erect a postcolonial republic. Theocracy is not democracy.

By contrast, the cultural approach emphasizes that millenarianism exhibits not political hopes but cultural disruption and an attempt by the colonized to restore cultural coherence. According to this view, the charismatic practice that everywhere distinguishes millenarianism is symptomatic of stress, which leads in turn to confusion, hysteria, desperation on the part of individuals, and widespread anomie.[21] The stress engendered by cultural collapse liberates monumental energies, which the adherents deploy in the tasks of "cultural revitalization," to use the term of Anthony Wallace, in order "to construct a more satisfying culture."[22] Bryan Wilson has insisted that, under these circumstances, individuals resort to nonrational means, especially magic.[23] Writing about an outbreak of Watchtower excitement in Zaire, Daniel Biebuyck placed mental confusion at the root of millenarianism.

> This confusion marks social organization, political organiza-
> tion, territorial and political division, the system of land tenure,
> power and authority, economic life, ceremonialism. It has en-
> gendered disequilibrium and instability, skepticism, apathy, an
> attitude of "so what?" [*l'idée de non-valorisation*]. From this one
> can explain the escapism on the one hand, and on the other,
> the passivity with respect to any innovation coming from the
> outside.[24]

For Biebuyck, nonrational solutions occur to peoples who are, to use his term, *mythomane*—"myth crazy." Without always going this far, advocates of the cultural approach generally follow Max Weber's suggestion that the extraordinary phenomena surrounding prophetic charisma are indigenous to situations in which the familiar world is in the process of collapse. In such situations the familiar has indeed met an apocalyptic "end," and masses of people orient themselves to the presumed "extraordinary" qualities of an individual.[25] In sum, the cultural approach understands millenarianism in terms of a scheme linking the mental clarity of individuals to cultural coherence—and of course obversely, where millenarians are concerned.

All the while advocates of these two approaches debate each other, they also concede each other's main points. Lucy Mair vigorously attacked Peter Worsley's account of cargo cult movements in terms he called barely "within the conventional limits of academic debate and ordinary civility."[26] But she nevertheless acknowledged that "all the messianic religions are in some way concerned with the distribution of power," although, following Georges Balandier, she claimed that their resistance, so far as it can be called that, was merely "verbal." From there, she went on to her main contention that such movements are not actually political at all.

> Their adherents belong to the section of the total society which
> has the least power, and in so far as we accept the explanation
> of these cults . . . as offering a fantasy compensation for prac-
> tical disappointments, we see in them, not a reinforcement of
> political action but a substitute for it.[27]

For Mair, the evidence that millenarian congregations are everywhere concerned with healing and moral regeneration pointed further in the same direction, away from politics. On the other side, Worsley's most important contribution conceded the main point of the culturalists—that we may question the political import of millenarianism, on the grounds that it does not embody rational means. He devoted by far the most imaginative part of his book to the task of rehabilitating his subjects' rationality. He contended that the fantasy aspect of cargo cults arose from his subjects' imperfect understanding of world market processes, and that their modes of action (however fantastic on the surface) were artifacts of a progression, still under way, toward modern forms of social movement. Predictably, moreover, since extensive conjuring with charisma is part of the position he challenges, Worsley mounted a penetrating critique of the uses to which this notion has been put.[28] So doing, and brilliant as his arguments are, Worsley conceded that the "problem of rationality" is central to any investigation of millenarianism.[29]

Debate over the rationality of millenarianism is perhaps the hottest part of the debate I am calling mistaken, its heat doubtless indicating its closeness to the core of the discussion. Lucy Mair caricatured Worsley's attempt to rehabilitate the rationality of cargo cult adherents by alleging that he attributed to them an independent discovery of the theory of surplus value. She evidently did not see that her own position could be caricatured in a similar way, as crediting villagers with the independent discovery of their ethnographers' theories about cultural coherence. And, five years after Worsley argued the rationality of cargo cult adherents, Bryan Wilson lambasted "self-hating" Western intellectuals who have so little faith in their heritage that they are ready to attribute rationality to what egregiously lacks it.[30]

According to advocates of the cultural view, if millenarianism has any political content at all, this content is expressive not instrumental, fantastic not practical, and certainly not rational. Those who put forward its political content try to explain away what seems to fit the culturalists' contention. But, so doing, they labor hard in a vineyard whose flora obscures the political import of baptism, prayer, and healing—the most characteristic forms of congregational practice. In fact, these receive at best very brief mention in political accounts. While culturalists minutely examine these as symbolic elements of ritual, which for them merges with whatever instrumental action there is, they, too, fail to look up from their labor long enough to note the sustained interest administrators had in mere symbolic action of this kind. Given the cultural standpoint, symbolic action could not possibly have had practical political consequences. Thus, whether one looks to the political approach or to the cultural one, the question of rationality obscures much of importance. And it promptly leads us astray. We do not learn to ask, What did the converts do and with what consequences? Instead we learn to ask the inverse, Why did they *not* do what it would have been rational for them to do? We thus gain a framework of description oddly premised upon what did not occur rather than what did. If we adopt it, we see the exploits of millenarians through a glass darkly, and backward.

In both kinds of discussion, we quickly lose sight of the fact I have emphasized from the beginning: that a supernatural threat could and did activate mundane police. And we can easily come away from both with the false impression that millenarianism in the colonies of three continents was a secondary phenomenon, accessible only to hardy researchers venturing along colonial back paths. The truth is otherwise. Scholars who could afterward write about a millenarian substitute for politics could obtain political intelligence about it from the moment they arrived in colonial capitals. They could interview veteran repressers of revival, or they could peruse police records that were sometimes decades thick. In this way, banal dispute has had the baneful result of providing a framework that almost guarantees the misleading portrayal of historical fact.

At bottom, the scholarly dispute is a display of antagonism among kin. The contested terrain of rationality joins rather than divides cultural and political hosts. Both take up their intellectual weapons at the seeming divide between rational secular action and its supposedly irrational religious opposite. Not surprisingly, the two views sometimes cohabit a single description—as, for example, A.J.F. Købben's often-quoted discussion, which harbors both the culturalist's confusion and the political analyst's protest.

> We may safely assume that one of the principle functions of all these movements is to offer relief to those who are, or feel themselves to be, humiliated or suppressed. Everyday life is too poor and wretched, too frightening and confusing, too degrading and oppressive to be borne without protest. A means of rising above it is sought; not, or anyway not altogether or always, through actions which we may regard as rational, but *through setting supernatural forces into movement.*[31]

Once again may we wonder what mobilized mundane police!

The common ancestor of both is the vulgar Marxist conception that social conditions cause religious ideology.[32] According to the political view, the cause of extraordinary belief lies in real social discontent; while for the cultural view, it is the stress occasioned by (real) cultural change. The family resemblance between the two is this: Wherever in reality the cause is sought, the sense of a senseless world awaits reconstruction at a considerable distance from what converts actually do and say. Since, in either case, millenarians cannot be conceived of as making sense in their own terms, whatever sense they may make to one another comes across this distance as garbled, faint, or even as not directly observable at all. Lucy Mair has gone so far as to invite depth psychologists to plumb the "similarities" she discerns between millennial visions and the "fantasies" and other "hysterical phenomena" characteristic of mental patients. And Købben repeated a widespread judgment, widely unsupported, that charismatic visionaries are generally gifted but "emotionally unstable" individuals (a judgment that, by the way, flies in the face of what the Bible repeatedly tells us, in great circumstantial detail, about the respectable ordinariness of the men called to prophesy).

Furthermore, each approach reasons that since millenarians cannot make sense of their own, they acquire sense only by means of scientific reconstructions, the one evolutionary, the other synchronic. But, from an adherent's standpoint at grass-roots level, as distinct from the uplands of academic abstraction, restoring cultural coherence may make as little sense as seizing state power and have as little practical relevance. Although our prophets are, by definition, articulate individuals, they do not articulate either aim. To "hear" such aims uttered, we must shift to the higher ground. But from there, the real voices are inaudible.

This scientific switching causes derailment, for, having identified millenarian *belief*—irrational belief in the unreal—as the object of explanation, we find ourselves locating what is to be thought of thenceforth as real in the abstractions, rather than in the historical circumstances that flesh-and-blood human beings inhabited. In short, a world is scientifically constructed in which an expression of real discontent takes on separate existence from its real content— which cannot be. In this way, the very act of making millenarian belief the object of explanation severs it from reality. Thereafter, the arduous and, I think, artificial task of explanation is to reunite them. There is a better way.

To begin correctly, any study of events in the past must reconstruct the horizon within which historical subjects thought and acted: "On doit la vérité aux morts," as Montaigne's maxim has it. Let us imagine that, for Watchtower followers, God really inhabited this horizon. Let us imagine furthermore that, for them, the hope of salvation guided responsible action in everyday life—as it did, say, for the Anabaptists of the sixteenth century or for Max Weber's Puritans of the seventeenth. If we do this, then we need not try to explain why individuals should have been impelled out of ordinary circumstances toward extraordinary belief. Rather, since belief would then come into view as routine common sense, we would try to see how the supernatural was embedded in mundane social relations. Christopher Hill has suggested that to orthodox churchmen of the sixteenth century, Anabaptists seeking the second baptism were the moral equivalents of Communists in our own age.[33] I submit that if we follow the doings of millenarians' God in this spirit, his appearance will no longer provoke confusion but will help us see the order of colonial societies in a new way. We then begin to see that the officials who did not scoff at missionaries' equating heresy and rebellion made perfect sense, while those who sat secure in the knowledge that prophecies were humbug did not. One consequence of following this course is that a commonly held notion that the colonial state was "modern" will wither away, for we will begin to compare it to the governmental systems of Europe's past. Taken as historical reality, the God of millenarians, who has sown so much disorder, can provide the key to understanding another order.

In arguing the approach I here oppose to the politico-cultural one, I raise and answer the old questions differently. Do the social relations within which millenarians routinely move stamp the distinction between religion and politics as real and important? Do they mark the supernatural as unreal and as requiring therefore a special leap of faith? And is it reasonable to distribute behavior between expressive and instrumental categories, according to eternally valid criteria? To show why all three answers must be *no*, in contrast to the *yes* of the politico-cultural approach, I will examine not only the extraordinary content of millenarian revival but also its ordinary context.

The context of Watchtower revival was a community where, as Hobsbawm said, the distinction between religious and secular things cannot readily be drawn. I intend to show that the colonial structure had a ready-made space for the God of the Watchtower millennium, because quieter but kindred gods were cemented into its very foundation, and because the propagation of belief helped maintain it erect. For a structure of this kind, revival is an inevitable byproduct of normal use. Given in such a structure is the possibility that baptism and "talking in the unknown tongue" can be reasonable—and effective—political tools.

Part 1 investigates this structure by considering the method by which the agents of colonial power ruled. To bring into focus their problem of order, I have found it fruitful to begin with the opposite and work backward. Since millennial revival exposes the lines along which order could break down, its analysis yields unusual evidence about the processes by which order was sustained. My reading of the revival episodes themselves suggested the importance of this evidence. The three case studies of Part 2 weigh, respectively, prophecy, baptism, and healing as disorderly political acts. Part 1 exhibits their counterparts on the side of colonial order. Since the species of religion that were the colonial regime's natural predators were akin to those which lived in symbiosis with it, Part 1 does not simply draw in the background of episodes to be recounted in detail, but presents a first account of them. It analyzes the distinct but complementary roles of the black and white, clerical and lay, officials who made the famous system of "indirect rule" work. Part 3 picks up these strands by examining millenarianism as a police problem, first as white agents of the colonial state faced it and then as their black collaborators did. In all this, I make no claim to having unearthed a great many hitherto-unknown facts. The African Watchtower movement has had sufficient chroniclers. But I do claim to arrive at a more adequate description of well-known and characteristic events than most studies of millenarianism have thus far achieved.

More adequate description is a step toward better theory. And better theory will guide our hands toward the pulse of the world in which we live. Sociologists of religion did not predict the political resurgence of "old-time religion" here in America, this most secular of modern societies. And we did not foresee that religion could fire a potent revolutionary engine in Iran. Indeed, we have done no better than economists have in predicting major new developments of our time. I do not know what ails economics. But I have become convinced that the problem of rationality, as applied to churches militant, is little more than a translation into scholarly terms of the native folklore about religious belief that is current in secular societies. My aim, at the end, is to have exposed this folklore for what it is.

I had to dispel this folklore from my own mental horizon in

1976, when I first wrote about the incident with which this study began (and which is fully treated in Chapter 4). Then, archival bits of vivid information led me to piece together in imagination the unfolding of a successful rebellion under the slogan God Is Great![34] But in 1979, what had had to be reconstructed in imagination as mere possibility could be witnessed live, in one's American living room, on satellite television. Along with millions of Americans, I watched as crowds of demonstrators shouting, "God is great!" exploded the foundations of the Iranian monarchy. Imagine the excitement of a scholar fascinated by the exotic deeds of Watchtower militants operating half a century and more ago, half a world away!

Part 1

THE PROBLEM
OF POLITICAL ORDER

◆

M ALAWI AND ZAMBIA FELL under the sway of the British Empire in the last decade of the nineteenth century. Britain achieved these conquests nonviolently, for the most part. Malawi (Nyasaland) became a protectorate of the Crown after some of its rulers put their marks to treaties of "protection." Zambia (Northern Rhodesia) was annexed on the Crown's behalf by the British South Africa Company, an extension of Cecil Rhodes' financial bucca-neering in the south, and was administered by BSAC employees until it passed to Colonial Office control in 1924. The empire's nonviolent methods of conquest are notorious. Working with the express, implied, or prospective support of the Crown, operatives of Rhodes' and other companies obtained treaties and land conces-sions from illiterate chiefs who had no way of knowing that they were signing away their sovereignty. Although the treaties thus obtained did not always provide an unambiguous legal basis for "protection," their defects were not crucial when the time came to create the Nyasaland Protectorate and those of North-eastern and North-western Rhodesia (legally merged in 1911). As the empire found its stride in Africa, even dubious treaties were not *de rigueur*. On the seizure of North-western Rhodesia (which included the future Copperbelt) for the BSAC, J. E. Stephenson wrote, "'We made no treaty; we referred to no treaty; we complied with no treaty. We walked in . . . and we forthwith started to 'administer' the country.'"[1]

While men like Stephenson led the patrols Rhodes required, men like Henry Hamilton Johnston (later Sir Harry) and Alfred Sharpe (later Sir Alfred) provided their treaty-obtaining services. All be-

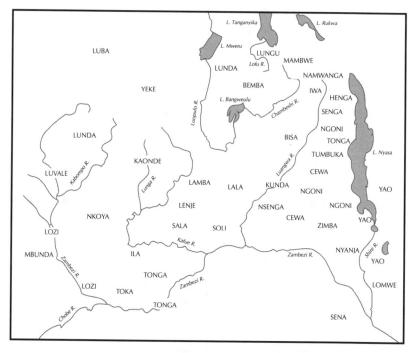

1. Peoples of Northern Rhodesia and Nyasaland

longed to a kind of adventurers' brotherhood that embraced, by
direct and indirect ties, agents of companies and of the British
government, as well as a disparate collection of explorers, hunters,
independent fortune seekers, and outright freebooters. It also included soldiers like the young Captain Lugard, who earned his
imperial spurs in East Africa during the 1880s.[2] Some churchmen's
exploits matched those of their secular brethren. By intrigue and
by making common cause with usurpers, the remarkable Father
Joseph Dupont (White Fathers) helped deliver both the enemies
of his friends and his friends into the grip of the BSAC. The
complex François Coillard (Paris Missionary Society) maneuvered
to the same event those whose confidence he had won.[3] After the
Berlin Conference of 1884-1885 set rules by which European nations would parcel Africa out among themselves, the "Scramble for
Africa" offered golden opportunities to men having the requisite
talents. The continent teemed with agents of Europe's worldly and
otherworldly interests.

An invisible hand guided individuals of diverse preoccupations
toward a common imperialism. For some it indicated gain. Men
crisscrossed territory thought to hold resources or strategic position

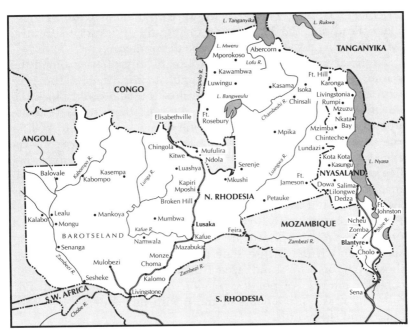

2. Towns and district centers in Northern Rhodesia
and Nyasaland during the colonial period.

of actual or future value to Britons. From his base in South Africa
as a gold and diamond magnate, Rhodes envisaged the exploitation
of Zambia's human resources as well as its copper; and he dreamed
of fathering an African empire that would stretch all the way to
Suez. For others, the pursuit of worldly gain took second place to
more exalted purposes. From the middle of the century until his
death in 1874, David Livingstone strove for an end to slave trading
and for its replacement by "legitimate commerce." The Scottish
businessmen who memorialized him by underwriting a Livingstonia
Mission (Free Church) on Lake Malawi also calculated the lake's
economic potential: It promised means of bringing their own legitimate commerce into the very heart of the region. The Church
of Scotland established Blantyre, its own memorial, upon the Shire
Highlands, where at first it bent nearly all its effort toward pi-
oneering the settler agriculture that speedily engulfed the local
economies.[4] When no obvious moral or material advantage presented itself, convinced imperialists sometimes chose to seize territory speculatively, in order to prevent a rival power from reaping
some as-yet-unforeseen colonial harvest, or in order simply to re-

strict its expansion. The Germans were on the move; the Belgians made headway; the Portuguese might still lay claim to Central Africa; the Arabs were not yet to be discounted.

As the Scramble pitched forward, many missionaries joined the clamor for empire.[5] Following a kind of *raison d'église*, the Free Church men saw that British control of the lake could block the advance of Catholicism and Islam, allowing them to concentrate upon war against "heathenism" alone. Besides, so long as African rulers enjoyed autonomy, all missionaries had to practice a respectful diplomacy in their capitals as the condition of propagating Christian benevolence in their villages. When on occasion diplomacy collapsed, the missionaries needed armed protection. They also had need of jails and other appurtenances of civil jurisdiction. Both Scottish missions and the London Missionary Society agonized under the pressure to provide their own—and this pressure could subside only if the British state built jails for the commitment of those Africans who scandalized British notions of justice. In sum, complex interests of politics, religion, and trade intertwined. For differing reasons, members of the British public demanded conquest; and they got it.

They did not always get conquest nonviolently. The conquest of Malawi and Zambia cost various wars of limited scale, notably those against the Ngonis under Mpezeni and the Lundas under Kazembe, certain Yao and Cewa chiefs, and the Afro-Arab forces of the trader-chieftain Mlozi.[6] But after the initial "pacification," no armed uprisings broke out in either territory such as shook the territories to the north and south. The problem of political order was to keep matters this way, in the teeth of a populace that was not uniformly content with its new circumstances. The British sought a strategy to perpetuate conquest with a minimum of force. To paraphrase Clausewitz, they sought the continuation of war by other means. They adopted the strategy of "indirect rule." Under it, black potentates, not white legions, would secure the day-to-day business of domination.

Money was the root of this strategy. When the pioneers took up the task of consolidating the British Empire in Africa, they quickly perceived that large-scale policing and extensive bureaucracy would cost much more than the British public was ready to pay. As Martin Kilson put it, they needed "colonialism-on-the-cheap."[7] Thus, even where power had initially grown out of the barrel of a gun, domination would not continue to do so year in, year out. Force of arms had permitted no more than the annexation of territory. The next step was to annex political power. Almost immediately following conquest, therefore, the architects of colonial order sought to redeploy African institutions. These pioneers quickly added an ethnographer's interest in the way chiefdoms and villages were built to an architect's interest in them as building material for a large colonial edifice. Since, to begin with, the "civilizing mission" respected little that was indigenous, the implementation of this strategy involved some about-faces. These about-faces are the subject of Chapter 2. I turn now to indirect rule and to its grand theoretician, Frederick John Dealtry Lugard.

1

INDIRECT RULE

The rulers of Great Britain were strongly opposed to extension of our territory in Africa, but the popular demand left the Foreign Office with no alternatives. The Government viewed with alarm the great cost of effective occupation. . . . But the British public never considers the cost of its demands, though it holds the Government to strict account for any disaster due to inadequate staff and insufficient force to protect its officers. . . . The staff, the troops, and the money were lacking, and neither the Colonial nor the Foreign Office had any knowledge or experience of administration in the interior of tropical Africa. . . . Above all, the statesmen of Britain had not grasped the incalculable virtue of the claims which the instinct of the nation urged them to peg out.

LORD FREDERICK LUGARD

INDIRECT RULE PROVIDED for a two-tiered structure, in which black and white rulers would occupy separate but interdependent compartments. The British regime would assign to African rulers many tasks of the new state—the census, tax collection, public works, law enforcement, and so on, in a gradually expanding list. At the same time, in all respects consistent with colonial law and order, and not "repugnant to British law and custom," the old way of life and its "native law and custom" would continue in the villages, with the blessing of the regime. Indirect rule was a conservative strategy designed to keep customary rulers and their subjects in place. It aimed to keep Africa's villages quiet while the colonial economy revolutionized them.

Indirect rule is so familiar that it requires no elaborate introduction. But, as with much that is familiar, we often take for granted its most problematic feature, that it should have worked at all. To the question, How did a notoriously small handful of white men

rule gigantic territories? indirect rule offers a simple answer: by
making black men with legitimate authority appendages of white
men without it—"mouthpieces," as Lucy Mair once wrote; "right
hands," as Paul Mushindo put a similar relationship.[1] This simple
answer is a bigger mouthful than it seems. For if it is the correct
answer to our question, we must draw an unfamiliar inference:
that black rulers constituted the State in a fundamental sense. Without them, the king's men who made up what A.H.M. Kirk-Greene
has called "the thin white line" could not render colonial law and
order effective. With them, the colonial state gained power to compel. Further, any attempt to unmake the state necessarily targeted
these men, for their ranks made up its vanguard.

The familiar notion conveys little of this. Every student of the
British Empire in Africa learns that indirect rule systematized the
transfer of power from the Crown to indigenous authorities, not
the other way around. Every student also learns that, despite the
appearance created by Lugard's formulas, the real power was not
transferred.[2] The real power remained in the hands of Britons—
territorial governors, magistrates, the officers who led colonial
troops or police, and perhaps above all, that personage endlessly
celebrated in colonial romances, "the lone-handed D[istrict]
C[ommissioner] . . . solely responsible for the administration of an
area the size of Wales or a typical British county," a veritable *roi
de la brousse*. Such a man could say, "I am the DC: *ergo quidque est.*"[3]
He could even imagine, as Louis XIV is said to have, *l'état c'est moi.*
Our familiar tableau has led reasonable men to give credence to
this notion, which I call the mystique of the few strong men. Thus,
Kirk-Greene lets the colonial aphorism "the DC is the government
and the government is the DC" slip as fact into his postcolonial
analysis. Since this mystique has continued to misguide reasonable
scholars,[4] I shall accept the risk of belaboring a point that is obvious,
once clearly stated. If indirect rule provides the answer to our
question, then African rulers, not the few strong men, belong in
the foreground of our tableau. And if our tableau is put right, then
new lessons emerge. Indirect rule was a way of making the colonial
state a consumer of power generated within the customary order.
It did not transfer real power from the Crown to African rulers.
Just the inverse: Real power issued from the ruled. Dame Margery
Perham once used a metapor that is neat, although it turns the
reality upside-down: "[Chiefs] took the strain of indirect rule,
breaking down, like human transformers, the powerful current
from above and distributing it in voltages that their people could

take."[5] Turned right-side-up, the image of electrical power generated and distributed is apt.

If the Crown did not distribute real power to African rulers, it did distribute powers, in the constitutional sense, not by any means the same thing. To think that the British began in possession of political power (singular) is to confuse fact with juridical artifact. It is akin to saying that the wealth derived from the Copperbelt mines originated with the men who passed out cash wages to the miners. None would fail speedily to diagnose and check the latter confusion. But the former propagates itself in various directions— in the myth that "direct rule" preceded its opposite, in the idea that missionary enterprise naturally seconded colonial rule, and in the failure to notice that successful rule depended both upon the ability of colonial officers to control African rulers and upon the ability of those rulers to control their people. Upon reaching this last point, I hope to have justified my proposal for altering the familiar tableau of indirect rule.

A word to specialists. This account does not aim to touch all the bases of past discussion—how the system fared in acephalous societies, how the assignment of uncustomary duties altered customary authorities, how official recognition of chiefs and headmen altered local institutions, or the other issues that have been dissected over many years in a large and important literature. What I attempt is neither a new ethnography of indirect rule nor a critical review of old ones, but a scheme by which to understand one mode of resistance to it.

THE THEORY OF INDIRECT RULE

Lord Lugard based his precepts upon his experience in the interlacustrine monarchies of Uganda and in the emirates of northern Nigeria. Although indirect rule worked best in such tightly organized political systems, it nevertheless became the official framework of administration in much of British Africa. By the late 1920s, Lugard's writings, *The Political Memoranda* and *The Dual Mandate in British Tropical Africa*, had become canonical books of British administration.[6] Thus, despite the prevalence in these territories of more loosely articulated polities than those in which indirect rule was devised, Zambia formally acquired the system in 1929 and Malawi in 1933.[7] With it evolved characteristic official functions: on the British side, district officers/commissioners, provincial commissioners, secretaries for native affairs, African clerks, messengers, and police, plus British legality; on the African side, native authorities and courts, native treasuries, and an expanding body of recognized provisions known as "native law and custom."

Unlike other canons, Lugard's did not prescribe virtue out of reach to living men; it made virtue of the necessity at hand. Only in cities and in labor compounds, or in territories densely settled by whites, was "direct rule" even imaginable.[a] For our regimes, the option of ruling directly existed only in imagination. Officials ruled indirectly, whether or not they recognized the fact, and whether or not the available institutions were readily adaptable to this use. In the real world of colonialism-on-the-cheap, every official had to work at the system's makeshifts, no matter how unsatisfactory and subject to breakdown. No one understood this better than Lugard. His *Dual Mandate* is a long reflection on the maintenance of makeshifts to which there were no practical alternatives. Some statistics will illustrate the point.

In 1960, when the provincial and district administration in Zambia reached its greatest numerical strength, it counted a mere 274 men, in a territory measuring 290,000 square miles (and by 1960, the British government was allocating vastly increased resources for economic and social development).[8] Between the wars, by contrast, at the high noon of the empire, fewer than half that number enforced the Crown's writ. In 1935, they numbered 134. The comparable statistics for Malawi, 48,000 square miles in extent, are 91 in 1960 and 45 in 1935.[9] Since they account for the regime's "white line" in the countryside, the provincial and district administrations are most important to us. But even if we add to these the other categories of Colonial Service employ—police and military, judiciary, medical, natural resources, public works, railways, and miscellaneous others—the sparseness of the imperial presence remains dramatic. (And we must be mindful, furthermore, that the technical functions tended to cluster in urban areas or in areas of relatively large white settlement, away from the rural majority.)

Combining all functions from the figures Kirk-Greene gathered from territorial staff lists, we again note the regime's small size. In Malawi (1939), 280 Colonial Service employees ruled in a population of 639,000 people; while in Zambia, 654 of their colleagues ruled 1,378,000. Relatively speaking, the regimes in Zambia and

---

[a] However, A. L. Epstein, *Politics in an Urban African Community*, Manchester, 1958, pp. 29ff., describes the attempt, following the strike of 1935, to import indirect rule onto the labor compounds and residential locations of the Copperbelt. See also Elspeth Huxley, *The Flame Trees of Thika: Memories of an African Childhood*, New York, 1959, which richly portrays the continued authority of African institutions in the midst of a settler colony.

TABLE 1

COLONIAL SERVICE COMPARED TO SIZE OF TERRITORY AND POPULATION

Country	Administrators per sq. mi.[a]	Total Colonial Service employees per sq. mi.[b]	Administrators per capita[a]	Total Colonial Service employees per capita[b]
Malawi	1:1,100	1:200	1:36,000	1:6,000
Zambia	1:2,200	1:400	1:10,000	1:2,000
Nigeria	1:1,000	1:200	1:56,000	1:10,000
Ghana	1:1,200	1:100	1:48,000	1:4,000

SOURCE: A.H.M. Kirk-Greene, "The Thin White Line," tables 7, 9, and 14
NOTE: Figures rounded to nearest 50 square miles and nearest 500 people
[a] Based on 1935 figures
[b] Based on 1939 figures

Malawi represented a "strong" imperial presence. As Kirk-Greene nicely put it, elsewhere "the thin white line" contracted into "a mere dot." In the Nigeria of 1935, 363 Colonial Service employees ruled 20,477,000 people in a territory of 373,000 square miles; in Ghana (Gold Coast), with its 92,000 square miles and 3,704,000 people, 77 ruled. Table 1 shows the approximate ratios.

The occupational category of blacks directly employed by the administration will complete the picture. These men worked as assistants of all kinds, and as clerks, translators, messengers, police, and soldiers attached to urban offices or to the rural *bomas*. Joyce Carey memorialized them in the semiliterate and semicompetent, but loyal and well-meaning, hero of *Mister Johnson*. Of their special predicament in time of trouble, we will learn in due course. For the present, let it suffice to hear the DC M. B. Otter's explanation of messengers' semicompetence: "Apart from . . . an easy going nature, he has probably at the back of his mind a fear of incurring the dislike and hatred of others, a hatred which may seek revenge in the employment of secret and supernatural means."[10] The proportions of tables 2 and 3 (for years before and after Indirect Rule) suggest that what the African majority thought of an unarmed messenger mattered. Roughly speaking, the Mister Johnsons in Zambia outnumbered their employers by about 6 to 1 and were outnumbered more than 2,000 to 1 by the African population.

These figures allow us to discern the grain of truth in the stereotype of many a feature film in which, time and again, a lone official in his pith helmet upholds the Crown's writ with the aid of a few African trusties in their tarbooshes. The falsity of this ster-

TABLE 2
ADMINISTRATIVE STAFF COMPARED TO POPULATION, 1928

| District | Administrative Employees | | Population | |
	African[a]	European[b]	African	European
Awemba	66	10	143,609	91
Barotse	120	13	301,824	154
Batoka	61	9	124,740	2,378
East Luangwa	54	8	216,706	501
Kafue	76	11	91,778	906
Kasempa	42	7	56,524	105
Luangwa	80	14	108,648	3,253
Mweru-Luapula	51	7	116,138	73
Tanganyika	45	8	102,005	75
On leave or traveling	4	17		
Totals	599	103	1,261,972	7,536

SOURCE: "Annual Report upon Native Affairs, 1928," appendix A

[a] Combines clerks and messengers

[b] Combines magistrates, district and native commissioners (including their "assistant" grades), cadets, clerks, and lady clerks

TABLE 3
ADMINISTRATIVE STAFF AND POLICE COMPARED TO POPULATION, 1934

| Province | Administrative Employees | | Police | | Population | |
	African[a]	European[b]	African	European	African	European
Barotse	92	11			332,093	132
Eastern	47	8			242,662	354
Northern	156	21			431,237	289
Central	97	21			163,676	7,443
Southern	94	20			196,757	3,246
On leave or traveling	3	14				
Totals	489	95	437[c]	56	1,366,425	11,464

SOURCE "Annual Report upon Native Affairs, 1934," appendix A

[a] Combines clerks and messengers

[b] Combines provincial commissioners, district officers (grades 1, 2, and 3), cadets, clerks, and lady clerks

[c] 1935 figures given in the *Report of the Commission Appointed to Enquire into the Disturbances in the Copperbelt, Northern Rhodesia, October, 1935*, London, 1935, p. 51

eotype lies in what it fails to portray: the dense, intense, and complex collaboration that went on behind the heroic scenes. And if this was true more in 1939, the high noon of the empire, than in 1960, its sunset, all the more so earlier. Yet men who did not want to see Indirect Rule enacted as a legal entity looked back to a direct rule that had supposedly gone before, when a man could write, "The native hardly recognized the existence of his chief and looked upon the officials residing in the country as representing all law and order."[11] Even scholars have imagined this imperial dawn, when still fewer Britons could have ruled directly.[12]

The dawn broke this way: Having quelled all local opposition to the transfer of sovereignty to the Crown, the new regime undertook every task of ruling—census and taxation; road building; land surveys; and the enforcement of controls upon hunting, fishing, agriculture, conservation, settlement, and internal trade. Further, its white magistrates went beyond their own immediate concerns and took jurisdiction over African court cases, not excluding inheritance disputes and divorces. In official theory, no area of African life escaped BSAC regulation. Summing up this theory, Justice P. J. Macdonnell declared, "We have governed the native and overgoverned him. We have taken from him the power of self-determination and have hedged him in with a network of rules and permits, a monotonous, highly regulated and very drab existence."[13] But in 1896, a total of twenty-seven BSAC men assured this "overgoverning" for the whole of Zambia. In 1898, one storekeeper and one administrator "overgoverned" the entire Fife District.[14]

Theory clouded the reality. Because the African population remained orderly, peaceful, and law-abiding to a remarkable degree, despite the thinness of the white line, the work actually being done by chiefs, village headmen, elders, and others of the customary hierarchy remained invisible. The work done by these Africans made it seem to pioneer British officials that their own strenuous activity brought this remarkable order about. After World War I, however, men like Justice Macdonnell began to penetrate the illusion. He argued for the preservation of "tribal authority"; without it, he "could see the abyss opening."[15] Not everyone did. Some officials strongly objected to the enactment of Indirect Rule. But one ground of their objection—that indigenous rulers had proved themselves unequal to the new responsibility—belies the notion that direct rule had previously been in force.

The census, state function par excellence, provides a good example. One objection called headmen too unreliable to be entrusted with it. For cause: When the regime began enforcing the "hut tax" (a tax that increased according to the number of wives a man had), many headmen began lying about villagers' marital status and even helped families to hurry through divorces so they could escape the burden of the tax.[b] Again, headmen commonly sounded the alarm at the approach of enumerators and tax collectors, thus permitting some villagers to escape being counted and others to escape imprisonment for tax arrears. Or a headman might protect a man liable to tax by claiming that he was absent working for some European, or seeking work, when he was in fact camped nearby. DCs' annual reports are full of such stories. To opponents of Indirect Rule, the unreliability of customary rulers argued against the legal delegation of responsibility to them. To us, the stories indicate that the census had been delegated before indirect rule evolved into Indirect Rule.

The BSAC's unsuccessful attempt to amalgamate Bemba villages shows the prehistory of Indirect Rule from another standpoint: that of rulers' effectiveness at established tasks of day-to-day order, rather than their effectiveness at novel ones. Traditionally, the Bembas lived for part of each year in temporary shelters—*mitanda*—near their fields. With the advent of colonial rule, they began residing in the scattered *mitanda* more permanently. Living in big, compact, often-stockaded villages had been the price of security in time of war—and in the last decades of the nineteenth century, Bemba country was a heavily militarized zone. But the *pax Britannica* freed people from the need to seek security in numbers and chiefly protection. Accordingly, they spread out. At first, missionaries and BSAC administrators alike applauded this development, which signaled for them that the despotic power of African chiefs had ended. They could reflect with satisfaction that people were enjoying the liberty British domination had wrought. But then they saw that the dispersion of the population worked against anyone who wished to rule, whether despot or DC. Moreover, they began to notice an upsurge of violent crime and adultery (not to mention nonpayment of the tax).[16] Missionaries saw that the new liberty worked also against those wishing to preach. The Reverend Dr. James Chisholm complained that a man would simply move "with a few friends" into the bush, separating himself from church and state alike. When the BSAC decided to amalgamate the villages, Chisholm and his colleagues heartily agreed.[17]

[b] Interestingly enough, the regime abolished "plural taxation" when it instituted Indirect Rule. The Annual Report of 1929–1930 notes the "popularity" of this move among chiefs and people alike.

People resisted passively at first, coming together when a BSAC man visited, dispersing after he left. Then in 1906, the BSAC inaugurated a policy of forcible destruction of the *mitanda*, coupled with a thorough reorganization of agriculture to make the fields more compact.[18] Their method, holding people at gunpoint while torching residences, succeeded in the short run. The power to herd people into concentrated settlements did indeed grow out of the barrel of a gun, but the power to keep them there in order did not. The headmen who lost out in the reorganization began agitating immediately. The chiefs who gained found the new villages ungovernable. Unending quarrels and feuds, poisonings, bewitchments, and accusations of witchcraft punctuated their failures. Then, nature and the dead found human voices in a violent outburst of possession, on a colossal scale.[19] When the spirits of the ancestors and the spirits of the land had had their say, the company understood that the plan could not work. It scrapped the policy of amalgamation and, with it, the possibility of easy direct access to the villagers. By 1915, the regime formally recognized that it had to be content with setting minimum limits to the size of new settlements—fifteen able-bodied men at first, and when officials saw that even this could not be upheld, ten.[20] (Even so, large numbers of unauthorized settlements were founded and tolerated.) In retreat from its offensive toward direct rule, the BSAC authorized chiefs to permit what it could not stop. New regulations made chiefs responsible for gazetting new villages.

Once again, officials noted chiefs' unreliability and incompetence. In practice, a chief was hard put to refuse permission to anyone wishing to establish a homestead. For him, granting permission was an easy route to popularity and influence. On the darker side, an unpopular chief not uncommonly came to grief at the hands of his subjects—nearer to him, for practical purposes, than the centralizers of the BSAC. As late as the 1930s, according to George Kay, "it was still more likely than not that a 'bad chief' would have a short life."[21] At the same time, a chief had few positive incentives to uphold the company's rules vigorously. "Ruling" did not necessarily mean one and the same thing to him and to the local administrator. Since all villages of his jurisdiction were theoretically under him, wherever they were and whatever their size, winking at the establishment of a minuscule village cost him little of importance. After all, the administrative problems of census taking and tax collecting were not, strictly speaking, his problems—at least, not until 1937, when the institution of Native Treasuries gave him new incentive. He did well to permit what he could not prevent. Inevitably, customary rulers who gave in to the villagers' pressure were weak in the eyes of many administrators. But, in their own solution to the problem of regulating domicile, the administrators themselves succumbed to the same pressures the chiefs had—albeit indirectly.

Given that African rulers had been depended upon all along to carry out the grass-roots work of the regime, administrators who argued against the legal creation of Indirect Rule were arguing for the perpetuation of a fiction. The question was how, not whether, indirect rule should be domesticated in the form of Indirect Rule. Lugard's system proposed nothing more, or less, than tidying up what already existed. By formalizing the rights and obligations of African rulers, he merely integrated them into the colonial state. He did not augment chiefs' independent (and "despotic") power, as opponents of the policy claimed, but channeled it. Neither did Indirect Rule diminish the power of local DCs in relation to chiefs; it enhanced their joint effectiveness by lending ragtag accommodations to local happenstance a degree of coherence. Furthermore, Lugard's precepts provided DCs with a professional method that counteracted the sometimes unruly aloneness of officials at work in remote stations. They spelled out the transition away from a charismatic era in which a "Bobo" Young could live in North-eastern Rhodesia "like an African chief" and operate "like a warlord"—the era Sir Percy Girouard referred to in 1910 when he pronounced in favor of recruiting university men, "no more cow-punchers."[22] As Margery Perham correctly pointed out, indirect rule has always been a rough-and-ready tool for imperialists of different epochs: Lugard's contribution "was to turn a rather widespread expedient into a carefully elaborated system, then to draw up a comprehensive code of laws with regulations and instructions and finally to rationalize the system in his later writings."[23] He gave it set principles, a clear hierarchy of functions, and mechanisms to assure a degree of uniformity throughout the system.

He also provided something else: a notion of respectability in which the Britons involved could share. Despite the practical need that dictated indirect rule as an expedient, it became in his hands part of a moral philosophy. The cardinal principle was the "dual mandate": to profit from rule *and* to civilize. A nation that failed to do both did not deserve to profit. Roman imperialism in Britain had "laid the foundations of modern civilisation and led the wild barbarians of these islands along the path of progress." Britons' duty now lay in "repaying the debt, and bringing to the dark places of the earth, the abode of barbarism and cruelty, the torch of

culture and progress, while administering to the material needs of
our own civilisation."[24] Thus did Lugard fearlessly claim that one
could do well by others by doing well oneself. But the most audacious part of this philosophy was its teaching that morality itself
demanded a partnership joining the civilizers to rulers lately
branded as despotic, bloodthirsty, ignorant, and utterly unworthy
to preside over "culture and progress." Men less worldly than Lugard in the ways of colonialism-on-the-cheap could still feel it to
be their mission to free Africa from its customary rulers and so
benefit the colonized.[25] Lugard pointed a better way. In 1931, the
political scientist Leo Marquard summed up this better way by
hailing Indirect Rule as "almost the theory of self-determination
applied to native tribes." It was nothing less than a "positive theory
of government based on the assumption that sound administration
rests on the traditions of the people."[26]

Thus, Lugard managed to turn the sunshine of moral correctness
on all elements of the imperial enterprise—crass matters of colonial
profit and high-flown principles enjoining colonization, adherence
to the principle of self-determination and the need to rule on a
shoestring budget. He managed to direct the sun's very best light
toward the customary ruler, the indispensable linchpin of the colonial state. In this light, the incorrigible autocrat of early propaganda
shone forth as the trainable guardian of tradition. *The Dual Mandate*
is a remarkable synthesis, and Lugard is justly famous for it.[27] Since
to behold the brilliance of the achievement is to behold its ironies,
let me quote at length from Lugard himself.

> The responsibility [to civilize] is one which the advantages
> of an inherited civilisation and a superior intellectual culture,
> no less than the physical superiority conferred by the monopoly
> of firearms, imposes upon the controlling Power. To the back-
> ward races civilisation must be made to mean something higher
> than the aims and methods of the development syndicate or
> the assiduous cultivation of new wants. The moral obligations
> to the subject peoples include such matters as the training of
> native rulers; the delegation to them of such responsibility as
> they are fit to exercise; the constitution of Courts of Justice
> free of corruption and accessible to all; the adoption of a system
> of education which will assist progress without creating false
> ideals; the institution of free labour and a just system of tax-
> ation; the protection of the peasantry from oppression, and
> the preservation of rights in land, &c.[28]

Thus did Lugard codify at one stroke not only a cheap adminis-

trative scheme but also a theory legitimizing rule in
institutional form that short funds imposed.

It is tempting to discount legitimizing theory as m‹
zation. In one sense, Lugard's further claim—that "‹
an individual, must have some task higher than th
material gain, if it is to escape the benumbing influence of paro-
chialism and fulfill its higher destiny"—exemplifies Max Weber's
remark about legitimizing theory. The privileged, Weber said,
never rest content merely to enjoy their good fortune; they always
demand to believe that it is merited.[29] But we would be unwise to
dismiss the moral principles without noticing their practical content. Not addressing himself to the ruled at all, Lugard aimed to
give the present and future actions of the rulers consistency and
order. By underlining the rule of law, the abolition of slavery,
religious toleration, the virtues of Christianity, the spread of education, the training of customary rulers, and however unsatisfac-
torily, limits to Europeans' exploitation of Africans, he helped the
regime to define itself. The ambiguous role of Christian missions
shows how such principles both advanced and retarded by turns
the consistent application of indirect rule. The combination of a
civilizing mandate with one of ruling through customary authority
made colonial rule a Penelope's fabric of doing and undoing.

THE AMBIGUITIES OF MISSION ENDEAVOR

On the one hand, missions served the regime. They aided it practically by mediating the spread of Western culture, and morally by
helping to legitimize colonial rule. But however great their utility,
they remained untidy tools. For on the other hand, they undermined the regime. Indirect rule presupposed the continuance of
customary authority; but the missions attacked as "heathenism"
much that was customary. In a system designed to maintain village
life and build upon its power structure, they were an anomaly.
By deliberate plan, mission Christianity was corrosive of African
village life. Tangibles such as imported clothing, cash crops, brick
houses, Western medicine, tombstones, books, and money were
part of its gospel. The intangibles of this gospel were not only those
pertaining to Christianity's transcendent God, but also individu-
alism, Western education, the nuclear family, middle-class values
and virtues, skilled trades, and ambition. All had religious value.
Christian conversion was a cultural, as well as a religious, conversion. The conventional language of Christians "coming forward,"

"setting themselves apart," and declaring for a "completely changed life" acquired new meaning.

The missions sought to create conditions in which they could carry out this cultural conversion intensively upon the individuals who would become Christian teachers. Especially in the early days, when there were no Christian groups in the villages, they tried whenever possible to transplant their pupils onto mission soil, so as to cut them off from village influences. It was partly to this end that the Free Church missionaries agitated for, and got, legal provisions for the indenturing of the pupil-apprentices who attended the Livingstonia Institution in Malawi.[30] For similar reasons, they provided haven to slaves and fugitives of all kinds—women escaping arranged or bad marriages, individuals harboring grievances against relatives, suspected witches unwilling to face trial by ordeal.[31] The point is not that such circumstances alone account for individuals' joining the early Christian communities (their motives were undoubtedly as complex as those of any convert to any religion), but that missionaries actively sought candidates who could be severed from their natal communities completely enough to permit a thorough Christian rebirth. The isolation would prepare them for a future role as witnesses to the "completely changed life" that resulted from conversion. When they went forth again to preach the Gospel, they would be a foreign element in the villages, in but not of them.

Some of the earliest missionaries had more grandiose dreams than the transformation of individuals, one by one. Catholic missionaries characteristically hoped to convert chiefs who would lead their people en masse to Christianity, as Clovis had led the Franks. Nor would Protestants at first have turned back this kind of success.[32] But chiefs were relatively slow to be converted, restrained in many cases by the prohibitions against polygamy, village rituals, and beer drinking (a hard-and-fast rule in evangelical Protestant groups). Worse, they sometimes put obstacles in the way of evangelism among their subjects. In these respects, from the missionary point of view, customary rulers represented all they had come to Africa to sweep away. Thus, even if sympathetic to the empire, they lost sympathy when it was embodied in the persons of non-Christian rulers. They felt chosen to do monumental battle against heathenism and immorality. If confronted with a choice between a pagan or Moslem order and disorder resulting from Christian evangelism, they repeatedly chose the latter, without hesitation.

Conflict between missions and the administration frequently broke out because the missions had declared war against custom,

while the administration was sensitive to breaches of custom that
led to breaches of the peace. For example, Catholic missionaries
and the administration did not agree on the question of divorce.
The missionaries interfered with the Bemba judges who based their
decisions on a customary law that did not make divorce difficult.
Since local administrators often thought it better to permit divorce,
and to allow chiefs to judge cases according to their lights, they
tried to restrain the fathers.[33] Another example: The White Fathers
sometimes made supernatural threats against chiefs or headmen
who resisted the construction of schools and chapels, or who persisted in the old religious observances side by side with the new
ones. Administrators fumed at this dangerous and irresponsible
cursing of the unconverted.[34] Some missionaries went so far as to
incite revolt among the young of a village in order to impose schools
upon unwilling headmen.[35] In other cases, disorder resulted from
the destruction of "idols" by Christian teachers, who scandalized
traditional opinion by desecrating ancestor shrines, breaking ceremonial drums and beer pots, disrupting communal rituals, and
insulting elders publicly. The *Livingstonia Mission Report* of 1906
admitted that teachers were "impatient and sometimes overbear-
ing." But the teachers only did, if sometimes overzealously, what
their employers condoned.

The employers could be convinced only some of the time that
there was such a thing as too much zeal in their campaign against
heathenism and immorality. They did not always agree with officials
about which acts by evangelists were excesses meriting punishment.
In 1908, the BSAC enacted a Native Schools Ordinance. Designed
to temper the enthusiasm of teachers by making white missionaries
responsible for giving them "adequate supervision," its immediate
stimulus was a violent confrontation between a young evangelist,
one Eron, and his assistant, Filipo. When the headmen Ntibasonjo
(Filipo's father) flogged the two for speaking and acting disre-
spectfully (among other delicts), Filipo broke his father's ceremonial spear. Then a local official arrested the two and upheld Ntibasonjo's punishment, adding his own. For his part, Eron claimed
that he had only resisted the headman's effort to block preaching
of the Gospel. Upon hearing the report, the Reverend Mr. Prentice
of Livingstonia defended the youths. There followed an exchange
of angry correspondence, in which the missionary upheld the
youths' right to preach and condemned the headman's action, while
the official insisted that it would shortly be impossible to keep order
if white men gave "easy credence" to the reports of young Africans
provoking scandal. The official, one Hall, went on to suggest that

Christian teaching would not be possible if such incidents were repeated.[36]

Prentice's colleague, the Reverend Mr. James Henderson, could see the elders' point. He understood why they tried to stop the young from joining Gospel classes or to "starve teachers out" by seeing that villagers provided no supplies: "No doubt there is some opposition that arises out of a healthy heathen conservatism dreading the disintegrating influence of Christianity." But this "disintegrating influence" alarmed him far less than it alarmed worldly rulers. Henderson calmly recognized that

> the new teaching tends to sweep aside, before it is able to make adequate compensations, customs not in any way wrong but apparently childish, which nevertheless are the real bonds of native society and the main safeguards of its moral code; but to attribute [weight to] considerations of this nature generally . . . would be a great stretch of generosity.[37]

The regime's concern about custom sprang not from "generosity" but from calculating the price of peace. Having calculated early, by the turn of the century, the BSAC forbade all missions to send evangelists into the Mwaruli District of Zambia. This area was the home of Shimwalule, official burier of the Crocodile Clan from which sprang the Bemba kings; and it was the site of the royal burial groves. The company feared that iconoclasm in Mwaruli might provoke riots in which it would be forced to intervene. In addition, it feared the consequences if Catholic and Protestant missionaries competed in that sacred area, as they were competing in the Chinsali district that enclosed it. As Robert ("Bobo") Young put it, "We don't want a row between the Christian (Catholic and Protestant) and Heathen Awemba [Bembas] over the next burial." But David Kaunda proceeded, with his group of evangelists, to violate this prohibition, and not outdone, White Fathers evangelists did likewise. It was not until 1909, when the BSAC obtained a joint and mutual withdrawal by both missions, that the threat to the BSAC's peace dissipated. Since Kaunda remained in the good graces of his superiors (he was eventually promoted to pastor)— and so presumably, did the White Fathers' employees—it would appear that all the Christians, black and white, felt themselves subject to an authority higher than that of the terrestrial regime.[38]

Some scrimmaging between evangelists and local notables did not fulfill a deliberate plan by the missions but occurred while evangelists were far from their bases. Like the regime, mission institutions were sparsely manned in proportion to the job they tried to do. And, like the regime, they depended upon African initiative. For example, before World War I, each of Livingstonia's stations claimed "jurisdiction" over from 40,000 to 100,000 souls; the headquarters in Malawi commanded an area 300 miles long and 100 miles wide with a white staff that numbered 49, counting missionaries' wives.[39] In these circumstances they had no choice but to practice "evangelism-on-the-cheap." Their version of the indirect ruler was the evangelist-teacher, product of the intensive program at the centers. He traveled widely, opening new schools, holding services, preparing candidates for baptism, and finding new talent. He could no more be supervised on a day-to-day basis than could his counterpart who served the state. (David Kaunda's group, which founded Lubwa Mission in 1905, did not receive a white missionary in charge until 1913.) Lugard, who was equally aware of the missionaries' zeal and their subordinates', put the problem diplomatically, in terms of inadequate staff:

> Christianity is, I think, sometimes apt to produce in its converts an attitude of intolerance, not intended by its teachers, toward native rulers, native customs, and even to native dress, especially when wholesale conversions have overtaxed the supervision of the European mission staff.[40]

Whatever BSAC administrators may have said in their hearts about the radicalism of a Prentice or a Henderson, they, too, talked about the inherent danger of missions—officially, at least—in terms of staff and supervision. In 1915, they enacted a new Native Schools Ordinance that specified what "adequate supervision" meant.[41] Naturally, the missionaries subscribed to the principle and promised to punish any misdeeds they uncovered. But, to them, the advantages of spreading the Christian net far and wide outweighed the disadvantages of an occasional breach of the peace—cure was less costly to their evangelical purpose than prevention. They did not have sufficient resources to apply the principle vigorously; and, in any case, keeping order outside the congregations was not, strictly speaking, their problem. It is fair to say that they never saw eye to eye with the regime on the matter of "adequate supervision."

Above and beyond scattered acts of aggression against customary order, mission enterprise contained a still more profound source of disorder: Jesus' message itself, which proclaimed the rupture of traditional ties and the assertion of an individualist conscience. Consider, for example, Matthew 19:29: "And everyone that hath forsaken houses, or brethren, or sisters, or father, or mother, or wife, or children, or lands, for my name's sake, shall receive an hundredfold." Christianity's individualist conscience gave people principled grounds for denying customary obligations of all kinds—arranged marriages and prescribed remarriages, customary labor, funeral observances, and obedience to elders. That such obligations had the support of supernatural sanctions did not mean they might not be onerous or irksome, or that people would let pass the opportunity to be free of them. A Bemba who refused to give aid according to custom gave this classic expression to Audrey Richards when he said, "I am a Christian; I don't do things for nothing."[42] According to Lugard's ponderous formulation, "The administration . . . insists that the profession of any creed . . . shall in no way absolve the convert from obedience to his customary rulers, or from the observance of native law and custom when not repugnant to his conscience."[43] I leave it to the reader to imagine what headaches for the local implementers of indirect rule lurked behind the phrase "when not repugnant to his conscience." By providing to converts legitimate grounds for denying formerly legitimate obligations, Christian teaching could plant the seeds of destruction in the pores of customary regimes.

Monica Wilson has shown how far such a community in southern Tanzania had gone by the mid-1930s toward creating a Christian state within a state.[44] Since she recounts systematically what we observe elsewhere in bits and pieces, and since the German mission she discusses was close enough doctrinally for Livingstonia to cooperate with it in many ways and then to take up its work in the crisis of World War I, her discussion is not out of place here.[45] The crystallization of a new policy was one aspect of this development. Mission members resolved disputes inside their group, bypassing the unconverted judges. And, in the midst of disastrous flooding, the congregation invoked Paul and Silas, bypassing the unconverted ancestors. Many of them continued to believe that cursing could cause misfortune but moved it into the new context. Some thought, for example, that a missionary could bring down God's wrath upon a wrongdoer by pronouncing an anathema, just as a traditional elder could.

At one stage in the growth of their little Christian polity, the members took a further step away from the non-Christian one. They declined to make the customary offering to their chief on the occasion of a relative's death. In not making the offering, Christians could recall Jesus' rebuke to the would-be disciple who asked permission to go first and bury his father: "Let the dead bury their dead" (Luke 9:60). Converts who followed this injunction courted ritual danger, including sickness and death, for such a dereliction could be punished by the legitimate use of witchcraft to secure punishment of the sacrilege. This sort of threat appealed to the missionaries, who set store by fiery tests of faith. Ever on the alert for means of blocking the retreat from conversion, they enjoined the dereliction enthusiastically. It constituted an outward and visible sign of new allegiance.

The violation of ritual had other practical results. When the *boma* called for supply carriers, chiefs learned to count upon their pagan followers and to avoid the Christians, although both were still theoretically subjects. On one occasion, when a chief called upon a Christian to fill a quota for workmen, the missionary immediately lodged an official protest. As logic demanded—the chief's ability to summon his subjects' labor rested upon a body of rights and obligations legitimated in religious terms. The local missionary saw that the Christian's compliance with the chief's political authority was tantamount to compliance with his religious authority, and the chief probably knew he was testing on this account. By protesting, the missionary was no doubt firing a message back to the chief. Thus, Christianity shifted the ground under indirect rule wherever the regime tried to set it down. For various reasons, then, the consistent application of indirect rule ought logically to have prohibited the work of missions. They simply were not natural supports to the state, given its peculiar structure. The idea that they were is the offspring of a flawed conception of indirect rule.

Despite the difficulties, however, missions were not excluded but tolerated, and usually more than tolerated, for the regime soon assisted their educational and medical activities with grants-in-aid.[46] The regime encouraged missions for both practical and moral reasons. Obviously, missions observed the civilizing morality of the dual mandate. And, in helping to produce the skilled and literate manpower the colonial polity and economy required, their presence was justifiable on utilitarian grounds as well. Finally, they helped to legitimize the regime. Not only before Africans; it was just as important to make the benefits of colonization a commonplace among the British themselves. Lugard showed how far this legitimation extended by quoting a Labour party foe of empire, who opined that while "the general effects of European policy in Africa have been almost wholly evil . . . experience and temperament have made the rule of the British over the non-adult races an example of everything that is best in modern imperialism."[47]

Christianity represented "what was best in modern imperialism." To ban missions would have been unthinkable. But if, in the heat of some local confrontation, their banishment was in fact thought of, powerful forces were at work in Britain to prevent this. Missionaries had thousands of sympathizers in Britain and more than a few distinguished patrons. Finally, Christian idealism must be given its due. Some British Christians valued the propagation of the Gospel for its own sake, pursuing it for no other reason and in the face of any obstacle. This is not the place to discuss in detail the extraordinary Christian character that the late nineteenth century produced or the revival of ascetic ideals that nourished it. But it is worth reflecting that Max Weber could observe firsthand this generation of militant Christians when he composed his famous essay on Protestantism. Such Christians lived inside and outside the missionary establishments of Africa. Lord Lugard himself could view them in the perspective of his own upbringing as the child of evangelical Anglicans at work in India.

Although the missions' civilizing ambition made them imperfect supports, they had a practical role to play on the regime's behalf nonetheless. Subtle, and for the most part unspoken, it derived from the practical circumstances of indirect rule rather than from its explicit theory. And it derived from a body of assumptions missionaries shared, or were presumed to share, with their kith and kin of the administration, the settler community, and all other whites in a colony. I have already noted the small number of officials in Zambia as a whole. Audrey Richards gives us a rough census of the huge Awemba District (about 22,000 square miles), in the north of Zambia. In 1934–1935, there were 289 Europeans, of whom only 7 worked for the regime, compared to an African population of 84,645.[48] The rest were an assortment of missionaries, traders, hunters, and drifters. Lugard assumed that in such circumstances, all whites had a role to play, including missionaries. While not addressing missionaries' practical role explicitly, he made clear his conception of a common task shared by all whites in an African land.

This conception appears in an admonition, directed to Pentecostalists in particular, against strict adherence to one of Protestantism's most creditable doctrines, the doctrine of Christian equality:

> Some few missions carry the ideal of the equality of man to a point which the intelligence of the primitive savage does not appreciate in its true significance. That a white man should come to Africa to do menial work in the furtherance of an altruistic ideal is not comprehensible to him, and the result is merely to destroy the missionary's own influence for good, and

to lessen the prestige of Europeans, upon which the avoidance of bloodshed and the maintenance of law and order so largely depend in Africa.[49]

Lugard's norm against manual labor by whites does not simply reflect a racist outlook. It reflects as well his practical thinking about how to lengthen and thicken the "thin white line." If, where he speaks of "influence for good," we understand "influence for good order," and if, where Lugard says "avoidance of bloodshed," we understand "avoidance of costly force," we begin to discern the missionaries' own peculiar contribution to the maintenance of order. Closer to the daily lives of African villagers than the "few strong men," they could augment the state's resources by playing their part in its stage-managed presence. They could bear the state's arms and its flag, in a sense, simply by wearing their white skins. In telling them not to do menial tasks, Lugard was telling them how to wear this uniform in such a way as to recreate daily the prestige that would make it serviceable. Lugard considered missionaries to be bound to this ritual in the same way as other Europeans. It had nothing to do with their particular beliefs. It had everything to do with the protection of the whole white community.

This ritual of appropriate uniform had a part for Africans to play. Not only were people of black skin set apart for menial work, but their skin was to be set off by distinctive dress. In the same passage, Lugard moved on from deploring Christian equality in work to deploring it in dress. Far too many missions took European dress as an outward and visible sign of conversion, but he felt heartened to note that some were beginning to abandon the practice. They must not foster "slavish imitation," he said, borrowing the phrase from a conservative Ghanaian chief. Africans should look like Africans, at work and in outfitting; Europeans should look like Europeans in all their doings. The European who hewed his own wood did not. The African who donned the wrong headgear did not. In a notorious incident of post–World War I Malawi, a European invoked this ritual by confiscating a pith helmet from a young African.[50] Reacting as he did, the European reached back historically, toward the sumptuary laws that once helped keep different ranks of white people separate and unequal. Those laws served as ritual supports of an old-fashioned "good order." But rituals do their work in curious ways. And they do not mean the same thing to all men or in all seasons. By urging African dress for the Africans, Lugard put forward a view now familiar as cultural nationalist doctrine. Forty years after *The Dual Mandate*, leaders of

the independence movement proclaimed it as an expression of
freedom; but Lugard proclaimed it to abort the expression of freedom, nonviolently.

I have emphasized the practical side of nonviolence, but it would
be wrong not to notice its moral side as well. Even if frequent use
of physical force had not been discouraged on financial grounds,
it would have been costly in the regime's soft currency as well. For
a corollary to the argument that colonization benefited the colonized was that force must be used sparingly. Too much of it too
blatantly applied would controvert the main thesis, and the *pax
Britannica*—the British peace—would lose all meaning. By falling
into step with the unwritten laws of colonial order—its etiquette—
missionaries could add to the nonviolent presence of the regime.
But, to the extent that they thereby sustained the logic of domination, they made themselves colonizers in their own right. And
since they, far more than officials, could make the empire felt as
a quotidian affair, one sort of opposition naturally targeted them.
Not surprisingly, missionaries targeted by militant revivalists heard
"blasphemy" as "sedition," and saw disrespect to themselves as revolt. But the line officers of the regime did not always shudder at
irreligion, nor did they always take action when they heard it from
missionaries who heard it from evangelists who heard it from revivalists haranguing the villagers. Most of the time, officials enjoyed
the luxury of greater distance than the missionaries' from the daily
peace work of the civilizing mission.

THE PRACTICE OF INDIRECT RULE

Customary rulers also carried out the daily peace work of the civilizing mission. To borrow Max Gluckman's nice phrase, they were
the regime's "noncommissioned officers."[51] Engaging the actual
and potential enemies of the regime in their villages, they laid the
platform upon which the DC erected his solitary might as well as
that confidence which Kirk-Greene illustrated thus: "As the DC
returning to London on leave said to his wife, as he strode mas-
terfully into the pell-mell traffic to cross Piccadilly Circus in the
rush-hour: 'They wouldn't dare!' "[52] Because such inattention to
reality was almost an occupational requirement, DCs often carried
on in this spirit, and the unwary can absorb the idea that audacity
counted for nearly everything. But correspondence among DCs in
the field went well beyond matters of efficacious bearing. It suggests
that they managed audacious presentation of self with one hand
and additional protection with the other.

dual articulation of I. Rule.

At times of millennial alarm, they wrote to one another and to their superiors about the ability of chiefs and headmen—not their own ability—to put an end to "irresponsible preaching." And "irresponsible preaching" carried with it forms of subversion to which one would not at first expect British rulers to be sensitive: clan incest and other forms of illicit sexual intercourse, failure to respect the dead, disobedience of wives to husbands, and refusal to participate in rituals of *African* kingship. Their correspondence sets out a catalog of norms that officials learned to regard as worthy of the Crown's recognition. Why should this have been so?

The answer lies in their method. The regimes built upon indirect rule were doubly articulated. One articulation made the African masses subject to customary rulers; the other made customary rulers subject to the Crown's representatives. The more fundamental articulation joined customary rulers and their subjects: For the regime to use chiefs as "mouthpieces" and "right hands" at all, chiefs had to be able to speak and act on their own behalf. The other, which joined customary rulers to white officials, operated the machinery whereby the regime sought simultaneously to control chiefs and to foster their control over their people.

pure rule

Interdependent in practice, these two articulations have not always been clearly distinguished. If we make the distinction, a static division corresponding to the racial aspect of the "colonial situation"[53] becomes a dynamic model capable of representing a complex, often dissonant ensemble of tactics and strategy. By using this dynamic model we can see, as Lugard did, that the central drama of indirect rule turned on keeping black rulers strong enough to control their people and yet weak enough to be controlled by the regime. The familiar conception of the system keeps the second articulation in clear focus, while directing attention to questions of chiefs' effectiveness or competence. It is a DC's view of subordinates in a quasi-bureaucratic structure. But if we focus exclusively upon the second articulation, our DC's attention to matters alien to the civilizing mission would remain inexplicable or, perhaps, to be explained away as Britons' irrational commitment to their national taste in ruling.[54] But Lugard's commitment to real-world experience was consummately rational. His mind never let the actual conditions of ruling out of focus. Still, he, too, was limited by a habit of seeing the white officials in the foreground. We learn from him about the first articulation through what he says about the second.

colonialism m the chief

Lugard transposed the question of chiefs' relations with their people as the question of finding the correct relationship between

Colon. in favor of polygamy because it keeps the chief in power

the administrator and the chief. In the correct relationship, the official interfered as little as possible with the activities of his black colleagues. Lugard preached what we can call a principle of calculated noninterference. In his words, there must be

> rule by native chiefs, unfettered in the control of their people as regards those matters which are to them the most important attributes of rule, the scope for initiative and responsibility, but admittedly—so far as the visible horizon is concerned— subordinated to the control of the Protecting Power in certain well-defined directions.[55]

Naturally, there were to be real fetters upon the power of African rulers—upon the right to raise armies, levy taxes, or try capital cases. By "the most important attributes of rule," Lugard meant custom, and even custom had definite limits. "We have put an end to . . . the slave trade and inter-tribal warfare, to human sacrifice and the ordeals of the witchdoctor," Lugard exulted.[56] Enslavement was excluded because it no longer suited British morals; warfare, because it lay beyond the pale of civilized ideals. However, some customs were excluded not only because they shocked but also because they contested British sovereignty. Thus, the regime prohibited customary rulers from administering the poison ordeal to suspected witches (which commonly resulted in the death of the accused person). British sovereignty meant that white rulers, not black ones, could claim the right to kill a subject, and to determine the proper grounds for doing so. In Lugard's formula, "If . . . any particular form of religion sanctions or enforces acts which are contrary to humanity or good order, the government intervenes regardless of religious sanctions."[57] But after the regime had pulled the teeth of customary regimes, customary law would receive positive encouragement.

Although Lugard envisaged the continued usefulness of a toothless customary law, he realized that if chiefs retained no more than symbolic means of enforcement, they would be unable to play their part. They had to retain methods of coercion. Thus, as he noted, British rule reduced to mere ceremony the obligatory state tours made by the Egba chiefs (in Nigeria). Only the "tinsel insignia of office" remained. No longer able to command obedience by force of arms, "on which in the last resort the authority of the law must depend," the Egba chiefs stood impotent when rioting broke out.[58] The regime had to move in and restore order.

Lugard's discussion of this incident reflects his preoccupation with nonviolent means. He leaves his discussion of the regime's

intervention for a later chapter devoted to the conditions in which
the use of force is permissible, to the regulations governing its use,
and (remembering always the British audience) to its humane ra-
tionale.[59] Lugard's immediate discussion of the incident embodies
his interest in adroit manipulation, which was always more sustained than his interest in force. He tells how the chiefs' power
might be buttressed after the restoration of order: by calculated
noninterference. Since, once again, to understand Lugard's view
is to understand its ironies, I shall quote him:

> The paramount chief might receive ceremonial visits . . . from
> the Governor, and even perhaps be addressed as "Your Royal
> Highness." . . . His right to impose tolls on trade, and to exact
> whatever oppressive taxes he chose from his peasantry, was
> admitted, but his authority was subject to constant interference.
> The last-joined District Officer, or any other official, might
> issue orders . . . and the native ruler had no legal or recognised
> means of enforcing his commands. He was necessarily forbid-
> den to raise armed forces . . . and could not therefore maintain
> order.[60]

Although in this passage Lugard was also deploring the existence
in Egbaland of theoretically autonomous realms (like the princely
states in British India), the main lines of his case are general ones.
Not only must local custom be left alone so far as possible, but a
chief must be left enough elbowroom to use whatever local forms
of muscle he could. The role of the local official was to be one of
"rendering assistance" and of serving as a "sympathetic advisor and
counselor," who must, furthermore, take care "not to interfere in
such a way as to lower a chief's prestige or destroy his interest in
his work." In plain English, the chief must be left free to exercise
his own power in his own way.

In the Egba case, the chiefs' taxes and tolls would stay (and with
them, presumably, the indigenous means of ensuring compliance),
the moralities of the "dual mandate" notwithstanding. That is, certain of the old exactions would be tolerated in practice (if temporarily) as a means of gaining chiefs' willing cooperation.[61] Excessive
interference would make it impossible for a chief to perform either
on his own behalf or on behalf of the regime. It would shift to
those who issued orders "through" chiefs the burden of enforcing
them. In sum, the regime had to choose between ruling directly
and restoring part of chiefs' effective power. Choosing the latter,
it worked at establishing an operational distance between officials

and customary rulers. By so doing, it could make the actual distance
between officials and the masses a smaller liability.

The possibility then arises, however, that chiefs would so harass
their subjects with exactions of all kinds that the oppressed would
rise in revolt, again necessitating costly force. Always alert to practical detail, Lugard takes up this inherent risk of calculated noninterference but, characteristically, in terms of the district officer's
role. This personage must tour his domain periodically, with the
manifest purpose of assessing taxes, supervising local improvement, and the like—but with an equally important latent purpose:

> [The district officer's] duties as assessing officer of the direct
> (income) tax effect much more than the mere collection of
> revenue. He is brought into close contact with the people, and
> gains an intimate knowledge of them, and of the personality
> and character of the chiefs and elders in every village. During
> his visit to each . . . he administers justice, inquires into and
> settles disputes, collects valuable statistics of population, agri-
> culture and industries.[62]

One pictures him as a combination administrator and *roi thauma-
turge*, whose annual visit marvelously erases the evil of the preceding year. Lugard's vision of his functions is an economical telescoping of development, intelligence, taxing, and public relations.
In this optimistic characterization, he does not attempt to conceal
a darker scenario at village level, where recalcitrant headmen might
disrupt both the first articulation and the second. This touring
official also "'uses every effort to detect oppression and extortion
if it exists, and impresses on the village elders the allegiance they
owe to their chiefs, and through them to the Government, and the
obligation to cease from lawless acts, and the right of every individual to appeal against injustice."

However we learn more from this about Lugard's reasons for
advocating periodic visitation than we do about its effectiveness in
tying local notables to their superiors further up the chain of command, or in preventing the misrepresentation of colonial laws. We
must not overestimate the political benefit to be reaped from such
tours, for how they succeeded must have varied from case to case.
But we can say for certain that they were, in large part, symbolic
displays. The DO's benign visitations were meant to imply, to both
ordinary villagers and their local rulers, the possibility of tough
ones. It appears from descriptions of their manner that these tours
were stage-managed as "progresses." Men went on palanquins (later

in Land Rovers), with entourages, and in the expectation that whole villages would turn out in stylized greeting.

It is important not to discount the symbolic aspect of touring. Every form of control not founded on continual and relentless violence is partly an exercise in suspended disbelief. (In a delightful paper, "Making Northern Rhodesia Imperial," Terence Ranger has shown how conscientiously British officials in Zambia toiled to strike the correct symbolic note.)[63] Nevertheless, however staged, the symbolic presence of the regime amounted in many areas, much of the time, to even less than a symbolic presence. Tours might occur quarterly or semiannually. They occurred less often than that in remoter areas, or at times when the DO's energy was absorbed in other work (as during wartime). According to the "Annual Report upon Native Affairs, 1933," the DO was "seen annually for a few hours," and he was the "only European ever seen at 90% of the villages." In the Chinsali and Mporokoso districts, villagers saw a white man "once or twice a year, when the DO [was] on tour or a European hunter travelled in the area."[64] An official who could write in one report after another that little had changed since his last visit and that all was "normal" was not, whatever he might have believed, either responsible for this state of affairs or in control of its evolution.

Indeed, some types of control were not feasible in the best of times, with the regime at close quarters. F. H. Melland, DO among the Lalas (Zambia), insisted that the ordinance that had "abolished the ordeals of the witchdoctor" was unenforceable and ought to be scrapped. He made a chilling argument: Illegal executions occurred "within earshot of the Boma," and yet he might not hear of them until years afterward. In the meantime, the reports of death came casually. The unsuspecting DO would make innocent notations as he crossed the victims off the census list, "died of pneumonia, killed by a lion, and so forth."[65]

Lugard recognized that the power exercised in the twilight zone between the administration and village authority, and between tours, could materialize in undesirable ways:

It is only by the advent of a British officer that scoundrels, misrepresenting the government's action, or extorting what they will from the natives in the name of Government can be caught; for the villagers in their ignorance, supposing them to be genuine, dare not as a rule complain. It has been abundantly shown that "unrest," resulting in murders and outrages inevitably take place among primitive tribes when districts are not regularly and systematically visited.[66]

Surely this reveals one of the deeper incertitudes of the second articulation. Lugard supposes that villagers would take the risk of entrusting themselves to the protection of an authority who appeared only intermittently (and who might well reject their complaints), rather than take their chances with the authority who sat within striking distance every day of the year. Besides, it is easy to imagine that the principled noninterference of the touring authority might cause him to wink sometimes at evils he suspected. And certain of them he could not suspect.

Lugard summed up these various practicalities in resounding language that does not quite cover the retreat he advocates from a plain-spoken, unsophisticated notion of a civilizing mission: "Principles do not change, but their mode of application may and should vary with the customs, the traditions, and the prejudices of each unit." Flexibility was administrative virtue, and he let it resound with other virtues in a Pauline flourish, "As Faith, Hope and Charity are to the Christian creed, so are Decentralization, Co-operation, and Continuity to African administration—and the greatest of these is Continuity." Decentralization was virtue because the tasks of administration varied from one locality to the next, and because the relevant "customs, traditions, and prejudices" were not the same pan-ethnically. If continuity was the greatest virtue, its sister was co-operation with customary rulers. "Co-operation," Lugard wrote, was "the keynote of success."[67] Continuity made it possible for a DO to familiarize himself with the local languages and local lore. (Zambia's District Notebooks are full of information, passed by official to successor, about local events, personalities, legends, myths, and more obviously practical data on weather, soil, crops, trade, and so on.) Continuity was doubly virtuous because effective co-operation with the men who counted locally presupposed that officials knew and were able to address effectively the people of their areas. In Lugard's portrayal, the DO must be capable of unusual diplomatic and rhetorical feats:

> The task of the administrative officer is to clothe his principles in the garb of evolution, not of revolution, to make it apparent alike to the educated native, the conservative Moslem, and the primitive pagan . . . that the policy of the Government is not antagonistic but progressive—sympathetic to his aspirations and guardian of his natural rights.[68]

Like Paul's ideal missionary, the DO was supposed to be all things to all the men (and sometimes, women) who were to carry forward the task of colonial domination. Viewed from the top side of the second articulation, their power to do so appeared only as power delegated. Viewed from within the first articulation, it grew upon its roots in the precolonial collectivity of African peoples and was imperfectly domesticated to British requirements. Thus the question with which I began—How did Britons rule?—is part of another: How did Britons rule in the company of Africans?

I do not claim to answer this question fully. My own answer is based upon the indirect evidence provided by official reactions to battle between revivalists and African rulers. It must remain provisional for two reasons. First, however rich in information, official testimony cannot replace testimony by the combatants themselves. Second, revealing though it may be, evidence derived from the analysis of battle cannot replace that derived from the analysis of day-to-day order. Having chosen to display order by working backward from disorder, I have not tried to draw the full circuit of African rule moving between the poles of voluntary compliance and coercion. Nonetheless, this indirect evidence about an aspect of the reality can supplement other findings.

The classic ethnographies that do set out to draw the full circuit of African rule do not place British officialdom alongside it on the same ethnographic footing.[69] In them, the world of ruling becomes a wholly African world, a world ordered by its own assumptions, contained within the limits of precolonial collectivity, and describable as if the British were not there—with one very large exception. Meyer Fortes and E. E. Evans-Pritchard state the large exception this way: "The sanction of force on which a European administration depends lies outside the native political system."[70] The "sanction of force" is thereby removed to a non-African world. It passes out of the ethnographic field and remains unstudied. By the same stroke, coercion within African polities passes as well; for although out of sight, the British presence has a highly visible effect. It interferes with the circuit of African rule between the poles of voluntary obedience and coercion. Arrogating to itself the sanction of force, the British regime seeks, as a matter of first principle, to freeze the motion of African rule at one pole, the pole of voluntary obedience; accordingly, it declares peace within the first articulation and countenances only those departures from peace there which are notarized by its own officials. As though incorporating this principle, Fortes and Evans-Pritchard rivet their attention upon voluntary compliance. Staked out this way, the ethnographic field takes its shape from the theory of the *pax Britannica*.

How far the resulting separation of black and white realms can properly define the scope of systematic description is open to question on both factual and theoretical grounds. Of some factual matters there can be no doubt: After the era of the adventurers, no one wrote from within a chief's enclosure during wartime, and no one stood idly by during an execution ordered solely under African law. Still, we cannot be certain unless we check that a sanction of force on which British rule depended disappeared from African polities. If we check, we are confronted by observations like Melland's, that actions defined as criminal under the *pax Britannica* continued and were punished only when—and if—discovered by British officials. Might not such actions expose to view relics and surrogates of force that remained available to African rulers of the British era? And is it not possible, in addition, that DCs and African rulers, working together and separately, found new methods of coercion—not all of them violent—for use within the first articulation? Despite their remove from many events, British informants can help us answer such factual questions.

The theoretical question arises from a well-established proposition: that institutionalized political arrangements tend, with the help of a legitimate order created by culture, to restrict the use of force. Ethnographies that have little to say about the use of force have much to say about voluntary compliance so created. In them, the constraints of culture build into individuals a bias toward obedience. A theory of culture so conceived substitutes for a theory of political power. Within such a theory, the first articulation is not defined in terms of rulers' ability to control their people; it is defined first and foremost in terms of people's motivation to control themselves. The passage of Fortes and Evans-Pritchard continues: "Sacred symbols, which reflect the social system, endow it with mystical values which evoke acceptance of the social order that goes beyond the obedience exacted by the secular sanction of force."

But to go beyond is not to do without. It is one thing to note the contribution of culture to orderly command, another to conceive of culture as automatically serving command. People are not "subjects" to culture as they may be to rulers. Rather, culture is subject to their purposes, and these purposes may lead toward novelty as well as toward repetition. Like language, culture is subject to the aims of users who are both constrained and empowered by its rules. At different times, the mystical aura around the sacred symbols of a culture may motivate people in different ways. In the episodes to be considered presently, we will see that sacred symbols did indeed evoke the social order, but that they sometimes empowered men and women who upheld the majesty of neither British nor African rulers.

Since I have relied upon European testimony almost exclusively, however, the image of events that emerges from my account is inevitably distorted and intermittent. Very often, for obvious reasons, the screen goes completely blank, and I can only hope to have filled in some of the gaps correctly. The complete story will have to be told by African investigators able to question villagers in detail, in their own languages, and from their own standpoints. Nevertheless, my limited evidence permits me at least to formulate an answer to the question, How did Britons rule in the company of Africans? in what I believe to be a fruitful way. This formulation hinges upon my conception of indirect rule as being *doubly articulated*.

Within the first articulation, black rulers' ability to command sat, so to speak, upon a cushion of culture—that is, upon routine ways of behaving and thinking that give to social life the relative predictability that members count upon for the conduct of their day-to-day lives. Culture in this sense provides the infrastructure of human social life, whose distinctive quality is that individuals must engage in practical reasoning every step of the way. To undertake a distinctively human social act is to proceed on the assumption that the consequences will be familiar and typical ones (like the act itself), and thus predictable. In other words, to undertake a human social act is to follow a known routine. I therefore suggest that Max Weber erred in assigning "habitual" action to the category of the "nonrational";[71] for if I am right, rational social action cannot even be conceived of apart from routine. We can view the contribution of culture to command in this light. Human beings daily recreate their interest in a given order simply by pursuing practical goals under known conditions. This interest is not easily forgone.[72]

The positions of African rulers commanded important nodes of routine—coming of age as a man or woman, marriage and divorce, access to property and livelihood, inheritance, cure, judgment of disputes, tax payments, repression of deviance, and religious rites that made collections of individuals into self-conscious units. These positions put them at necessary crossings of men's and women's ordinary lives. And there, sources of power other than mundane physical force opened up. African rulers tapped these sources, not

simply in order to serve foreign overlords but, obviously, for reasons they could defend before all of their subjects at least some of
the time. The colonial official began to learn this lesson, at first by
trial and error. So doing, he discovered that indirect rule joined
together what the civilizing mission put asunder: avoidance of clan
incest and road maintenance; witch cleansing and tax payment;
and veneration of ancestors and loyalty to the Crown. In short, the
first articulation enclosed a politics of custom that, properly tapped,
could distribute political power upward. It is this species of politics
that I propose to examine now.

2

THE POLITICS OF CUSTOM

Throughout history there have been circumstances in the extension of imperial power when it suited the conquerors to preserve and utilize the institutions of the conquered and especially the kingships and chieftaincies which could be used as ready-made economical agencies of coherence and order.

MARGERY PERHAM

BEFORE PROCEEDING, LET us agree that neither human expansiveness nor intellectual commitment disposed our official toward accommodation with African custom. Philosophy urged the speedy displacement of an "inferior" culture. Science seconded philosophy. Science placed most Britons in the "best" white race. It established descending ranks of white "lesser" races before identifying the "highest" colored ones and set these above another hierarchy of African races.[1] While science disposed our official toward contempt for Africans and their culture, human expansiveness disposed him, at best, toward the "uplifting" of men and women deemed to belong to humankind's childhood. Late-nineteenth-century human expansiveness longed to remake all humanity in its own image. If our official flew in the face of these influences, and sought to learn, he did so because he had to. He had to because the kingships and chieftaincies that might serve as "ready-made economical agencies of coherence and order" had coherence and order of their own. Ignorance could defeat the enterprise. Anthropologists helped to defeat the ignorance. As their science outgrew the sterile evolutionism and the ethnocentric certainty of its beginnings, they evolved an appreciation of coherence in cultures not their own.

CUSTOM AND THE POWER TO COMPEL

According to Malcolm Hailey, "practical reality" led anyone toward "Lugardism," including the French. Never mind the renowned French commitment to "direct rule" and to "assimilation," he said. And never mind their philosophical lukewarmness toward "theories of 'differentiation.' " Men like Lanesson, Gallieni, and Lyautey discovered early that they could not do without the collaboration of indigenous rulers. To push home his point, that "practical reality" necessarily qualified the civilizing mission, even as conducted by his Lugardless French colleagues, Lord Hailey quoted remarks Lyautey made in 1902:

> [There is need] so far as possible to keep intact the indigenous governmental machinery [*rouages indigènes*], institutions, serviceable customs [*usages à utiliser*], and traditional chiefs, leaving to them the direct exercise of police, administration, even justice and tax collection, under the simple control of a single agent attached to the chief. It is through this agent, in constant contact with the indigenous chief, that the horizon of the latter, and that of his people, will progressively broaden.[2]

We may take as an instance of French "Lugardism" the strategy Félix Eboué used when he arrived in French Equatorial Africa. In 1910, administrators still confronted widespread refusal to pay colonial taxes, and worse, periodic assaults upon *concessionnaires* or their agents. The young administrator had instructions to arrest the recalcitrant chiefs of this not-yet-fully "pacified" area. More intelligent than the men who urged arrests, he conducted an ethnographic study (which was later published) and came independently to the Lugard-Lyautey conclusions. In a series of palavers with the rulers he had identified through his research among local informants, he offered various inducements, such as 5 percent of the tax collected. Thereafter, the chiefs did what was necessary to assure the payment of taxes.

The same strategy led him to visit Ngokala, the supernatural head of an influential secret society called the Somale. After first sending gifts of salt, machetes, and cloth, Eboué set out. The incident recalls Macbeth's encounter with the three weird sisters on the heath in one respect—a strange, howling storm arose during the journey. At the audience, Eboué exchanged messages with the redoubtable Ngokala, who never showed himself bodily. Then the mortal parted company with the immortal. The storm had already convinced Eboué's interpreter and sole traveling companion of the being's supernatural power. Eboué himself was soon convinced of the being's worldly power, for it accomplished what the Frenchman could not. After he had offered the spirit an appropriate quid pro quo, Eboué later said, its "cooperation was promised, and I must admit that the contract was faithfully executed, the orders were given in the way I desired ... after which the difficulties disappeared like magic."³ Magic helped to erect more than one of Kirk-Greene's "rois de la brousse." Eboué's kinship to Macbeth does not end with the happenstance of a windstorm. Like Macbeth, he had no legitimate right to rule. To "be king hereafter," he had to venture for supernatural help into the twilight of official usage. Fair was foul and foul was fair.

Collaboration with African rulers followed from a political logic that immediately took colonial administrators a step further; collaborators did not come simply as usable "mouthpieces," detached and portable everywhere, but as leaders geared into *rouages indigènes*. And even if African leaders began merely as willing collaborators, with no legitimate claim to preeminence, they, too, could accomplish little unless they became enmeshed in the same *rouages* and availed themselves of the same *usages à utiliser*.⁴ Not surprisingly, therefore, we hear from officials repeated warnings not only against excessive interference in chiefs' work but also against ill-thought-out cultural disruption. The word of an Ngokala was good only in context.

Black rulers' ability to command rested upon routine ways of behaving and thinking. This routine included techniques, products, expectations, rituals, usages, conventional emotions, concepts of scandal, rules of etiquette, ranks, rights, rules, and obligations that together delimited order within the first articulation. The legitimate authority of customary rulers—that is, their ability to obtain voluntary obedience—stood only if mounted on this foundation. When the technicians of indirect rule saw that by reckless pursuit of a civilizing mission they might destroy this foundation, and thereby colonial power, they reconsidered. The intelligent drew back from the triumphal Hobbesian vision that the state rightly tames an uncivil society. They had had the quite un-Hobbesian nightmare that the state might be forced to try. As one governor, Sir Percy Girouard (Nigeria), put it:

If we allow the tribal authority to be ignored or broken, it will mean that we, who numerically form a small minority in the country, shall be obliged to deal with a rabble, with thousands of persons in a savage or semi-savage state, all acting on their own impulses, and making themselves a danger to society generally.[5]

Not all officials were equally apt students of this practical reality. But even if all had been, forces innate to colonialism shifted the cultural footing of colonial order. As the new economy altered productive activity in the countryside, it inevitably changed the context of customary authority. And by setting customary rulers to work at tasks without precedent in history or custom, officials necessarily crosscut what they had learned about the cultural context of legitimate rulers' power: Not all commands may be legitimately issued even by a legitimate ruler. Nevertheless, the British went to considerable lengths to recognize the legitimate inheritors of chieftaincies and headmanships. For a state born illegitimate and forced to scrimp all its life, chiefs' legitimacy was the best available makeshift.

Anthropologists assisted officials in the difficult tasks of discovering the rules applicable to position and succession, and of threading a way through innumerable permutations and exceptions. The often monumental difficulty of these tasks was an artifact of their formulation. Taking colonial law and order as premise, officials sought rules that promised to contribute thereto—and that would help to advance Britain's war by other means toward bureaucratic predictability. Furthermore, they meant to bypass the uncertainties of politics. For most of the colonial period, the regime recognized no African politics as such, but only "native administration." As Karl Mannheim said so well, "The fundamental tendency of all bureaucratic thought is to turn all problems of politics into problems of administration."[6]

But the practical reality that confronted the British had no inherent tendency to conform to bureaucratic thought. For example, a notation in the Chinsali District Notebook, dated in the early 1930s, states the finding of "an anthropologist" (probably Audrey Richards) that the Bembas' Shimwalule was to the Citimukulu as the Archbishop of Canterbury was to the British Crown: an anointer of kings without temporal power.[7] Here then was a rule with a British equivalent that promised, at first glance, to smooth out rough places in a nonpolitical "native administration." Then again, in view of the tempestuous relationship between church and state in England (not to speak of Europe more generally), it promised no such thing with certainty. Discovering and trying to manipulate such rules, officials found in native administration political drama they had not sought.

Before the *pax Britannica*, the application of formal rules to cases was not the only method of choosing new leadership or settling disputed claims; war and migration cut through legal and moral tangles. But the new dispensation halted wars of succession, feuds, and the founding of new chiefdoms by simple migration—all available methods thitherto. While describing the formal rules of succession, Richards paused to remark that "admittedly in the past the Chitimukuluship (the Paramount Chieftaincy) was often seized by force, yet it is important to realize from the point of view of present-day administration that a mechanism for the peaceful settlement of this question of succession actually existed."[8] But the decisiveness of such rules did not arise full-blown from the traditional society of the past but was the creature of colonization. It was part of the theory and practice of indirect rule to convert African ways of doing into a formulized "custom," the museum display we gaze at in much ethnographic writing. Lugard assigned constraint within the first articulation to the domain of "native law and custom." When he wrote that chiefs would be "unfettered as regards matters . . . to them the most important attributes of rule," he was stating the peculiar form in which custom would finally reign in the world of indirect rule.

This world corresponds remarkably to the functionalists' world of norms, rules, and overarching values, a world without a place for the Macbeth who liquidates his opposition or for truly heinous kin. Genuine struggles for power occur in this world, if at all, in pantomime.[9] (For officials, in a similar way, politics could only intrude on this world as an alien element—in the persons of "detribalized" Africans, other troublemakers, and the occasional untrustworthy chief.) Customary order is encapsulated in ritual and supernatural belief, in traditionally legitimated norms, in flamboyant ceremonial and magic incantation—all these animate humans toward ordered social life from beyond the body politic.

But insofar as this portrayal corresponds to anything real, it was the plan of colonial rule that reoutfitted the customary order to look this way. Only in consequence of colonial rule did it become possible for a Bemba disrespectful to his chief merely to suffer the

Crown's arrest. When Richards visited Lubemba in the 1930s, rule was based upon "supernatural sanctions," but old people were still alive who had been mutilated for such crimes as *lèse-majesté*.[10] Paradoxically, the role of the "supernatural" increased as Africa's history joined that of a secularized modern society. Thus, the rule-governedness of human behavior that is central to anthropological theorizing converged with the theoretical implications of indirect rule. Both accounted for collective order without recourse to politics or war. But at the dawn of the colonial era, there were despots the equal of Macbeth. It took conquest to reduce them to mere repositories of custom. And it took the political logic of indirect rule to impart to custom as such the substance it gradually acquired.

DISPOSSESSING AND RESTORING CUSTOMARY AUTHORITY

At first the regime was satisfied simply to dispossess the chiefs. To facilitate the penetration of old sovereignties, it made common cause with usurpers. Father Dupont helped the BSAC penetrate the heart of the Bemba kingdom by befriending a rebellious son of the Citimukulu.[11] Chief Chuaula hurried to befriend agents of the BSAC as well as missionaries, because his people despised him—according to rumor, he had committed adultery and murder in order to come to power.[12] For their part, the British hurried to befriend the Tumbukas and the Tongas of Malawi by freeing them from the overlordship of the Ngonis.[13] They then proceeded further against all chiefs by stripping them of the right to customary tribute in labor and products, and by taking over their judicial functions.[14] Robert Codrington, an early *roi de la brousse*, even rendered judgments in divorce and property cases. It seemed at first an excellent sign that people began to take their private disputes to men like Codrington—whatever worked against African authority worked for British power. Conquest seemed complete and completely effective.

But before long, men of the regime noticed a certain unwholesomeness in some Africans' enthusiasm for the new arrangements. For example, Chuaula's co-operation was one thing, his people's another. His chiefdom remained for years troubled and troublesome, a land in which one Watchtower preacher after the other gained active converts. The enthusiasm of Codrington's superiors cooled when they understood that some Africans were only too willing to come to his court, there to let the ignorance or interests of this alien judge violate to their advantage local notions of simple justice. Codrington was making "great mistakes," his superiors realized, and he was creating disorder rather than a predictable new order.[15] They curtailed his legal jurisdiction.

Again, British officials rethought their attitude toward chiefs' customary rights in tribute labor. At first, the principle seemed straightforward. Customary labor was a form of servitude. As such, it deserved condemnation and abolition—after all, the commitment to stamp out slavery had provided imperialism with one of its rationales, and the abolition of customary labor carried the bonus of further expropriating the independent authority of chiefs. But as the regime came to depend upon their dependent authority, the disadvantages of this principle revealed themselves. Officials soon realized that a chief's authority among his people rested in part on his ability to collect tribute. Customary labor was so fundamental an attribute of customary authority that one way of identifying one's chief was in the formula "I do tribute labor in so-and-so's village." Unfree labor of this kind had been an important resource in the execution of essential public works, in warfare, and in the maintenance of a body of men capable of enforcing a chief's will throughout his dominions. Further, a chief called on tribute labor to produce famine crops, whose distribution in time of scarcity was his obligation. By causing chiefs to fail in such obligations, the regime undercut their moral influence, which in turn undercut their effectiveness.[16]

Richards records a case in which tribute labor was inseparable from the performance of legitimizing ritual, precisely the sort of custom that the regime wished to underwrite.[17] She reports that the Citimukulu, Paramount Chief of the Bembas, was widely blamed for the economic distress of the early 1930s, which was aggravated by a serious infestation of locusts.[18] Calamity had come to pass, people said, because the Citimukulu had failed to build a new capital upon his accession, as custom demanded. He had failed to do this because he had not been able to assemble the builders or, before that, to grow surplus crops for their provisioning. In addition, the Citimukulu had no money to pay the builders, and he could not compel them to work for nothing. Although reputedly very strong throughout the colonial period, shared sentiment for chieftaincy and its symbols proved insufficient to mobilize the needed labor. The chief complained that his influence was waning as people found in his ritual tort a ground for disobeying him and, indeed, for expressing their contempt to his face. These developments provided the backdrop of the spectacular *mucapi* revival, whose indirect use by the regime I shall return to.

Since Britons had been prominent in the international campaign against forced labor in the Congo Free State (a fact that Lugard set in the context of Britain's moral mandate), they could not easily countenance the restoration of tribute labor.[19] Since they could not easily forgo it either, they arrived at the principle that any such labor should be remunerated at set rates. This principle raised a new difficulty. Prescribing even nominal rates of payment aggravated the problem of financing chiefs.[20] In 1934, the Citimukulu was receiving an annual "allowance" of sixty pounds, equivalent to the salary of an African clerk or cook.[21] Leaving aside the anomaly of a chief's paying people who owed him tribute, the problem remained that the allowance did not go far enough. Solving this problem led, inter alia, to increasing chiefs' salaries and to the introduction of a system that authorized chiefs to retain a share of the taxes they collected, for use on authorized local projects. But tax farming, even in modified form, inevitably raised the dual specter of tax extortion and conversion of public funds. Various local officials opposed the establishment of Native Treasuries on these grounds.[22] Given the practical problem of making indirect rule work, their objections were less invalid than irrelevant.

Sometimes the regime's need to restore customary prerogatives coincided with its interest in promoting colonial development. Seeing that they could redeploy chiefs' traditional function of assigning manpower quotas to the headmen under them, the British put chiefs to work recruiting labor for colonial enterprises before World War I.[23] And during the war, African policemen and *boma* "messengers" frequently used force to back up chiefs and headmen in this task.[24] Villagers' unpaid labor proved useful in the execution of public works—road building and maintenance, canal digging, clearing, terracing, and so forth. During World War II, the regime used customary tribute labor in the production of surplus food. Since local administrators could define such projects as being in Africans' interest, this labor was rebaptized "communal labor," that is, stipulated amounts of unremunerated work.[25] Both the recruitment of workers and their supervision typically fell to chiefs. Those who succeeded and showed enthusiasm earned the qualifications "progressive" and "competent." Not all succeeded.

Their failure forced the DCs into action. During World War II, when resistance to the forced production of famine crops reached large proportions, we find these men querying the rectitude of

THE POLITICS OF CUSTOM

using unfree labor—their understanding of local dissatisfaction no doubt grew in step with local resistance. The probability that the difficulties of enforcement put the question does not alter the point: The regime found it difficult to justify either to Africans or to itself what amounted to the forced labor that had supposedly been abolished. The regime met the problem by enacting regulations designed to limit the quotas of famine production legally assignable to villages.[a] The burden of execution always fell first upon customary rulers. And when strong enforcement seemed indicated, administrators kept to the logic of this arrangement by pushing chiefs forward as much as was practicable. Because administrators so often stood hidden in the rear, it is sometimes difficult to follow the logic of local actions.

For example, Watchtower converts in the Luapula Valley usually phrased their opposition to the chiefs in the ancient language of Protestant dissent. Like the seventeenth-century Quakers who refused to doff their hats to worldly authority, Watchtowerites refused to perform customary obeisances to chiefs. For them, performing customary labor was the same as obeisance; and both belong to the "idolatrous" ritual they execrated. In accord with the Biblical injunction to "get out from among them and be clean," the Watchtower faithful formed separate little communities of the saved. When such things happened, local officials usually stepped up from the rear in order to enforce the chief's position or to compel expressions of respect. In Luapula the regime prohibited disrespect to chiefs and the establishment of unauthorized villages. It gave the native authorities license to punish individuals for breach of customary decorum. Thus authorized, the chiefs gathered their loyalists' support and burned to the ground the Watchtower settlements. Upon returning to minority status in their original villages, these Protestants moderated their tone and attitude immediately.[26] But they fought back. They "fulfilled and overfulfilled" their quotas of communal labor but made their every move the opposite of deference.

[a] Given the strategic importance of surplus food production, I imagine that such regulations need have existed only on paper wherever enforcement presented no acute difficulty. Where, on the other hand, quotas could only be enforced at great cost, their relaxation could be justified as British fair play. Some local officials argued that crops destined for territory-wide use could not legitimately be defined as "famine production" in the same sense that purely local stocks could be and that, therefore, the former did not fall under the rules governing unpaid "communal labour" (see NAZ, Sec/Nat 312, vol. 7).

The nonconformity of the Watchtower also interfered with chiefs' ability to summon soldiers. When conscription for military service in the East African theater was at its height, the Watchtower saw a dramatic upsurge in its popularity. Large numbers of people found themselves in accord with Watchtower doctrine about killing; and the commandment "Thou shalt not kill" reverberated everywhere. According to Alex Muwamba, a clerk and a loyal Malawian member of the Livingstonia Mission, the commandment fell from the lips of men inconspicuous thitherto in their devotion to the Christian God. "I do not think they join the movement to become Christians," Muwamba informed the secretary for native affairs (Zambia), "but to avoid death by being killed."[27]

The complementary phenomena of resistance by refusal to conform to custom and of punishment through the instrumentalities of custom took other forms. At first glance, the domain of kinship regulations would appear to be a matter in which the regime would have little serious interest. Yet Africans attempting to bypass customary control of marriage ran into British officials attempting to reinforce this control. In Kasempa District, we find district commissioners listening carefully as old chiefs recite for them the degrees of kinship within which sexual relations were prohibited. Chief Kasonso said, "We have [Watchtower] men here and they have committed incest here and spoilt the country." The DC asked the prohibited degrees of kinship. Kasonso replied, "[Classificatory] mother, niece, sister, daughter." Although some of these classificatory relatives were remote, from the Western standpoint, from that of Kasonso and his colleagues they were not; violating the rules was an abomination. According to Kasonso's brother chief, Muiji, Watchtower heretics had even given incest ritual meaning: "They do commit incest and cheat them by saying that they have a spirit if they do or die if they do not."[28] Rancor and conflict erupted in the villages of two Copperbelt chiefdoms because young people were engaging in adultery and incest. According to the recognized chief, their immorality had caused women to become barren and the fields to stop yielding as they had done in the past; the Watchtower was spoiling the land. This immorality worried administrators because it worried chiefs.

The chiefs worried not only about scandal in families but also about the erosion of their own prerogatives. It was a function of customary authority to regulate marriage and preside over the transactions connected with it, to keep track of family relationships, and sometimes to control the transfer of property belonging to a lineage. The regime early returned questions of marriage and in-

heritance to African judges. It periodically took steps to prevent
this ancient competence from falling into disuse, even if it meant
scotching missionary plans for the expansion of Christian marriage.
(Indeed, as part of the attempt to institute indirect rule on the
Copperbelt, the regime went so far as to impose allegedly "traditional" marriage arrangements upon urbanites.)[29] To let marriage
escape from customary control was to expropriate further what
authority African potentates still preserved.

Sexual immorality could threaten colonial law and order in another way as well. It might force a chief or headman into lawlessness. In villages where the chief had a large contingent of loyal
followers, he might not sit idly by while young people flaunted
abomination in everyone's face. He might march against the sinners. It was one thing if a chief marched, with British authorization,
to burn a city of destruction. It was quite another if he acted on
his own or at the urging of his scandalized subjects. In the second
case, the sufferers could march to the *boma* to demand British
justice; and then the DC, to uphold British justice, would be hard
put not to act, even if it meant prosecuting his African right-hand
man. Such potential trouble put administrators into close conversation with the like of Kasonso, Muiji, and their colleagues.

Some Watchtower congregations instituted free love among the
faithful. In classic antinomian fashion, the vice of the unredeemed
became the virtue of the redeemed; free love became part of a
"baptism of love" (in some groups, a "baptism of fire").[30] Accompanied by loud and intrusive ritual, these practices shocked conventional rulers and their supporters. Although orthodox members
of the sect excoriated free love, the correspondence of the missionary L. V. Phillips shows that the practice was still alive in some
conventicles in the mid-1940s.[31] Not explained simply as lewd excess, free love must be understood, I believe, as part of the resistance against customary control of marriage and the custodianship
that went with it. As Lévi-Strauss showed long ago, the prohibition
of incest is fundamental to the integrity of all families—and to the
integrity of the wider systems in which families are inserted.[32] The
prescription of incest thus provides a weapon against any authority
grounded in kinship. It is hard to conceive of another action, short
of death, that might remove an individual beyond the pale of
earthly kinship as swiftly and definitively—or one that would as
effectively burn the convert's bridge back to kinship-based society.[b]

[b] Incidentally, in 1 Cor. 5:1, Paul makes reference to incest in the Corinthian
congregation (a congregation that, we recall, had carried "talking in the unknown

Since the regime sought to protect marriage custom, ritual incest and free love hammered against its very foundations. Quite literally, sexual morality became a police problem.

One official, J. Moffat Thompson, said as much, almost in so many words. Just after World War I, he encountered a Watchtower preacher, one Lamek, who desired to marry a classificatory relative. Even though satisfied that the marriage did not constitute incest under European law, Thompson argued that a prosecution in the case would "set a good example." "Let these people see," he wrote, "that they have to comply with the customs of their elders and the people in general notwithstanding their belonging to the Watchtower Church."[33] The records do not say with what success officials enforced conventional sexual morality.

Nonconformity with custom was not limited to Christian elements of the population, or to nonconformity based upon religious commitment. The spread of the modern economy into rural districts did damage of its own. On Chiluŵi Island, in the swamplands of the Mbereshi River, the Bisa people took up significant amounts of cash-crop production before World War I. When the buying and selling of land as a commodity, capitalist fashion, grew up alongside the new market activity, customary rulers complained to local officials that these practices were eroding their authority to distribute land annually for use. In this region of relatively dense settlement, the authority to distribute and redistribute lands was a substantial prerogative that carried with it control over people's livelihood. Loss of this prerogative meant loss of practical authority. The administration saw the point; it moved to block the purchase and sale of land in order to preserve the leverage of customary authorities.[34]

Thus, in many ways the customary prerogatives of African rulers saw a new, if transformed, life. While the colonial regime took from customary rulers some means of enforcing their will, it also restored some, left others intact, and added new ones. For example, it became possible for Africans found guilty of offenses under native

---

tongue" and women's participation in services to an indecent extreme). Paul said, "It is reported commonly that there is fornication among you as is not so much as named among the Gentiles, that one should have his father's wife." Like African Watchtowerites, the Corinthians, too, had to transcend clan ties in order to enter into a fellowship as reborn children of God. I suspect that clan incest may be the natural concomitant of rupturing clan organization and replacing it with group membership based upon shared faith—that is, voluntary rather than imposed membership or, in Toënnies's expression, *Gesellschaft* rather than *Gemeinschaft*.

law and custom to face terms of imprisonment and hard labor in His Majesty's jails. At the same time the regime countenanced sentences by native authorities to fines and flogging, in addition to imprisonment. Native law and custom stood beside other laws valid in the territory as a whole. Customary rulers bore responsibility for enforcing two sets of laws, although the extent of this responsibility varied from area to area and from time to time. But if the logic of indirect rule drew customary rulers into the colonial order, the same logic drew the administration into the customary order. To protect African rulers as keepers of the colonial peace, it had to buttress them as repositories of custom. Custom in this sense was not a discretionary matter of correct and incorrect usage, punishable only by the bad opinion of others and conscience. It became legally obligatory.

Mission activity violated this logic by displacing the religious foundations of African rulers' legitimacy. The colonial economy further violated the logic of indirect rule by displacing people from their village economies into the paid labor force. By withdrawing villagers from the moral and physical authority of the customary order, it created "masterless men," Middleton's term for a comparable group in early modern England.[35] These contradictory movements intensified the political importance of custom. The regime's vacillation on the subject of witchcraft is parallel to its vacillation in the case of customary tribute labor.

WITCH DOCTORS

Between 1930 and 1934, the administration of Malawi and Zambia went back and forth between opposing and tolerating a spectacular antiwitchcraft revival led by medicine men called Bamucapi. The familiar chain of events recurs: African rulers have a customary prerogative to cleanse their lands of witchcraft; they lose purchase on their people if they fail to exercise it; they do exercise it; the regime at first opposes the prerogative, hesitates, and finally supports the chiefs; it is then drawn onto the territory of witch doctoring, just as it was drawn onto the territories of unfree labor and sexual morality.

The responses of officials to witchcraft ranged from a compelling curiosity about "primitive" beliefs to a hardheaded readiness to redeploy even witchcraft in the interest of colonial order. Félix Eboué remained fascinated by the Somale society for thirty years. District Officer F. H. Melland produced an amateur ethnographer's study arguing the logical coherence of witch beliefs some fifteen years in advance of E. E. Evans-Pritchard's classic *Witchcraft, Oracles and Magic among the Azande.* Autobiographical works by others devote long passages to accounts of their dealings with the weird practitioners of an esoteric craft.[36] John Nottingham, a DO in Kenya during the 1950s, proposed that Kenya officials study witch doctors' methods systematically, in order to fashion a political weapon against Mau Mau guerrillas. In the course of his argument, he revealed that Britons had suborned the services of witch doctors in the past—although not always with the results they hoped for.

> "Please help us get rid of witchcraft" must be one of the hardiest annuals on the agenda of Chiefs' meetings all over Africa, and it is too often politely passed over by administrative officers who feel it is too thorny a subject to dabble in. But at this particular juncture [1959], as clear indications came in that Kikuyu and Kamba Mau Mau were using and adapting Kamba "witchcraft" in their campaign of subversion, the District Commissioner of Machakos felt that the opportunity which a properly controlled inquiry might give to learn something of its techniques and their alleged effects should not be missed.

Since Nottingham reveals what never was, or could have been, explicit policy, his argument offers rare testimony about the inner workings of indirect rule.

> It was decided early on that it would be wrong to import a reputedly all-powerful wizard from say the Giriama at Kilifi, to overawe the local demons. Two blacks do not make a white, and publicly to admit that witchcraft could only be cured by further witchcraft, of whatever color, would only thicken the already dense enough clouds obscuring the subject. Furthermore, it would foster the impression that Government disapproved only of Kamba witchcraft. . . . It was on this reef that some previous officials' efforts had foundered, such as the wholesale "*kithitu*" and "*kabisu*" cleansing ceremonies conducted under Government auspices shortly before the war, which did little except line the pockets of the witchdoctor concerned.[37]

In Zambia and Malawi, a few officials and a very few missionaries set forth coherent arguments in favor of taking a broader view of witchcraft and witchcraft eradication than was suggested by Lugard's exclamation that the *pax Britannica* had "abolished the ordeals of the witchdoctor." Sometimes they went further than merely taking a broader view. In the wake of the *mucapi* revival, some officials began to doubt the wisdom of the Witchcraft Ordinance, and some attacked it forcefully.

In 1935, F. H. Melland, an experienced DO, attacked. The Witchcraft Ordinance was ethically wrong, politically foolish, and unenforceable. His insight as a line officer charged with enforcing an unpopular regulation probably accounts for his blunt conclusion that the ordinance was, indeed, "divorced from reason." The climax of Melland's argument is this remarkable proposal:

> Everyone who has intimate knowledge of such matters knows that the word of a witchdoctor has infinitely more weight with the majority of Africans than that of an official or a missionary. *Is it not common sense that we should make an alliance with him— get the use of his power and of his services? From personal experience in individual cases I have found that the better-class witchdoctor can so co-operate and is perfectly willing to do so.*[38]

One may not draw the same practical conclusion. But his contention that the official attitude toward witchcraft was illogical, given the premise of ruling through preestablished leadership, is thoroughly convincing:

> *Is it not recognised . . . that in this system of indirect rule we are making the position untenable.* We tell headmen to try cases, but not when they refer to a non-existent thing like witchcraft, the greatest evil in all their eyes. We tell people to listen to their headmen, and to abhor the witchdoctor. The two may be one and the same. I know of such cases. Even when they are not, the *sub rosa* trial will still take place, for the headman not being allowed to try such a case in open court dare not try to prevent a trial . . . lest he be accused of being a witch. *As regards this particular matter we have put the headman in an impossible position, and that is ethically wrong while politically it is a very serious introduction of "foreign matter" into the machinery we have established.*[39]

The regime never systematically tolerated the antiwitchcraft functions of customary rulers, but its pragmatic handling of the *mucapi* revival came close to Melland's reasoning. By the time of the Bamucapi, officials had come to realize that, like the precolonial units of allegiance, witchcraft was not easily wiped off Africa's map.

In the days before the *pax Britannica*, a chief could try those accused of witchcraft by applying the poison ordeal, but the regime suppressed ordeals from the beginning. The Witchcraft Ordinance of 1914 systematically attacked the whole complex of witch belief.[40] It removed the offense of witchcraft from the purview of the law altogether. Whereas murder and theft were crimes before and after the advent of British rule, witchcraft went from the status of a crime to the status of a superstitious belief that merely generated recognized crimes. The execution of a convicted witch counted as premeditated murder and its perpetrator(s) could hang. The ordinance also made it unlawful to divine the mystical cause of a misfortune. If a person lamented, for example, that a witch had caused his crops to wither, or that adultery had caused his brother's death, he committed a crime; and so did the doctor who diagnosed his misfortune. The law was intended to stop the violence that sometimes followed such diagnoses. The law also prohibited the naming of witches, because naming could lead to vigilante justice against those so accused, to rulers' exercise of authority that the regime had stripped from them, or both. But even if unconnected with violence of any kind, the purveying of medicine and skill in witchcraft and witch finding was actionable—as fraud. Convicted persons faced severe penalties—imprisonment, fine, flogging, or a combination of all three.

Scientific writers on witchcraft generally agree that the Witchcraft Ordinance was widely considered unjust and even as deliberately harmful.[41] It put the regime that claimed to uphold law and order in the position of shielding known criminals. It put customary upholders of justice in the position of outlaws. And it made the ordinary villager who obtained a charm for self-defense, much as an American householder might obtain a pistol, subject to prosecution. Under a colonial law that assumed the innocence of the witch the villager feared, victim and perpetrator changed places—the "victim" stood accused of an impossible crime; the "perpetrator" was one who (falsely) alleged that the impossible crime had been committed. Thus, colonial rule opposed two idioms for the handling of conflict under the law. Anyone wishing to advance the British idiom had to bypass the logic of witchcraft. Anyone wishing to advance the African idiom had to enter into this logic.

F. H. Melland entered in. He traveled the same road as Thomas Hobbes, who wrote, "As for witches, I think not that their witchcraft is any real power; but yet that they are justly punished, for the false belief they have that they can do such mischief, joined with their purpose to do it if they can."[42] Melland claimed that many actual murders went untried because Britons and Africans failed to understand one another. Villagers were sometimes afraid, he said, even to report murders by poisoning since they thought of poisoning as a species of bewitchment. Countering the observation that the bodies of victims often bore no signs of murderous violence, he suggested that the traces of the exotic pharmacopeia available to African poisoners disappeared so quickly from a corpse as to render autopsy useless. (It is difficult to be sure, however, that Melland was not duped on this point by the very ambiguity between witchcraft and poisoning he pointed out himself: Conceivably, the blurring could work more than one way—physical substances being sometimes but not always used to bring about a victim's illness or death.) In any case, Melland meant to impress upon his readers what Africans tried to impress upon British skeptics: Witchcraft killed. By this route, Melland entered the actual syllogizing of African villagers.

Melland contended that the regime had misplaced sympathy for the "victims" of witchcraft—the accused witches. No matter what Britons believed, it was proper to bring accused witches to justice in some orderly, official way. If A confessed to having bewitched B, for instance, it was right and necessary for a community both to purge him and to receive the regime's support in so doing. Whether A had actually harmed B, A was rightly considered a threat to the community, because he had resorted to evil doings. But, instead of that, colonial law freed the culprit while punishing the upholders of public tranquillity: "It is largely for these 'innocent' men and women that our withers have been wrung, while we have, officially, given no pity to the ordinary man and woman living in constant dread of, and actually suffering from the machinations" of witches. In bracketing the innocence of those accused of witchcraft, Melland stepped deep into the local logic. In arguing the efficacity of the African legal procedure by which the guilt or innocence of a suspected witch was customarily established, he went deeper still:

> It cannot be too strongly stressed that in a native witch trial by ordeal (a most ceremonious affair, formally conducted), the belief in witchcraft and the faith in the ordeal are so complete, that not only the accusers—the sufferers—believe in the righteousness and efficacity of the trial, but the convicted witch . . . believes in it just as implicitly, and so do the witch's nearest and dearest relatives.[43]

For African judges—and for Melland also—the external correctness of the procedure was a warrant for its justice. It does not seem
to have occurred to him that the authoritative performance of the
correct procedure, backed up by might, could provide an effective
surrogate for people's "belief" in its justice, while simultaneously
putting into the hands of those who administered the procedure
a formidable weapon. Then again, perhaps this did indeed occur
to the able and practical-minded Melland.

It has been widely attested that witchcraft and witchcraft accusations serve as weapons of struggle within the customary order,
and that people often wield them in support of purely personal or
sectional claims.[44] Like all forms of ideology, the principles of witchcraft can serve opposite positions. In other words, the progression
from rules to cases is not merely logical; and not all tangles undo
themselves before the correct rule. Thus, Melland's proposal and
supporting arguments exemplify the reification of custom under
colonial auspices. For him, there was an ultimate "right" side in a
witchcraft case, and that right side corresponded to norms and
rules that were tied in turn to principles of justice, peace, and
order—just as, for Richards, the "right" ruler was to be identified
by applying formal criteria. Substantive judgments that might have
emerged from conflict and a matching of forces now derived, in
Melland's conception, from immutable truths about danger to a
community. But Melland's reification of witch belief was not a logical fallacy but a logical practicality. He merely took a side, the side
of constituted authority: The regime had chosen chiefs and headmen as executors of colonial order; it was up to them to control
social evil in their own terms and up to local administrations to
support them.

SUBORNING WITCH DOCTORS

The position of chiefs and headmen was particularly difficult during the Great Depression.[45] The colonial economy had taken many
young men out of the customary order. (Percentages of the able-
bodied male labor force absent from rural areas sometimes ranged
as high as 70 percent and commonly reached 50 percent.) Now the
economy returned these men to the old conditions of village life
suddenly and in large numbers. At the same time, it demanded
that they continue to pay taxes. Customary rulers had the unen-
viable tasks of enforcing the tax law and reimposing customary
discipline upon those who had breathed the freer air of the towns.

When, in the 1930s, Audrey Richards reported widespread disobedience to chiefs, she reported that many people gave their
chiefs' ritual failures as a reason for open disobedience; but actual
disobedience preceded the ritual tort. It began when the colonial
regime broke the chiefs' independent power. The regime left them
with no right to command labor, no armies to compel the payment
of tribute, no right to administer the poison ordeal, no right to
inflict awe-inspiring punishments, no freedom to liquidate political
opposition or to dispatch powerful rivals to remote frontiers. Above
all, it left them no way to keep the Bembas within Bemba country—
that is, within the physical and moral jurisdiction of the Bemba
state.

Thus, the Bemba chiefs faced the disobedience of the Depression
era with few resources. As the means of compelling customary
obedience evaporated, such things as the mystique of kingship and
of kinship, fear of ancestral vengeance, and the like hung high and
dry. The burden of compliance fell increasingly upon people's
capacity to be bound subjectively by abstract conceptions of right
behavior. Few social systems limit themselves to this. What remained of the chiefs' power was the capacity to achieve new popularity, to realign people on their side, and then to transform a
newly created public consensus into new power. The same would
be true further down the line, for headmen, senior members of
family groups, and other local notables. The appearance of a Mucapi offered a solution. Customary authority might yet reassert
itself by operating within the illegal idiom of witchcraft and witchcraft eradication. Disobedience phrased in ritual terms set the stage
for the restoration of authority in the same terms. The Bamucapi
found and exploited these conditions.

At the root of the word *mucapi* is the idea of cleansing. *Mucapi*
denotes both the cleansing medicine and the medicine man. (*Bamucapi* is a plural form referring to the people.) The medicine
originated in Malawi in 1930 with a chief who claimed to have
bought the medicine from a European.[46] To meet the demand that
arose immediately, the chief hired distributors, who worked for
commissions.[47] These assistants purveyed the *mucapi* far and wide
and in turn hired others. The *mucapi* spread to Zambia, Tanzania,
Mozambique, Zaire, and Zimbabwe.[48] It came to the attention of
officials in Zambia in the spring of 1933.

Audrey Richards, who witnessed the arrival of the Bamucapi in
Bemba country, emphasized their modernity. Their youth and European dress contrasted with the age and "greasy bark cloth" of

their traditional prototypes.[49] They carried the *mucapi* in glass bot-
tles, rather than in horns or leaves. They used store-bought mirrors
rather than basins of water. Reverend James Chisholm (Free
Church) described them as "more or less educated," and identified
some as lapsed mission Christians.[50] In this modernity they were,
in a sense, products of the colonial order. They were products of
the colonial order in the additional sense that, in a time of economic
retrenchment, the sale of the *mucapi* yielded them cash incomes
with which to pay taxes and other expenses. The Bamucapi toured
village after village, claiming that by means of the medicine, all
witchcraft would be cleared away. Clearing away witchcraft would
simultaneously free villagers from all the misfortunes of witchcraft.
After everyone had taken the medicine, one Mucapi said, everyone
could be sure that further misfortune came only from God or from
natural causes—not from the machinations of witches.[51] They proceeded by first securing the permission of a chief to cleanse his
domain and then touring village by village. In one sense, the Bamucapi did what they claimed. By demanding the surrender of all
magical objects, they did in fact cleanse—everything was deposited
in a hideous pile on the outskirts of the village. One official said
he had had to ride around in the medicine men's wake and remove
horns, charms, and philters by the truckload.[52]

The method of the Bamucapi varied, but in general it consisted
of a collective rite with hymns and preaching,[53] followed by a command that people surrender all their old medicines, regardless of
whether these served bewitching or healing (black or white magic),
and finally a form of divination. In some cases, the villagers would
be commanded to file past the Mucapi, who sighted witches with
a mirror but usually avoided naming any.[54] In other cases, the
Mucapi would divine by tasting the surrendered medicines in order
to determine whether they were healing medicines or tools of witchcraft. He would then neutralize all by applying some of the *mucapi*
to them and calling upon all the villagers to consume the *mucapi*
together. Thereafter the village was pronounced clean. Further
misfortunes due to witchcraft would now be impossible. Any witch
who took the medicine and backslid would automatically be killed
by the *mucapi* inside him. For these services, villages paid cash sums
as high as four pounds, five shillings, as well as presents in kind,
meals, and lodging.[55]

The testimony as to the virtues of the *mucapi* medicine and ceremonial may be read as a catalog of internal conflict in some villages.
In one case, a young migrant worker lay seriously ill in his village

until the Mucapi arrived.[56] He had been bewitched by an uncle, to whom he had refused to give a "present" out of his earnings.[c] Other cases involved competition and envy that led people to "grumble in their hearts." Such grumbling was a conventional prelude to the use of black magic. A large number of accounts refer to conflicts formulated as jealousy between co-wives of polygamous men. The migratory labor system left a preponderance of women on the land, who bore with their children and the elderly, but without their husbands and brothers, a heavy burden in agricultural production. Nearly all accounts refer to adultery, which was not a civil matter according to local understandings but a crime that might eventuate in the death of an innocent person.

The colonial tax created pressure of its own. As a matter of principle, the regime maintained that the unemployed should continue to be liable to the tax—in cash, even at a time when wage work was hard to get. Some local officials sided with villagers arguing that the tax was unfair in the circumstances. At least one requested permission to grant a reprieve from the tax during the crisis, or at least to permit a temporary return to payment in kind. The authoritative view held that tax payment was too important as an affirmation of allegiance to permit any relaxation of its burdens; any relaxation would create an undesired precedent.[57] The tax therefore stayed. And when one considers that an employed man was often responsible for paying the taxes of various relatives, the magnitude of the difficulty is evident. Richards reports that men competed vigorously for the relatively few cash-paying jobs available in the countryside, and that people resorted to white magic in the effort to procure favorable outcomes in the competition.

The return of young men from the towns must have intensified whatever strife was endemic to the villages. To the former urbanites, the authority of custom could no longer pass as the mainly invisible constraint of long habituation and no obvious alternative. To them, the uncle who insisted on his present became an armed robber; and the neighbor who invoked ancestors' help through white magic to get a job might as well have used black magic against his competitor. Thus the picture of what people hoped to derive from the *mucapi* reflects an infernal atmosphere of violence and interpersonal strife, as well as every sort of economic, social, po-

[c] This "present" was probably a nonvoluntary transfer, required by custom, to a mother's brother—an example of what Marcel Mauss called a *prestation* in his famous *Essai sur le don*, Paris, 1925.

litical, and moral insecurity. Since all such conflict, its expression, and even unexpressed emotions ("grumbling in one's heart") implied witchcraft, it is beyond doubt that there was witchcraft in the villages, and witchcraft rampant. Archdeacon Glossop remarked that "telling the Native that witchcraft doesn't exist is like telling a Londoner that Communism doesn't exist."[58] He could not have chosen an apter comparison.

The following is one description of the proclaimed virtue of the *mucapi*, written by a villager eager to see his village cleansed. Addressed to a DC in support of a future visit by the Bamucapi, it is part of a paper titled, in advance, "A Brief History of the Proposed Visit of the Mucapi People."

> Results from mucapi: (1) No one will ever attempt to bewitch him or her, if one does so, he will die himself. If he or she eats bad food or poison will never die. (2) If a person was a wizard, and has drunk this medicine he will never return to do or practice those bad medicines again. If he does so he will die the same day. (3) He will never be angry at any offence, nor show signs of being disappointed. If he does so, he will die. But to be happy always with anybody though your enemy. (4) No one will attempt to have sexual intercourse with any woman in the bush [a reference to adultery]. If he does they will both die at the same time. (5) If anyone who was a wizard has drunk this mucapi he will be declared clean. No one will be afraid of him any more. He will be congratulated for casting away his bad medicine. After the man has undergone all these instructions he goes home full of joy and hope that he will never die of any kind of poison, and has now conquered the difficulties.[d] All the family in the house rejoice all the day. They will never be afraid of anyone at all. Only god himself, that is all.[59]

Chiefs and headmen responded enthusiastically. According to the DC at Chinsali, all the Bemba chiefs openly invited the Bamucapi into their areas to distribute the healing medicine.[60] The chiefs "welcomed it," he said, and the medicine was "praised all around" by the people. Village headmen also supported the movement. One witness (of the Malawi revival) said that "all the headmen of all the villages and all the people were fond of these mucapes."

---

[d] Note the inclusion of poisoning among the ills to be cured by an antidote to witchcraft.

Richard Stuart has concluded that it became critical for headmen to "seem to be leading" in the matter of *mucapi*, whatever their personal attitude. The possible gain to be made by a chief or headman who accepted the cleansing had a negative counterpart if he refused. As one chief put his dilemma, "If I don't agree with my people about mucape, they will say I am not their chief."[61]

As might be anticipated, the Christian element in some villages inhibited the ritual politics of the customary order by blocking unanimity about the *mucapi* revival. The observer who proclaimed the popularity of the medicine all around added, "But the Christians did not like them. The Christians said, we must not take this mucape or it is bad for us."[62] They faced an ominous choice, between the missions' strict opposition to the *mucapi* and many villagers' strict support of it. On Likoma Island (Malawi), Stuart reports, Christians who refused to take the medicine were suspected of continuing willfully in the practice of witchcraft. The regime in Malawi joined the issue when violence erupted over Christians' refusal to undergo the ritual. Some Christians underwent the ritual and suffered in consequence. Certain elders of the congregation at Likoma who were also village headmen were cut off from communion for refusing to swear in advance that they would abstain from taking the *mucapi*. Others took the medicine unofficially, as the price of remaining unmolested or unsuspected in their villages. Episodes of this kind underscore the incompatibility of mission Christianity with the *rouages* of the customary order.

Administrative documents do not show clearly whether similar conflicts occurred in Bemba country or elsewhere in Zambia. Mission records confirm that Protestant and Catholic missions lost substantial numbers of adherents to the *mucapi* revival, especially in areas on the periphery of a given mission's sphere of influence.[63] But they do not report violence against those who refused to take the medicine. On the contrary, an official document that urged toleration of the revival supported its case by stating that "few would refuse it in Bemba country."[64] Since both Protestants and Catholics were extremely active in Bemba country (and if this is not a somewhat sinister reference to the remaining power of the Bemba chiefs), this expectation poses a difficulty. In some cases, the Bamucapi themselves made specific provision in their ritual to exclude Christians from the need to take the medicine. Wilson Ngwata testified that one of them said, "Christians have already drunk their mucape."[65] How widespread this attitude was or how much it was conditioned by the proximity of a *boma* or a mission station is hard to assess. It is certainly possible, too, that some Bamucapi sought to protect their commerce by minimizing their unattractiveness to administrators. Nevertheless, the Bamucapi seem to have made such provisions for Christians only some of the time. Therefore, unlike their brethren of the administration, missionaries never warmed to the Bamucapi. Church publications convey the fear that gripped them during the episode—and the consternation: A group of parishioners obtained written permission from their chief to invite a Mucapi right into the Mbereshi Station of the London Missionary Society.[66]

Despite the complications that the existence of Christian minorities created within chiefdoms, the establishment eagerly embraced the witch cleansing. In doing so, they ignored their superiors. One witness testified to the following conversation with a Mucapi: "On [the Mucapi's] coming I asked him the power with which he does this work and he refused, that it was not the power of the Government, but the power of the Chiefs of the country and they allowed him to clean all the villages of Mwase (a Cewa chief), he gives his people medicine to drink."[67] The peddler, who was convicted in this case, admitted that he had "erred in listening to the word of the Chief and not the word of the Boma."[68] All the Bemba chiefs beckoned the Bamucapi without first obtaining official permission.[69] They beckoned together, in flagrant violation of the Witchcraft Ordinance.

At first the administration strove to prosecute the medicine men. The case just referred to was tried under the Witchcraft Ordinance in the summer of 1933. By a year later, the majority of officials had changed their position. The Provincial Commissioners' Conference of May 1934 concluded that, all things considered, unless the movement proved itself to be "harmful to public order and good government, it was better left alone."[70] Thus the regime made another of the about-faces that reveal how vacuous is the notion that a few strong men prevailed alone against the multitude. Watching the Witchcraft Ordinance, that peculiarly emblematic law, bob above and below the surface of events, one sees how much depended upon collaboration.

Officials had good reason to suppress the Bamucapi. First there were the more or less clear-cut violations of the Witchcraft Ordinance and all the dangers it was designed to block. In the summer of 1933, J. Moffat Thompson was quoting the language of the ordinance as grounds for arrest: The Bamucapi "represented themselves as having and exercising the power of witchcraft" and

"professed by non-natural means and subtle craft to deceive . . .
the villagers."[71] Second, whites feared that violence against witches
might grow into violence against themselves. A disheartening rumor had it that the medicine conferred immunity from bullets, like
the medicine the Maji Maji guerrillas had used in Tanzania a generation earlier. One Mucapi proclaimed the imminent end of the
tax and said that, meanwhile, the medicine gave prisoners the ability
to escape.[72] Such claims reflected the unrest of which the regime
was all too cognizant.

Sensible people realized that they had every reason to expect
trouble from the thousands of young men who had been thrown
out of work. And since the collection of the tax continued unin-
terrupted, many served terms of imprisonment for tax arrears. At
Isoka, for example, in 1933, the DC was arresting an average of
sixteen tax defaulters a day.[73] A letter from the Reverend Dr.
Chisholm to the DC at Isoka expressed the fear experienced by
people who could see that African unrest was justified. The DC's
reply reveals the scantiness of the local machinery he controlled:

> The apparent popularity of the "medicine" and prophecies
> likely to prove acceptable to Watchtower adherents, makes the
> presence of these men in a Watchtower stronghold such as
> Isoka somewhat disquieting, at a period when the difficulty of
> finding money and the Government's increasing pressure on
> tax defaulters had created a degree of discontent which might
> prove very fertile soil for the sowing of discord . . . I do not
> seriously anticipate any possibility of serious disorder; but I
> do fear that sooner or later some subversive element will have
> the intelligence to realize that we cannot put the whole district
> in prison for tax default, and that a policy of passive resistance
> will have us completely beaten.[74]

Upon receiving Chisholm's letter, the DC considered amending his
relatively casual attitude toward the revival. The most principled
argument for suppression came from the provincial commissioner
of Northern Province, where the *mucapi* enthusiasm was rampant
during the summer of 1933. "If we permit this 'cleaning' of villages," he wrote, "we almost admit that witchcraft exists."[75]

But to favor suppression was not to accomplish it. Officials soon
recognized that the logistical problem of suppression exceeded
their resources. The Bamucapi traveled rapidly through remote
areas outside the immediate radius of district *boma*s. Officials could
not hope to catch them without the active co-operation of villagers

and local leaders. This they did not get. Villagers usually failed even to inform the authorities of these visits; the first rumors generally reached a *boma* long after a Mucapi had done his work and moved on. Of ten Bamucapi known to be operating in Chinsali and Isoka early in 1934, only one was caught and identified.[76] The DC at Kawambwa, who intensified his touring, complained that the information frequently failed to reach officials, period. To make matters still worse, the unmolested passage meanwhile of the Bamucapi through the villages implied official support. This, in addition to the considerable social pressure for acceptance, intimidated villagers who might conceivably have complained.[77] Villagers neither complained nor informed DOs about the movements of Bamucapi. And when called by a DO who had the facts, they showed great reluctance to testify at trials. Thus, at best, officials could hope for a few arrests and prosecutions carried out haphazardly; and that might do more harm than good. To some extent, colonial legality itself inhibited suppression. The provincial commissioner at Kasama suggested that the Alien Natives Ordinance might be used to deport Malawian medicine men. But locals rapidly took up the trade.[78] He warned, furthermore, that cases against local Bamucapi must be carefully prepared; a verdict of not guilty or a conviction quashed by the High Court would give a Mucapi "undesirable prestige."[79] His fear was realistic. The Bamucapi became adept at conforming to the letter of the law.

It gradually became clear that any attempt systematically to crush the revival was bound to fail. Thoughtful men pondered the ramifications of trying hard to enforce existing law and failing in full view of the villagers. The immense popularity of the medicine raised the stakes higher. Isolated arrests would generate ill will without yielding significant results. Drastic suppression would force it underground, where it might well develop into something worse. In the face of these difficulties, the provincial commissioner of the Northern Province came to see the "openness" of the revival as a "redeeming feature."[80] In the spring of 1934, he recommended a four-point policy: to deport aliens; to ignore the "mere sale" of the medicine; to use messengers to ridicule and discredit the Bamucapi; and to prosecute sedition and witchcraft accusations. In the early months of 1934, the regime was already well into its about-face.

Villagers, their leaders, the Bamucapi, and some of the regime's black employees forced the regime to make its about-face complete. In many areas, a Mucapi's arrival was heralded from afar and "eagerly awaited."[81] In mid-1934, the DC at Abercorn characterized the movement as a "fad, like the Charleston or mahjong in England some years ago."[82] In addition, he noticed a "cheerful atmosphere" in the villages, fostered by the belief that "something [was] at last being done about witchcraft." A middle-aged villager testified simply, "I paid 1d. for the mucape, as I believe in witches and witchcraft, and any medicine that can ward off the dangers of witchcraft must be very good medicine."[83] The *mucapi* was so popular that the policy of systematic ridicule did not work. Ridicule by *boma* messengers was impractical because the messengers themselves were chary of the surrendered medicines.[84] Ridicule was doubly impractical since, as one DC said, "The Native has little sense of humor where witchcraft is concerned."[85] But neither had the Briton, who had begun to see the abyss opening. His toleration for witch beliefs broadened apace.

If it was true that *mucapi* was popular, it was also true that the Bamucapi were skilled salesmen able to create a climate favorable to the reception of their wares. The DC at Kawambwa claimed that existing dissension at Mbereshi Mission was "fanned to white heat by the salesmen."[86] We must take into account their salesmanship and showmanship when we read the conclusion of a DC: "[The fact] that the Native believes it [witchcraft] still exists is shewn by their willingness to tolerate, encourage, and pay these 'cleaners.' "[87] Chiefs' enthusiasm met that of the villagers. One chief was found to have taken the medicine himself. Probably, he and others supported the Bamucapi out of political calculation if nothing else. Even if he had wanted to suppress them, he would have had to think twice. He had little to gain if he managed to suppress the revival and a great deal to lose if he tried and failed. His dilemma was the same as the official's. The Reverend Dr. Chisholm stated the position nicely:

> I don't for a minute suppose this "mucapi" will succeed in engendering a lasting belief that all the everyday minor and major calamities are due to natural causes. The craze for it will—as the D.C. Chinsali suggests—die a natural death. But in the meantime we have to deal with the possible consequences of the movement . . . and consider what capital the suppliers of the "medicine" may make of any action on our part to prevent them from supplying their stuff to people who have a superstitious faith in it, and whom [sic] seem anxious to get it.[88]

When officials saw that chiefs whose abilities they had come to count on were determined to bring the Bamucapi into their chiefdoms, they had to pay attention. Therefore, after many months of the de facto toleration that scant resources imposed, the Provincial Commissioners' Conference of May 1934 decided to make toleration, plus watchfulness, a general policy. The conference took its cue from the chiefs, whose openness in inviting the Bamucapi inspired confidence. The list of the important Bemba chiefs, including the renowned "progressive" Nkula, inspired further confidence. The fact that Malawi officials had not tried to suppress the movement wholesale created additional momentum toward official toleration. The DC at Mzimba (Malawi) had provided the model. He tolerated witch cleansing on two conditions: first, that the Mucapi be invited by a chief; and second, that the chief be held responsible (for aiding and abetting) if violence resulted from the visit. Chief Chimtuongo had officially invited a Mucapi under those conditions. Others seemed ready to follow suit.[90]

Such conditions may have reacted upon the witch-cleansing technique. Some Bamucapi exempted Christians from the ritual, and instead of naming witches, some of them tested the surrendered medicines, not the people, pronouncing which were "good" or "bad."[91] Since villagers knew who had surrendered what, this amounted to naming without actually doing so. But since all the medicines were neutralized afterward, violence against a suspect could be avoided, while, at the same time, a suspect could be warned. Max Marwick noticed in a similar movement, which sprang up in 1947, a further development: The liquid medicine taken orally was replaced by a solid one applied through incisions. He suggested that this was a deliberate attempt to reduce the resemblance of the medicine to the outlawed poison ordeal.[92]

The eventual solution grew out of many delicate transactions. Whatever resourcefulness the administration brought to bear had its counterpart in that of villagers, their leaders, and the Bamucapi. The revised opinion of the provincial commissioners vindicated the DC in Chinsali, who arrived at "doubt that legal action [was] necessary since the mucapi [were] not violating the law." In contrast to earlier attacks on the Bamucapi as swindlers and easy livers fraudulently exploiting the credulity of the villagers—or worse, as potential revivers of a Maji Maji-like nightmare—he suspected that "the price [of the mucapi was] not excessive and the folly of their belief [would] not be impressed on them by withdrawing the supply."[93] The use of such arguments for changed policy brings us 180 degrees from the early arrests under the Witchcraft Ordinance. The Bamucapi helped the regime see how it must apply its own rule to an actual case. Support grew for a less rigorous attitude toward witch cleansing. The *mucapi* revival created an intellectual climate in which an F. H. Melland could publicly recommend co-opting the "better-class witchdoctors."

In the official records of the colonial regime, the curtain rarely opens so wide as this upon the meaning of the co-operation with local authority that Lugard so deliberately underlined. I imagine it took years for a local officer to plumb the deep and hidden meanings of Lugard's insistence that "principles must vary with customs." Yet, indirect rule had its own peculiar logic, and those whose job it was to implement effective rule were drawn inexorably into it. Melland conceived the idea of accommodating old-fashioned witch doctors. Another official realized that it would be advantageous for the district officer to have villagers deposit harmful medicines officially and publicly at the *boma*—in effect transforming the DC into a Mucapi.[94] Every now and then, too, a missionary adopted the same expedient if he found his congregation caught in a witch scare.[95] Still others, Elizabeth Hopkins suggests, attempted to tar with the brush of witchcraft prophetic healers regarded by the regime as politically dangerous, hoping thereby to discredit their abilities in the eyes of the populace.[96] The more logical and supple-minded of local officials may well have reached such conclusions more frequently than the records indicate.

Although the desire to keep the chiefs operating and the recognition of limited capability together dictated a practical plan to tolerate the Bamucapi, the obvious dangers of such tactics doubtless limited their use. No matter how initiated, antiwitchcraft activity could always generate violence. People might be killed, commit suicide, or suffer fatal ostracism from their village communities. The exposure of witches might bring factional disputes within villages to the point of open fighting. Thus, from a coldly practical standpoint, it was probably best to let customary rulers bear the risks, as the DC at Mzimba did. For them, the potential advantages probably outweighed the risks. Customary rulers could embrace witch cleansing in order to enhance their popularity and public confidence in their capacity to rule. In making this accommodation possible, the Bamucapi indirectly aided the regime. As indirect rule engaged the *rouages* of the first articulation, it called into action powers of this world and powers of worlds beyond.

WHEN the Watchtower movement came, it rattled a colonial edifice that stood upon two kinds of religious foundation: missions on the one hand and customary polities on the other. Each called in the supernatural to sanction natural behavior. And each could batten on revival or succumb to it. In physical edifices, the forces that tend to maintain equilibrium move along the same pillars and beams as do those which tend to destroy it. The art of architecture is to prevail, always temporarily, over the destructive effects of gravity, the elements, and above all, use. Lugard's social architecture was subject to a similar dynamism. One stress after another upon indirect rule's pillars and beams required one repair after another. They also required a succession of additions not envisaged in the original plans. The makeshifts required for it to withstand prophetic thunder and charismatic fire reveal the bits and pieces it was made of. They are the subject of Part 2.

Part 2

THE POLITICAL PROBLEM

OF EVIL

━━━━━━━━━━━━━ ❖ ━━━━━━━━━━━━━

FOR MUCH OF ITS HISTORY in Central Africa, the Watchtower movement was unified neither by fixed leadership nor by the same reading of a common theology, still less by common practice. Between 1908, when Watchtower missionaries became a significant factor, the details of doctrine and practice discourage generalization. In some congregations we find instances of ritual incest; in others, mores indistinguishable from missions'. We encounter some adherents refusing even to greet their chiefs, and others cheerfully doing their quota of tribute labor. Some made a fetish of European dress and education; others kept their children out of school, refused to wash or groom their hair, and went about in zebra-striped paraphernalia. To compound the variation over space, groups varied, often dramatically, over time. In short, instead of common doctrine and practice, we confront a body of imported ideas percolating through an immense land and undergoing continual modification.

The main Watchtower ideas were imported from twentieth-century America, the same fertile garden of religious novelties and religious fossils that de Tocqueville discovered two centuries ago. Charles Taze Russell, a native of Allegheny, Pennsylvania, founded the movement in the 1870s, amid the widespread religious revival that crisscrossed the radical politics of the time.[1] He acknowledged an intellectual debt to William Miller, founder of the Seventh-Day Adventists, who had inspired crowds with the prospect of Christ's imminent Second Coming. (The Millerites put on their ascension robes in 1844 and waited, in vain.)[2] At the age of thirty, Russell left a successful career as a haberdasher to devote himself to Bible study, writing, and pastorship. *Watchtower Magazine* appeared in 1879, under his editorship. His six-volume work, *Studies in the Scriptures*, became the common text shared by a proliferation of Bible study groups. Russell's colleagues published a seventh volume after his death. In 1884, the study groups were incorporated in the United States as the Watchtower Bible and Tract Society. In 1914, English groups in existence since 1880 were incorporated as the International Bible Students Association. These two corporations publish and distribute *Watchtower Magazine, Awake!* and other publications in many languages, in addition to Bibles, Bible translations, and a number of reference books. Since 1931, members have called themselves Jehovah's Witnesses.[3]

At first known variously as "Russellites," "Millennial Dawnites," and by other names, members were united by a hostility to established denominations, and especially to the churches' hierarchies. Counting among their precursors all groups that have opposed hierarchy in religion, they reserved special animosity for the Catholic church. In common with others rooted in the broad evangelical tendency of nineteenth-century America, they affirmed the literal truth of the Bible, believing that it contains a comprehensive divine plan for all history. They also condemned doctrines and practices lacking specific warrant in the Scriptures. During Russell's time and that of his successor, Joseph F. Rutherford, the society developed, besides, a vivid political rhetoric. Both believed revolution to be inevitable and part of God's plan. At the same time, both argued against political participation, on the grounds that the world's institutions are dominated by Satan. They counseled neutrality in all battles except the final battle of Armageddon. For forty years, the movement riveted its joint attention upon 1914, the year in which, according to Russell's calculation, Christ would return to earth and Armageddon would begin. When the End did not come in 1914, the date was redefined as the inauguration of Christ's Kingdom on earth. Human intelligence was fallible; God's plan of victory, not so.

Russell died in 1916 and was succeeded as president of the society by Joseph F. Rutherford, a lawyer who had for many years conducted the society's legal affairs. Rutherford proved to be a prolific and forceful pamphleteer. His anti-Fascist pamphlets were so powerful that a colonial administrator joked that they probably yielded dividends among Africans as an aid to the war mobilization.[4] But they had an important drawback: Rutherford's invective against the "satanic alliance" between the established churches and the

capitalist world order was as virulent as that against Hitler. It un-
settled a polity in which churches played an important role. After
Rutherford's death in 1942, the tone of the society's literature qui-
eted somewhat. Nathan Knorr, formerly manager of the business
and legal activities of the American corporation, succeeded him.
At Knorr's death in 1977, Fred Franz became president.

Today the Jehovah's Witnesses are integrated into a vertical organization of companies, circuits, assemblies, and so forth, up to
the president of the society. The old emphasis upon group study
continues. Company servants lead congregations at the place of
worship, called the Kingdom Hall. Theoretically any member may
be elected to the position of company servant. Rotation of this role
among members is encouraged. In theory, there are no fixed pas-
torships. All members being preachers, all are encouraged to lecture on Sunday mornings using the lessons prescribed in *Watchtower
Magazine*. In addition, they are enjoined to carry on the all-important door-to-door ministry, to distribute the society's publications, and to spread the good news that the world we know will
soon end.

Witnesses read the Bible actively. To make the most of what they
read, they carry their Bibles and notebooks to meetings.[5] Members
ask and answer questions during the service, using the *Watchtower
Magazine* as a basic text and the Bible as a reference book. In
ministers' meetings, they train one another to meet the questions
and objections they are likely to encounter in door-to-door work.
In these meetings, they carefully polish such details of personal
presentation as speech, dress, and style of argument. Similar practices were common on the Zambian Copperbelt at least as early as
the late 1940s.[6]

Consistent with their primary interest in Bible study, Witnesses
despise religious ritual and tradition as "false religion." Kingdom
Halls are modestly furnished, services are plain. Members believe
that religion should be approached rationally, through study, and
that the Bible is literally true. Witnesses join other fundamentalists
in rejecting the theory of evolution, not simply because it contra-
dicts Genesis but, more importantly, because it excludes a moral
interpretation of the earth's history. Consistent with their ration-
alism, Witnesses do not cultivate religious enthusiasm as do some
American fundamentalist groups. They condemn it as mistaken
and regard the divine origins of ecstasy and speaking in tongues
as questionable. The status of faith healing is ambiguous. While
not denying the reality of healing—to do so would be to deny the

omnipotence of God—such events are considered possible, but rare.[7] Faith healing now has no part in Watchtower ceremonial.

Major ceremonials common to most Christian denominations have been abolished. Witnesses reject Holy Communion as un-Biblical, specifically denying its traditional symbolism and the priestly mysteries associated with it. A "memorial supper" held annually has replaced Holy Communion. Christmas and Easter are ignored on the grounds that the Bible does not justify their cele-bration. Considering themselves servants of a theocratic regime headed by Jesus Christ, Witnesses acknowledge worldly authority only insofar as it does not interfere with their primary tasks and allegiance. For this reason, they refuse to salute national flags, vote, or do military service. For the same reason, they ignore as irrelevant movements of social uplift and political change.[a] They are com-mitted to taking a side in war only at Armageddon.

Although they avoid political activism, Witnesses have frequently become embroiled politically. During World War I, the society's seeming "pacifism" led members into violent confrontation with mobs that enjoyed the tacit consent of local law enforcers. One member from a small town in Pennsylvania recalled to me that Witnesses used to carry heavy walking sticks to meetings at their Kingdom Hall, for self-defense against patriotic mobs. During the same period, six of the society's top leaders were convicted under the Espionage Act and sentenced to twenty years' imprisonment, on the grounds that their literature had given aid and comfort to the enemy.[8] A federal appeals court overturned this conviction, but only after Rutherford and five others had served nineteen months in federal prison at Atlanta. Three new journals, including *Awake!* magazine, were born in prison. Although litigation regarding con-scientious-objector status and numerous other civil rights issues aligned Witnesses with liberal causes, Witnesses undertook these struggles for their own reasons. The American Civil Liberties

---

[a] Incidentally, Eric Hobsbawm noticed that some of the radicals among the south Italian villagers whose political history he studied were attracted to the Watchtower. He found one individual who was both the Communist party cell leader and leader of the local Jehovah's Witnesses. Hobsbawm commented that such dual responsi-bility is somewhat embarrassing for the Communist leadership to admit. It is equally the case that, by accepting secular office or even espousing secular political goals, the man was far from the "line" of the Jehovah's Witnesses (see *Primitive Rebels: Studies in Archaic Forms of Social Movement in the Nineteenth and Twentieth Centuries,* New York, 1971, p. 73).

Union has sided with them on many occasions, but the Jehovah's Witnesses acknowledge no common ground with this group.[9]

During World War II, meetings of English Witnesses were sometimes banned in order to prevent factional fighting and mob violence, as well as to silence their agitation against military conscription.[10] Perhaps because of the Watchtower publications' strong rhetoric, the British Criminal Investigation Division undertook an investigation to see whether the International Bible Students Association was a Communist organization.[11] It forwarded the result to Zambia, where officials had a similar worry. A circular exonerating the IBSA of Communist connection arrived in Zambia in 1942; the view of the Belgian missionary Father von Hofwegen that Witnesses were "decidedly bolshevistic" could thus be taken as a mere manner of speaking.[12] In Germany during the war, the Nazis interned large numbers of Witnesses—Rutherford claimed 6,000.[13] Bruno Bettelheim has commented upon the Witnesses' capacity to survive the concentration camps with their beliefs intact and with their sense of self, meaning, and purpose unaltered. They continued to proselytize and to make whatever arrangements this required. According to Bettelheim, Jehovah's Witnesses co-operated with political prisoners in obtaining such necessities as food and heat.[14] Like the political prisoners, the Witnesses seemed able to fit the experience into a coherent understanding of history.

Witnesses read the Bible as a guide to worldly events. Back in the 1870s, Russell calculated that Armageddon would begin in October 1914, and that the Consummation would occur soon after. The failure of this prediction led to a number of schisms.[15] Witnesses now teach that the last battles preceding the establishment of Christ's Kingdom on earth have already begun: Twentieth-century war and other disasters are "rounds" in the last great match whereby the army of Jesus Christ will finally enthrone their leader as King and hurl Satan and his army into the depths for a thousand years. There is a characteristic Watchtower gloss for everything from earthquakes to the breakdown of the nuclear family; all disasters constitute signs that prophecy is being fulfilled. Since the great events of Armageddon and the Consummation of all history are imminent, all believers have an urgent duty to preach. Witnesses vow to ignore all battles but this one. Meanwhile the evidence of Satan's power in the world is everywhere.

The reality of Satan's actual power in the world follows from the premise that the forces of good and evil are at present locked in strenuous combat. Thus, although Jehovah's Witnesses do not cultivate religious ecstasy, they do not deny the reality of spiritual manifestations.[16] Consistent with a literal reading of the Bible, Watchtower publications urge rejection of "spiritism," rather than skepticism regarding it. Indeed, early converts testified to physical bouts with the Devil. This aspect of Watchtower theology fit the assumptions of its African hearers. An African preacher could accept the reality of spirits, without departing from the orthodox views of the American movement, and then demand that converts place their trust in God. He could find support for such a position in the society's publications. Testimony published in the *Watchtower* of November 1913 describes a man's physical possession by Satan, an affliction that caused him to interrupt prayer meetings with violent dancing and senselessness; a pamphlet of 1925 took up the question of communication with the dead.[17]

The Jehovah's Witnesses practice adult baptism, by total immersion, as a sign of commitment to the Kingdom. They do not recognize previous baptisms. Through baptism, a convert signals the desire to work in Christ's "earthly organization" until his coming. Affirming that the Garden of Eden was on earth, Witnesses say that the ultimate victory will lead to the reestablishment of an earthly paradise, of which their theocratic organization will be the basis. They deny the existence of heaven and hell, together with the doctrine that an individual goes to one or the other upon his death; both are priestly inventions. They define hell as a state of death only, its reputed torments being another invention. People will go either to eternal death or to eternal life only on the Last Day. Consistent with these views, Witnesses assert bodily immortality and reject as pagan the idea that humans possess an immortal soul.[18] On the Day of Judgment, all those previously dead will return to life. Then a great "dividing work" will be done, as described in Revelation. The "sheep" will live forever, the "goats" will die, and the New Age will begin.

These ideas were taken up spectacularly in Africa. One Central African people assimilated this American millennium to their own eschatology in which a New Age would be heralded by the coming of Mwana Lesa, the Son of God, and by the return of the ancestors. Elsewhere people translated the vision of the End into terms that referred directly to colonial exploitation. During a revival in 1918, an administrator claimed that African believers failed to see the contradiction he saw between the end of the world and a thriving Africa without European rulers. In fact, there was no contradiction.

Witnesses everywhere claim that the Final Judgment will not end all world history. It will gloriously begin a new one.

It is often suggested that an exotic African movement drew merely a distant inspiration from its American forebear.[19] This is not entirely true. Much that seems "fantastic" in the African movement exists in the American one as well: belief in the reality of spirits, in the sudden return of the dead to life on earth, in the battle involving heavenly and earthly armies, in a this-worldly paradise to come—all these tenets belong to Russell's early inspiration and remain the theology of American Jehovah's Witnesses. Further, both movements have always had an implicit political potential. Whether they have realized this potential has owed more to external factors of context than to internal differences of doctrine; the theocratic doctrines of the Watchtower have engendered conflict with civil authorities in and outside of Africa. Finally, a drive for intellectual coherence is built into Watchtower theory and practice wherever adherents are. This drive for coherence impels them to search day-to-day events, as well as the Bible, for evidence that they are correctly fulfilling their tasks until the Consummation.[20] This feature has been as evident in the American movement as in the African movement that sprang from it. It is a classic search for the sense of a senseless world.

I emphasize these connections. The idea that African adherents of the movement merely invented under the vague impulse of the American movement has led to baseless argument about the literal-mindedness of African converts, in contrast to others, and about their special propensity to clash with secular authorities. But the literal-mindedness of American Witnesses, where Scripture is concerned, takes second place to no one's; and I have described their clashes with American and German governments.[b] Although less spectacular, these conflicts in the West have taken some of the same forms observable in Africa: factional conflict with nonconverts in small communities; de facto sedition as a result of passive resistance to military mobilization; and provocative expressions of religious scruple designed to underline the sect's difference from other bodies. (Recently, for example, a Witness went to court in New Hampshire testing the state's right to compel the display of the motto

---

[b] The society's publications claim the underground existence of coreligionists in the Soviet Union, converts who returned from the camps of the Third Reich and those they in turn converted. Barbara Grizzuti Harrison, *Visions of Glory: A History and a Memory of Jehovah's Witnesses*, New York, 1978, p. 330, quotes a 1959 estimate of 100,000 Witnesses in the Eastern bloc countries.

Live Free or Die on his automobile license plate.) Outstandingly, Witnesses everywhere exhibit an elaborate rationality that looks like irrationality. Reasoning from premises that non-Witnesses do not accept, they acquire the unsavory aroma of fanaticism.

From a sociological point of view, the question of why the ideas of the Watchtower in America did not always result in widespread official repression is as important as the question of why they so often did in colonial Africa. If a literal interpretation of the Bible's revolutionary passages could account for this result, then we should expect to find the same results everywhere. Since such is not the case, we come back to the importance of context. Let us turn now to the religious and political context of the first Watchtower revival in Central Africa.

3

PROPHETIC THUNDER:
THE REVIVAL IN MALAWI, 1908

And it shall come to pass in the last days, saith God,
I will pour out my spirit upon all flesh: and your sons
and your daughters shall prophesy, and your young
men shall see visions and your old men shall dream
dreams. . . . And I will shew wonders in heaven above,
and signs in the earth beneath; blood, and fire, and
vapour of smoke. . . . And it shall come to pass, that
whoever shall call on the name of the Lord shall be
saved.

ACTS 2:17, 19, 21

E LLIOT KENAN KAMWANA,
the first Malawian prophet of
the Watchtower millennium, is mainly remembered by historians
as an intellectual who made Watchtower ideology into an ideology
of anticolonial revolution.[1] For good reason: His contemporaries
of the colonial regime so feared his influence that, between 1908
and 1914, they deported him to remote sectors of the country; and
in 1914, to the Seychelles where he remained for twenty-three
years. Yet, despite his reputation as an early messenger of African
nationalism, he did not advocate attack upon the regime. He told
his countrymen to be baptized and to look forward to the day when
God would overturn the established order. Even though popular
excitement carried Watchtower adherents no further than this,
Kamwana's movement threatened colonial rule. How was it possible
to shake a colonial regime by baptizing thousands and by preaching
a revolution that demanded no human participation?

Kamwana's vigorous anticolonial rhetoric can lead us to forget
that he enjoyed immense success as a Christian preacher, and that
baptizing was as much part of his career as his anticolonial speeches

and the prophecy that God would rout Malawi's invaders. But it is not enough to listen to Kamwana as a nationalist while ignoring him as a preacher. The nationalist succeeded because the preacher did; the anticolonial movement was powerful because the revival was. It is not enough, either, to listen to the message while ignoring the hearers. Mass involvement and excitement made the preacher visible and audible to colonial authorities. Thus, both the revival and its message command our attention.

A mission product, Kamwana carried on his most successful work in areas that British missionaries had already evangelized. He was therefore a "revival" preacher in the very specific sense of being an insider who demanded that Christianity as practiced in Malawi purify itself. He preached the "true" religion, administered the "true" baptism, and excoriated as "false" religion various practices that had grown up in Christian communities. If the regime had stood indifferent to heterodox religious teaching, the revival of 1908 would have remained a church matter only. Kamwana would have suffered excommunication, perhaps, but not deportation. The regime did not stand indifferent, however, and the revival of 1908 showed that the preaching of religious reform could threaten colonial order. If Kamwana was dangerous, then he was dangerous where he succeeded best. He succeeded best in areas under the influence of missions. Thus, missions gave his work its political context. The Free Church mission at Livingstonia, with its far-flung stations, provided the most important target of Kamwana's revival.[2]

THE POLITICS OF MISSIONARY ENTERPRISE

In general, the Christian mission played a significant political role, no matter what its denomination. As the empire's cultural right hand, it aided the flow of good things from Britain into African villages. And it propagated the idea that empire was a good thing, both by being a pacific presence and by teaching this specific lesson. That the mission provided general legitimation to British rule requires little argument. How it functioned politically at ground level is less obvious. For if missionaries willingly performed useful ideological tasks, they did not willingly accept concrete political ones. The earliest instructions of some groups warned emphatically against political involvement.[3] And one important reason that Livingstonia missionaries clamored for the establishment of a protectorate was precisely their wish to be rid of political tasks that complicated their performance of spiritual ones.[4] But, despite their intentions, missionaries came to perform political tasks. What were they, and how were they performed?

Let us agree, first of all, that missions aimed primarily to evangelize—that although *in* the flow of imperialism, they were not *of* it. The political work missions did day in, day out is best seen partly as a condition of their primary endeavor, partly as its outcome, but not as an agenda followed in its own right. Even the ideological aspect of missions' political work went together with their primary task of evangelization: To evangelize, they had to create a permanent organization to accommodate their churches, schools, hospitals, mission stores, and so forth. All mission activities required, in addition, a network of enduring ties with chiefs and administrators, with evangelists and other mission employees, with church members and potential members. Therefore let us agree, secondly, that organization and intention are different matters. If missionaries inculcated belief in the rightness of colonial rule, their ability to do so presupposed this organization and its effectiveness; neither belief nor talk accomplishes anything by itself; and a willing helper is not necessarily an effective one. Besides, individual missionaries differed among themselves in the degree to which they acknowledged or accepted an active part in upholding colonial domination. But even if they had sought purely religious ends without exception, a manifold political role would have been thrust upon them. Such were the effects of a mission's successful integration into the society of the protectorate.

Some of these effects were as intangible as the ties of goodfellowship and common culture that missionaries shared with Europeans outside the missions. Others were as concrete as the need to command sufficient funds and the support of overseas notables. Sometimes what was required was a certain pragmatism in religious matters, a church statesmanship that permitted fruitful compromises. Since the Free Church mission usually met these conditions, it was able to carry out informal political functions rather well.[5]

Livingstonia's political role grew up organically. It was natural for Livingstonia to bargain with Cecil Rhodes for land concessions on which to build schools, chapels, hospitals, missionaries' houses, and workshops. In return, the British South Africa Company gained a continuous supply of trained manpower—clerks, masons, telegraphers, interpreters, and so on.[6] It was natural also for the BSAC to offer Livingstonia a tract of land at Chitambo (Zambia), the site of David Livingstones's death, and to stipulate that a white missionary must run it.[7] Since mission medical facilities not only aided religious work among Africans but served Europeans as well, it was natural that the company should contribute to their support. Thus, practical relationships between Livingstonia and the regime gradually knit together according to practical needs. Because these practical relationships evolved gradually and informally, it is difficult to read directly from them those structural factors which permitted missions to aid the regime and those which inhibited their doing so; hence the common supposition that missions easily seconded colonial rule.

These structural factors became more noticeable when, for some reason, a particular mission could not fit into the framework of rule. The political dangers that the Watchtower eventually posed are foreshadowed by the structural weaknesses of poorly integrated groups. Although often politically conservative, fundamentalist missions could not always perform conservative political functions. Their vicissitudes allow us to peel away ideology and thus lay bare the joint political functioning of church and state at ground level. For the Watchtower did not stand alone in uneasy relationship to the colonial administration and the Free Church's Christian "establishment"; other nonconformist groups did as well. There is a further reason for treating the new fundamentalist missions in a study of the Watchtower. The Watchtower and a variety of small missions began their history in Malawi through the efforts of an unusual character, Joseph Booth. Joseph Booth was an English-born businessman who, during the 1890s, turned Christian militant in Australia. George Shepperson has fully recounted Booth's career as a reformer in Africa. I will sketch here only Booth's ill-fitting additions to the universe of religious institutions in Malawi.[8]

From the moment of his arrival in 1892, Booth's activities disturbed the quiet Christian consensus and institutional integration that had begun to unite missionaries with officials in the protectorate. Moving from group to group, Booth campaigned for and received support from a succession of small American denominations, including the Seventh-Day Adventists and Seventh-Day Baptists. He drew up various plans for the establishment of "industrial missions" aimed at encouraging African self-help. At the same time, Booth criticized the relaxed style of life into which the older missions had sunk and the elaborate social etiquette that defined the separation between black and white Christendom. It would be easy to attribute the hostility Booth quickly aroused to his outspokenness alone, but there was more to the story than that.

The new missions were typically small and underfinanced compared to the older ones. Finance in itself had important structural consequences. To begin with, field missionaries often could not maintain a style of life in keeping with the established norms for whites. In a society ruled in part by a prestige expressed in material attainments, these small missions would have proved an embarrassment even without Booth's outspokenness. With it, they put many ill at ease. Their relative poverty had a second result. Strained finances would have blocked the deployment of a well-disciplined hierarchy to guide home and field mission committees even if their principles had allowed it—and they often did not.[9] Third, not surprisingly, small missions did not respect the preestablished division of labor among missions—it did not include them. A well-disciplined hierarchy was one condition of using resources efficiently over a large area. Such a hierarchy was also indispensable if missionaries were to retain control over the armies of evangelists and teachers they hired. Otherwise, these employees might create unforeseen difficulties in the villages and provoke the intervention of local officials. Taught without adequate supervision, the pure message of the Gospel, even in its most quietistic forms, might lead to dissension and violence. Outside a well-controlled organization, ordinary Christian teaching could subvert order every bit as readily as anticolonial sedition.

The disorder these missions might cause was not always the teachers' doing. Typically, breakaway fundamentalist sects broadcast a loud polemic against established churches, pitting the scriptural against the unscriptural, the true against the false. For this reason, their methods of proselytizing in Malawi were often aggressive and heedless of previously well-respected spheres of influence. Still, to cause disruption, they did not have to be aggressive. Simply by existing, they could undermine the discipline of established missions. By offering alternative Christian membership, hitherto unavailable in a given area, they could loosen all churches' collective hold on their surrounding populations. If benefits withdrawn or withheld by one congregation could be sought elsewhere, the established missions' threat of suspension or excommunication lost its sting.[10] Observing this same phenomenon in the United States, Max Weber commented that destructive competition has often generated pressure toward the formation of cartels among competing denominations.[11] In the first decade of the twentieth century, cartelization among missions—that is, such comity arrangements as would come—lay for the most part in the future.

For structural reasons, then, small Christian groups acquired a reputation of unsavoriness, regardless of whether they took up revolutionary causes on behalf of Africans—and even though, with the exception of Booth himself, their missionaries were typically conservative. For example, Thomas Branch, a black American Seventh-Day Baptist whom local officials long regarded with suspicion, was in fact the epitome of staid respectability.[12] The less sophisticated of these missionaries received summary treatment on occasion. A white South African nurse who had received a "call" to become a faith healer was deported first from Malawi and then from Zambia. The grounds: her presence, her style of life, and her free-lance activities would inevitably ruffle the public calm.[13] Officials gradually recognized that the disturbing effect of small missions stemmed not from the ideology or the political aspirations of those who ran them but from their peculiar misfit in the structure of the protectorate. They were too small, too poor, too late arriving, and perhaps too fundamentalist to slip easily into the fraternal intercourse with colonial officialdom that the older missions enjoyed; and their intercourse with the older missions was often anything but fraternal. Most of all, such groups could not, or simply did not, organize their activities to the satisfaction of the administration. In the aftermath of the Chilembwe Rising (1915), groups that the administration called "eccentric" missions came in for specific condemnation, not for active sedition but for failing to maintain suitable control.[14]

By dint of energy and what the Reverend Walter Elmslie ruefully called his "well-known plausibility," Booth founded seven eccentric groups between 1892 and 1907.[15] He was expelled from the protectorate once, in 1899, but was permitted to return if he would desist from his unsettling activities. He continued to initiate projects and then pass them on to others, black and white, who ran them after he had moved on. Booth left the country finally in 1902, but his spirit remained at work in the schools and churches he had helped to establish and in his African colleagues. In their turn, Booth's African colleagues had a lasting impact upon church-state relations in Malawi. The foremost of these colleagues were John Chilembwe and Elliot Kamwana.

John Chilembwe traveled with Booth to America in 1897, returning three years later as an ordained Baptist preacher.[16] With the help of some black American Baptists, he founded the Providence Industrial Mission and established a network of schools and commercial farms. In line with the ideas Booker T. Washington and others were popularizing in America, he committed himself to racial uplift through labor and slow but steady accumulation. The spirit of the Tuskegee and Hampton institutes also entered homes. Chilembwe's elite colleagues joined him in emulating the material style of middle-class black Americans. Pastors affected stiff Edwardian collars; their wives, corsets and silk stockings.[17] (And one imagines that they acquired front parlors dressed up with doilies and whatnots, as well.) Together they propagated in Africa the respectable substance of Afro-America's "talented tenth," along with the Protestant ethic of Washington. But, in a remarkable train of events, Chilembwe led in 1915 the first armed revolt since the conquest. This incident helped to harden into active repression the regime's annoyance with eccentric missions under the influence of black American or maverick white missionaries.

Despite his physical departure from Malawi in 1902, Booth's spirit continued to hover over the colonial rulers of Malawi. While Chilembwe was yet busy advocating hard work and gradual uplift, Booth was busy in South Africa with new proselytes from Malawi. In 1906, Booth convinced Charles Taze Russell that his society should extend its field of operations to Africa. Inaugurating its base of operations in Cape Town, Booth taught the society's doctrines to a number of migrant workers, who then returned to their homes to preach.[18] Thus it was that Elliot Kamwana arrived home late in 1908 preaching that Armageddon and the End would come in October 1914.

Kamwana was a Tonga from Chifira, the district of the Free Church station called Bandawe. A product of the church's schools, he was among the most promising pupils of the 1899 middle-school class, and his name appeared on the Livingstonia honor roll in 1901.[19] But he became dissatisfied with the mission when it introduced school fees, in 1898. The introduction of the hut tax in his area the same year probably accentuated the impact of the move.[20] In 1902, Kamwana left for South Africa to work.[21] By 1907 (according to an account of Kamwana's career written by the Reverend Mr. R. D. McMinn), he was employed in a hospital and living an "openly immoral" life. Booth taught "half-castes" early on, but by 1907 he had turned his attention to "Nyasa boys" working in the mines—in order, McMinn wrote, "to undo the missionaries."[22] Kamwana received eight months' instruction from him before returning home.[23]

Reverend A. G. McAlpine, another Livingstonia missionary, thought that Kamwana's and others' Watchtower conversions could be explained by their exposure to the morally corrosive atmosphere of the urban work situation in South Africa and to the influence of "Ethiopian," or pan-Africanist, churches that proliferated in South Africa. (But it should also be noted that schismatic churches were also prevalent among the white lower classes in South Africa; these equally may have influenced the South African blacks' tendency toward religious separatism.)[24] In his report to interested people in Scotland, McAlpine took pains to say that Kamwana was not really one of Livingstonia's own; even though he had excelled in the mission's schools, he had never been in its employ. "The lad possesses some natural ability, but his moral character was rated very low by his Tonga fellow workmen till at least a few months before his return to the Lake [Nyasa]."[25] Elmslie reaffirmed the point McMinn and McAlpine made about Kamwana's "moral character."

Missionaries often meant by "immorality" something more than the sins of polygamy, beer drinking, and licentiousness. Disloyalty to the mission or disobedience to a missionary might also reflect on a member's moral character; both could carry heavy physical and psychological penalties. When the African teachers at Ekwendeni Station refused in 1919 to work three extra weeks without additional pay, several of them were summarily fired.[26] When the Ngoni evangelist (later pastor) Daniel Mtusu once rebelled against the distasteful assignment of going to a strange and distant area alone, without his trusted colleagues of years' standing, he was visited by a frightening apocalyptic dream. As if the dream and Mtusu's penitence thereafter were not enough, the Reverend Mr. Elmslie deliberately held him in prolonged suspense as to his Christian future, then gave him a severe "talking to" before sending him off a second time on exactly the same task, in exactly the same circumstances. In short, "morality" implied obedience to the orders of individual missionaries as well as to the rules governing employees' or members' behavior. Although commanding the personal obedience of African members was part of the mission's functioning as an effective organization, it also entered into missionaries' definition of "morality."

An antinomian rebellion that occurred in 1900 further illustrates this point. A talented and well-trusted teacher at Livingstonia was caught engaging in "immoral acts." Instead of repenting and accepting the church's discipline, the wrongdoer presented before the Kirk Session a carefully argued written defense of his action. The teacher's remorseless defense of the (unnamed) "immorality," of which he was found guilty, weighed as heavily upon missionaries' minds as the actual offense. His pride dismayed and offended

them, and his independence of mind set a bad example. To hu-
miliate him, they removed him from teaching to gardening work.
The *Livingstonia Mission Report* described the case as a "fall from
the highest position attainable here to almost the lowest possible."

> He had much done for him and an earnest effort was made
> to bring him back, but his intelligence and wide reading, we
> fear, now make him a dangerous person to those less in-
> structed. His defense before the session, when charged with
> one of several fresh sins, was not a denial, but an open confes-
> sion and an attempt to justify his request to be received back
> by propounding an antinomian law of Christian liberty which
> he did in a long paper submitted to the session.[27]

At Livingstonia, independence of mind was a virtue when it led a
person to break with "heathen" tradition: The Reverend Mr. Elmslie fondly told the story of a courageous woman who refused to
pray at an ancestor shrine, despite her Job-like sufferings, and in
the teeth of unremitting pressure from her relatives and neighbors.[28] But the same quality of independence was vice when applied
to the judgments of missionaries. Thus it was possible for Elmslie
both to deny that Kamwana's movement was actually "Ethiopian"—
that is, adhering to the political slogan, Africa for the Africans—
and yet to affirm that it possessed the "spirit, if not the principles
of Ethiopianism."[29]

The morality of obedience underwent further tests when issues
of public policy separated missionaries from their African parishioners. One of these issues was colonial taxation. Africans regarded
the tax as an oppressive imposition. The Western Lundas (Zambia)
are said to have rioted when the principles of taxation were first
explained to them.[30] A Tonga witch doctor fomented violent resistance. And numerous accounts show that the regime had recourse to raids, house burnings, and kidnappings in order to compel payment of the tax. According to J. E. Stephenson, the Lala
people (Zambia) were told that the *pax Britannica* meant "no more
war, no more witchcraft, no more slavery," but when tax collecting
began in earnest, a Lala princess exclaimed to him, "Why, this is
just like war!"[31] Because the protectorate administration was aware
that Africans might not submit to the tax without a struggle, it
imposed the tax upon the Tongas first, reasoning that in seeing
their old enemies the Ngonis disarmed, they gained from colonial
rule more than they lost. Perhaps reasoning that the Ngonis had
lost more than they had gained, the administration waited several

years before introducing the tax among them, in order to permit
the full "pacification" of this old military people. Applauding the
introduction of the hut tax, Free Church pastors took it upon
themselves both to explain its "benefits" and to minimize friction
in its collection. The Reverend Dr. Robert Laws, head of Livingstonia, made the argument to his theology students that the hut
tax was actually less burdensome than the chiefly tribute it replaced.[32]

Laws and his colleagues favored the tax not only as a normal
and natural sign of allegiance to the empire, but also because they
favored a tax of three shillings a year as a means of prodding
Africans to work for cash. Africans would actually profit from this
indispensable nudge toward "self-improvement."[33] Further, the assessment of tax on the basis of the number of "huts" a man had
was a bonus to Christian culture, for it placed a financial obstacle
in the way of polygamy. However, in 1902, when the administration
began to discuss doubling the tax to promote migration to the gold
mines of the Transvaal, Livingstonia missionaries disapproved.[34]
Laws called the measure "scarcely veiled slavery." The problem, he
philosophized, was that an "indigenous stimulus" to work was lacking. Rather than coercion through tax, Africans needed an "internal motive": "Most powerful of all is that of a new spiritual life.
Combine this with education, and new needs will be felt, requiring
more work, and eventually steady industry to supply them."[35] Laws
based his objection upon the realistic fear that the tide of labor
migration would bear away Livingstonia's constituency. It would
thus destroy the dream of creating around the mission a buzzing
center of modern economic enterprise. Livingstonia aimed to "seed
the villages" with cadres embodying a Protestant ethic. It could not
succeed in this if the South African economy continually removed
the most progressive elements. In this, as John McCracken has
pointed out, history has fully vindicated Laws' fear. Today northern
Malawi combines economic backwardness with an unusually high
level of literacy.[36]

Despite their opposition to the doubling of the African tax as a
tool of labor recruitment, the missionaries did not oppose monetary
constraint as such. The mission's one great gift of the Gospel began
to merge into the growing stream of colonial commodities. It was
mission policy to make African congregations self-supporting as
soon as possible. And Africans were to pay fees for health and
educational services as soon as they had the means or could be
induced to work for them. (In 1908, Livingstonia set a charge of

3 pence per medical visit.) These policies had a practical origin: rising costs plus an inadequate flow of contributions from Britain. But they also had a philosophic origin. Elmslie argued that, without the institution of fees for services, Africans would get the idea that missionaries were "incalculably rich, or soft, to be bled."[37] From the standpoint of many Africans, the mission's policies must have appeared to be of a piece with the exactions of the regime. Decision on such matters of basic philosophy did not require consultation with African members, or even with the elite who sat side by side with missionaries in the Kirk Session. Philosophy and practicality alike went by fiat.

Of course, African Christians were not well placed to appreciate the philosophical issue. Elmslie and his colleagues brought, with the Christianity that no Malawian had initially requested, pieties about anything that smacked of welfare. They belonged to the era of Booker T. Washington (and of Max Weber, who could observe Washington's spiritual kin around him as he composed *The Protestant Ethic and the Spirit of Capitalism*). Some came from those happy working strata who saw themselves rising by dint of hard work and abstemiousness. For example, Laws read medicine and religion in the dark hours of the morning and while working at his lathe. McMinn struggled and finally rose from missionary artisan to pastor. Both understood material wonders as arising from self-mastery and spiritual dedication. And, as Free Church men, they belonged to a spiritual elite, for whom material advance was one outward sign of election.

They and their colleagues saw their decision to evangelize in Africa as sacrifice. But, no matter how poor missionaries were in their own eyes, and in the eyes of some settlers, they were conspicuously wealthier than their charges. Households, household help, clothing, transportation home, guns, and other amenities— not just schools and hospitals, Bible translations and equipment— came out of mission funds. Only some of these came from parishioner's contributions, which did not come close to paying the whole bill. But, to a man like Elmslie, the principle mattered. To his African colleagues, it did not matter in the same way.

Financing mission work was a different matter—and a constant headache. The necessity of raising funds from the local powers that be helped to tailor many missions' role over time.[38] Not only did these funds come from local taxation, which allied missions with the administration's tax policies, but their use was also subject to other administrative policies. Sometimes these policies were not the missions' first choice; at other times, black and white Christians made different first choices. In various ways, money put black and white Livingstonia at odds. It was the root of different evils.

At the turn of the century, many were alive who remembered the Free Church missionaries' behavior in the early days when they had offered gifts to young people in order to secure attendance at mission schools and hearers' classes. But, by the time fees were introduced, Christianity had become virtually a way of life among the Tongas, and the Free Church had achieved wide acceptance. (As early as 1898, some congregations even began to finance their own missionary expeditions into Zambia.)[39] In the aftermath of the crisis precipitated by Kamwana, Elmslie summed up the situation: "The Watchtower could not have succeeded at all had there not been a widespread general knowledge of Scripture truth."[40] But the church was more than an affair of "Scripture truth" without significance for physical well-being. It had thoroughly entrenched itself in African life. Educational and job opportunities were tied closely to mission membership. By 1908, the mission's schools were handling some 30,000 pupils per year[41]—and the first state-financed schools did not appear until well into the 1920s. Moreover, Livingstonia had become a significant local market for agricultural produce and a center for cash employment as well.

Now that the church had achieved importance and wide acceptance, it raised the ante of membership. Elmslie made baptism contingent upon ability to read the Scriptures. As early as 1906, he refused schooling to children of nonmembers and members under suspension. If he so chose, he suspended from Holy Communion parents who failed to pay for their children's schooling.[42] He demanded a set monthly contribution (using the threat of suspension), and he required members to buy Scripture texts. A few years later, the church as a whole adopted a policy of suspending members who declined to marry under the Christian Native Marriage Ordinance of 1912. (If persons married under this law subsequently "lapsed into polygamy," they faced not only suspension from Communion, but also a five-year jail term.) In short, because Livingstonia controlled access to things people had come to need or want, it could set conditions and rules in their acquisition. Inevitably, then, the imperatives of spreading the Gospel fostered obedience and conformity. In this way, Livingstonia accomplished political goals while pursuing religious ones.

To emphasize the ways in which the church shaped mundane life is not to deny the import of its salvation, however understood.

People responded not only to the material benefits of membership but also to the message about sin and salvation. There is not much written evidence of the message the missionaries taught to their earliest converts, and obviously less evidence still of what these converts actually made of it. But Monica Wilson observed firsthand the preaching style of African evangelists at work in southern Tanzania. "Do you want to burn? Do you want to burn?" they would shout, as they rushed into a village. After drawing a crowd, they would proceed with loud enthusiastic preaching that no doubt made salvation from eternal punishment seem attractive. Such extravagance did not originate with African evangelists.[43] They shared the style of belief that colored Protestant and Catholic practice in the second half of the nineteenth century, a style that produced the fear-ridden musical literature that E. P. Thompson has analyzed so perceptively in his study of Methodism.[44] When harmonium playing was at last introduced into the rigorously plain Free Church service, the Reverend Mr. McAlpine enthused that Tonga Christians were now singing "There Is a Fountain Filled with Blood" to instrumental accompaniment.[45] The British evangelical conceptions of fear, guilt, and sin so resounded locally that, as early as 1898, the first African revival occurred.[46]

Having arranged that church membership seemed to many vital, the Free Church missionaries now limited access to it. They enforced a long period of study and waiting before baptism. Often as long as four years, the progression from "hearer" to catechumen to baptized member never took less than two. People even had to apply for admission to the catechumens' classes; in 1902, Elmslie rejected 60 out of 140 applicants.[47] It was a task of the Kirk Sessions, the "self-government" institutions into which the African mission elite was recruited, to narrow various bottlenecks to membership so that only persons deemed to have the correct reasons for seeking conversion might pass through.[48] The Kirk Sessions also investigated the private character of candidates for baptism, which took time. And, even if such an investigation cleared the way, an application was not necessarily successful. Livingstonia simply did not believe in admitting large numbers of people at once. In 1904, McAlpine baptized 151 out of 300 applicants.[49] In 1910, Robert Laws sifted the aspirants by refusing to baptize people who had not contributed to the church while they were not yet full members. Livingstonia's Protestants thus arrived at what amounted to a doctrine of salvation by works. So doing, they cleared the way for their own Luther.

After the Watchtower episode, Livingstonians still embraced their exclusionary policy as an effective method of purging the "slacker elements."[50] It was these "slacker elements" whose entry they tried to prevent by establishing the strictest possible requirements. Even if they had no objection to a particular candidacy, the missionaries mistrusted and therefore resisted the tendency of villagers to join the church collectively, progressing through the several stages together. This communal tendency disturbed them, for the Free Church had the sect's emphasis upon individual conversion. It disturbed them the more because villagers who joined as a group typically fell away as a group. The church's publications deplore the fact that the "declension" of a particular teacher or church elder often led to "backsliding" by his entire following.[51] This problem was acute where African members disagreed with missionaries on matters of social convention, and where all that held disobedience at bay was strong conviction. In such a case, an individual decision, tempered if possible in the fire of persecution, promised to be the most durable one.

While some norms blocked entry, others pushed people out after they had been baptized. Disagreement about social convention continually produced "discipline cases," which typically involved the sins of polygamy and beer drinking. Members suspended for polygamy were unlikely ever to return.[52] But suspension did not necessarily mean that beer drinkers or polygamists ceased to consider themselves Christians, or that they subscribed to the mission's view: Livingstonians repeatedly condemned the "lack of public conscience" about these "evils."[53] The remark of a well-known village headman nicely sums this up. Asked his religious affiliation by a court official, before being allowed to swear on the Bible, he said in correct English, "I am a Christian, but I am not a church member."[54] "Here spoke the inconsequent African," commented a missionary, who went on to brand the Christian a "notorious polygamist" and a "bloated beer-drinker." But the man had expressed an important truth. Christianity had a wider following than just those who bore the mission's seal of approval. Many people excluded from the church's fellowship questioned the justice of their exclusion.

Not all suffered exclusion for Christian reasons. Large numbers of people lost out by virtue of historical chance in the initial location of mission stations.[55] Outlying areas were visited only periodically by evangelists and teachers, and by missionaries at still longer intervals. For example, converts gained in Zambia by the Malawian evangelist David Kaunda, beginning in 1904, had to wait until 1911 to be baptized. No European missionary could be sent from Malawi before then—and, at that time, only white hands could perform the rite.[56] Some areas did not benefit from mission schools, employment, and markets because the Free Church was never able to cover its whole sphere of influence with equal attention. It is for this reason that Livingstonia's missionaries applauded the BSAC's program of village amalgamation.[57] But even if the amalgamation policy had succeeded perfectly, the problem would not have been solved. The Free Church "jurisdiction" embraced too vast an area to attend to with the available personnel and funds. Their establishment near some villages thus created a mainstream that shifted other villages into remote backwaters.

A writer in the 1907 report of the Foreign Mission Committee described the condition of an outlying village, where evangelists alone made periodic visits. In the midst of a calamitous drought that year, some of the old people, including several deposed chiefs, urged the revival of spirit worship. But even though under suspension from Free Church membership, the present chief urged the people to pray to the Christian God alone. The report continued:

> While one rejoices at such evidence of the wide and deep influence of the Word of God among the people, the position of these people is very pathetic. Once upon a time, and not very long ago, they ruled the opinions and customs of the people and now, quietly, yet surely, they are left out of account.[58]

In many such areas, nothing more durable than intermittent visits by teen-age evangelists replaced the disestablished religion. One chief outspokenly demanded more. He wanted a church in his village and a white missionary to run it.[59] Temporary schools and churches, run by mission pupils during their vacation times, subject to closure for no evident reason, appearing and disappearing unpredictably—these were the price of living in the backwaters of Livingstonia's world.

The excluded opened the mission's flank. Needless to say, the disgruntlement of those not receiving the material and spiritual benefits of church membership exposed the Livingstonia polity to attack from inside. But, equally important, in fringe areas the polity itself could not form cohesive Christian communities fully integrated into the network of mission control and therefore reachable as units by the regime beyond. Where such networks existed, they could exert powerful influence at moments of crisis. For example, during World War I, a young Ngoni chief refused to aid the regime's campaign to recruit carriers and buy grain. When the regime threatened the chief's village with an armed patrol, the chief took refuge in the nearby mission. But he did not find sanctuary: Reverend Donald Fraser persuaded the chief that he must turn himself in and accept being deposed. Thereafter recruitment proceeded, without use of force, and the food requisitions were met in less than a week. To a British missionary, of course, the duty to defend the empire against German encroachment was self-evident and should have been so to Malawi's chiefs. After the incident, Fraser observed, "His brother chiefs have awakened to the fact that they must work if they are to retain their positions."[60]

Where close Christian polity did not exist, the mission was less than useful to the regime, not only because it could not supplement the regime's ability to neutralize discontent arising from state action, but also because it generated its own. Elliot Kamwana's home area of Chifira was a place where Christian polity faltered. Discontent continued there into the 1920s, when it was still a headquarters of the Watchtower organization in the district.[61] Kamwana's revival produced a landslide among the disadvantaged or excluded groups. It was the lapsed Christians, the hearers, the eternal catechumens, and those who lived on the fringes of mission influence who responded most avidly to the new creed.

KAMWANA AND THE WATCHTOWER MILLENNIUM

Kamwana arrived on the scene in mid-1908. By April of 1909, he claimed to have baptized over nine thousand people. By the time of his banishment later in the year, the newly baptized numbered between ten thousand and twelve thousand people, in his own home area and as far afield as Nkota Kota and Usisya. In addition, Kamwana and his colleagues made determined but largely unsuccessful efforts away from the lake, in Ekwendeni District. Like subsequent groups of heterodox revivalists, Kamwana and his colleagues gave aliens a wide berth and concentrated their work in more distant areas. In that way, they could free themselves to make war on "heathenism" and "false Christianity," while avoiding skirmishes with the authorities. Very often the news of these activities only reached missionaries and officials via African employees at work in outlying areas. The Reverend Mr. McAlpine first heard the bad news of Christ's imminent Second Coming from a Tonga evangelist.[62]

Groups of assistants quickly flocked to Kamwana and the Tonga colleagues who had accompanied him from South Africa. According to one mission report, these were "flighty young men" who already had "a history."[63] Reverend T. Cullen Young declared that this group "aimed more at undermining the white men than belief or understanding of the Adventist propaganda of the Watchtower." He may or may not have been right in this characteristic expression of missionary bewilderment and offense; it was also true, as he himself reported, that people were attracted to the movement by the promise of free books and their own schools. Many saw substance in Kamwana's charge that the established missions were simply extorting money instead of performing their appointed task. Some years later, Isaac Muwamba, a hostile observer of the Watchtower, made the point that many people were dissatisfied with the missions' contribution to their material betterment, a benefit that the missionaries constantly touted. Muwamba claimed that during the Kamwana revival his father, a village headman, had been hoodwinked by Kamwana's band of liars, who promised him and his villagers vastly improved living standards.[64] (We shall encounter Isaac Muwamba and his brother Ernest again, for both served as informers against Watchtower preachers in Zambia. They also repudiated their cousin, Clements Kadalie, founder of the first African trade union in South Africa.)

If Kamwana's mission is not fairly summarized as a plot against white men, it is certainly true that he expressed popular discontent with both missionaries and officials. He is reported to have told enthusiastic crowds, "Officials, you will see no more. We shall build our own ships, make our own powder and make or import our own guns."[65] And two of Kamwana's colleagues dogged the itinerary of an African mission teacher, denouncing all Africans who prayed for whites.[66] Preachers foretold that Africans would manage their own affairs in church and state. It was wrong, they said, to compel school attendance, to require fees, and to demand a long probationary period before acceptance into the church. And they speedily branded missionaries' efforts to block this teaching as religious persecution.[67] While pointedly criticizing Livingstonia's policies, Kamwana made the blanket indictment that is characteristic of the American Watchtower movement: All "etablished churches" are inextricably bound up with the political authorities of "the world." Kamwana applied this argument to the Christian establishment over which Livingstonia presided. The Reverend Mr. Elmslie responded in kind. To him the Watchtower was bent on undoing the missionaries; and if they went, so would the fiber of colonial society in Malawi.[68]

Still, Livingstonia missionaries could not report direct attack against Europeans. To make the connection between their own work and colonial law and order, they emphasized Kamwana's political aspirations. To persuade an administration that was at first inclined to see the episode as merely a church matter, they reported that not only the mission, but also backward heathen chiefs were disturbed by the preaching. "The political aspect of the movement became so prominent that even heathen chiefs and headmen denounced the ruinous tendency of the new crusade," reported a mission publication.[69] As we have seen, however, at least one village headman responded favorably to the promise of free schooling and other material benefits. Although it may be true that many customary rulers disliked the movement, this qualification should be kept in view. At the same time, some chiefs doubtless saw Watchtower preaching as intrinsically hostile to them, for a simple reason: Watchtower preachers typically shared the missionaries' contempt for heathen observances. Chiefs' attitudes were further complicated by their need to be at least as attentive to what was countenanced by the administration as loyal mission adherents were to what was approved by missionaries. Although I cannot confirm this, I think it possible that chiefs were at some point commanded to break up Watchtower meetings and arrest troublemakers. Such was certainly the case later in Zambian revivals.

Whatever may have been the ultimate political ambition of Kamwana and those who supported him, baptism was the centerpiece of the campaign. We cannot understand his campaign at all if we fail to understand why people accepted baptism. For many, the rite was an unquestionable good. An old lady was heard to exclaim, "We have seen baptism today, and our hearts are light and happy."[70] So widespread was this idea that even loyal mission members seem to have assumed at first that missionaries would support it. Elmslie found it necessary to make his opposition clear. Christians held aloof from the movement, he explained, "as soon as it was realized that the mission would have nothing to do with it"— apparently not before.[71] Even then, some within the mission's orbit seem to have discounted this as the prejudiced personal view of Elmslie and others, insisting that even if local missionaries opposed it, the great Dr. Robert Laws, head of the Livingstonia Institution,

would not. In fact, a rumor circulated around Bandawe that Laws
was on his way with seven Europeans to serve the sect and vanquish
its opponents.[72]

Extraordinary displays of religious emotion accompanied the
baptisms. Fraser gave the following eyewitness account of the proceedings in one area:

> Great audiences were assembled everywhere. The response to
> teaching was immediate and often with sobs and tears ... a
> strong tendency to expect the blessing of God through spasms
> ... silly rumors were spread by ignorant people that fire was
> to come down from heaven to burn up all those who concealed
> their sins. Exaggerated desires for wild physical emotions were
> evident ... a youth rose and began to pray with a tremor in
> his voice and I ordered the man to stop at once. ... Soon two
> or three began to pray at the same time. ... I stopped them,
> forbidding more than one at a time to pray. But during the
> struggle of those few minutes with the force of disorder and
> emotion, one felt as if we were passing through a powder
> magazine, and some were trying to light matches.[73]

Although an observer like Fraser would be disconcerted by "the
force of disorder and emotion," then and always, he would not
possibly have disapproved the classic testimonies confessing and
renouncing sin. And although the crowd's conception of fire that
would punish the unrepentent may well have been too concrete
and too immediate to suit Fraser's sensibility, hot fires burned in
the correct evangelical Protestant theology he embraced. The
thought of those fires would soon be pulling sinners off the "mourn-
er's bench" at the mission, during the Inwood Revival of 1910.
Fraser would then see religious enthusiasm differently: "With the
conversion came wonderful experiences, conviction of sin, pros-
tration of multitudes, the leaping joy of those 'who saw the Lord.' "[74]

BAPTISM AS A POLITICAL ACT

Kamwana's success did not rest simply upon his anticolonial politics.
If the ambitions of Kamwana and his followers were political, then
so must have been the act of baptism. And if baptism itself was a
political act, we are still not free to ignore the many senses in which
those who received it treated it as an ultimate good connected with,
but distinct from, their feelings about the regime. Even if the baptism was directed to political ends, it cannot be regarded as a tool

devoid of significance in its own terms. Effective tools of mass mobilization never are. What, then, is to be made of Kamwana's campaign of baptism? The answer has several layers: the Watchtower's theory of baptism; the mission's more general social meaning of the sacrament; and the connotation of baptism in terms of preexisting African conceptions. Although baptism has its own traditional meaning of death and rebirth, an African convert to Christianity was not considering for the first time the problem for which it proposes solutions. Africans lacked neither the ideas of sin and repentance nor the practice of confession. Traditional ceremonies of purification corresponded to these aspects of baptism. Bengt Sundkler has beautifully shown how they transit into independent African churches.[75]

At one level, an anticolonial translation of Kamwana's baptisms comes easily, and he provides a key to it himself. Expressing popular resentment against discrimination, and again at the church's restrictive policies, he astonished and excited crowds by claiming, "I have baptized seven thousand whites in the south. I have denied Members of Parliament."[76] Kamwana, who could deny this unexcelled benefit to South African whites, was now offering it to any African who would come forward! He also capitalized on the high valuation of baptism, as inculcated by the missions, and then criticized the many barriers they placed in the way of achieving this spiritual good. He claimed, furthermore, that missionaries had withheld from Africans the Truth contained in the millennial message of the Watchtower: The Jews would reoccupy Palestine when the End came; the End would come in October 1914; only those who had joined the sect would be saved from the ensuing holocaust; only the baptized could hope for admission to the Kingdom that God would then inaugurate on earth.[77] Baptism always signifies entrance into a new "community," but the Watchtower understands this in a more concrete and immediate sense than do other denominations. It expects the establishment of a new polity on earth with Jesus Christ as its head. In this way, the Watchtower theory of baptism provided a Christian vehicle for the assertion of political independence. Its practice earned Elliot Kamwana the religious label "heretic."

Missionaries considered him an antinomian. "The youth who is commissioned to carry on the propaganda," a church report said, "preaches salvation by baptism, irrespective of character." Whereas the missionaries required sustained proof of what they liked to call "a change of heart,"[78] Kamwana advanced the outrageous doctrine that "the one thing needful was baptism, and that baptism could save people from sin and its consequences." In some areas there was a noticeable return to dancing and beer drinking—practices long outlawed by Livingstonia but condemned by no widespread "public conscience" against them. People started to reverse the cultural transformation that was part and parcel of the "change of heart." Polygamous spouses accepted baptism together instead of being divorced and accepting it separately. By offering baptism without regard to the mission's rules, Kamwana discredited for some people the mission's equation of sin with the traditional way of life.

Furthermore, by baptizing indiscriminately, he devalued the mission's all-important instruction, together with the officials whose task it was to educate and screen the people. Naturally, the enthusiasm of the would-be baptized Christians upset the orthodox. As one said, his preaching "awakened fear and great excitement" as "the ignorant came under his spell."[79] In common with other new sects, Kamwana's Watchtower opened wide the doors to Christian allegiance. His new church offered relief from the same fears; it encompassed the same hopes, but it did not make the Free Church's relentless sobriety the condition of their fulfillment. The popular response to this heresy demonstrated to the missionaries a widespread "unhealthy desire to seek entrance" and an unforeseen complexity of people's "true motives for seeking Christian membership."[80] However, it would be wrong to see the extraordinary emphasis upon baptism solely as a popular rejection of the mission's demands. Africans worried about African forms of sin that the church systematically ignored.

All episodes of Watchtower revival replicate Kamwana's "false emphasis on baptism." This emphasis is not restricted to the Watchtower. A common practice in African independent churches, baptism by total immersion is adopted, in part, as a weapon in the struggle against witchcraft.[81] In many such baptisms, a promise to renounce the practice of witchcraft accompanies the rite. Other participants confess it to all present by publicly giving up charms and medicines (although this concrete expression need not be part of the proceedings). In Africa, baptism "for the remission of sins" has often melded with ancient procedures for the renunciation of witchcraft. (The orthodox teaching of modern Jehovah's Witnesses specifically rejects the doctrine of baptism for the remission of sins. For them it is uniquely a symbol of new membership and the convert's future life in the theocratic organization. I cannot tell whether

Kamwana preached the remission of sins, or whether his and his successors' preaching was simply "heard" in this way by people habituated to it through the teaching of many missions.)

Although I do not think Kamwana's baptisms differed from his successors', I must admit that his missionary critics failed to mention any such synthesis of baptism and the cure of witchcraft. If their failure to mention it means that no such synthesis had yet occurred in Malawi, then my explanation of the popular enthusiasm for Watchtower baptism must be qualified. I think it more likely, however, that missionary observers were blinded by a naive belief that they had done away with the reality of witchcraft—or by ignorance of its implications.[a] They may not have been able to take in the full meaning of this account, by an evangelist, of an exchange between a villager and himself, written in about 1900:

> And another came saying, "Why don't you teach that it is wrong to bewitch people? I hear you teaching it is wrong to kill. Do you mean that this witchcraft is murder too?" And I said "Indeed God forbids poisoning too and says that to be angry with your neighbors without cause is to kill."[82]

My best evidence that Kamwana's revival contained this element appears in a letter from Isaac Muwamba to a district administrator some years later.

> While at home [from a job in Zambia], I at times pointed out to Watchtower people that they seemed to think that they had found a true church of "salvation" and yet it was curious to notice some of them going to cemeteries [sic] at night for the purpose of digging up the dead for their pots: did not part away with divination.[83]

[a] A Scots clergyman told me the following anecdote dating from the 1950s. The missionary's daughter was killed in an automobile accident, and not long afterward his son suffered an ugly head wound in a fall. African Christian elders assisted the family to get medical treatment. After the danger was past, the church members began to pay the customary visits to the family. Since this pastor belonged to a younger generation of missionaries, living close to their parishioners in a style similar to that of the local people, conversation was always in the vernacular, even when church people were fluent in English. As they sat one evening discussing the affair, one of the elders made the startling remark that if the son had not recovered, they would have begun to look for the witch. The missionary told me how grateful he was that the venacular required no more response from him than the conventional acknowledgment "Eeee, baba" [an Ngoni equivalent of "Yeah, uh huh"]. So surprised was he by the discovery that witch belief survived among the very best Christians of the parish that he could not have managed more.

Muwamba implies that ordinary Christians baptized by the missions, in the normal way, did not leave behind the belief in witchcraft or its practice either. There are two further reasons for believing that Kamwana's baptisms had this significance. If this conception of sin had indeed been submerged in 1909, then in 1919 it had reemerged. At the height of the influenza epidemic that year, there was such a scourge of witchcraft that even Donald Fraser was forced to take it seriously. The reverend invited the *nganga* (medicine man) to church and asked people to bring their charms and magical objects there.[84] Finally, in many African societies, spirit possession takes place in the formal procedure for exposing witchcraft. It may be that the mass possessions that accompanied the mass baptisms served temporarily at least, and symbolically, to affirm that all sin and all evil had been discovered and banished from the midst of the new converts.

This hypothesis, that Kamwana associated baptism with the cure of witchcraft, would explain why some people who were already church members should also have been interested in the movement. The missions offered no solution to the evil of witchcraft. Just as the regime dropped witchcraft from the list of recognized crimes, so the missions dropped it from the list of recognized sins. Thus, even if church members did not seek baptism for themselves, they might well have wanted it for relatives, friends and, conceivably, for ill-intentioned or envious neighbors. Some people might have associated material goods with baptism in a magical way. Some might have fully accepted the mission's elevation of baptism as a goal to be sought at all costs. And if by baptism a person publicly showed himself to be free of witchcraft and other sins, the same pressure that motivated others to accept the *mucapi* would have motivated him to accept baptism. These factors, combined with the ease of being baptized, would have made Kamwana's offer difficult to refuse. During one of the subsequent movements, villagers testified that they had been baptized both because they thought the preachings good and because they wanted to prove they were not witches. If my interpolation of witch cleansing into Kamwana's baptisms is correct, then the Watchtower fit into the cycle according to which the problem of evil inevitably found its resolution in political terms; and it pointed back to the religious communalism that the missionaries had long feared and mistrusted. If this is true, then the Watchtower may be seen as attacking recurrent problems of village life as well as novel ones that arose from colonial rule.

All I have said about Kamwana's baptisms has shown the complexity of Kamwana's appeal. To say simply, as many writers have, that the 1908 outbreak was an early expression of African discontent with colonial rule is so obviously true as to be misleading. It singles out and incorporates only what most exercised contemporary white observers. While we can readily appreciate the limitations of their view, we need not limit ourselves in the same way. For the participants themselves, joining Kamwana's movement need not have been solely a means of achieving revolutionary ends—even one as comprehensible as the sudden disappearance of the Reverend Mr. Elmslie. They may well have set themselves the religiously respectable task of abolishing evil. Exposing evil and prevailing on people to renounce it are sensible means to that end.

But uncovering people's likely motivation does not exhaust the fundamental problem. Wishing to shake an order and actually doing so are different things. Watchtower converts did not have the power to move the polity at will any more than they could prevail at will over witchcraft. Whether they sought to purge the land of evil or of the alien presence, this problem remains. The consequences of their actions are not directly attributable to what they may have desired to accomplish. These consequences took form and direction from factors given historically. One such given was the religious universe of Livingstonia Mission: its points of congruence with the evolving colonial regime, its internal structure, and its methods. A missionary writer in the *Livingstonia Mission Report* denies that Kamwana's spectacular influence flowed from his preaching. "[He was] a strategist and struck the weak points of the situation very cleverly."[85] What were these "weak points" where baptism is concerned?

Baptism gave definition not only to the work of church officials but also to the activities of those who aspired to become members. As the rock on which stood much worldly work, it signified much more than an individual's spiritual conversion. It was the centerpiece of missionary labor. If suddenly available, at the low cost of stepping forward, baptism lost its utility as a collective means of recognizing an individual's change of heart. It could no longer stand as a goal in pursuit of which a candidate would be repeatedly examined, disciplined, tested, and slowly woven into the mission's social fabric. Kamwana's speedy baptizing and his doctrine of baptism as the one thing needful inflated the church's hard currency. He thereby jeopardized the effectiveness of one resource in the mission's dealings with prospective Christians. The mission's effectiveness as an informal agency of political rule declined accordingly.

The outlook of the Anabaptists and the Church's ferocity in repressing them may be understood analogously. To deny the validity of infant baptism, as the Anabaptists did, was to deny the Church's right to recruit new members automatically and as a consequence of their being born on the physical and spiritual territory of Christendom. To condemn infant baptism on religious grounds was simultaneously to undercut the Church's control over immortal souls and over mortal bodies. In the early 1900s, the cultural part of Livingstonia's enterprise required at least that no competitor with whom no prior arrangement had been made should undertake to recruit in their place. In its own way, the mission had the pretensions of the medieval Church thrust upon it. Kamwana brought in both the thunder of Luther and the water of the Anabaptists.

AFTER KAMWANA'S REVIVAL

For their part, the missionaries were convinced that the mission had saved the day. Elmslie claimed credit for the movement's relative harmlessness from the standpoint of the regime. "But for the solid work done by the Mission," he declared, "the Government would have had a large thing to deal with. The movement failed whenever it was seen that the church people and the catechumenate ignored it."[86] Kamwana carefully sounded elders and teachers at the outset of his campaign, but these did not budge;[87] one area showed no defections among students; by 1915, although the movement continued to be "very influential among the unconverted," not more than one percent of the church's full members had fallen away. In most cases those who joined were "merely" catechumens and hearers, people under discipline, and inhabitants of areas less favored by the mission's institutions, not members; and it was the baptized members who counted. Livingstonia's Christian elitism stood confirmed. Officials saw things otherwise. The governor ventured the criticism that Livingstonia's strictness had been an important cause of the outburst. Elmslie retorted that it was precisely this policy that had ultimately saved the situation.

> When the Governor, Sir Alfred Sharpe, was here and discussed the movement, he expressed the opinion that it was a revolt against our strict discipline: and but for that it would not have taken root. We were able to show that the methods we follow,

apart altogether from the spiritual necessity for following them, have been, by producing a sound church and class, on this occasion the safety of the country.[88]

Although mission and administration shared an interest in political order, these interests did not move in synchrony. Elmslie's remark underlines this fact. Where missionaries performed a civic role in buttressing colonial order, they did so in the interest of their own work and not as appendages of the regime. If their interest had matched the regime's, they would have followed a laxer policy of admission and a more flexible discipline. Exclusion from church privileges surely caused discontent, but such was not their main concern. The Livingstonians looked forward to new harvests among the excluded, and then to ever renewed winnowing of these harvests. Thus, although they admitted the dark side of the episode—that "intense bitterness had been sown in the hearts of many—bitterness toward their friends and associates of former days, and toward the white man,"[89] the episode fed a strange optimism. A valuable time of trouble had come to test the resolve of church members. Moreover, they observed a redoubled interest in the Word and a dramatic increase in the number of candidates for all categories of mission adherence. The mission did not alter its restrictive policies, which the episode seemed to have vindicated; they stood ready with their winnowing baskets. There were irreducible limits to the mission's functioning as a territorial institution.

Nevertheless, Livingstonia had resources that enabled it to prevail over the Watchtower. Whereas Livingstonia was well organized, the Watchtower's structure, such as it was, had grown out of the enthusiasm of the moment. And, unlike Livingstonia, the Watchtower preachers had no prestigious directorate to resolve differences among them. Before long, the spectacle of infighting among the sect's leaders had Elmslie smiling: "As the sect is already at sixes and sevens among themselves, the natives will have an object lesson on how impossible it is for them to cut off their first teachers and leaders and build up an independent church."[90] Further, Livingstonia was able to apply to its own account the new interest the episode had generated. In September 1910, they brought in the revival preacher Charles Inwood. The fire came down again, this time in a respectable institutional context. The effects of the Inwood Revival lasted well into 1911. As the demand for both baptism and admission to hearers' classes recovered, 1,181 people were admitted to full membership.[91]

Apart from initial advantages of finance and organization, Livingstonia had its good relations in the protectorate to fall back on. Hard upon the description of the Kamwana episode in the *Livingstonia Mission Report* of 1909, we read that a Mr. Alexander laid out a golf course at Ekwendeni Station, and that a "European rest home" was under construction, with pupils fulfilling a subcontract by making the 70,000 bricks needed.[92] Work of this kind supplemented church income and aided the expansion of other activities, while continuing the established pattern of mutually beneficial co-operation. This co-operation highlights the difference between established missions and fundamentalist newcomers. The fate of the Seventh-Day Baptists' schools after the Kamwana episode offers a case in point. After Booth's departure, Charles Domingo (once a teacher for the Free Church) ran a district of the church's schools, using American funds.[93] In the aftermath of the crisis, American representatives arrived on the scene to investigate. As a result of their local consultations, they withdrew the funds, whereupon most of the schools had to close. Similarly ill equipped to compete with Livingstonia's varied resources, the Watchtower lost adherents. Nevertheless, in some areas many remained. By August 1914, there were 51 such churches with 1,000 members in West Nyasa District (near Bandawe).[94] They maintained correspondence with the society's headquarters in South Africa, and the society regularly sent them its publications.

IT IS beyond dispute that the principle of "Africa for the Africans" was a significant part of Kamwana's message. Nevertheless, as much as the mass displays of enthusiasm disturbed those on the scene, and despite repeated contemporary references to Kamwana's political aroma, no civil disobedience occurred. And when the opportunity came to join Chilembwe's revolt, Kamwana refused. A mere handful of his followers were implicated and those few as individuals only. Why did Kamwana and his followers stand by?

It is possible, as some have suggested, that Kamwana believed human action to be unnecessary, and that his followers sought in ecstatic practice the direct experience of divine power, perhaps as a foretaste and an assurance of greater things to come. On the other hand, he may have believed armed revolt to be doomed to failure. Chilembwe alluded to failure and heroic suicide when he said, during a crucial deliberation, "Let us strike a blow and die."[95] Still another possibility is that Kamwana believed in present spiritual regeneration as the means of future advance. Or perhaps the two men had no common religious ground. Then again, the whole question may seem baffling only at a safe distance from the flesh-and-blood reality of the armed patrols of the regime and white settlers: In defeat Chilembwe and his followers suffered hideous floggings, imprisonment, exile, and death. What we know for certain is that, from about 1898 on, Kamwana no longer accepted Livingstonia's Christianity as the wave of his people's future, if he ever had. When he returned to Malawi in 1908, it was the church, not the state, that he sought to challenge directly.

Whatever Kamwana's reasoning, the action that followed from his preaching was admirably calculated to unsettle the protectorate's regime. Taking his cue from the heavily Biblical rhetoric of the time, Ian Linden has suggested that Kamwana's method (and Chilembwe's for a long time) followed from the literal-minded religious culture of African intellectuals of the period.[96] But like those who argue Kamwana's primitive nationalism, Linden focuses upon the political content of religious ideas without giving proper weight to their political context. A more complete formulation of this history would be that the religious culture of the time thrived within a religious polity. This polity worked informally and almost invisibly, to be sure, but it worked nevertheless along the front lines of the colonized order. Making this polity effective, missions co-operated with the administration and manipulated their always ambiguous community of interest with other European-run institutions. Above all, missions provided an integrated context of day-to-day activity for their adherents, while providing channels for the achievement of both mundane and transcendental goals. When churches are implicated in such arrangements, heresy spells political danger.

Kamwana did not stop with spoken heresy. He devalued the prevailing currency of this- and other-worldly salvation by offering baptism to all and sundry, regardless of character. He undercut Livingstonia's practical creed of salvation by works. Not stopping there, he let it be known that those who received Watchtower baptism could do so in the hope of attaining benefits uniquely associated with Christian allegiance. Kamwana failed among those fully integrated into Livingstonia, but succeeded among those rejected or neglected by it. Finally, he seems to have offered a baptism that, by confronting witchcraft, could claim superiority to the mission rite. Whether this multifaceted attack was wholly the result of a deliberate strategy is difficult to say. Some missionaries thought so. Equally, it may be that Kamwana did only what came logically in the kind of religious community Livingstonia was—his kind of heresy has ancient predecessors. In any event, it does seem clear that, for large numbers of people, religious innovation was a natural result and expression of religious discontent. But religion stood together with polity. Since ruling was too large a matter for colonial officials alone, some political tasks fell to the church. Livingstonia carried on from day to day in a state of permanent contradiction. On the one hand, it had a civil role thrust upon it; on the other hand, it sought to fulfill its own stringent spiritual ideals. This contradiction provided the fissure which the first wave of Watchtower enthusiasm crashed through.

4

CHARISMATIC FIRE:
THE OUTBREAK IN ZAMBIA, 1917

> If therefore the whole church be come together in
> one place, and all speak with tongues, and there come
> in those that are unlearned, or unbelievers, will they
> not say that ye are mad?
>
> 1 COR. 14:23

THE SECOND MAJOR WATCH-
tower outbreak comes alive
in colonial records as repeated bright flashes of charismatic excitement, which began in late 1917 and reached their climax early in
1919. If the earlier incident centers the mind upon an articulate
man addressing enthusiastic followers, this one centers it upon a
seemingly inarticulate mass: Some eight hundred converts gathered in a "New Jerusalem" on a hill, "shouting" and "talking in the
unknown tongue," defiant of this-worldly authority, transported
into other-worldly rapture, mad. But, if mad, they displayed political method in which prayer and calling upon God became weapons. As the heavenly tongues of fire touched down to ignite suc-
cessive knots of believers, unbelievers witnessed a leaping fire of
civil disobedience. When groups of shouting believers brought the
northern districts of Zambia to a state of insurrection, the unbelievers of the BSAC brought in armed police to dismantle the Jerusalem and scatter its citizens.

Recalling the incident four years later, the administrator of the
colony termed the Watchtower "at present the only *political* movement with any following."[1] He thereby acknowledged the political
capacity of a mass who seemed, even to some who saw the fires
close up, as merely mad—at first. In time, these on-the-spot observers saw that the injunction "Pray to God alone!" might as well
have been "Down with Tyranny!" and how the inarticulate sedition

of tongues and shouting—*chongo* in local parlance—could galvanize militant action as effectively as its articulate counterpart.

THE SOCIAL CONTEXT OF THE REVIVAL

Since not every descent of the Spirit ignites rebellion along with revival, we cannot grasp the revolutionary significance of *chongo* without grasping the peculiar features of political order in Zambia. Anyone who has witnessed ecstasy and talking in tongues in our own society knows that these things are profoundly disconcerting to see, and that they feel like a huge pulsation of collective power. But he also knows that they fit without difficulty into the wider social order. The sense of power belongs to the décor of the prayer meeting; it begins and ends there. Moreover, adepts in our own society typically renounce the world's political struggles as solemnly as they renounce the World. The suggestion that charismatic practice could build effective rebellion here would be laughed at; the Spirit benefits political order by opening a safety valve through which the sign of the oppressed creature wafts impotently toward high heaven. Robert Rotberg's mistaken assessment of the Zambian Watchtowerites' praying in 1918 is probably true of many others': "Happily content in their sublimation, their beliefs offered an escape from the realities of colonial rule."²

During the revival of 1917–1919, however, praying to God alone did not mark a fantastic escape route from the powers of the world but a collision course with them. Like their predecessors in Malawi, the Zambian Watchtower adherents who obeyed God alone ceased to acknowledge the authority of missionaries. And, surpassing the Malawians, they defied customary rulers so successfully that the regime found itself suddenly adrift in a lake of charismatic fire. Watchtower converts' prayerful exertions reveal the particularity of a regime in which *chongo* constituted a political act. Once again, missions stood on the front line of colonial power; they played their role in the regime's intermissions.

Intra-Christian Warfare in the Northern Districts

From the beginning, the northern districts of Zambia lacked the kind of missionary "universal church" that the Free Church became in its share of Malawi. In Tanganyika and Abercorn districts, the western portion of the area, the London Missionary Society (LMS) vied with the White Fathers for the allegiance of the surrounding villagers. In the east, a thinly stretched network of schools defined the area claimed by the Free Church, headquartered at Mwenzo, outpost of Livingstonia's Zambian frontierland. Before 1913, this immense area included Chinsali, in addition to Isoka and Fife districts. The White Fathers operated in the east, too, in areas marked off from those of the Free Church on a map established by the BSAC administration.[3] In Malawi, as we saw, the arrival of small interloping missions tended to disrupt the order of communities dominated by established mission societies. In the northern portion of Zambia, however, almost from the beginning, missions that enjoyed comparable finances and equal status in the eyes of the administration competed. Everyone interloped.

Until the outbreak of World War I (and continuing as soon as possible thereafter), all these missions proselytized strenuously. They directed their efforts as much against Romanism/Protestantism as against their common heathen enemy. This religious Scramble for Africa borrowed language from the secular one. Missionaries spoke of "aggression," "encroachment," and "retaliation." Villages were "effectively occupied," for purposes of evangelization, by the establishment of a school or chapel. Mission "spheres of influence" existed. In the opinion of Livingstonia missionaries, there was need in 1901 to "claim the country for Christ and save it from Heathenism and the Pope."[4] They pleaded for more money and missionaries, "because the Jesuit [sic] White Fathers are coming in great numbers . . . and, if the Church will only enable us, we long to give the people the Gospel of Jesus Christ before it is too late."[5] The effort to head off Catholic influence spurred Livingstonia to rapid expansion and to the wide deployment of African evangelists with orders to "hold" large areas for future work by white missionaries. This they did by running village schools until a missionary could be sent. In 1902, Livingstonia's *Report* warned supporters in Britain that "our schools, as conducted, are the most potent barrier against the inroads of Roman Catholicism and Islamism, both of which are at work at our very doors."[6] A school had strategic importance, not only as a wedge into a heathen community, but also as a barricade against Catholic influence. According to a report of 1909,

> the indigenous people have given their verdict on the work of
> the Livingstonia mission, as compared with the Romanist mis-
> sion there, in that they have requested the government as well
> as Dr. Chisholm to secure for them the schools and other

departments of our work against the encroachment of the Catholics. This shows that if the Protestant Church at home will only adequately support educational-evangelistic work there will be no danger of the spread of Roman Catholicism.[7]

Catholic missionaries kept abreast. Competition with Livingstonia and the LMS led the White Fathers to abandon their original strategy of establishing residential missions, in favor of using African catechists extensively.[8] They also reported on the titanic struggle that opposed ancient rivals, and marked its progress on their maps. Missionaries, who in the early years often resorted to bullying reluctant headmen into accepting mission schools, did not hesitate to bully these men to obtain advantage over other missionaries. This they did both directly and through their African employees. The latter followed through by sowing the relevant hatreds in the groups for which they were responsible and by organizing the faithful accordingly.

A complaint by Father Peuth (WF) to the administration illustrates some of the methods used. According to Peuth, LMS missionaries summoned at least one headman into their Kawimbe station to reproach him for having accepted teachers from Kayambi, a White Fathers station. Peuth claimed that Kawimbe teachers had gone so far as to incite the villagers to violence against their Kayambi competitors. Peuth continued:

> And lastly I hear that they have recently been sending their teachers throughout the Mambwe villages to enroll them, telling the people that Kawimbe teachers would come to instruct them, that those of Kayambi would be driven away. . . . But the Kawimbe missionaries may rest assured that we will not withdraw, and retire before them, if they enter our territory we shall advance into theirs. . . . As to the means they employed to attract the people to their mission, allow me to tell you that they are simply disloyal.[9]

This war between Kawimbe and Kayambi must have been a puzzlement in one neighborhood and a stumbling block in the other.

No one excluded damning rhetoric. Thus the Reverend Mr. Fell of the (Anglican) Universities Mission wrote in the 1920s that the White Fathers were propagating the doctrine that Fell was not only unqualified to give the sacraments but even to receive them. "Imagine the effect on the [mission] station!" Fell exclaimed.[10] Refereeing this hard-fought contest became a task of administration. When, in the 1930s, there was talk of an official policy of tolerating small, heterodox movements, a veteran official argued against further additions to the competitive scene of all against all. "If they [the missionaries] had had their way in the past," he remarked, "they would not have tolerated each other."[11]

It is easy to overlook the fact that Watchtower revivals in Zambia usually occurred on social terrain prepared by such intra-Christian struggles.[12] Sholto Cross writes that an attack by Father E. Peuth on the Watchtower "began a long tradition of hostility between the Roman Catholic missions and this movement in Central Africa, with each side occupying a prominent position in their opposing demonologies."[13] Not quite: Catholic catechists and Protestant evangelists had long since been deployed against "opposing demonologies." The struggles of 1918 simply provided new grist for an old propaganda mill—one centuries old if we count the long tradition that activated missionaries. In 1920, Father Peuth insinuated that Kawimbe could be charged with responsibility for the outbreak, by virtue of its religiously unwholesome teaching.[14] A Jesuit missionary later made this charge explicitly, when he identified the Watchtower as a consequence of "that Satanic revolt of the sixteenth century."[15]

Reserving the sharpest rhetoric for Catholic missionaries and converts, preachers of the African Watchtower simply took their own outlook from the resolutely Protestant outlook of the American movement, which has always regarded the Roman Catholic church with special contempt. *Watchtower Magazine* (from which African adherents fluently borrowed hostile phraseology) never fails to append the adjective "Roman" to "Catholic church." This merely states the other side of "that Satanic revolt of the sixteenth century"—the custom in many Protestant denominations always to add "Roman," to deny the universality of the church headed by the pope. Missionaries planted militant sectarianism long before the Watchtower had been heard from. Watchtower preachers merely reaped—and replanted.

For different reasons, officials as well as missionaries deplored interdenominational strife. A magistrate to whom Peuth wrote one of his many complaints about the LMS feared that conflict between missions might cause serious friction in African communities.[16] (Similar views surfaced in the mid-1930s, when the administration decided to ban the entry of new mission societies into Zambia.[17] By then the number had reached twenty.) At least one missionary drew a lesson about the advance of the Watchtower movement among

African Christians bewildered and fatigued by constant feuding. He wrote:

> When we have different missions scrambling and falling over each other to open schools within sight of each other . . . and have teachers of different churches at war telling the people in one village that the other church is no use and that they have the only Gospel then we are reduced indeed to a sorry spectacle. . . . A Bantu Church with Bantu leaders on their own lines would be more agreeable to the Bantu people than either Congregationalism, Methodism, Anglicanism, or any other ism. The Watchtower movement may point this way.[18]

The "Bantu" Christian leadership to whom the missionary referred was being formed in the competing missions. Whether constructive or aggressive, and whether working against heathen or Christian enemies, these men were on the front lines of the struggle to establish schools and chapels as beachheads of competing Christian confessions. In consequence, African troops called up in the scramble for Africa's souls were fully equipped to turn the training they had acquired against rival missions and conservative villagers against their missionary supervisors. Such men were to make themselves conspicuous in the events of 1918. Meanwhile, their work for the missions gave them training in the mentality as well as in the skills of aggressive religious organizing. The missions delivered into their hands an offensive capability that they could later use as they saw fit.

Like those who administered indirect rule, missionaries tended to regard the Africans on whom they depended as mere extensions of themselves and as activated only by themselves. Chiefs and headmen were "mouthpieces." Similarly, the evangelist Paul Mushindo (later a pastor) was the Reverend Mr. R. D. McMinn's "right hand."[a] According to Monsignor (later Cardinal) Lavigerie, founder of the White Fathers, "By using catechists as intermediaries, the missionaries gain the additional advantage of communicating with the natives in native disguise."[19] But mission evangelists and catechists

---

[a] Mushindo collaborated with McMinn on a Bemba Bible translation that took sixteen years to complete. His statement merits full quotation: "If there were some people he (McMinn) loved, one of them was me. But he did not love me as a friend according to Christian principles, but he loved me as one can love his or her best tool which is useful for his or her work. He said very often 'Mushindo is my right hand' " (J. Van Velsen, ed., "The Life of a Zambian Evangelist: The Reminiscences of the Reverend Paul Bwembya Mushindo," Lusaka, 1973, p. 49).

were more than mere appendages of their missionary employers. We will presently see these men in action; but first, let us examine the consequences of World War I and its aftermath.

Intra-European Warfare in the Northern Districts

World War I transformed missionary work. In September 1914, fighting broke out at Abercorn and Fife, areas bordering Tanzania (then German East Africa), and troops remained quartered in the vicinity throughout the war.[20] In these circumstances, missionary infighting took a back seat to the world conflict. When the mass mobilization took many young men who would otherwise have been its pupils or teachers, the Free Church drew in its carpet of village schools. The Reverend Dr. James Chisholm, the missionary in charge at Mwenzo, urged his flock to join the effort, as did his colleagues in Malawi. After leaving Mwenzo station in October 1915, Chisholm (also an MD) ran a field hospital, while the evangelist Yohane Afwenge Banda (for twenty years Chisholm's right-hand man) tended what remained of Mwenzo's affairs. Even after the early fighting came to an end, the uncertainty continued. Reports of the time refer to sinister "moonlight flittings" in the neighborhood of Mwenzo and to raids back and forth across the border. On more than one occasion, Banda had to vacate Mwenzo with whatever could be carried into the bush.[21] The work of the Catholic mission suffered comparable disarray. White Fathers tried and failed to obtain immunity from war service for those directly employed by their mission. For the most part here, too, evangelization became a spare-time activity. In 1915, four priests joined the army. By 1918, most priests and almost all catechists had been called up.[22] On various occasions, the skeleton staff of Kayambi had to flee into the bush and live in the once-outlawed *mitanda* (garden shelters) of parishioners.[23] Later, the White Fathers stations of Kayambi and Chilubula would be sacked and burned by enemy troops.

The political order also underwent traumatic changes during the war. The regime forcibly removed people living on the border, sometimes by the expedient of burning their homes. In consequence, the Mambwes lost their cattle, for they moved into tsetse-infected areas.[24] There they found themselves not only destitute but also dependent upon the hospitality of the very Bemba chiefs who had raided them in the days before the *pax Britannica*. At the end of the outbreak, when convicts were being flogged, the Citimukulu turned from his spectating to call the revolt the doing of "mannerless slaves."[25] Mambwe, Iwa, and Namwanga inhabitants of the northern districts were prominent among the rebels. Few Bembas joined.

Besides the forced evacuation of border areas and the consequent mixing of populations, the war also demanded various kinds of labor. Supplies for troops operating near the border had to be transported for the most part by thousands of men, each carrying a hundred-pound head load. Other carriers provisioned these workers.[26] Still other laborers built and maintained roads and worked on various public projects. To secure the required manpower, the regime hoisted the African tax from three to five shillings.[27] According to official estimates, every available man in Tanganyika District did an average of five months' work between 1916 and 1917, earning about seven shillings and six pence per month. Of 162,982 men who worked during this period, 138,930 came from the northern districts.[28] As elsewhere in the world during this war, women also streamed into the paid labor force. Thousands worked in casual transport and in grinding grain bought in other areas.[29] The civilian sacrifices occasioned by the war belong to our story because the regime resorted to an unaccustomed degree of internal violence to obtain them. And since familiar sorts of exaction gave way to unfamiliar ones, the quality of internal violence changed as well. Finally, the disruption of peacetime routine eventually exposed the weakness of the men whose business it was to enforce the unfamiliar demands and the familiar ones. Their weakness was to become the Watchtower's strength.

Villagers disliked portering, because the work was extremely hard and sometimes dangerous, and because they were subjected to the violence of white foremen while on the job. In addition, men were reluctant to leave their farms during phases of the agricultural cycle when their labor was required for tree cutting, fencing, breaking new ground, and the like.[30] When increased taxation failed to bring out the required labor, the regime added direct impressment, hostage taking, house burning, and general terror to the incentive of the increased tax.[31] According to one postwar report, villagers not uncommonly bolted at the very sight of a white person.[32] Other reports tell of violence by white labor recruiters and more violence by African *boma* messengers striving to fill their quotas. Hanoc Sindano, a Watchtower preacher, summed up his experience in this way:

> There they are, they who overburden us with loads, and beat us like slaves, but a day will come when they will be the slaves . . . God only is to be respected and obeyed, nobody else on

earth has any right to it; no more the European than the native chiefs. The English have no right whatsoever in the country, they are committing injustice against the natives in pretending to have rights.[33]

The massive redeployment of manpower dislocated village production. As the administration drew away manpower from the villages, an increasing burden fell to women, children, and old or disabled men exempt from war work.[34] Women and juveniles joined the shouters of 1918 in large numbers. Inevitably, since the technology remained unchanged, smaller acreages were cultivated. Average yields declined as existing sites were exhausted and new areas could not be broken. Nevertheless, the administration had to find, on these crippled farms, some of the provisions for the immense corps of porters and soldiers. Food requisitioning began in 1914. The grain sales of 1914 resulted in shortages the following year and some famine. By 1916, villages that had quartered refugees were facing desperate shortages and even starvation.[35] Here again, violence supplemented cash incentives. Thus a district commissioner wrote after the war that there had been "some forced sales," robbery, and assault.[36]

To meet the various wartime contingencies, the administration deliberately increased the legal authority of customary rulers. Prior to the war, chiefs and headmen had been encouraged, by means of bounties, to assist in labor recruitment for white enterprises in the south. For a time, a chief or headman pocketed five shillings annually if he succeeded in recruiting thirty-six men. During the war he performed the same task gratis.[37] To tie the interests of customary rulers securely to those of the administration, a new ordinance empowered officials to hire and fire chiefs and to "call upon [them] to supply men for the defence of the territory and for suppression of disorder and rebellion within its borders." As customary rulers answered the call, their interests diverged from those of their people.[38]

Chiefs and headmen exercised their new formal powers without much supervision or help. Since the wartime duties of European administrators made touring infrequent, district messengers—direct employees of the district *bomas*—supported customary rulers in these new tasks.[39] The messengers often resorted to strong-arm methods to fill their quotas in labor and foodstuffs, usually with the connivance of these local rulers, but sometimes over the latters' impotent objections. Thus one report revealed that a headman had been tied up by a messenger because he had failed to produce carriers. And the DC at Fife saw messengers bring in a hundred men at a time tied together on a rope like captured slaves.[40] Such incidents must not have been uncommon, for the militants of 1918 singled messengers out for special opprobrium. The argot of the faithful insultingly dubbed them *malakoshi*, meaning "drops of rain falling from the trees": When the End came, the messengers would amount to no more.[41] After the war, Justice P. J. Macdonnell condemned the excesses committed under these wartime arrangements for indirect rule:

> Thus the Administration of the division had been left to messengers unaccompanied by an European. But not only delinquencies of the messengers. . . . The delinquencies of the messengers . . . were as nothing to what had been done by Europeans. All through the War this unfortunate division was being traversed by the Nymns and Pistols of the fighting forces beyond, the meanest of mean whites who would now, could they but have their desserts, be serving long terms for assault and robbery and rape.[42]

In the meantime, Mwenzo viewed the wartime labor coercion, from its own special religious viewpoint, not as part of the descent from a civilizing cosmos into a murderous chaos, but as the source of spiritually corrosive prosperity and a declining sense of spiritual need.[43] In the face of the evil that proceeded from this prosperity (based upon carriers' wages, grain sales, soldiers' pay, and the like), there could be no relaxation of the Free Church's rigor. Accordingly, while the tides of war bore away some adherents, the church purged itself of others. In 1915, the Reverend Dr. Chisholm reported that many backsliders had been ejected and that practically no suitable candidates for admission to baptism were among those who had presented themselves. A dramatic increase in the use of beer seems to have been the reason for many suspensions; military porters particularly fell to this offense.[44] (Ironically, though, the same new prosperity supported a 370 percent increase in church contributions over the years of the war.)[45] Thus, by deliberate policy, the mission added new wounds to those inflicted by the war. It increased the tempo of moral purges while refusing to let the congregation grow. Not surprisingly, a number of former teachers and pupils found that their way to rejoining their prewar pursuit was blocked by the mission but not by the Watchtower. As to the frustrated candidates for baptism, the remarks of Visiting Commissioner H. C. Marshall echo those of Alfred Sharpe a decade earlier:

> Missionary bodies generally are slow to grant full membership and insist upon a long probationary period. In my opinion the readiness to immerse "converts" explains to a large extent the success and rapid spread of the Watchtower movement.[46]

Having created a vigorous demand for a religious good, missionary bodies restricted the supply. They laid themselves open to challenge by new suppliers offering a vauntedly superior good at less religious cost.

THE REVIVAL IS LAUNCHED

What most distinguished the Zambian episode from its Malawian predecessor was the impact of World War I. As in many nations at the end of that war, it was impossible in Zambia simply to return to a status quo ante; war had distorted and destroyed the old institutions, while displacing the habits of mind that had made them at least endurable. Zambia's postwar upheaval coincided with others that occurred in the lands of the victorious no less than in those of the vanquished.

Despite the many privations of the war years and the withdrawal one by one of the previously touted benefits of the *pax Britannica*, however, Africans co-operated in the military effort to a remarkable degree. F. H. Melland went out of his way to inform his countrymen about Africans' monumental part in the salvation of the empire.[47] Although the work was compulsory, it was nonetheless "cheerfully done," in his opinion. Cheerfully or not, there was no whisper of rebellion. But the silence was unnatural, and it did not last. Just as the war was ending, a wave of unrest broke over the north of the country. Fueled by inflated prices, food shortages, and a murderous epidemic of influenza (which arrived from the south along the line-of-rail), this unrest led the administration to reinstate wartime measures. In 1918, it revived impressment for public works as a way of curbing the unruliness of demobilized military porters and soldiers, who had begun to return to their villages.[48]

Watchtower ideas appeared in Zambia in late 1917 when, on the warning of an intelligence report, forty-three adherents of the Watchtower were expelled from labor compounds in Zimbabwe.[49] Most of them hailed from Malawi, but seven were Zambians. As "alien natives," the Zambians and Malawians were issued with exit permits rather than passes and deported in October 1917. The Malawians traveled home along the important labor route via Feira and Fort Jameson. The Zambians passed through Livingstone, Mazabuka, Mkushi, and Serenje districts—preaching along the way, we may imagine, as did many a subsequent Watchtower preacher. Hanoc Sindano, Leviticus Kanjele, and Shadrach Sinkala were among this latter group. The others are identified as Pesa, Yaponga, Simuchimba, and Makomba.[50] Sindano emerged as the leader most visible to the administration, while Kanjele became his right-hand man. Sinkala gathered a following of his own in Chinsali District, but he left the area in 1919 and chose not to return.[51] His determined preaching helped spread Watchtower doctrine in the Southern and Eastern provinces of the country. He became the notorious Shadrach.

Like his seven colleagues, Hanoc Sindano had been a pupil at Mwenzo. After hearing of the Watchtower while working in Zimbabwe, he journeyed to Cape Town to learn more.[52] Once at home, he immediately began preaching. According to Father Peuth, Sindano moved to Mengo's village on his return, where he converted and baptized everyone except the headman.[53] Even at this early stage, village headmen stood aloof from the movement because, unlike other Christian enterprise, it lacked the sanction of the *boma*. From Mengo, Sindano moved to Tukamulozya's village on the Saissi River, where again everyone but the headman accepted baptism. He built churches in both villages. From headquarters at Tukamulozya's village, Sindano worked the district in the style of a missionary in charge of a central station. Like them, Sindano dispatched evangelists and appointed a regular teacher to a village whenever the baptized reached a certain number. Many of these teachers were recruited among present and former employees of Mwenzo. Most, an observer said, could read and write, and some could read and write English.[54] They are also described as "young men of the military porter class."[55] The two indications are not, of course, contradictory; many mission workers had become warriors.

At the early stage, villagers heard the usual Watchtower doctrines: the imminence of the End and the urgent need for baptism. Sindano and his colleagues taught that the end of the world would inaugurate an era of peace and plenty. The missions had withheld the true religion from the people, all the while taking the people's money during the long probationary period before baptism. When the End came, those who had been baptized would put on immortality, while those who had not been faced destruction. Europeans would be enslaved or routed from the country.[56] The missions had only supplied part of the truth. In the light of Watchtower prophecy, many preachers and hearers could think about already familiar texts in a new way—Matthew 24:6-8, for example:

> And ye shall hear of wars and rumors of wars: see that ye be not troubled: for all these things must come to pass, but the end is not yet. For nation shall rise against nation, and kingdom against kingdom: and there shall be famines, and pestilences, and earthquakes, in divers places. All these are the beginning of sorrows.

In many respects, Watchtower teaching resembles the missions'. Sindano and his colleagues fulminated against polygamy and beer drinking. When they insulted old men for their continued allegiance to heathen customs, destroyed ancestor shrines, publicly ridiculed the beliefs of village elders, and execrated "beer-bloated" and "lascivious" traditionalists, they fell into missionary commonplaces. Not even their millenarian extravagance was a Watchtower invention. As George Shepperson has pointed out, Livingstonia created a climate of millenarianism from the time of the first loud, enthusiastic outpourings in 1898.[57] It repeated them during the Inwood Revival of 1910. No less sober a personage than Justice Macdonnell noted the similarities. Watchtower preaching was "harmless," he said, until the fall of 1918, and "not different from what they [the villagers] had always heard from the Mwenzo teachers."[58]

However, preaching and the response to it did not draw exclusively on Christian polemical styles. Those who refused baptism and conversion were also said to be bewitched and were called *wasatani*, or devils, against whose malignant influence the faithful made and took protective medicines. The baptized were sometimes said to become invulnerable to bullets, which (as in the Maji Maji revolt) would turn to water provided the convert also abandoned the use of European utensils.[59] These local interpretations joined the ideology of the orthodox Watchtower movement: Those who were baptized, the saved, became the sheep described in Revelation; those who remained unbaptized were goats. The African Watchtower added a third term, *snakes*, for application to Catholics refusing baptism. All but the sheep would be doomed at the End.

The new converts held nightly prayer meetings near their villages, and the noise of *chongo*, hymn singing, and drumming could be heard into the wee hours. Their loud services intruded upon

the peace of nonmembers, while the Watchtower's preaching immediately caused dissension in the villages. Complaints sped to the
local administration. Converts' very meeting in the bush, outside
the ritual circle of the villages, was scandalous—it was the local
rulers' duty to purify village sites from the natural and supernatural
evil rampant in the surrounding wilderness.[60] Beyond this obvious
challenge to the prerogatives of customary authority, Watchtowerites' actions had a disturbing ritual tinge. Persons wishing to be
inhabited by spirits or to perpetuate evil by witchcraft went seeking
in the bush after dark. Watchtower converts made themselves conspicuous to their unbelieving neighbors by daring to travel along
bush paths at night, fearless of harm from bewitching spirits or
wild animals. While some transgressed established norms governing man's relationship to nature, others transgressed those governing human relationships. The rules that prohibited romantic
attachment within certain degrees of classificatory kinship lost their
authority. Children ignored their parents. Ordinary villagers discounted their elders and headmen. Excitement mounted as one
sleepless night of drumming and rapture succeeded another.

An assistant native commissioner reported hearing of village elders' complaints early on; but the administrative demands of the
war effort prevented his or his colleagues' paying much attention
to complaints that reported "vaguely" on the "general, sorry state
of the country" or that charged Watchtower enthusiasts with "spoiling the land." Not having grasped as yet that customary rulers'
notions of propriety and order must be their own, officials let the
complaints about noise and ritual scandal pass as parochial matters
limited to certain villages.[61] Other matters seemed more pressing.

To meet the complaints that reached him, the DC Charles Draper
merely activated legal machinery. He promulgated an order against
"irresponsible preaching." As usual, enforcement fell to chiefs and
headmen. Draper's order gave them legal authority to disrupt
prayer meetings, make arrests, and inflict "light chastisement" upon
the offenders.[62] The order was a mistake. Customary authorities
set to work ordering men formerly associated with the mission, now
with the Watchtower, to cease promulgating the Word of God, thus
creating the appearance that they were now legally empowered to
reassert their heathen conservatism against the type of upstarts
they had battled for years. Chief Kafwimbe went so far as to punish
several Watchtower followers by confiscating their store-bought
clothes, besides flogging them. Draper later acknowledged his mistake. In an area where various species of the Word of God had

long competed, with the *boma* as referee, the order to disperse praying Christians enabled Watchtower followers to raise the cry of religious persecution. This cry they had doubtless learned to use for missionary battles in heathen villages with one faith and one religion.

Since in earlier struggles, mission adherents must have become accustomed to overriding the opinions of customary rulers, Draper's move must have appeared to them as blatant discrimination and sudden aggrandizement of chiefly authority—in short, as a new escalation of local oppression. Draper's application of indirect rule made it seem that rulers had been given the legal right not only to dictate against Christian teaching but also to do what they chose to the persons and property of the faithful. Worst of all, to give customary rulers legal "power" to stop "irresponsible preaching" was not to give them the real power to do so. Draper's chiefs and headmen failed to enforce the order and, while failing, created much ill will. Their powerlessness stood exposed to all, whether Watchtower adherents or not. Thereafter trouble spurted from other quarters. Parents of juvenile Watchtower converts blamed Chief Terefya for their children's disobedience: "You have made our children mad, better that you should look after them."[63] In short, Draper's order made this lever of the regime's political machinery ineffective. When he tried to use it, the mystique of these men crumpled. From that other ill effects followed.

Draper sent out *boma* messengers next, both to reinforce the chiefs and to correct the impression that the chiefs had acted on their own initiative and in pursuit of their own selfish interests. The messengers' implementation of Draper's order produced "startling reading," as Justice Macdonnell commented when he reviewed their reports. "Accused called them to come and pray and hear the Word of God," one testified. "I arrested him and told him that it was forbidden to preach lies to the people." In another case, the accused man beat a drum. "He sang by himself and then all the others joined in. He is the leader. We arrested him. Gathering the people like that was defiance."[64] Unfortunately for the regime, the *boma* messengers—the *malakoshi*—fared no better than those born to rule. When this second lever failed to work, the stage was set for one of the BSAC's "petty kings" to wield power directly, along with his handful of white colleagues. The time was approaching when a rebellion that had at first proceeded in remote shadows, with black struggling against black, would burst into prominence as a rebellion pitting black against white.

But the regime did not reach this pass until late 1918, many months after the seven deportees from Zimbabwe had begun their work. When it did, the logic of indirect rule offered two complementary strategies—the resuscitation of customary authority and visitation by the DC. Draper did both. He attempted to arrest Watchtower converts for desecrating a village headman's ancestor shrine, a fateful attempt that eventuated in the "hut of defiance" episode. And he summoned a large meeting for the purpose of clarifying to villagers the danger of "irresponsible preaching." This meeting, or *ndaba*, at Chunga Village led him to witness *chongo* firsthand. By this time, the last quarter of 1918, Watchtower adherents had been active in the villages for nearly a year. They had had the time to go very far before white functionaries of the colonial state gave the revival their undivided attention.[65]

THE COLLAPSE OF INDIRECT RULE

Praying, preaching, and assembling the people unlawfully were only part of the problem. Sindano and Kanjele were arrested in July 1918 for refusing to work as porters and again in September for illegal preaching.[66] They continued urging people to ignore the demands of the administration for porters and grain and to drop the conventional show of respect and cheerful greeting when Europeans arrived in the villages. White Fathers found Dominico Pitala, a dismissed Catholic catechist and close friend of Sindano's, inciting villagers around Kayambi to stop fetching wood and water for the mission and to stop sending their children to Kayambi's school. Father Tanguy said he heard an unnamed preacher exciting villagers with the slogan, Africa for the Africans, which Marcus Garvey made famous. "Tous les hommes sont égaux," wrote the shocked Belgian. "Le noir est égal au blanc. Soyons nos propres maîtres: l'Europe à l'Européen, l'Afrique à l'Africain." Wherever people listened sympathetically, the atmosphere in formerly cordial villages froze into a cheerless quiet upon the approach of a missionary. Showing the collective face of growing passive resistance, their very quiet trumpeted rebellion. Since rebellion might claim White Fathers as its first victims, these men sounded the alarm. When, in November 1918, Tanguy found a man crying in the wilderness, "Take care, God is great, pray to God alone,"[67] he swung into action, trying first to hand the man over to justice, then flogging him. By that time, the revival was nearing its climax and Tanguy, together with his brethren, must have long since placed himself on permanent alert. Violence was indeed on the way—but from a white enemy.

Imperial Pride Purged

In September 1918, a guerrilla column led by General Paul von Lettow-Worbeck suddenly turned south. They burned the *boma* at Fife, sacked the Kayambi and Chilubula mission stations, raided widely for supplies among the villages and finally, to the great humiliation of the regime in Zambia, they burned the Kasama District *boma*, whose garrison had been removed to more strategic duty elsewhere.[68] The pace of Watchtower baptizing quickened dramatically, impelled by this evidence that prophecy was being fulfilled. After the sack of Kayambi, those about to inherit a Kingdom of plenty began to uproot their crops—they were no longer needed. Chiefs, missionaries, and officials became nonentities. Throngs of villagers hurried to put their trust in God alone.

Draper's colleague Dewhurst struggled to convey the seriousness of the situation after Lettow-Worbeck's incursion. His report slid from a claim that the "preaching coming at a time when Germans were marching through the country destroying Bomas, etc. was in my opinion seditious, if not treasonable," to the idea that the Germans were actually behind it: "In my opinion the date of the end of the world coinciding with the German invasion cannot be dismissed as a matter of mere chance."[69] He urged that the Central Investigation Department in Salisbury be contacted for more details about the "exact circumstances" in which the original group had been deported. There is no reason to assume, however, that Watchtower prophecy needed the help of German intelligence to enhance its prestige.

If, in 1908, the Watchtower's ideas of Armageddon had been free-floating prophecy about the course of history up to 1914, in 1918 they settled upon an ugly reality. People had witnessed the killing of blacks and whites, the devastation of their crops and homes, a raging epidemic of Spanish influenza, the dissolution of normal productive activity, and the discrediting of rational planning for individual and collective survival. Now they witnessed the actual breakdown of civil order. As Justice Macdonnell later put it, they "[saw] the King's Writ disappear overnight."[70] Anyone awaiting demonstration of Watchtower claims could have it both subjectively, in the descent of the Spirit, and objectively, in the evident fulfillment of prophecy. Fear became the midwife of faith. By the end of 1918, the chief tenets of the movement were, first, that there would presently be a new chieftainship under God; and, second, that converts must maintain an attitude of passive resistance to all orders of chiefs or Europeans—it was not possible to obey two masters at once. According to Dewhurst's later report, these teachings had a "devastating effect":

> The power of the chiefs was at an end and the authority of the Boma was seriously threatened. . . . The preaching of these two tenets combined had resulted in administrative, tribal, and domestic chaos. In fact, the natives were out of hand, and the situation was getting worse every day.[71]

The "devastating effect" Dewhurst referred to followed not from fantastic belief but from the strategic action of converts. If the End was imminent, then it was urgent to be baptized. Dewhurst said there "was evidence to show that the end of the world was foretold at an early date."[b] The whole movement to the end of December 1918 was an imitation of John the Baptist. A time arrived when "every river became Jordan," and there was a "massive rush" to be baptized. Gone was the missionaries' long (and quite unscriptural) waiting period of study and moral perfection; Watchtower preachers conducted their rite as simply as John the Baptist had. A villager would be immersed in a "Jordan, instructed in a few things which a baptized person should not do and would then return the same day to his own village."[72] One thing he should do, however, was to obey God alone, for the world's satanic rulers could no longer claim his loyalty. The devastating practice of *chongo* may have been derived from the same Gospel. Matthew (3:3) speaks of "a voice crying in the wilderness saying, Prepare ye the way of the Lord." Converts took to leaving their houses, and even their villages, so as to pray and shout unceasingly. By the very act, they left behind the physical and ritual authority of headmen and elders. Once people found themselves outside the jurisdiction of their former rulers, it was obviously not these who were to be obeyed. Since, in the short run, obeying God meant obeying God's representatives on earth, authority passed to inspired Watchtower prophets and their deputies. Not surprisingly, therefore, Hanoc Sindano and Shadrach Sinkala eventually came to be treated like chiefs.[73]

---

[b] The year 1914 became the target year of a millenarian "count down" in 1876, when Charles Taze Russell published the results of prophetic calculations based upon his study of the Bible.

If, by discrediting the fear of earthly punishment, belief in the imminence of the End was an incentive to civil disobedience, it was also a disincentive to work: The End heralded a new era of plenty. Dewhurst declared that the faster conversion advanced, the more starkly famine threatened, for large numbers of the baptized followed the logic of their new belief. So doing, they in effect went out on a general strike. Like all general strikes, this one had more than economic ramifications. Work as usual and fear of famine presupposed an untransformed future, in which only unbelievers still believed. In the transformed present, the cessation of work further unraveled the authority of all those responsible for supervision. Headmen seeking to organize cultivation, foremen seeking to direct wage workers—the rulers of worldly work had come to naught.

One baptized woman sued to divorce her unbaptized husband. If she continued to live with a *satani*, she feared that she would be barred from collecting her share of clothing in the New Era. Women converts such as this one exerted powerful leverage on their employed husbands and, through them, upon the powers of the world, including the army. In early 1919, two privates, Sefu and Malipenga, deserted their unit and then refused to be arrested. They ignored a summons to return to camp. Instead of the usual procedure, whereby the arrested person responded voluntarily to the summons delivered by an unarmed constable, a patrol had to be sent for the two. They and other soldiers explained that their wives had been baptized and had refused to sleep with them unless they, too, underwent the rite. As baptized Watchtower Christians, they said, and therefore pacifists, they could no longer be soldiers; nor were they subject any longer to military orders. Sergeant Sibold, who reported the incident, foresaw "enormous difficulty" for the army if the movement was not quashed immediately.[74] Since nearly all the villagers near the camp had been baptized, the stage was set for trouble between the people and the army. The unbaptized soldiers, now also *wasatani*, were ritually separated from the neighboring villagers, including their own families, to whom furthermore they were now ritually dangerous: thence Dewhurst's "domestic chaos." If, on the other hand, the family prayed together and therefore stayed together, the domestic gain was the army's loss— and the state's. If all arrested persons ceased to arrest themselves by answering a summons voluntarily, the regime would have to do so directly—or else leave the lawbreakers in peace.

Observing such developments, Dewhurst became convinced that Watchtower baptism was "not really religious at all."

> The baptism . . . can almost be considered as a sign that the subject was a member of a community which was to receive a novel form of government; rather than of a purely and simply religious sect. After baptism the converts returned to their villages and slept outside altogether in order to avoid being taken unawares by the end of the world.[75]

We need not concur in Dewhurst's denial that Watchtower baptism was "really religious." Baptism always signifies entrance into a new community—and into a new Kingdom—eventually. In the present case, by the very act of being baptized and joining a new community of the faithful, adherents immediately received "a novel form of government." For them, as for the Anabaptists, who accepted the notorious second baptism, membership in a new community of the faithful automatically canceled the old allegiance. Thus, the immediate reality of a new dispensation arrayed heathen rulers, missionaries, administrators, and the military against the rite: Baptism in imitation of John the Baptist was anathema to them all.

Dewhurst also suggested that the faithful gave a political interpretation to the story of John the Baptist.

> The passive resistance displayed by the cry which went through the country that it was necessary to hear the word of God and not to worry about the chiefs and headmen, may be due to the account of John the Baptist's dealings with the Pharisees and the Sadducees who, together with other non-converts, were in for a hot time at the end of the world.[76]

Considering the chiefs' dealing with the regime, the parallel was not inaptly chosen. The chiefs were Pharisees and Sadducees; and a Watchtower hymn of the time dubbed the administration *Aloma* or "Romans."[77] Customary rulers had allied themselves with imperial aliens, as they had in Biblical times. Now, at a critical moment in history, they not only refused conversion but also colluded with the aliens in persecuting the faithful. It must have dismayed the missionaries to hear this logical interpretation of a well-loved Gospel.

Official accounts repeatedly state that the movement remained "harmless" until the fall of 1918. In fact, however, the movement had already done great harm to authority in the villages. After having toppled the "Pharisees and Sadducees," the people of the

Watchtower found themselves face to face with the Aloma. But all the local Aloma could report to their superiors elsewhere was "dangerous" preaching that sounded harmlessly scriptural from a distance. Ironically, just as the chiefs and headmen failed at first to make district administrators really "hear" the noise that undermined their authority, so eventually did the administrators fail with their superiors. Distance from the actual scenes transformed the harm into harmlessness. Only hearing was believing.

Sitting safe at the High Court, Justice Macdonnell later reprimanded the men on the spot by quashing some of the original sentences when these came up for review. In his long opinion, the judge added insult to injury by calling the blanket orders against "irresponsible preaching" both legally questionable and politically inept. But the judge was no expert on the local political reality. He had neither heard nor seen. Dewhurst responded with his firsthand knowledge.[78] Against "his Lordship," who permitted himself to chuckle at the messengers' testimony as "startling reading," Dewhurst maintained that the preachers gave nonconverts as well as converts graphic proof that the power of worldly rulers was at an end: "The messengers sent out . . . were defied directly they gave out the order [to stop preaching]. . . . A native would show his defiance by beating a drum to collect the people to do exactly what the messengers had been sent out to prohibit." It was well and good for Macdonnell to insist upon arrests for "specific offenses," rather than for violation of a general order. But who would or could bring complaint? Even the charge of unlawful assembly was impractical, Dewhurst continued. The very idea of "assembly" implied a non-participant group, but "the individual was not committing a grave crime as an individual." The whole population was offending in some way. Besides, "the non-converts were so outnumbered that opposition was out of the question. There was no chief concerned who was in a position to put up a shew of authority." Macdonnell simply could not imagine the happenings he had not seen and heard.

During the heat of the revival, neither could those in a position to send reinforcements to their beleaguered line officers. Early requests for help were blandly denied. Wrote the DC at Kasama, "Such measures [of supplying reinforcements] I cannot advise and I feel sure will not be approved unless there is very much more definite evidence that the movement is actively seditious and openly hostile to government."[79] It appears, however, that the Watchtower strategists had been astute enough to keep the followers out of direct confrontation with the administration as long as possible.[80] To make do, Draper had recourse to the Lugardian strategies of touring and buttressing customary authority. Trying the first, he summoned a *ndaba*. Also, by targeted questioning, he probably hoped to get the "definite evidence" his superior required. Such evidence was not easily obtained, even at the *ndaba*. When converts spoke of the "government," meaning the *boma*, their tone was careful; but, when speaking of the chiefs, their contempt knew no limit. Since Draper did not yet see clearly that the government did not only mean the *boma*, the Watchtowerites at the meeting told the truth of their sedition openly, but with impunity.

The Ndaba at Chunga Village

Draper's description of the meeting shows his struggle to make remote superiors see what he did. However harmless the teachings might appear in writing, he insisted, it was not so much the content of the message but the Watchtower manner, which was literal and loud. "The danger of the teaching is the absolute literal interpretation of a text, e.g., 'the last shall be first and the first last' was taught to the detriment of the European." Conventional-sounding doctrines that were "harmless in themselves when properly and quietly taught" were transformed in enthusiastic Watchtower gatherings, awesome affairs. Draper's description of one reads much like that of the Reverend Mr. Fraser a decade before:

> A youth got up and commenced to preach in an excited manner, which became more pronounced as he proceeded. One of his companions would read out a Bible text, and he would dilate upon it. The congregation consisted mostly of young women and children—most of the village being stricken with Spanish influenza. From what I could gather there was no harm in the actual words used, but the preacher became more and more excited, appeared to work on his audience, and soon three youngsters started shivering and groaning. . . . When this stage was reached, the preacher made repeated calls on Leza (God), but much of what he said was then incoherent.[81]

When Draper stopped this preacher by grabbing him, another took his place. Fraser had spoken of "passing through a powder magazine, and some were trying to light matches." Draper felt that "it would have been necessary only for a prophet to arise and say that the end of the world had now arrived, and that it was only necessary for the adherents to seize their promised inheritance."

In his conversations with those present, Draper noted that there were many dissatisfactions—about the high price of goods in the wake of the war, the prevalence of disease, and the hunger in some areas. When nonconverts expressed themselves against the Watchtower, Draper observed firsthand the dissension that had engulfed many villages. Watchtowerites began to sing then and there. When ordered not to interrupt, there was a "display of rolling eyes on the spot by individuals defiantly stepping forward."[82] The attempt to remove these hecklers created an uproar, and fighting was narrowly averted. As Draper continued his warnings to the people, Laban, formerly a teacher at Mwenzo mission, stepped forward. A passionate exchange ensued:

> LABAN: We learnt at the mission schools [which] were brought by the white men [where] we were taught—stop fighting, committing adultery, and drinking beer and thought such teachings good. We were taught to read the Bible and buy books and teachers beat us to make us attend school. We submitted—we learnt to teach others. Dr. Chisholm told us we did good work, we taught the children and beat them to make them learn. Now Watchtower teaching tells us war is bad, adultery is bad, beating children is bad. Then the chiefs turned against us and we wish to build separate villages.

When Draper asked whether the Watchtower revival was hostile to "the government," Laban distinguished carefully between the government of the chiefs and that of the *boma*:

> DC: Have you any grievance against the government?
> LABAN: No. But the chiefs beat us for our teaching.

When Draper pressed his question, however, some members of the crowd frankly stated their grievances against the government:

> DC: Have you any real grievance?
> A VOICE: Yes, there has been the war, and some of us have died.
> ANOTHER VOICE: Yes, but the bwanas have also died. . . .
> THIRD VOICE: Yes, but the white men deserved to die for it was the white men who started the war.

Laban went on to insist that the chiefs had trumped up the charges against Watchtower adherents. "These chiefs then lied to you and told you we cursed the white men and the chiefs, and demanded that we be sent away or killed."

In this, Chief Kafwimbe seems to have been an outstanding of-fender, perhaps because he still had a sizable following loyal to him. Laban and his colleagues, it appears, received a summons from Fife Boma (Draper's headquarters) via district messenger. Like Sefu and Malipenga, they did not voluntarily answer it, as they might have in ordinary times. But when they heard that Draper was going to Chunga Village, they decided to meet him there. (When questioned at the meeting about their apparent con-tempt for a summons, they declared that urgent business had de-layed their leaving for the *boma*.) On the way through Kafwimbe's area, they continued to preach. Kafwimbe caught some of them, beat them, and confiscated their clothes. People present displayed the marks of those beatings. Draper then asked if it was true that the Watchtower was defying chiefs, and if it was responsible for a slanderous rumor that Chief Kafwimbe was really a woman, and pregnant with Satan. Laban denied this insult to the chief and said, "Let any chief stand up and accuse us. Chiefs are only against us because of our religion. We are peaceable and annoy no one. But we do preach at night and shout outside our village." Laban shrewdly transposed all the stated grievances into a question of religious liberty.

Draper then asked if the Watchtower would stop "irresponsible preaching." Loud negatives and a stir followed. The reply turned about the mutual hostility between chiefs and Watchtower follow-ers. Jacob said, "We do not want to stop. We will stop if the Bwana kills us. Headmen and chiefs say we have caused lack of rain and brought the disease (influenza)." Jacob was responding to what amounted to a grave political insult. In earlier times, such an ac-cusation might have led to a trial for witchcraft and possible exe-cution, if the followers of the chief were strong enough. Otherwise, if the forces on both sides were equally matched, prolonged fac-tional fighting might have led to the breakup of the village, a very serious blow to a chief. When Draper pressed his initial question, someone else shouted out, "We have chiefs and headmen with whom we shall fight. We shall kill each other." Still the DC insisted, and Laban answered, "We do not want to hide it from the Bwana. We are going to shout and sing at our camp [located outside of a legally established village],"—to which Solomon of Chiwale village added, "Is not the Boma under God?" As the crowd dispersed, there was a scuffle, which might easily have turned into a riot,

Draper felt, if the two white officials present had not succeeded in preventing some of Kafwimbe's followers from seizing a drum that belonged to a Watchtower adherent.

Thus a battle between chiefs and Watchtower adherents had been engaged that had far more serious implications than the "ruinous tendency" reported by Malawian chiefs ten years earlier. The reason is not far to seek. During the war, the chiefs and headmen had emerged as the regime's agents among the people, rather than as customary rulers to whom customary respect was due. A widening gulf separated their interests from those of their people, a gulf that their unbaptized state made uncrossable. Now their attempts to put down the Watchtower revival were leading to violent factional divisions within villages. Mission networks were unavailable in this second episode, as they had been in the first, to moderate these antagonisms, since their influence had been greatly attenuated during the war. In fact, the manpower that might have made their influence effective had left the missionary side. Dewhurst summed up his analysis by noting the preponderance of former mission teachers among the Watchtower leadership. He emphasized the dynamism that pushed them forward to more and more forceful action.

> In normal times these men were of no importance. During the Watchtower movement they became possessed of real power, having usurped the authority of chiefs and headmen. I argued that this would be an incitement to their ambition. *Having defied the chiefs and headmen with ease and success, it was only a matter of time before they would realize their strength and defy the authority of the Boma also.*[83]

A group led by Shadrach Sinkala defied the authority of the *boma*. The court proceedings refer to the event as the "hut of defiance" episode.

The Hut of Defiance

In December 1918, Shadrach Sinkala's wing of the church militant descended upon the village of Musamansi.[84] There, pronouncing anathemas against idolatry and against Musamansi himself, they razed the headman's ancestor shrine to the ground. Someone went for help, and Shadrach was arrested. Someone else went for help, and Shadrach was rescued by a squad of sympathizers, who took him to a friendly village nearby. Draper stood in the midst of this

African melee, a handful of *boma* messengers on one side, on the other a crowd of Watchtower militants that blurred into a crowd of bystanding villagers. When he reached out to grab one of the rescuers, a hand reached out from the blur and struck him.

The act must have electrified the crowd, for the next day some put it out that he had been struck dead. Draper presided over a political order in which whites struck blacks but not vice versa. Blacks, not whites, could be sentenced to corporal punishment; whites routinely escaped punishment for assaulting blacks; white employers even claimed the right to "thrash their boys."[85] But these days in December were the Last Days, when, as prophesied, God would "overturn, overturn, overturn." The hand from the crowd did to the mystique of the man what Sinkala had done to the mystique of the shrine. One part of colonial law and order stood in seeming majesty only so long as it stood untouched and untested. It stood because the would-be rebel hesitated. When actual rebels reached out, that part toppled over. The next day, Draper tried again to make arrests—and again failed. "You will not take this man [Jacob Kasuya] today," said a voice from the crowd. "If you take one you must take all." Recognizing Draper's helplessness at that moment, people went on, "Also when you go you must send us bicycles and motor cars. We will never be taken to another country [that is, Kasama], we will be killed in our own country. If you come back bring a maxim gun. Talk will not move us."

As the news spread, new squads of sympathizers joined Shadrach in his sanctuary. Meanwhile a squad of African *boma* mesengers arrested Shadrach and his rescuers and started to escort them to the provincial headquarters at Kasama, for trial and punishment. But the messengers worked, as usual, unarmed. Kasama was distant. And the group traveled on foot. The accused broke away from their escort. Dewhurst managed to rearrest them, and then shut them up in a hut covered with a hunting net, but the ten people in the hut "went absolutely mad inside":

> Messengers! Come into the hut and we will beat you! Whiteman! Come into the hut and we will beat you! Mr. Draper was beaten at Mwika Village, he is now dead at Mwenzo. The white man persecutes us, we are slaves, therefore we want the askari [soldiers] to be called up to kill us. We want to die. The recognised missions of the country deceived us by withholding part of the truth. Now we know the truth. We want to die, we want you to kill us.[86]

While some defended the narrow entrance to the hut, others broke the walls. Then with the help of sympathetic villagers, who lifted the nets, all ten escaped in a body. Five got clear; Dewhurst managed to arrest eleven people. Dewhurst wrote ominously to his superior: "I must now state that if the natives continue to see that nothing effective is done to restore the prestige of the Administration in the Fife district, I can not hold myself responsible for future happenings."[87] Father Peuth wrote no less ominously: "This movement, although presumed to be entirely of religious significance—but this is yet to be proved—is fraught with many and perhaps unforeseen dangers, and may lead to the lapse into disaffection of a large number of natives, at present waiting to see, what measures the government may adopt."[88]

Armed police finally removed some 800 of Hanoc Sindano's followers from a camp on top of Kapililonga Hill and made possible the arrests of 119 people. While it is true that they thus restored order, the very necessity of dispatching police marked the former regime's collapse. Requiring force to disperse a "Jerusalem" on a hill was a thing to be avoided. In repeatedly throwing line officers Draper and Dewhurst back upon their own resources, the BSAC's general staff must already have recognized what Lugard would later make very clear: Recourse to the kind of political power that grew out of the barrel of a gun would destroy the empire rather than save it. In sending reinforcements, BSAC administrators confronted events that were without precedent in Zambia. For the first time in thirty years, Africans had openly contested the power of the regime; and, by using their superior numbers to advantage, they had touched the political nerve of colonial rule.

With this dramatic confrontation of white and black, the end of the rebellion of 1917–1919 was unlike the beginning. At the beginning, Africans battled Africans, while the administration neither saw the conflict nor heard its noise. Indeed, the conflict did not directly concern whites at all. Even when it had reached midcourse, clear cases of antiwhite propaganda were hard to find. White men became targets of hostile action only when they stepped in to protect customary rulers from insult and outrage. At the end, armed force guaranteed effective repression. At the beginning, talk rather than force made the rebellion effective. Throughout, the rebellion was built upon religious theory and practice, upon prophecy, baptizing, and above all, upon *chongo*. Having seen that *chongo* helped to dismantle the regime's unarmed political power, we cannot leave this discussion of the episode without considering why *chongo* worked.

The Natural in the Supernatural

External and internal features of *chongo* account for its effectiveness as political method. The most striking external feature of *chongo* was its noise. In scene after scene, a crowd of Watchtower converts ascended into a Babel of inspired utterance. Lost to ordinary fear thereafter, they felt empowered to defy nonconverts. Fully grasping only what was visible to the naked eye, Draper attributed the progression behavioristically to the noise of *chongo*. The noise led to madness. The noise transformed familiar scriptures into rebels' slogans:

> All teaching seems to be drawn from the Bible, some of it probably quite harmless, if properly and quietly taught, but I am certain many texts are entirely misinterpreted, and the frantic and constant preachings, prayings, and yellings at night . . . is having a bad effect. It is creating a spirit of open defiance such as one has never dreamt of in this part of the world. It is easy to *see* [Draper's emphasis] that these people take no notice of headmen or elders, and this same spirit of disobedience and defiance of authority is spreading.[89]

Justice Macdonnell picked up the point about noise in his long second-guessing of the men in the field. For him the noise of *chongo* was merely noise. Draper would have been on better ground, Macdonnell thought, if he had had the legal imagination to see that the adepts of *chongo* were committing the common-law misdemeanor of disturbing the peace. Since every legal system recognized some version of this offense, Draper could thus have avoided the charge of religious persecution that attended his abortive proclamation against "irresponsible preaching." That way he could have avoided handing Watchtowerites the moral advantage. But was the noise of *chongo* just noise? Some of Draper's own remarks about the "madness" connected with the noise suggest the internal dimensions of *chongo*.

The Order in the Disorder

Draper pronounced the rank-and-file shouters mad but guessed that the leaders sometimes counterfeited madness to suit their own purpose, to usurp power and authority.

> Personally, I think a lot of the frenzy, particularly amongst adults, is assumed. . . . It is apparently believed that one who

gets one of these mad, gibbering, shivering, and generally mad
fits, has seen a vision, and is at once termed a prophet.[90]

This new "prophet" could then impose his inspired leadership upon
his fellow villagers. When he became God's representative on earth,
receiving instructions directly from on high, God's followers owed
him obedience; he could claim that his ascendency was right and
merited. If Draper was right, Watchtower leaders drew upon Old
and New Testament models of authority dependent upon God
alone. They fit Max Weber's model, in which an individual's extraordinary power, or charisma, justifies a claim to speak independent of tradition and office. Such power, Weber says, may be
"actual, alleged, or presumed."[91] Insofar as the men who emerged
as leaders had formerly been subordinates of the missions, Weber's
pattern was reproduced almost term for term. Those men had been
previously "of no importance"; the "office" of evangelist was unex-
alted. But now, under the influence of the Spirit, they acquired
power in their own right. Although Christian establishments have
an inherent tendency to divest themselves of the Spirit's power, its
possibility is part of their raison d'être, and they preach it quietly,
but they are obliged to preach it nonetheless. One internal dimen-
sion of *chongo*, therefore, was that the missions had long since
created the conditions in which it could flourish as the basis of
using power legitimately. They had introduced into the milieus
they influenced the new currency of communion with the Holy
Spirit. Even if some individuals always, or all individuals sometimes,
merely feigned their transports into "mad, gibbering, shivering,
and generally mad fits," that very semblance tells us as much about
the missionary religious environment as it does about the ulterior
purposes of would-be prophets. No one counterfeits bills that do
not exist.

The semblance also tells us something about the traditional religious environment that the missionaries struggled to change. The
idea that people could become closed to mere mundane communication and have their bodies ravaged by unseen power was not
without precedent in indigenous African conceptions. Traditional
Africa had theories of possession and mediumship, along with established procedures for authenticating these.[92] And ecstasy existed
as a desirable form of religious practice. In fact, missionaries early
noted (and deplored the fact) that their African converts so readily
translated new Christian belief into the cultivation of visionary experience. The fact that they seemed to transfer what they knew

about possession into a novel context raised a natural concern about keeping the new faith purged of old influences.

But the same indigenous conceptions left an opening into which missionaries could place their supramundane God, his Son, and the Holy Spirit. Evangelization in Africa did not require argument as to whether extraordinary Power existed, as it must have in much of contemporary Britain. Less for African hearers than for their mission mentors did the point need emphasizing that supernatural forces could transform one's life for good or ill. Missionaries, after all, were products of what Weber called a "disenchanted" world. I imagine that it was with a certain double-mindedness that they taught as the real truth Paul's proclamation about transcending the world: "Behold I shew you a mystery. We shall not all sleep, but we shall all be changed" (1 Cor. 15:51). As representatives of a scientific-industrial world that had transcended mystery, they had to teach the New Testament as really true but not literally true. In a sense, Africans were in a better position to receive an ancient, non-European religion than their European mentors were to give it.

If Africans were amenable to new ideas about a transforming Power, it was because they were already subject to extraordinary powers in everyday life. Spirits assured the invisible work of witches and witch doctors. Spirits communicated through human mediums and determined the outcome of divination; they also administered rewards and punishments directly. A chief's ancestral spirits had especial power. So did those of a village headman or elder, although they were of lesser importance. And, in general, as every ethnographic text tells us, authority in traditional Africa was buttressed by supernatural sanctions. These intertwined with "natural" sanctions and so with the order of the ordinary. Thus, the Watchtower adepts of *chongo* attacked customary authority by putting its supernatural currency to new uses. The seeming disorder of *chongo* concealed another order. Far from constituting madness, the inarticulate sedition of *chongo* communicated meaning in a conventional political language.

We heard this language during the remarkable *ndaba* at Chunga village. Laban spoke of the chief's desire to "have us killed." To do so, the chief had mystical as well as physical means. Those of traditional high status had the right to curse a troublemaker before the ancestral shrines they controlled, with evil consequences for the person so cursed.[93] But tradition also provided a mode of response: The widespread making and taking of medicines against the power of the *wasatani*, which Draper reported, probably aimed at meeting this and similar threats. Chiefs could also seek to discredit dissidents by attributing hostile ritual power to them. Thus Jacob reported an accusation that the Watchtower adherents had caused lack of rain and widespread sickness. The Watchtower adherents countered by insisting that they "harmed no one" but would not stop praying to the Christian God and shouting in their New Jerusalem.

Shadrach Sinkala carried the fight into the enemy's camp. By destroying Musamansi's ancestor shrine, he killed two birds with one stone. The faithful need no longer fear Musamansi's supernatural power, since the shrine was no longer sacrosanct, and everyone saw the perpetrators walk away whole. The faithful need not fear Musamansi's natural power, either, since everyone saw the headman and his loyalists fail to prevent or punish the outrage. And, if any lingering doubt troubled Shadrach and his colleagues, the deed must have given them a powerful injection of certainty. Disastrously for Musamansi's mystique, only the intervention of a white man troubled the iconoclasts, and not at first impressively, at that. As the political argument shot back and forth across ritual terrain, notions about deliverance from evil mingled the natural and supernatural. Rumors circulated that the baptized put on not only a general immortality but also a specific immunity to bullets. With such an idea, Maji Maji rebels had held out against fear and bullets for two years at the turn of the century.[94] At various levels, then, the thrust and parry of the fight engaged a known ritual discourse about authority and power.

The Disorder in the Order

Anthropologists have usually emphasized the conservative features of ritual within the customary order. In his book *Ecstatic Religion*, Ioan Lewis argues that spirit possession offers subordinates a method to extract concessions or other benefits from their social betters. This method, which Lewis calls "indirect attack," is used where direct means against superiors, such as physical coercion, ceremonial recourse to ancestral spirits, the practice of witchcraft, and the like, are barred to the lowly.[95] Possession—seeming madness—thus gives a safe and well-understood front to the commoner who insults his chief, the child who insults his parent, and so on. It permits the expression and sometimes the redress of grievances.

Max Gluckman's classic "Rituals of Rebellion in Southeast Africa"

makes a similar but more general case about public ritual.[96] He
claims that traditional polities contain real conflicts by providing
their expression in public ritual. By being stated or acted out in
public, conflicts are resolved symbolically and are thus prevented
from ripping apart the body politic. Although Gluckman highlights
the symbolic resolution of conflicts, the conflicts themselves are real.
Thus the chief who is symbolically strangled at his investiture for
oppressing his people has the real possibility of suffering this fate
once he holds the reigns of power. For the present purpose, Gluckman's argument can be carried a step further.

We would expect any form of ritualized rebellion to perform
conservative functions only when carried out under conservative
auspices—that is, under the auspices of constituted traditional authority maintained within a preexisting consensus. If rituals of rebellion are indeed genuine public political processes, not gratuitous
artifacts, then the inverse must also be true. When the basis for
widespread agreement is lacking and when constituted authority
does not control the proceedings, rituals of rebellion are free to
become blueprints of rebellion. They would automatically chart the
course of dissolution. Although rooted in otherwise acceptable ritual practices, these would cease to be mere rituals, which have a
predetermined beginning, middle, and end. For if ritual processes
solve actual political problems, then they are to be compared with
other forms of rational enterprise—and not, let us say, with the
ritual processes of bees. The rituals of bees are automatically and
inevitably conservative. Human rituals need not be. The king may
be strangled in fact.

It seems clear from the record of our case that Watchtower adherents opposed and then overthrew the power of customary rulers
by using the ritual idiom that pervaded everyday political discourse.
In this they resemble the Puritans in the English civil war, who
combined ritual with physical attacks upon church and state. English men and women of the seventeenth century did not yet inhabit
a "disenchanted" world. They could still witness the supernatural
in the natural: Cromwell instructed his followers to "pray to God
and keep your powder dry." And, as Christopher Hill has shown,
the radical sectarians pursued their egalitarian ideals in a hierar-
chical society to the accompaniment of prophecy, quaking, and
talking in tongues.[97] For them, as for the charismatics of the Watchtower, the extraordinary formed part of the ordinary world they
sought to overthrow and transcend. I imagine that it was as unthinkable for them to oppose it politically by the merely secular

means and language of a rational-legal order as it is for the secular militants of our own day not to do so.

In 1917–1919, Watchtower pastors, deacons, and elders displaced the earlier leaders of the people. Shadrach Sinkala "was treated like a chief, as to his people he undoubtedly was." Justice Macdonnell called him a fanatic but "an honest fanatic," who was prepared to "brush aside as irrelevant any duties he might have to his chief or to the Boma that conflicted with what he thought were his religious obligations."[98] Hanoc Sindano, too, became "something like a chief." After repeated unsuccessful attempts to break up his large following, Sindano was allowed to form a village under the jurisdiction of Chief Tukamulozya. This Jerusalem survived intact into the 1950s.[99] Although officials carried out a systematic restoration from above, they were keenly aware that an extraordinarily clean sweep had been made. Visiting Commissioner H. C. Marshall commented on the situation with unintentional irony. His reply to a proposal that loyalty to the regime should be conspicuously rewarded was No, it need not be. In getting back their positions, he said, chiefs and headmen had received payment enough.[100] Justice Macdonnell described the Watchtower's New Era in apocalyptic language: "As one listened to the pleas and evidence, which shewed that the old words, obedience to elders, headmen, and chiefs, obedience to the Boma, had lost their meaning, one realized the delicate and fragile nature of our hold over these people and at times we saw the abyss opening."[101] Chiefs and headmen did not suffer alone at the edge of the abyss. After the high court quashed many of his sentences, Dewhurst went to Kasama to ask that a telegram be sent to the administrator of the territory. After insisting upon his "success" against the Watchtower by the legal methods he had chosen, Dewhurst went on: "This success rendered abortive by ruling of Judge that my order unlawful impossible for me remain at Chinsali in any case leave necessary after strain of last four months alternative to this is resignation."[102]

The Reverend Dr. Chisholm had suffered great strain as well. But, although in broken health, he optimistically pointed his mission's way ahead as soon as quiet returned. It was time, he thought, for a revitalized Livingstonia to complete the work of sweeping away the pieces of a moribund customary regime:

> In my opinion the people, especially the younger people, have reached a stage when their old religious customs and beliefs

have no power over them. They are restless and looking for something to take the place of the old superstitions.[103]

But although the Watchtower wave had receded, Chisholm's suffering was not over. The men of the BSAC did not receive his proposal warmly. For if customary rulers had lost control, so had the missions, and outstandingly Mwenzo, which had come through the events even worse off than the regime. The administration at least had kept the leaders when it lost the people. Mwenzo had lost both. When the question arose of restoring Mwenzo's activities, the administration closely scrutinized, and found wanting, the mission's arrangements for guaranteeing the loyalty of its employees.[104]

As the colony returned to quiet, officials took steps to insure that the missions could aid in the maintenance of order or, at the very least, not harbor a bomb against it. In that climate of official opinion, the unfortunate Dr. Chisholm found himself having to defend the most fundamental principles of his mission:

> After eighteen years of schools in Fife district there must be very few who have any book knowledge or are able to read, who do not declare themselves as our "teachers" or "scholars." We have given them the power to read. ... We accept the responsibility of having given this education, but not of the Watchtower Church doctrines or the disturbances arising therefrom.[105]

But what the mission had offered the people could be used in more than one way. Once someone had the power to read the Gospel for himself, what he might then do with it transcended prediction and control. The capacity of human endeavor to undo its human agents has rarely been more poignantly stated. Missionaries often spoke of themselves as "planting" Christianity in Africa. But after they cultivated God's field, an uncertain work was done. As Rilke said so well, "A farmer may work and worry, but where the seed turns into summer he never reaches."

IT DOES NOT follow from the fact that the second Watchtower outbreak was directed against customary authority that it must necessarily do so. One chief, Shimwalule, is known to have accepted Watchtower baptism in 1918. His case is significant for two reasons. First, the parts of Chinsali and Isoka districts that were tributary to him were the only part of Bemba country where any significant Watchtower activity occurred at all.[106] Second, as guardian of the royal burial groves, he possessed traditional religious authority. Only after being made to understand that the *boma* was hostile to the Watchtower did Shimwalule drop all interest, so that in mid-1919 he could report with his brother chiefs, "I am living happily with my people again. They obey and respect me. My troubles are over."[107] In the next chapter we will see how troubles of the Lala priest-king Shaiwila led him to seek the witch-cleansing services of a Watchtower baptizer. The same practices that here provided a blueprint of rebellion against chiefly power there provided a blueprint for its violent restoration. Let us keep in mind the comment of an informant who reported to Father Peuth that Watchtower preachers were saying, "When we are more numerous then things will change, more so if a big chief like Nsokolo or any other paramount chief comes in with us. In 3 or 4 years there will be something new."[108] In 1925, Shaiwila joined the Watchtower, and there was something new.

5

THE WATER NEXT TIME: WITCH CLEANSING IN ZAMBIA, 1925

Think not that I am come to send peace on earth: I came not to send peace but a sword. For I am come to set a man at variance against his father, and the daughter against her mother, and the daughter in law against her mother in law. And a man's foes shall be they of his own household.

MATTHEW 10:34–36

THE SINISTER FIGURE OF one man dominates most accounts of this episode: Tomo Nyirenda, who used the Watchtower's baptism by total immersion to drown persons accused of witchcraft, who terrorized villagers, first in Zambia and then in Zaire, and who at the end stood in the dock with both arms amputated, because a terrified *boma* messenger had bound his arms too tightly at the moment of his capture. But two men, not one, actually dominated events. Shaiwila, who was recognized by the Crown as chief of the Western Lala people, engaged the witch-killing services of Tomo Nyirenda, confirmed him in the gruesome title Mwana Lesa—Son of God—identified persons to be executed, and secured widespread complicity in the killings. Shaiwila's part reveals a chief's calculated attempt to raise himself to effective power, despite the restrictions of colonial rule, by forcibly establishing a consensus on the basis of supernatural sanctions. The two men's collaboration offers insight into the political mechanism of witchcraft eradication.

The story of their collaboration exposes a part of the colonial state whose machinery turned from day to day in a pervading

dimness, out of the sight and earshot of local whites. Shaiwila succeeded in making the ties within the first articulation so tight for
a time that His Majesty's law and order atrophied and dropped
away; for many months he and Nyirenda managed to kill, and then
to keep the killing secret. When their deeds finally came to light,
making the villagers' nightmare that of the settlers, a painstaking
pretrial investigation showed how the natural and the supernatural
intertwined in the plot Shaiwila entered with the Son of God.

Tomo Nyirenda's Career, February to September 1925

The social context of Nyirenda's career differs in some respects
from that of his two precedessors. First, for many years, jurisdic-
tional disputes between the Universities Mission to Central Africa
(Anglican) and the Dutch Reformed Mission prevented the formal
establishment of any village schools in Shaiwila's area. At times, the
dispute was four-sided, since the Jesuit mission and Livingstonia
also exerted claims. The "scouts" of the UMCA—military language
remained the vogue—did not prevail until 1925, when a station
was finally opened at Fiwila. Shaiwila immediately sought to establish friendly relations with his new neighbor.[1]

Second, unlike the areas in which the two earlier revivals occurred, Shaiwila's had many white settlers. Large portions of Lala
country had become "European farming areas," with the result that
some Africans had been forced to leave their land, and others found
themselves reduced to the status of tenants.[2] Third, Lala country
was close to the main centers of large-scale wage employment. Local
people had relatively quick access to the town of Broken Hill, built
around lead and zinc mining, as well as to the towns of the Zairian
and Zambian copperbelts. Migrant laborers from other areas frequently traversed it on their way to and from urban jobs. Tomo
Nyirenda was one of many uprooted villagers who passed through,
came under the influence of Watchtower ideas, and spread them
while moving from job to job.

Tomo Nyirenda, a literate Tumbuka from Karonga District, Malawi, was well educated, by local standards.[3] He had the advantage
of six years' schooling by Free Church teachers at Bandawe (Kamwana's home). From Bandawe he went to Broken Hill, where he
worked as a cook, and from Broken Hill to Jesse Mine, near Mkushi.
The preachers already active in this important crossroads area included Isaac Bright Malenga, Harrison Nyendwa (now esteemed
by the Watchtower Bible and Tract Society as a founder of the

Zambian Jehovah's Witnesses),[4] Gabriel Phiri, and others. Baptized by Phiri in February 1925, Nyirenda soon became a valued colleague who corresponded with the others, as well as with his own followers, throughout his career. Shortly after his baptism, Nyirenda was arrested for "harmful preaching." Actually charged for the technical offense of failing to register as an "alien native," Nyirenda served a few weeks of imprisonment. Upon his release in April, he resumed his preaching, this time in the rural districts around Mkushi Boma.

He began at a village called Mondoka, where he taught the basic message of the Watchtower millennium, tailoring it to fit African conditions in the usual ways.[5] Aliens would be driven from the country. Taxation would cease. By 1925, the "Americans" were to do this revolutionary work. Watchtower teaching pictured them variously as all black or as blacks and whites living together in peace and equality.[6] Until the Americans came, villagers should either stop cultivating or make especially large gardens: In the first case, there would be no further need to toil; in the second, the people would grow rich by selling surplus produce.[7] Like his predecessors, he placed great emphasis on all-night hymn singing. He told the faithful to watch in the bush until the evening star set. Christ would soon arrive in a beam of light shining through the trees.[8] The divine Mwana Lesa would arrive from the east, while the people's enemies would depart to the west. Apparently, Nyirenda's version of Watchtower teaching absorbed some elements from a traditional eschatology, for the mythical personage Luchele had departed to the east, promising to return one day. (The first BSAC administrators seem to have benefited from the same myth.)[9]

Nyirenda also taught rules of conduct. According to one of his preachers, he told the people that they must "love each other, must not commit adultery, must not practice witchcraft nor refuse to give food to a neighbor." Further,

> [Tomo] said that if people did not throw away their witchcraft medicine he would know them for witches and would kill them. He said the Americans were coming and would give wealth and power . . . to the people if they were living well in their hearts.[10]

He also instructed people to be hospitable to strangers, to give food to needy neighbors, and to pray for the sick.[11,a] Emphasizing that

---

[a] Ranger suggests that the commandment of hospitality offered Christian uni-

these teachings of the Watchtower were a preparation for something more vast, another preacher said that Tomo repeatedly taught that "[O]ur 'church' was coming. The Watchtower was the house of the Church."[12]

Often Nyirenda repeated hygiene rules taught by mission and *boma*. Thus:

> Tomo said I have come to tell you the words of God. It was bad to steal, smoke bhang, good to obey the boma, to keep the villages clean. Food must be covered when taken outside and eaten.[13]

He sometimes claimed that he had been "sent out from the school"[14] or that his work had been authorized by the *boma*. Some people appear to have accepted him as a run-of-the-mill Christian evangelist.

> I went to Chondoka . . . to be dipped because the people who came advised us to be dipped, and it was good for people to know one another. When we got to Tomo's camp he himself said, "I bring you good news . . . I have come to baptize the people and make you repent in your hearts, to know one another and to be baptized." I thought it was a mission like any other. So we all went to the stream where we were baptized.[15]

In the orthodox teaching of the American movement, baptism signified entry into a special community that alone would be saved at the End, but Nyirenda went further. He branded the unbaptized as *bayendeni*, "ashes," "worthless ones," "witches," or "snakes and witches," to be shunned by the baptized.[16] "Repenting in the heart" came to mean, more and more explicitly, abstention from witchcraft:

> Anyone who does not come to be baptized by me in this country, he shall be killed by the wrath of God on his coming. If *everyone* will be baptized you will not be dying now and then all witches with charms must throw them away.[17]

Baptism and actual physical life were thus powerfully connected, while the boon of physical life was made contingent upon "repentence" by all. Those who did not throw their charms away threatened those who did—hence the equation of "ashes" (those

---

versalism in opposition to the particularism of the Lala clans. Equally, however, this commandment served the interests of Nyirenda, a stranger from the east, and his fellow travelers.

who would burn) and "witches." An understandable pressure to be baptized resulted, comparable to that which reinforced popular acceptance of the *mucapi* medicines. Anyone reluctant to be baptized fell under suspicion. Headmen led entire villages to be baptized. On one occasion, Tomo sent for a child he had accidentally missed; no one would eat with him until he, too, had been "dipped."[18]

Nyirenda worked through the outer fringes of Mkushi and then moved into Chief Mulungwe's country. For some time, his teaching on baptism must have resembled that of other Watchtower preachers: He simply told people to renounce witchcraft and to give up their charms and medicines. As he progressed through Mulungwe's villages, however, the baptisms underwent a change of nuance. They came to be credited with the power to unmask witches. Those who failed to be immersed completely became suspects whom Nyirenda questioned. If the subject found no satisfactory alternative explanation, he could be exposed as a witch. Usually no more than three to five people at a time, nearly all elderly, were so exposed. Their floating constituted an indictment. Sometimes those indicted were already under suspicion in their villages. Once the witches were unmasked, Nyirenda and his helpers took no further action themselves. But if opinion was united on a person's guilt, he might suffer ostracism, which often drove a person to suicide, or to death by exposure, or by tooth and claw of wild animals.[19]

Nyirenda's reputation as a witch finder spread rapidly. While in Chief Mulungwe's area, a headman of Shaiwila's invited him to find the witches in his own village, called Musakanya. According to the arrangements, Nyirenda would come accompanied by four deacons recruited at Mulungwe's. Musakanya was also one of dozens of people who came in person or wrote letters to request Nyirenda's services.[20] When Nyirenda later began to kill witches, he was sometimes asked to return to villages visited in earlier days to complete the work. A resident of Syaluka wrote, "I pray you do not miss us. I pray you. You only danced you did not pick out the weeds . . . come on Friday. I pray you even unto God."[21]

"Picking out the weeds" had a positive purpose: healing. The subordinate pastor Sukuta related that at Musanla village, where three people had died, "the witches were killed . . . because the village's men and women asked that this be done as the people were not giving birth to children."[22] Sometimes he was approached by individuals with personal complaints. While still in the vicinity of Musakanya's village, Nyirenda was visited by Chawala, the fourth

and youngest wife of Shaiwila. Chawala had come because she had
not been able to conceive in four years of marriage. She was baptized together with several female companions, who in turn begged
Tomo to visit their own villages. When Chawala returned home,
she refused to sleep with her husband until he, too, had been
baptized.

Shaiwila was baptized seven days after Chawala had visited Tomo
Nyirenda.[23] Shaiwila first satisfied himself that Nyirenda would be
suitable, then authorized him to kill witches. Shaiwila provided
Nyirenda with a list of people to be killed. Only after this first
group's liquidation was Shaiwila himself baptized. The agreement
with Shaiwila was critical. Tomo Nyirenda only began to kill witches
after he had been authorized by the chief to do so. Following this
encounter with the chief of the Western Lalas, Nyirenda's baptism
underwent its final change of nuance. Having begun as a sign of
repentance and of new Christian membership, it became a way of
distinguishing the saved from the damned, then witches from non-
witches. At the final stage, it became, like the outlawed poison
oracle, a means of destroying witches.

Nyirenda ordered his assistants to sustain the myth that baptism
took away the guilty, sometimes in conjunction with a book to which
infallible powers of detection were attributed.[24] Hence, only
preachers assisted at the killings. One later testified that he had
maintained a lookout to assure that no one surprised the group
before the drownings were over.[25] To sustain this myth, Tomo
threatened to kill those responsible if a witch escaped.[26,b] Sometimes
the relation between sin and death as a witch was stated as the
automatic result of a transgression. Thus, the death of one victim
was attributed to his sin of smoking bhang.[27]

Having won the traditional title of Mwana Lesa—Son of God—
Nyirenda was treated as prophet and savior. As Mwana Lesa, he
was showered with gifts and provided with food and shelter for
himself and his entourage wherever he went.[28] The entourage
grew. A large camp following from the villages swelled as he moved

---

[b] Bearing in mind that his remark was elicited in court testimony, it is well to
retain a certain skepticism, for it is difficult to be sure that a threat of death always
meant a promise of murder. The pastors had an obvious interest in creating the
impression that Nyirenda coerced them, thereby minimizing their own responsibility. It is not possible to disentangle these things. Even when alone in the company
of his close associates, Nyirenda preserved the mystique of his own baptism. During
the drownings, he would pray, "My Father, God, look down on these people that
they may die." I do not know what is to be made of this.

along. Sometimes he demanded that headmen produce helpers for him in the manner of traditional (and colonial) labor levies.[29] These followers became Mwana Lesa's deacons, elders, pastors, teachers, and choristers, each assigned definite tasks. This division of labor led to paradoxes, like that of the doctor or the priest who assists at executions. Sukuta said, "My job was to pray for the sick. I saw all the corpses of the witches."[30] Many women joined the group, sometimes abandoning husbands who refused to be baptized. They became choristers, prepared food for the group, and were sometimes given in marriage to preachers.[31]

During this time, officials knew little of the group's activities, which the villagers subordinate to Shaiwila carefully concealed. Others joined the conspiracy of silence. Africans merely passing through Mulungwe's country knew about the killings in Shaiwila's while officials and missionaries actually stationed there did not.[32] Though not subject to Shaiwila, travelers kept silent. One of Mulungwe's people explained, "It was not my country and not my business."[33] Husbands whose wives divorced them told the *boma* but did not report the reason or complain.[34] Justice Macdonnell commented later:

> The people came to the man . . . they fed him, built shelters for him, let their young men go with him, let him baptize them, and let him kill their brothers, fathers, and mothers as he wished—and concealed everything from the Boma. So they were to find happiness and so their country was to be cleaned! Today [the day of the trial verdict] they see the fullness of their gain.[35]

Although Macdonnell's remarks misleadingly suggest that villagers were free to refuse what Nyirenda demanded, they fully convey the co-operation accorded to a Watchtower preacher by the Western Lalas. This massive co-operation distinguishes Nyirenda's campaign in Shaiwila's country from those of other Watchtower preachers, as well as from his own activities among the Lenjes near Mkushi and the Swakas to the west.

After all of Shaiwila's villages had been baptized, Nyirenda moved into the country of the Swaka people of Ndola District, where no chiefs and only a handful of headmen co-operated. Chief Chitina immediately sent a letter of complaint to the *boma*, which repeated almost word for word the complaints of Kafwimbe, Terefya, and Nsokolo in 1918.

I want the Boma to make a case against all those people of mine who were baptized. They do not obey me now and they refuse to tell me anything although they are my people. They call me "muyandani" (ashes) because I was not baptized.

His nephew Mwashe reported that Watchtower adherents "told me that the chiefs would be driven away by the Americans and 'Wachitawala' put in their place."[36] Despite official opposition, Nyirenda baptized many people of the area. Others came to his meetings from across the border in Zaire.

During this crusade Mwana Lesa overreached himself. He killed Chibuye, an elderly woman whose son denied that she could have been a witch. "My two people [relatives] were healthy people," Mukalwe objected, making a strong prima facie case for his mother's innocence. "They were not sick people. No relatives of Mwelwa or Chibuye [both victims] have been accused of being witches. All Chibuye's people are alive." Mukalwe had led a party of five men and five women to the village of Chondoka to be baptized. To his surprise, Chibuye had been among the four witches named at the baptism—all had floated. Yes, he said, "my mother was not properly immersed because she is an old woman and not a witch at all."[37] But Mwana Lesa killed her, together with Chondoka's mother, Namasale, also in the group. Chondoka who, together with his wives, had refused baptism, now arrested Mukalwe and sent him to report the killings at the boma. Whereas in Shaiwila's country, headmen sided with their chief against what they knew to be their obligation toward the boma, Mukalwe's headman immediately asserted his duty under indirect rule: "This country belongs to the white men and now you have killed my mother, there is a big case in my village."[38,c]

While the boma was being alerted, Chief Mufumbi arrived from Zaire, inviting Mwana Lesa to "cleanse" his villages, too.[39] When a message from Shaiwila warned that a detachment of plainclothes police were on his trail, Nyirenda accepted the invitation and departed for Zaire with some 60 followers of his own.[40] When Mufumbi supplied him with about 40 more helpers, the combined group must have constituted a formidable bodyguard.[41] He re-

---

c The case was more complicated even than this. The examining official discovered that headman Chondoka had suborned witnesses to say that they had been indicted by Nyirenda and then rescued by their headman. In fact, he "made no attempt to save even Namasale [his own mother] and even called Tomo to his village to find witches" (NAZ, KSM 3/1/2, ex. no. 10, Finding).

mained in Zaire during June and July, killing witches on a colossal scale. Perhaps as many as 174 Zairians as compared with 17 Zambians died.[42] When Nyirenda questioned the advisability of killing witches in such conspicuous numbers, Mufumbi, according to a witness, insisted that killing witches was "permissible in the Congo."[43] It was not, of course. Armed patrols were sent out toward the end of July to arrest Tomo. On hearing this news, Nyirenda boasted that God would destroy any patrol that tried to capture him.[44] His prophecy was fulfilled. Surprised in camp by a patrol, everyone escaped, owing to a freakish accident. A shot intended for Nyirenda grazed his chest but shot a member of the patrol dead. When members of the party started to flee, Tomo seized the dead man's gun and threatened to kill anyone who abandoned him. Although he dispatched armed followers to bring back the deserters, he recrossed the border into Zambia with a diminished party.

Tomo resumed his preaching, joined by other Watchtower pastors, Patterson Nyendwa and one Sebelous, both of whom had large followings.[45] But he spent the next month in a long flight eastward. Still ignorant of the killings in Shaiwila's country, Zambian constables tracked him in co-operation with the Belgian authorities.[46] During this time, hundreds of villagers helped Nyirenda make his way through the bush, supplying food and warning of danger. They kept his activities in their own villages secret from the authorities, even reburying the victims at remoter sites. They lied about the deaths. Since most had been elderly, the deaths could be attributed to some common affliction. Or they said simply that the person had left for Broken Hill. Mwana Lesa was finally caught in Petauke District by the same messenger who had caught him prior to the fateful meeting with Shaiwila.[47]

Not only Nyirenda, Shaiwila, and their subordinates stood accused but also "every man, woman, and child" in twenty-nine villages.[48] The defense, which included someone identified as "Melland," argued that Nyirenda had genuinely believed in the benefits of his campaign. He was "ignorant," "not reasoning as white men reason," and hence not punishable under white men's law.[49] If the court were black, Nyirenda would go free. In his address, Justice Macdonnell cited this defense only to refute it. Nyirenda had "lived on other people" ever since leaving Karonga. "He is a clever man, a strong man, who can reason well and dominate others for his own gain." Turning to Shaiwila's case, Macdonnell recalled that the chief had given the witchfinder a list of names. "Is that black man's law?" he demanded. "In the old days the people would have re-volted." In the end, the court came to the same conclusion as Wanga, the wife of Mwana Lesa, who said simply, "This killing was done by one Tomo met Shaiwila. Tomo did this murder himself for his own power."[50]

In the spring of 1926, Nyirenda, Shaiwila, and fourteen others were convicted of murder and sentenced to death. Two others were acquitted.[51] Nyirenda and Shaiwila were hanged, together with one Nkufye, a headman who had submitted the names of two personal enemies subsequently killed. The regime commuted the sentences of the others to corporal punishment and terms of imprisonment—except Jere, one of Nyirenda's most notorious assistants, who escaped to Zaire and was never punished. "Every man, woman, and child" in twenty-nine villages was sentenced under the Collective Punishment Ordinance to collective fines later commuted to forced labor.

THE ANATOMY OF A REBELLION

The technical details of the Collective Punishment Ordinance had been worked out in Ireland, England's oldest colony.[52] Its specific provisions caused some difficulty in the Mwana Lesa case, since they required that an attempt at rebellion be demonstrated. Wide-spread and systematic violation of the law, such as had occurred in Shaiwila's country, did not quite suffice. The effort to meet this legal test probably biased the investigation. So far as I am aware, no one except the court and the white settlers who lived near Shaiwila's villages has tried to interpret the Mwana Lesa episode as tantamount to anticolonial rebellion. They reasoned from the villagers' silence: Any collective ability to keep a secret itself pointed toward the abyss. Besides, some passed along rumors that obtaining the support of a strong chief was only the first phase of the plot; the *boma* and the settlers would be next. J. E. Stephenson was perhaps the most outspoken proponent of this view.[53] But Africans, not English and Boer settlers, fell, and no antiwhite plot came to light. Academic commentators have favored a cultural interpretation.

Terence Ranger reminds us that the Lala chiefs were priest-kings and suggests that, perhaps more than other peoples, the Lalas lived within a "witch-dominated spiritual economy." If we add the prevalence of witch fears, made more virulent since the regime's abolition of witch trials, both Shaiwila's reception of Tomo Nyirenda and Nyirenda's wide popular reception become neatly explicable. The manifold disruption and uncertainty caused by the British presence leads us further, to the psychological anomie that cultural interpreters of millenarian tumult unfailingly discover.

But cultural interpretation will not do. The question is not why witch killing was conceivable and desirable to the Lalas under Shaiwila but how it could be carried out despite colonial prohibition. Cultural interpretation portrays only the presumed "mind" of the episode, not its "body"—and not the anatomy of the body. But it is the body of the episode—the ability of Shaiwila and Nyirenda to redeploy existing organization—that sets it apart. Furthermore, the episode is not at all distinguished by its mind. Fear of witches, belief in the power of witch doctors, and "witch-dominated spiritual economy" existed elsewhere. And all Watchtower baptizing in our region connoted deliverance from the evil of witchcraft. Gabriel Phiri, who had baptized Nyirenda, preached to the Lenjes he baptized that they must "give up horns and charms"; probably, he preached this to Nyirenda himself, an "alien native" from Malawi. Neither Shaiwila's duty to protect his people from witches, nor the supernatural sanctions that upheld his preeminence sets him apart as a priest-king different from his royal colleagues of different ethnic origin. Finally, no particular kind or structure of action against witches follows from simple belief in witchcraft, any more than recognition of crime dictates a particular means of punishment.

A cultural interpretation will not do. Even if popular fears of witchcraft accounted for the willingness to accept Mwana Lesa's baptism, the acceptance of Nyirenda's indictments and sentences would not automatically follow. Could an ordinary person have managed, within the system of beliefs, to distinguish between murder and execution? If one could, amid the general enthusiasm for Mwana Lesa's baptizing, then something more than belief must account for the details of the campaign. We already know that one could and did.

Chibuye accompanied her son to Mwana Lesa's ceremony in order to witness the "weeding out," not to be weeded out herself. Mukalwe complained afterward that his mother had been weeded out unjustly. He did not deny that witches were killing people; he denied that Chibuye was doing so. No one Chibuye could have harmed, if she had been a witch, had in fact been harmed: "All Chibuye's people are alive." Nor could any relative have passed on a latent trait that remained as yet invisible: "No relations of Mwelwa or Chibuye had been accused of being witches." According to the conventions of witch belief, Mwana Lesa was clearly a charlatan, and he had perpetrated a gross miscarriage of justice. If Mukalwe's mother could be executed as a witch, despite Mukalwe's evidence and solely on the basis of Mwana Lesa's baptism, then something more than the generalized fear of witchcraft was at work.

Sholto Cross's observation that "what is most striking is the chief's wholehearted support" provides a clue.[54] Mwana Lesa's work among Shaiwila's villages differed from his work among those subject to Chief Chitina: Chitina refused to support the movement. Mukalwe's complaint reached the *boma* because his headman required it and because customary authority at all levels resisted the revival. What counted among the Western Lalas was Shaiwila's decision to co-opt a Watchtower preacher who promised a radical solution to the political problem of evil and, so doing, to restore his own effective power. Shaiwila the politician had several reasons to seek restoration of his effective power, some of which he shared in common with other customary authorities, some his own. Shaiwila followed up his decision to "radicalize" Nyirenda's solution by making a series of calculated moves that created the consensus so impressive to most writers.

The Fall of the House of Nyendwa

Like their colleagues elsewhere, the Lala chiefs had been weakened by the colonial regime. They lost the perquisites of office—such as their privileged position in the trade of ivory and slaves—and with them an important part of what distinguished chief from commoner.[55] War was outlawed. And with the advent of settlers, young men who would have been available to work the chiefs' lands and fight their battles went to work for Europeans. Portions of the older domains of the Lala chiefs had been taken over as Crown lands in 1924 and then distributed to settler farmers and entrepreneurs. The regime also limited chiefs' power over their subjects in various ways. The Lala chiefs responded as chiefs did elsewhere by attempting to impose new, unauthorized exactions. Summing up a missionary's account of their predicament, Ranger writes,

> Striving to retain something of their old prestige they found themselves endeavoring to exact from commoners tribute that no longer had legal sanction—demanding "at least one day's tribute-labor from every able-bodied commoner"; demanding a tribute of "at least five shillings" from those who had been

fortunate enough to obtain paid employment with the whites; and extracting rather uncertain income from "fines" from law cases which are not recognized by the government.[56]

But people did not readily accept these novel demands. Nor did they have to. The new dispensation offered them various lines of resistance. If the demands were illegal, they could complain to district officials. They could simply fail to comply. Or they could leave the jurisdiction of their chief. The colonial economy offered a choice between customary forms of oppression and uncustomary ones, while the possibility of earning a livelihood elsewhere destroyed the most fundamental restraint available to any social system, the absence of practical alternatives. The economy contested the customary system in a deeper way. Subjects wise in the ways of the alien world could deny chiefs' moral authority and thereby erase their own sense of obligation to obey. As this support of authority became less effective, external coercion had to increase, but the chiefs confronted their declining situation with few weapons. They could no longer prevent subjects from leaving their jurisdiction. The colonial economy demanded the mobility of labor, and the incentives of the cash economy had for years been destroying the particularism of clans, on which the Lala chieftainships were built. When Nyirenda enjoined friendliness to strangers as part of Christian conversion, he was merely giving religious value to the universalism that the colonial economy demanded as a practical necessity. Thus, the dissolution of the old social organization diminished the effectiveness of the political levers native to it, while chiefs were not free to devise new ones. The colonial regime disarmed customary authority against old and new sorts of internal opposition.

Customary rulers had to be disarmed in order that the British Crown might reign supreme. J. E. Stephenson vividly describes his own campaign to expropriate the Lala chiefs in his autobiographical work, *Chirupula's Tale*. It was part of Stephenson's task as a BSAC administrator to enforce colonial laws that forbade chiefs to order capital punishment or even to try capital cases. Doing his duty, Stephenson arrested one chief and several accomplices for carrying out half a dozen executions in 1911. On another occasion, Chief Mbowoka fled into exile to escape imprisonment for carrying out a similar sentence.[57] Obviously, there was no alternative to these measures. Either the Lala chiefs possessed sovereign authority or the Crown did, and the right to condemn a subject to death is a fundamental attribute of sovereignty. The attendant diminution of the chiefs' day-to-day power over their subjects was a secondary issue the significance of which escaped colonial officials for some time.

Early officials such as Stephenson did not hesitate to intervene in the more humdrum judicial functioning of the customary order. People brought all kinds of legal cases to the *boma*—accusations of theft, complaints of assault, suits for divorce, and so on. It seemed to so enthusiastic an imperialist that ordinary villagers had instantly recognized the superior wisdom of British law. Direct rule was evidently succeeding. Stephenson reported with satisfaction that the justice handed down at Mkushi Boma enjoyed immense "popularity."[58] People preferred him to the judges of the customary order. His rough-and-ready justice at the *boma* introduced appealing novelties. In particular, Stephenson said, villagers approved of flogging as a punishment for a variety of offenses. (His nickname *Chirupula*—"the flogger"—derived from his work as official executioner.) The availability of justice at the *boma* as an alternative to that of the customary order deprived chiefs of additional political tools. By demonstrating to ordinary villagers that chiefs could be dispensed with or circumvented, the *boma*'s justice achieved indirectly what the expropriation of chiefs had achieved directly. Both pressed the assault upon chiefs' sovereignty. The chiefs need no longer be feared by the empire, and their own subjects might be free of their authority. The danger inherent in commoners' not fearing rulers whom the Crown did not fear was not apparent so long as it seemed possible to dominate the African masses directly.

Incredibly, Stephenson and others like him imagined they could handle all the judicial matters of thousands of African subjects, and as a part-time activity sandwiched between many others. Stephenson joined the BSAC at a time when reality seemed to support the belief that there was nothing that Great Britain, or Britons, could not do. R. J. Short, a DC in Zambia for many years, could still write in the late 1960s that the demise of the British Empire had resulted from a loss of character and toughness.[59] Such beliefs of Crown officials partly account for their actions and for gaps in their vision.

Even during Chirupula's time, before World War I and long before Indirect Rule was enacted, customary rulers could not be dispensed with. Stephenson vividly recounts a public meeting in which he scolded chiefs and headmen for failing to produce carriers as requested. When the meeting began, Stephenson had already decided to carry out some exemplary punishments but had not yet decided upon whom. After listening for some time, Chief Lwimba stepped forward to be punished on behalf of his people. Chirupula personally administered the flogging. After this incident, there was no further difficulty in obtaining the necessary "volunteers" from the villages.

Stephenson expatiates on the chief's nobility—Lwimba was a Nyendwa, one of the Lala royal clan, and his gesture evidently appealed to the Briton's ingrained sentiment for aristocracy. But the deed and this attitude illustrate the inconsistent view of British officials toward the hereditary rulers whose power over Africans they at first implicitly, then explicitly, upheld. Since officials thought of themselves as ruling directly, transferring to chiefs bits of power as need arose, they saw no danger in removing still another tool of the chiefs' authority, the mystique of royalty. The mystique of royal blood did not prevent public assault upon Lwimba's person and, more important, upon his royal personage. Though Stephenson could write with obvious feeling about the special properties of noble blood and breeding, he treated Lwimba not as a prince who could be king, but as an African. Flogging was an acceptable punishment for Africans but not for Europeans.[60] Lwimba's people were "never cordial thereafter," Stephenson said. They quaintly "believed that a chief should not suffer corporal punishment." In such performances, the regime asserted the equality of all Africans, in its own eyes, but also before the eyes of African commoners. The regime contradicted itself. It laid low the persons who had to be exalted if they were to be effective in their separate sphere.

Shaiwila's Descent

Shaiwila's descent paralleled that of other Lala chiefs, but it had advanced further by the mid-1920s. His was the first chiefdom to receive the *pax Britannica*, as borne by J. E. Stephenson.

> Of the Zambian Lala chiefs, the weakest was Shaiwila, holder of the first chieftainship to come under European rule. Ordinary Lala were flouting his authority: one man, a veteran of the First World War, went about in his army uniform as if to assert his independence of the chief; another killed a village headman, going unpunished because the chief no longer had the authority to try capital cases.[61]

British rule also curtailed Shaiwila's ability to perform important ritual duties. According to Ranger, these included the annual performance of fertility ceremonies in each of the villages under him.[62] Nyirenda's summons to point out witches, because "women were not giving birth to children," suggests that the fertility ceremonies were tied to the cure of witchcraft. If so, then by making witch trials illegal, the regime had outlawed not one but two important ritual duties at one stroke. (Recall that a witch had allegedly prevented Shaiwila's wife from conceiving.) Apparently, Shaiwila could not even travel freely in his own domain. After the first killings, he commented, "Now I can visit Musanla's in safety." Later it was said that Shaiwila would not drink in a village where Tomo Nyirenda had not killed someone.[63]

Shaiwila's personal enemies included certain elders who disapproved of his accession to the chiefship. They regarded him as a sacrilegious usurper. The missionary report quoted above continues:

> Shaiwila had committed the unpardonable sin of sleeping with one of his uncle's wives before the old chief's death. . . . The Lala believed that he would die because of his breach of the taboo. Sharing these beliefs he lived in fear that untimely death would overtake him.[64]

Since, under matrilineal inheritance, a man succeeds his maternal uncle and since, according to conventional ideas, adultery could bring about the death of a spouse, Shaiwila himself may have stood accused of murdering his uncle in order to succeed.[65] Sometimes the retribution was seen as arising automatically from the act; the scandal of it stirred protective ancestral spirits to action. At other times the curse of an elder before the ancestral shrines was required. Either way, we need not assume that Shaiwila's enemies stood idly by until these mystical forces took effect.

Probably Shaiwila lived in fear not only because he shared elders' beliefs about sacrilege, but also because he knew the elders. And if he feared physical harm from certain of his subjects, the way to remove the fear was to remove the people. We need not accept at face value the accusation that Shaiwila had committed adultery with one of his uncle's wives. Because of its association with premeditated murder, adultery with a chief's wife was a charge that could legitimate strong opposition. The old chief's death may well have stood as "evidence" of the machinations an unpopular new Shaiwila (whose position was guaranteed by the regime) had resorted to, in the same way that death or illness of Chibuye's relatives would have supported her guilt.

The rite of touring villages annually presented opportunities for political work on both sides. If a chief was strong and popular, he could strengthen his alliances and purge his enemies. If he was not so, eating and drinking in tributary villages offered numerous opportunities for enemies to conduct a purge. Or the considerable ritual power that elders of high status wielded might always make a guilty chief succumb to the ancestral spirits' anger at his misdeeds. Shaiwila might have had little to fear if he could stay home. But the clever customary arrangement had a built-in mechanism for assuring the widest possible consensus on the accession of a chief: He could not remain at home among loyal supporters and retain the allegiance of all his subjects. A sort of plebiscite in which subjects could pronounce a fatal *No* had to be conducted annually.

The arrival of Tomo Nyirenda presented a challenge and an opportunity. A challenge: With declining authority, Shaiwila himself probably could not refuse baptism, let alone prohibit it to others. An opportunity: He could reap the advantage of providing a service in demand. Although Shaiwila had to take certain steps to seize control of Tomo Nyirenda's baptismal campaign, his actions already cast doubt on any simple notion of a "witch-dominated *spiritual* economy." Shaiwila was weak politically and had definite human enemies. Faced merely with a spiritual problem, he could have enlisted the services that Nyirenda initially offered. He did not actually have to destroy witches. Instead, by inserting witchcraft into a local political discourse, Shaiwila, a shrewd politician, dared to take advantage of an opportunity. He played his hand with care.

The Ascent of Shaiwila and Mwana Lesa

Shaiwila learned of Nyirenda's preaching from several sources. A man whose relative had been unjustly indicted as a witch had gone to the chief to complain and had even threatened to go to the *boma* unless the chief did something about it. Shaiwila sent the man home with a promise that he would take care of the matter. The Anglican missionaries at Fiwila, with whom Shaiwila was rather friendly, had requested their sympathetic neighbor to call a halt to the Watchtower baptisms underway at least since the previous fall.[66] Finally, as we saw, the chief's own wife went out to seek Tomo's services as a healer.

To investigate, Shaiwila sent Muswalo, his divisional headman, who ordinarily collected meal from the villages for sale to the *boma* and the mission.[67] Well known to people as the chief's representative, he wore a fez that symbolized his good relations at the *boma*. He was a messenger, or *kapasu*. Thus, the people Muswalo and his party encountered on their way to Nyirenda's prayer meeting bolted into the bush to avoid interference. Muswalo noted many people abroad on the paths. After a time, Muswalo instructed his party to be quiet, removed his fez, and entered the bush as if he were an ordinary villager. Slowly making his way toward the sound of hymn singing, he found Nyirenda with a large gathering of hearers. Accusing Tomo of lying to the people, Muswalo arrested him, but the crowd protested as the two moved away.

Delegations from a number of surrounding villages were present. The large delegation from Letele village included the headman's wife.[68] According to Muswalo, "All the people of Letele said that I must not take Tomo away as they wanted him to make things good in the village and hear more about the witchcraft." Muswalo underwent baptism, "in order to find out what was being taught,"[69] and then stayed on for a time, according to his testimony, to hear the preaching, which, he said, concerned adultery and stealing. Subsequent testimony revealed that Muswalo's fact-finding went deeper. Tomo's assistant Sukuta testified that Muswalo specifically asked to "hear the hymns" used in witch finding and to witness an exhibition.[70] Tomo obliged, naming several people from Letele. The *kapasu*, as Sukuta called Muswalo, then set out with Nyirenda for Shaiwila's village, instructing the people to follow. On the way, they received an order from Shaiwila to take Tomo to a remoter area, where Shaiwila would meet him. Shaiwila worried that the noise of so many people would alert the missionaries at Fiwila that something was afoot. Already they had asked him why mission attendance had suddenly plummeted.[71]

Later that evening, Shaiwila asked Muswalo whether he had seen the witch finding himself and whether it had been successful. He especially wanted to know whether the hymns were efficacious. Shaiwila expressed satisfaction with all of Muswalo's replies. Then, in the presence of some of his people, Shaiwila authorized Nyirenda to "weed out" the witches in his country and announced that soon he, too, would be baptized. Muswalo's role as Shaiwila's right-hand man continued. A villager testified that when Muswalo arrived at his village to collect meal, he also announced the time when baptisms would be held by the side of the Likosi Stream, where the chief himself had arranged to be baptized.[72]

Shaiwila put in his appearance after dark. He immediately expressed dissatisfaction with the noise the large crowd was making. "Why are you only coming with your wives?" he demanded—a detail that suggests *chongo* and the prominence of women shouting and talking in tongues.[73] "Now there is going to be trouble." The chief recovered from his misgivings, however, and he was duly baptized beside the bodies of Mwana Lesa's first five victims, drowned earlier the same day. When he had seen the bodies, he said to Tomo, "You have done well to kill these witches. I am pleased, and now I can visit Musanla's in safety." Referring to Chawala's complaint, he told the witch finder, "At Leza's [village] there is one who has made my wife barren."[74] He then directed Nyirenda to his next targets. At Leza's village, Nyirenda subsequently killed Mufulwe, an elder with whom Shaiwila had an old grudge, together with Mufulwe's wife and a kinswoman.[75]

In addition to directing Nyirenda to the next witches to be unmasked and killed, Shaiwila thanked him formally. He gave Tomo the right to wear the red *nduba* feather, traditionally worn by the slayer of a lion or a man, and promised to give him a red cloth to wear around his head, an additional sign of high esteem.[76] Headman Musanla, who witnessed these proceedings and who might have been expected to resist the slaughter of his relatives, marveled instead. "When I heard that," Musanla told the court, "I said that Shaiwila had indeed given Tomo power." Musanla decided not to oppose his chief by reporting the affair to the *boma*.

Shaiwila then instructed Nyirenda to "weed out" all the villages, saving his own for last. He announced to those present that "Tomo, his father, was killing witches, but that the Boma must not be told, otherwise he [Shaiwila] would be killed."[77] All those killed were old people who, according to one informant, had been accused by the women of keeping them barren.[78] The chief's interests thus coincided to this extent with public opinion. But to secure his interests further, Shaiwila took a crucial step vis-à-vis his headmen. Pointing to the bodies, he said to them, "See, you headmen are unlucky. See what you have done?"[79] "You send Tomo to kill witches when Tomo was already arrested by a kapasu," said Shaiwila, according to the headman Koni. For his part, Koni replied, "You are also unlucky." Shaiwila then ordered them not to report to the *boma*.

With this exchange, a definite chain of command was developing. The headman Koni further testified that as soon as Tomo had killed the first witches, he immediately wrote a letter to Shaiwila saying, "Shaiwila, that was you told me to kill the witches in your country; I have killed one." The message was read aloud to the illiterate Shaiwila by the teen-age preacher Faifi (Fife). Thus, Tomo had witnesses to his accord with Shaiwila. It seems he did not intend to be blamed alone for the destruction of the chief's enemies. What Tomo did to Shaiwila, Shaiwila then did to his headmen. When ordering them to report nothing to the *boma*, he said he would deny prior knowledge of the crimes. After all, the headmen, not he, had witnessed the execution of the first five witches. Koni used a similar tactic with his villagers. In a bit of testimony that took twenty minutes to elicit,[80] Koni at last admitted that he had been present with all his people at Chipanga's village on the day Tomo arrived. Possibly he had even led them there, for he was baptized at the same time. One of Koni's people had been indicted as a witch at this meeting, but Koni happened to be "taking meal to the *boma*" when the killing took place. Like Shaiwila's, Koni's absence seems to have been calculated. Had the court not pressed him, he would not have admitted going to the baptism at all. Koni told the court that he had not reported the affair at the *boma* at first because, when he heard of it, he assumed that Shaiwila would. Shaiwila then told him to report nothing. Koni testified that he was following Shaiwila's orders when the local official, one Brown, inquired about an old man named Lipereto. The women told Brown that Lipereto had gone to Broken Hill. Koni did not contradict them.[81]

Muswalo, the messenger who had originally arrested Tomo, was also caught in the chain of command. He was requestioned when it became clear from other testimony that his role had been bigger than he had at first intimated. He then admitted having known about all the events. He said that if he had reported to the *boma*, he would have been blamed by the chief's brothers for anything that happened to the chief. Furthermore, if he had failed to co-operate and do exactly as the chief ordered, he feared that "the chief would complain about [him] to the boma and have [him] removed from [his] position as Divisional Headman."[82] Muswalo's role thus seems to have been assured by his interest in keeping his job, which depended in large part on Shaiwila's recommendation, and by his fear of Shaiwila's supporters.

Headman Musanla learned of Nyirenda's activities from Muswalo who, as divisional headman, was his superior. Musanla's predicament was similar to that of other headmen. He was under pressure from villagers who demanded baptism. At Musanla, Sukuta reported, "the witches were killed . . . because the village men and women asked that this be done as the people were not giving birth to children."[83] Once at the meeting, five of Musanla's people were indicted, including a close relative of the headman. When Musanla tried to save the relative, Tomo sharply reminded him, "Did you not yourself call me to find the witches? I am the roof and the aeroplane."[84] (Another witness was questioned as to the meaning of this formula. "I know what an aeroplane is; it is a thing made by white men that flies and kills people . . . He said he was a roof because it meant he had strength."[85] And Tomo used this formula as a threat: "Tomo used to say he was an aeroplane and a roof and that he would kill anyone who opposed him." A line in one of the hymns used when Tomo was baptizing said, "The aeroplane is roaring.") Musanla probably understood Tomo's words as an implicit threat that he, too, could be unmasked as a witch. He was also influenced by Shaiwila. Musanla heard Shaiwila promise that he would be blamed if anything happened.[86] In sum, as in other cases, Musanla's lips were sealed by a combination of his own complicity, his chief's and Nyirenda's physical threats, and the pressure of public opinion. The villagers supported Tomo in his demand that all those indicted in Musanla's village should be killed, and they threatened to leave him if he did not permit it.[87] The headmen Leza and Chungwe had similar experiences.[88]

After arranging the meeting between Nyirenda and Shaiwila, Muswalo discreetly continued his work of collecting meal. Although he had no further direct part in the events, his work kept him close to all parties until the end—and one imagines, vulnerable to them. Messengers had no entourage to carry equipment or set up independent encampments when spending the night away from home. When asked again why he failed to tell the *boma* what he knew, he replied that he feared the bad opinion of the chief's relatives and supporters: "I was afraid to speak because Shaiwila and his people would hate me."[89]

The witch finding dramatically changed Shaiwila's position. If he had been a weak chief whose people defied him at will, the opposite was now true. Again and again, both villagers and village headmen told the court that they went to be baptized, permitted and remained silent about the killings, lied about them, and aided Nyirenda because their chief ordered them to. Headman Musakanya said, "I did not report the death because I was a fool. Tomo said he had Shaiwila's authority."[90] Ironically, duty now compelled ordinary villagers to disobey their chief by doing what he told them not to do: by reporting at the *boma*. At least once, Nyirenda met their predicament halfway, creating the impression that he was acting legitimately in the regime's eyes—or so a villager testified. According to the villager, Tomo preached obedience to the sanitary regulations supported by the *boma* and even claimed to be sending to the *boma* a list of the witches of whom the country had been "cleansed."[91] Reporting that Tomo had created this impression was admirably adapted to the villagers' defense. They were able to say that, ignorant as they were, they took him to be yet another Christian visitor with the *boma*'s prestige behind him. Nyirenda was actually collecting names of all those baptized, to be sent to Watchtower headquarters in Broken Hill. Meanwhile, many preachers, in direct communication with white Watchtower officials in Cape Town, were also at work.

Just as Shaiwila proceeded by inculpating his headmen, and Nyirenda the chief, so Nyirenda and his assistants made certain that the villagers shared in the guilt of the murders. They were invariably called to see the bodies of the drowned witches with their own eyes: "All the people knew that Tomo was going around killing witches, because after he killed them he made everyone go and look for them."[92] At the same time, the villagers were warned by the very actions that inculpated them, for they were told that if they tried to report to the *boma*, they would be killed. A number of villagers testified that Nyirenda claimed to have laid a spell on the road that would cause them to be killed by lions if they ventured away for the wrong reasons.[93] The faithful, however, could travel along bush paths day or night. A Christian boy unsympathetic to the baptisms passed on a rumor about the remarkable faith. A group of Watchtower converts who were journeying down a bush path at night suddenly confronted a leopard. There and then they prayed for deliverance; after a while, the leopard went on his way.[94] Other witnesses gave no elaborate reasons for not reporting Nyirenda's activities, but pleaded instead low status in the polity. The wife of a murdered man said simply, "I did not report the death because I'm only a woman and Shaiwila had forbidden us to do so."[95] A youth said, "I was only a young man of the village."[96]

Although Shaiwila and Nyirenda together manipulated prevailing beliefs and fears, villagers did not accept baptism or support the killings solely because they feared these two ruthless men. Ordinary villagers testified to the combination of factors that motivated them. Some people went in order to silence gossip that they bewitched people or to prevent such suspicions.[d] "The people all

---

[d] One case is recorded in which a woman stood up to the immense pressure to be baptized. She braved total ostracism by her friends, relatives, and neighbors (NAZ, KSM 3/1/1, ex. no. 22, Chungwe).

went to be dipped," said one witness, "to show they were free from witchcraft."[97] But people who feared an accusation of witchcraft if they were not baptized also gave positive reasons. "We went to be baptized to find out who was free from witchcraft," one man began. "Tomo told us that Americans were coming and we were to grow much food to sell them."[98] Then he returned to a negative reason: "All who were unbaptized were 'bayendeni' and on the coming of the Americans they would be burnt, as they were snakes and witches." Back to the positive: "He said the Americans and white people were 'sons of sisters' [that is, like close relatives] and lived together like one people and that the baptized would live with them." Then the mixture: "First he told us to be good people and not commit adultery and to be kind to one another. I went to be dipped because Tomo said that every person unbaptized was a wizard or a witch. I believed it was a good thing and that people would not die." Another witness testified that "the people all went to be dipped to show that they were free from witchcraft, also because Tomo said only those who had been baptized would see God."[99] Many said that people had gone of their own accord; no one had been forced to go. Nyirenda's teen-age assistant, Kunda Chinilankwa, reported that customary rulers experienced the same mixed motives: "The elders and headmen kept the information from the government officials because they approved of the witch-finding and killing and also because Tomo said if people went to the Boma lions would eat them on the way."[100]

Thus, once Nyirenda's career of witch killing had begun, powerful political forces joined the ideological and psychological. Constraint cemented willing co-operation. Private interests went in the guise of praiseworthy public duties. Team players appeared from every direction. Dissent was silenced. Once the campaign of killing had begun, it was far from difficult for skeptical people to join in. But the key phrase is "once Nyirenda's career had begun." Shaiwila took over the campaign after assuring himself of Nyirenda's popularity and effectiveness. Only then did he decorate Nyirenda, now Mwana Lesa, with a red *nduba* feather. Shaiwila would use Nyirenda as a tool in the pursuit of his own interests only because the idea of "cleansing" the country had firm roots.

The Witches

The Mwana Lesa files reveal two kinds of witchcraft accusations: accusations against individuals already under suspicion when the witch finder arrived, and politically motivated accusations made as a consequence of Nyirenda's campaign. As an example of the first, consider an old man, Lipereto, whose position had become difficult in the normal course of life in his village; of the second, consider a young man, Shaŵomba, who appears to have been liquidated by a competitor.

In a fashion not unfamiliar in matrilineal villages, an old man was suspected of having caused his sister's barrenness.[101] Fellow villagers alleged that, before Nyirenda's arrival, Lipereto had placed a magical horn on a path she often took.[102] According to Lipereto's wife, Nyirenda's promised visit offered a way out of a difficult situation. Lipereto intended to ask to be made a preacher, in one stroke to absolve himself of guilt and to achieve power over others.[103,e] Unfortunately, he was at a funeral when his fellow villagers were baptized, and they no doubt told Nyirenda the gossip. When Lipereto at last went to be baptized, accompanied by his wife and daughters, Tomo greeted him strangely: "You have come, Lipereto? Today you are going to die." Lipereto's hope of becoming a preacher perished when he floated. "All right, if I am a wizard, I must die," said Lipereto. Although he did not confess responsibility for his sister's sickness, he admitted that he had some "medicine." "I have a little horn of jealousy," he said—medicine to stop the jealous bickering between his two wives.[104] Perhaps Lipereto was convinced of his own guilt when Nyirenda "discovered" the existence of this hidden witchcraft. Perhaps he merely saw that his social existence was at an end with his unmasking by means of this highly reputed new procedure. Women later told the DO that Lipereto had gone to Broken Hill.[105]

The second example concerns real conflict and hostility, well known to neighbors, and the use of the witch finder by one of the parties. Unlike Lipereto, Shaŵomba was not generally suspected of witchcraft; and a fellow villager, rather than Nyirenda, carried out his execution.[106] Shaŵomba lived in a village, Mwaluka, which appears to have been in the throes of a three-sided struggle among equally eligible successors to the headmanship and the headman himself. Mwaluka, the headman, had two nephews, Shaŵomba and Matanga, who were married to two daughters of Mwaluka's. Since Shaŵomba was married to the elder of the two,[107] he was probably older than his cousin, and perhaps had a greater claim to succeed.

e Mary Douglas has shown that elders likely to fall under suspicion of witchcraft commonly adopt this tactic of arming themselves with official status in a new cult (see "Techniques of Sorcery Control," in John Middleton and E. H. Winter, eds., *Witchcraft and Sorcery in East Africa*, New York, 1963).

But it was Matanga who had begun gradually to take over the chores of headmanship from his weak and ailing uncle. He hunted, for example, and he acted as spokesman when officials visited. (Mwaluka later claimed that he had tried to tell the DO that Shawomba had been killed and that Matanga had exhumed and reburied Shawomba's corpse in order to prevent its discovery. But, he claimed, "Brown would only listen to Matanga.")[108]

The cousins were "always quarreling," and the quarreling followed a conventional theme. Matanga allegedly coveted Shawomba's wife; he had even been charged with adultery. And Matanga was creating more general disharmony. Mwaluka told Matanga to leave the village because he was troublesome and "undesirable,"[109] but Shawomba left instead. Meanwhile, said Mwaluka, "Someone had bewitched [my] eyes."[110] When questioned by the court, he denied that he had ever made any accusations against either of his nephews, even when two horns were discovered in his house.

When Tomo arrived, Mwaluka's people went to a nearby village for the services. Mwaluka claimed to be too sick to go. Besides, he added, he had decided to remain behind "in charge of the village": "Two," he said cryptically, "cannot be in charge." He sent Matanga to meet Tomo. At this time Shawomba was living at his garden shelter with a friend, Mwape. Possibly he had chosen to retire from the village, away from the scene of strife. It appears that the two friends passed their days tranquilly—Shawomba and Mwape were great bhang smokers. When Tomo arrived at the village, he asked about them, for they had not been present at the baptism. Matanga replied that Shawomba smoked bhang and that Mwape cursed at children and said, "If I could kill persons I should kill Shawomba because he smokes bhang."[111] Shawomba and Mwape were not indicted as witches in the normal way, but were punished in a way Tomo sometimes used to enforce his new directives about proper behavior for converts.[112] Matanga splashed water in Shawomba's face until he drowned. Mwape received similar punishment for cursing but was rescued when he fainted. Afterward it was said that Shawomba had died from smoking bhang.

The story had undercurrents of extortion and bribery that, along with other details of the crime, investigators were never able fully to sort out. The village of Mwaluka suffered exceptionally severe punishment partly because the cover-up continued to the end and partly because the political motivation of the killing was obvious.[113] It was clear that the villagers had not acted simply out of superstitious fear. Furthermore, as the magistrate noted, this internally troubled village had produced more of Nyirenda's close followers than had any other. The most important preachers—Sukuta, Jere, Kalunga, and others who were responsible for the "baptizing" and the drowning, and who had accompanied Nyirenda into the Congo—all came from Mwaluka.

Witch Finders

Nyirenda's assistants were all young people. At thirty, Sukuta was not only the oldest of the inner circle of preachers, but the only one not under twenty-one years of age. No traditional elders were taken into the officeholding levels of Nyirenda's Watchtower Church. Thus the movement provided opportunities for ambitious young men with education or experience in the world outside the villages.[114] Perhaps the struggle in Mwaluka included both a conflict between the two possible inheritors of the headmanship and a series of moves against the old man. At the trial, the judge was already calling Matanga by his uncle's name, "Mwaluka Junior," and old Mwaluka complained of having been bewitched. Either of the cousins would have had a motive for bewitching him if they were ambitious to succeed. When asked directly, however, Mwaluka denied that he suspected Matanga, although, probably, his earlier effort to banish Matanga had been based on such a suspicion. If so, he had a reason to try to shift the blame onto Matanga by sending him to summon Nyirenda and then by allowing Matanga to lie about the killing.

Possibly the administration was deliberately favoring younger men like Matanga as more efficient and more progressive than their elders. Brown, we recall, was treating Matanga as the headman. If so, administrative policy would have amplified preexisting intergenerational cleavages. And Nyirenda's Watchtower revival would then represent an effective new synthesis. In its organization it deliberately favored the young, and yet its ideological platform contained elements attractive to elders as well. Everyone could cherish the idea of a new world of plenty, cleansed of all forms of interpersonal strife. The stage was set for the young to usurp part of the elders' power and remove certain elders without displacing them altogether and without overturning the principle of eldership.[115]

Young people were deliberately favored in the operation of the baptisms. When a young woman called Mwelwa floated, Tomo stated his opinion that she was "too young" to be a witch,[116] whereupon she suggested that she had been "made so by touching." "Perhaps," she added, "my aunt put medicine in my porridge." The aunt floated and was later killed. Another youth accused his uncle. A woman left her husband and married the sixteen-year-old preacher Kalunga, without seeking her parents' permission. Kalunga himself was instrumental in the deaths of both his parents. Many young women also joined, leaving husbands or parents. One, according to her husband, was baptized and immediately took to sleeping on her mat. The man went immediately to the *boma* to have their names stricken from the marriage register. "I did not want a Watchtower wife in my house."[117]

Those who joined Nyirenda's band enjoyed extraordinary freedom from the normal drudgery of village life. But membership in the group carried heavy demands of its own. Tomo Nyirenda had to maintain stern discipline to prevent lapses by individual converts. There was no going back. When one asked permission to return home and attend to farm work, Nyirenda threatened him with the sinister formula, "I am the roof and the aeroplane." He then turned and reiterated to those who still felt tied to their homes the importance of their task. "My foot is my house," he said, in a classic expression of the evangelist's total commitment.[118] Not all his followers shared his commitment in its totality, but they continued for less exalted reasons. Reluctant to go to Zaire, one member of the group was told:

> No it is not a matter of refusing. You are thinking about your own business but what about our own. We have left our kaffir corn and millet and we have not built any barns for it and we have come, we did not refuse. If you refuse you will die.[119]

Two young men claimed at their trial that they "were against Tomo, but that Tomo had preachers," that is, the inner circle of helpers who always traveled with him and acted as "enforcers."[120] According to Mulakasa, Tomo would say, "I have my preachers, and if you do not do as I have told you, I will tell them to take you and kill you like a witch."[121] That is, he threatened to arrange their demise in such a way that no one would be in either a moral or a physical position to protect them. Once a person was indicted as a witch, colleagues, relatives, and friends would be powerless to intervene. "For that reason," Mulakasa continued, "we were afraid when he told us to follow him. That is all I have to say. We were foolish to be afraid of him." One wonders.

A youth from Chungwe village testified that the people were

singing hymns all night when Shaiwila's messenger arrived and arrested Tomo. People believed, he said, that Tomo was being taken to the *boma*.[122] But instead of passing out of their lives, he returned a week later and baptized the whole village, pointing out three witches. He left again, but suddenly reappeared a third time and killed those who had been previously named, including Kalunga's mother and father, who had a longstanding quarrel with Shaiwila. Since the headman had already been eased into acquiescence, the spotlight turned upon their only other living relative, their son. Only he was likely to make a case about it at the *boma*. Nyirenda asked Kalunga if he thought they should be killed. Kalunga said *Yes*, but it is hard to imagine that he could safely have given any other reply. Witnesses said that Kalunga "stood trembling with fear" while the other villagers "sang and sang."[123] Kalunga later became one of the inner circle of men with direct responsibility for carrying out the drownings.[124] Part of his compensation was permission to marry, although he was only sixteen.

Makwati, a man who tried to defend a relative, was killed "like a witch" to prevent his reporting Nyirenda's activities to the *boma*. Makwati protested when his cousin was accused of causing the ailment that had preceded the death of a preacher. Makwati declared that Nyirenda was "bad" and that he would report to the chief and to the *boma*. Shaiwila assured Makwati that he would take care of the matter. He did: He ordered Makwati baptized and killed. But Makwati refused to answer Tomo's summons to be baptized. Instead he fumed about the village. Unfortunately, he chose to make an angry visit to Tomo's headquarters just when the preachers returned.[125] After a fierce fight, they overpowered him. One later said, recounting his duties, "If a witch was strong, we helped to hold him."[126] An elder testified that he heard the fight, but "I did not go with this party as it was not my work. I had to write down the names of the baptized."[127] As usual, the next morning all the villagers were invited to go to the stream and behold the body of the witch.

Since Makwati's wife provided the important information, ordinary villagers were probably aware of the real reasons for Makwati's removal, even though they may have agreed entirely with the principle of witch killing. Thus they sometimes co-operated out of fear, even if they also had positive motives. Negative and positive reasons for support amplified one another. Certainly there were powerful reasons for not going to the *boma*. As one said, "Tomo killed people, while the Boma only makes us pay taxes. We were more afraid of Tomo than of the Boma. We were foolish to be afraid of him."[128] But the *boma* was distant; a person had to live daily in the village. Anyone who blocked Nyirenda's popular activities as a healer and the preacher of an attractive millennium for mere personal reasons would find himself in difficulty.

By helping Nyirenda try to cover up his crimes and escape, the people were obviously helping themselves. Tolani, a headman who stored Nyirenda's belongings in a house at his village, denied doing so when confronted by the *kapasu* Ntembelwa. Ntembelwa said, "I used pressure and [Tolani] finally admitted that he had been storing Tomo's things for him and had been sending food."[129] Tolani even offered Ntembelwa five shillings not to report this to the *boma*. "None of the headmen would help me at all to find Tomo, and tried, till they saw it was too late, to put every obstacle in my way." Thus Matanga exhumed and reburied the body of Shawomba; after his arrest, Mwaluka sent him silence money in jail.[130]

WATCHTOWER ideas did not necessarily subvert customary order. An artful chief might deploy them to increase his power and forge new unity in the villages, for good or ill. Watchtower preaching advocated peace and neighborliness and new reconciliation among the people, despite its paradoxically violent means. But although killing was a paradoxical means in the midst of Christian revival, it was not illogical, given indigenous habits of thought; and in the history of the Church, of course, it was not unprecedented. Although people explicitly joined the revival to gain plenty and peace, the line of causation did not go directly from aspiration to reform, or from thought to reality. The mechanisms that moved the villagers toward new unity did not derive from the content of the revival but from its organization. New consensus came about because key individuals activated a series of existing ties, while imbuing them with new strength drawn from shared guilt and hopes. Specific political links steadily tightened: those between the chief and his headmen, between headmen and their subjects, between Nyirenda and his followers, and, finally, those manifold and complex links that connected villagers and kinsmen. With shared beliefs and fears as a starting point, all these relationships could be focused effectively to produce the result—but only by daring and determined leaders in available institutions.

The evidence remains difficult to interpret. It consists of court testimony designed by witnesses so far as was feasible (one imagines) to conceal facts, to shift responsibility, and perhaps to take advan-

tage of the examiners' naiveté about witchcraft and the inner workings of the villages. Hence, any interpretation must be tentative.
But two points can be made with assurance. First, any explanation
based upon generalized hysteria or fear of witchcraft must be rejected. Under the canopy of witch fears and witch beliefs, the participants behaved in intelligible ways and had complex motives.
Nor did Tomo and Shaiwila simply join forces to exploit the fears
of superstitious villagers. Many had their own aims in joining the
movement, and ordinary villagers pushed hesitant superiors forward. J. E. Stephenson reported with dismay that even uninvolved
villagers expressed sympathy for those implicated in Mwana Lesa's
crimes. He feared not hysteria but the considered opinions of the
upright and the law-abiding.

> I am certain that EVERY native in the countryside regards us
> white people as merciless tyrants determined to protect
> witches, who, as you will know, are regarded by natives as
> beings so unspeakably vile as to merit slaying without com-
> punction.[131]

Second, Stephenson was partly right when he called the Mwana
Lesa episode "as near an approach to open rebellion as will be
without the actuality occurring."[132] If murders that were common
knowledge, seditious utterance, and recurrent and massive violation of the Witchcraft Ordinance could be kept secret, so could
conspiracy against the aliens. He could see the handwriting on the
wall. The central drama of indirect rule was to keep customary
rulers strong enough to control their people and yet weak enough
to be controlled by the regime. Tomo Nyirenda's campaign tipped
this balance. By enhancing Shaiwila's power and fostering new unity
in the villages, it shut the door of the Western Lalas in the regime's
face. For this reason, officials took an added precaution after all
the sentences had been executed. The new Shaiwila was made to
rebuild his village close to the *boma*, lest he, too, be tempted to go
his own way.[133]

The outbreaks of 1918 and 1925 demonstrate that indirect rule
was doubly articulated, dependent upon the maintenance of effective links between officials and customary rulers and between
customary rulers and ordinary villagers. In the earlier case, the ties
of the first articulation were broken, in the later one, those of the
second. Either way, the colonial political machinery ceased to function.

Part 3

ELEMENTARY NORMS
OF THE RELIGIOUS LIFE

❖

THE MWANA LESA EPISODE
occurred amid a large Watch-
tower revival during the mid-1920s. During the Great Depression
and again during World War II, Zambia's rulers confronted new
outbursts. Each time, preachers accented their message—and hearers listened to it—in light of contemporary developments. In 1922–
1924, the colony experienced an economic downturn that threw
many out of work. The man who faced the obligation to pay taxes,
without means of earning the cash to do so, listened intently to
news of things to come. He listened more intently still, perhaps,
when the Colonial Office took over from the BSAC in Zambia.

As the transfer went forward, settlers mobilized to press for closer
union with the white-dominated territories to the south. (This agitation finally bore fruit in 1953, when Malawi, Zambia, and Zimbabwe were joined in the Federation of Rhodesia and Nyasaland.)
In 1924, the Colonial Office resisted the mobilization and made
the resounding promise that African interests would be kept "paramount." It immediately set a land policy that resounded otherwise.
To make the colony "pay for itself," the new regime promoted
white immigration and land sales. Land surveys followed by white
settlement created dramatic unrest in some areas. In parts of the
Eastern Province, a land squeeze resulted almost immediately.[1] As
protection of some Africans' access to some land, inalienable re-
serves came into being. Those who had seen Zimbabwe and South
Africa knew well what this portended. Thus, the mid-1920s saw
widespread ferment about what ought or ought not to come next.
Blacks and whites differed.

In 1924, blacks witnessed something positively new. The Phelps-

Stokes Fund dispatched from America a commission that generated grand excitement. Not only did it investigate African education, the object of intense popular interest, but it also asked Africans their opinions; and not only did it tour rural areas as well as towns, but it also toured with an African member, the Ghanaian educator James Kwegyir Aggrey. Aggrey's speeches made a deep impression. Old people interviewed in Malawi some forty years later could still recite what they heard.[2] As young people, they must have spread the good news of the Americans' commission far and wide, to others who spread it in turn. At about the same time, the Watchtower exiles of 1919 began returning on foot to their homes. Some were still bursting with the good news of their American revelation. Preachers and hearers savored the prospect of a transatlantic alliance to come.

Meanwhile, the early 1920s had given the regime a bright new Monday morning. As the turmoil of the war and the scare of 1919 receded, Monday's brightness exposed the previous Friday's mistakes. Men drew lessons about what ought to have been done against Watchtower excitement and about what ought to be done in the future. They concluded that evidently "harmless" preaching had combined with something else to produce the scare of 1919. From this conclusion followed a practical policy of divide and rule: remove the harmful elements; tolerate the rest. According to Justice P. J. Macdonnell, religion "per se" was not only tolerable but was guaranteed the protection of the law. The rest stood exposed to the law's rigor:

> I start, as one must, with the proposition that a religious movement or a religious sect or church is something to which *per se* the law is indifferent. . . . A uniform course of jurisprudence for at least 100 years has deprived Courts of Justice of any excuse for expressing opinions on the merits or demerits of religious bodies. It is a region of human activity into which Courts of Justice do not enter. But these courts have their definite sphere, positive law. Once show that a prominent leader of [a] religion has broken that positive law, and the Courts will interfere, not because he belongs to some particular religious body but because he has broken the law.[3]

Over the first few years of the decade, as the regime continued its repacification of the northern districts, the distinction between harmful elements and the rest seemed easier to make than it presently would. In 1924, the repeated success of Watchtower preachers in bringing together new collectivities suddenly exhibited so much more than religion per se that officials often doubted that they preached religion at all. The "uniform course of jurisprudence" to which Macdonnell referred presumed that religion per se was inherently quiet and quieting, that it was indeed the opium of the people. A different result pointed to a different cause. Thus, when faced with revivals that led to disorder, officials inclined to the belief that Watchtower preachers hid their real motives behind religious language. At no time did they entertain the idea that their presumption about the tone of religion in social life might not be founded upon universal truth about the nature of religion. They forgot Britain's own constitutional past and the untamed British ancestors of religion per se who had flourished in a not-yet-secular society.

Born into a secular society, Macdonnell and his colleagues took for granted that religion inhabits a definite "region of human activity." To their minds, definite norms governed religious behavior, which in turn governed and were governed by private matters of conscience and belief: mere conscience and mere belief. But in the African real world, these inward matters kept leaving the quiet region of the mind. Conscience did not know its place. Belief moved about as loud voices preaching without permission, or as congregations gibbering in tongues one moment and attacking some colonial bulwark the next. (Of course, it moved about also when missionaries taught their hearers to render unto Caesar the tax he demanded or when, in 1914 and 1940, they joined the patriotic din. But, in the colonial context, not to do these things was departure from religion per se.) The constitutional ideas that guaranteed freedom of religion also set standards as to its social effect.

L. V. Phillips, an agent of the Watchtower Bible and Tract Society, studied this freedom and drew his own lessons about the norms of religious life. No, he said in 1944, when it was proposed to hold a Watchtower assembly on the Copperbelt. An assembly would inevitably run the society afoul of colonial law and order. The first difficulty was the prospect of an enthusiastic crowd. The crowd's own momentum would carry it outside the realm of proper religious behavior:

> We will have swarms of Africans, thousands in fact, all turning up, women, babies, etc. . . . If this large convention be held up there it is my honest conviction that more harm will be done than good—Mwanalesa, the foolish Isoka people who shouted

"Jehovah" on the mountainside until the military had to come
and shift them and compel them to plant crops . . . all had wild
elements in them because an impossible proposition is huge
crowds.[4]

The second difficulty was the ease with which African preachers
stepped beyond religion per se. Even Manasse Nkhoma, one of the
society's best-trained preachers at the time, could not be counted
upon to stand to attention in religion's proper sphere.

> I still recall, with a shudder, an occasion not two years old
> when Manasse, of all people, stood up on the platform, where
> I was sitting, and told friends not to do the farm work and . . .
> it was as much as I could do to stop him. Outside and after-
> wards it was easy enough to deal with him . . . and suspend
> him until he had cooled down and learned reason.

In order to protect the society, Phillips and his colleagues kept
struggling to push their African colleagues back into the region
that colonial norms defined.

The word *norm* has two meanings. A norm may be an explicit
rule, or it may be an underlying pattern. When we discover a
pattern, we discover what behavior actually is, whereas a rule only
states what behavior *ought* to be. Sometimes, as in the theory of
Max Weber, the discovery of a pattern allows us to infer a rule;
individuals following a rule produce a corresponding pattern.
Hence, for example, if a population is generally law-abiding, it is
because most individuals orient their behavior to a system of rules,
a "normative order." Even the thief does, insofar as he proceeds
by stealth and does all he can afterward to conceal the deed.[5] But
sometimes rules and patterns cannot be related in this way. Colonial
societies brought together more than one set of rules and patterns;
different normative orders were in force in all aspects of life, including religion.

Chapter 6 investigates the formal and informal rules the regime
in Zambia attempted to apply to religious life. Chapter 7 investigates the pattern of religious life that permanently challenged these
rules. I will show, in accordance with Emile Durkheim's famous
discovery in *The Elementary Forms of the Religious Life*, that religion
in colonized Zambia did not only symbolize society; it was society.
And, in the peculiar circumstances of indirect rule, religion was
also polity. While examining the various ways in which rule and
pattern failed to correspond, I will show the truth of Durkheim's

less well-remembered discovery—that religious ideas represent for individuals not only society itself but also "the obscure but intimate relations which they have with it."[6] Religious ideas, and ideas about religion, defined a battleground among colonial officials, customary rulers, and Watchtower converts within the society and polity they shared.

6

COERCIVE TOLERANCE: ADMINISTRATIVE STRATEGY TO CONTAIN MILITANT REVIVAL

> If a Watchtower preacher says that only those who
> enter the sect will be saved, that the end of the world
> is coming shortly . . . what have Courts of Justice to
> do with such sayings?
>
> JUSTICE P. J. MACDONNELL

THE BRITISH EFFORT TO control the social effect of religion posed theoretical as well as practical difficulties. Scant resources posed the practical difficulty, which remained whether the religious target was traditional African or Christian. Law posed the theoretical difficulty, which differed between traditional and Christian targets. In the first case, the formula "repugnant to British law and natural justice" rather precisely guided the civilizer's onslaught against practices considered intolerable. In the second, it offered vaguer guidance. Bible-quoting preachers and their hearers might be loud and heretical in one place, arrogant and rude in another, simply inconvenient elsewhere; but the principle of religious toleration hovered over all attempts to contain them. Their repeated cry—Religious persecution!—brought the hovering principle down to earth. When Watchtowerites stood against religious persecution, they were not alone. For although the law in colonized Zambia served rule, it did not always bow low in this service. Its practitioners stood committed to higher ideals of legality, among these the principle of religious toleration, whose roots go deep in British constitutional tradition—and which in fact grew up with it. Thus, officials who sought to restrict Christians faced two problems: how to do so effectively and how to do so lawfully. In reviewing the sentences of 1919, Justice P. J. Macdonnell showed the way.[1]

USING THE LAW TO REPRESS THE WATCHTOWER

Macdonnell tackled the theoretical issue by defining the lawful use of the Native Schools Ordinance (Proclamation 8/1916). In the face of *chongo* and mounting defiance, Draper and Dewhurst had issued blanket orders that Watchtower preaching must stop, and that anyone who disobeyed the order was subject to arrest. But, according to the judge, Proclamation 8 was a "weapon in reserve" and, as such, not to be used promiscuously. To invoke it as the basis of an order, an official had to have "clear evidence" of sedition or subversive tendencies. But in the hands of those two men, it had become an instrument of "purely religious persecution," which was unlawful. Accordingly, Macdonnell upheld only the convictions in which specific crimes had been proved. In those cases, punishments were severe: a combination of corporal punishment, hard labor, and exile. (For his part in the "hut of defiance" episode, Shadrach Sinkala received twenty-four lashes, three- and-one-half years' hard labor, and deportation until 1924.)[2] But although fully aware of the likely repercussions, Macdonnell quashed all sentences in which the only crime proved had been disobedience to orders made under Proclamation 8. Macdonnell was convinced that formal legality could be preserved without damage to practical policy. He criticized Dewhurst and Draper as much for their "poverty of resource" in collecting evidence as for their indiscriminate use of the Native Schools Ordinance. "Resource" meant the use of sharp legal instruments instead of blunt ones; it meant a few harsh penalties to deter, instead of many minor ones to annoy.

Greater resource also meant the careful collection of evidence. It included such practices as mail censorship (always on the authority of proper warrants),[3] infiltration, and personal surveillance. "Spying and opening letters," the judge wrote,

> are not pretty things as everyone knows, but everyone also knows that most of the criminal cases tried with all the pomp of justice and with scrupulous attention to open and fair dealing have these things as the basis on which they are built. Out of sight they may be, but without them the criminal would not have been brought to trial.

Furthermore, liberty of individual conscience was not inconsistent with administrative regulation of religious groups. Macdonnell went on to suggest amendments to Proclamation 8 that would bring both preachers and teachers into its purview.

If it be objected that the law does not affect to deal with religious issues, but with educational ones, that no native who is
not authorized by some one or other recognized European
missionary—they could be specified in a schedule—shall *preach
or teach* unless he be in possession of an annual permit from
the D.C.[4]

Macdonnell was recommending what we can call selective toleration: Preachers and teachers chosen by a European supervisor
would be allowed to work, provided they kept within the limits of
what the administration recognized to be "religious" preaching or
teaching. Other proposals specified what adequate European supervision would mean. The amended Native Schools Ordinance
(1921) made it an offense to preach or teach without certification
by a "recognised European missionary."[5]

Macdonnell's ideas were applied over the next few years as part
of the general drive to stamp out what remained of the Watchtower
in the northern districts. Hanoc Sindano and Leviticus Kanjele,
who escaped imprisonment, were barred from preaching because
they did not belong to a recognized denomination.[6] Robert Simpelwe, an African detective, infiltrated Sindano's clandestine congregation in Tanzania.[7] Police kept the known Watchtower leaders
under surveillance until 1923. Magistrates issued warrants to permit the inspection of letters to and from exiled Watchtower adherents. DOs and police made inquiries into the personal histories
of individual adherents.[8] In addition to extending the regime's
resources of detection, all these measures would solve evidential
problems in court, should further legal repression seem indicated.

In keeping with Macdonnell's emphasis upon specific charges, a
variety of other provisions allowed for "technical arrests." Use of
the Native Tax Ordinance, the Vagrancy Act, the Alien Natives
Ordinance, and the Native Labour Ordinance made it possible to
sidestep altogether any reference to religion. (Tomo Nyirenda, we
recall, was imprisoned early in 1925 for failing to register as an
"alien native.") Dozens of preachers were jailed for tax default,
especially in times of widespread unemployment, as in 1922–1924
and 1930–1935. The Labour Ordinance permitted numerous prosecutions in 1924, when a large-scale exodus of baptized workers
threatened colonial enterprises. All these provisions had minor
sentences: for example, tax default carried a maximum sentence
of one month's imprisonment; failure to register, two months.

The law against sedition carried harsher penalties, but sedition was harder to prove. As time went on, however, sedition received more imaginative legal definition. One magistrate argued that in an "industrial community" a call to leave the work place (even for baptism) was sedition.[9] But redefining terms offered no panacea. The preachers had to be reckoned with. If an arresting DC shouted "Sedition!" and a preacher shouted back "Religion!" as he was taken away, it mattered what village bystanders thought. Thus, whatever their legal aspects, trials for sedition had political drawbacks. The governor in Malawi recommended toleration. But if it was necessary to arrest a preacher, then the grounds must be thoroughly explained. Moreover, if seditious elements occurred in a sermon, both the preacher and his hearers must be carefully told what they were. Again, if a man was arrested not for preaching but for tax default, this, too, should be made clear. Above all, if sedition was charged, the case must be airtight.[10] Quashed sentences were dangerous.

By contrast, technical prosecutions were easy to carry out, and for this reason were applied wholesale, but their ease proved illusory. Since only a small proportion of the known offenders could be arrested, no one was fooled as to the real intention of these prosecutions. For example, in 1924 the preacher Thomas exploited his arrest for tax default effectively; his audience was fully aware that in a year of widespread unemployment, many men were unable to pay their taxes on time.[11] Soon preachers were using their technical arrests so skillfully that officials were instructed to avoid them. As one native commissioner said, such arrests "only serve[d] to advertise the movement."[12] As of old, the blood of the martyrs was the seed of the Church. When the legal approach to controlling the Watchtower met this obstacle, practical politics reinforced the liberal principle of toleration.

Meanwhile, perceptions had also begun to change. Four years after the episode in the northern districts, the administrator was able to tell the high commissioner for South Africa that although the sect was still active, its "more objectionable features" had disappeared.[13] "It was the attempt inherent in these doctrines to subvert all authority which necessitated government action." The administration could now note with satisfaction the "changed demeanor" of the returnees. But since Watchtower activists did not stop their preaching altogether, the amended version of the Schools Ordinance soon engendered new embarrassment: The now-quiet returnees were still lawbreakers by the ordinance's definition. Since there was no way for men like Sindano and Kanjele to comply, they repeatedly broke this law but were careful to break no other. Once

again the administration found itself in the position of punishing
people for religion alone. When administrators insisted that they
had nothing against religion per se, they did not specify that they
meant mission religion only. The ordinance must have been galling
to men like Sindano, who aspired to recognition as religious leaders
in their own right. It presently gave rise to a new form of crimi-
nality, the use of certificates forged by an African printer in Zimbabwe and transmitted up the labor routes.[14]

H. A. Sylvester, a perceptive native commissioner, insisted that
the ordinance was unenforceable and therefore dangerous. The
proliferation of unenforceable laws led to a

> lessening of responsibility [on the part of officials], thereby
> allowing the natives to see that the government is not all pow-
> erful. . . . The native is altering. . . . [He is now] realizing that
> a white man is not to be feared simply because he is white.[15]

The proportion of arrests under the Native Schools Ordinance (and
other laws, such as those regulating the sale of African beer, timber
cutting, breach of contract, and shooting game) to violations was
"infinitesimal," Sylvester said, and inconsistent enforcement would
only erode the regime's prestige.

> These may be valuable laws for use under certain circum-
> stances, but I doubt if a native would realize the distinction
> between a law for breaking which he will be punished and a
> law for breaking which he may be punished if he is unfortunate
> enough to commit the crime under certain circumstances the
> nature of which he has no chance of knowing.

Partly to avoid the obvious injustices and partly because it could
not stamp out the renewed revival, the regime moved to liberalize
the Native Schools Ordinance. Proclamation 28 of 1924 gave local
officials authority to certify local preachers, whether or not they
were members of a recognized denomination.[16] The reasoning:
Preachers anxious to avoid prosecution for noncertification would
flock to their local magistrates to receive certification. Thereafter,
they would comport themselves in such a way as to keep it. Justice
Macdonnell hailed this new move as likely to achieve effective control of the movement, on the principle, he said, of "*divide et im-
pera.*"[17] He was to be disappointed. Undoubtedly, many adherents
realized that an administration that could certify them might also
refuse to do so. Why, therefore, present themselves to an official

when it was still possible to work for long periods in outlying areas without discovery?

Others were unimpressed by the law itself and would not condescend to apply to a worldly ruler for the right to preach the Word of God. So argued J. B. Manda and two colleagues at their trial.[18] Asked his authority for preaching, Manda contemptuously said, "I refer the Court to 1 Cor. 1:19–20." Asked to quote it for the court, he did so:

> For it is written, I will destroy the wisdom of the wise, and will bring to nothing the understanding of the prudent. Where is the wise? where is the scribe? where is the disputer of this world? hath not God made foolish the wisdom of this world?

His colleague, Isaac Nyasulo, declared that his right to preach came from the Spirit, as described in Isaiah 61:1:

> The spirit of the Lord is upon me because the Lord has approved me to preach good tidings unto the meek . . . to bind up the broken hearted, to proclaim liberty to the captives, and the opening of the prison to them that are bound.

The defense went on in this vein. Reminding Manda that certification was required to form a church, the judge asked where the headquarters of the Watchtower were. After replying that he did not know, Manda added, "John the Baptist had no church."

Another defendant recanted with malice aforethought. David Gareta easily obtained his release in 1923 by apologizing for his activities and promising to mend his ways. Rearrested for illegal preaching the following year, he coolly told Native Commissioner Cholmeley that he had recanted earlier simply "to avoid trouble."[19] When Cholmeley taunted him with the charge of cowardice, Gareta shot right back that Peter (who denied Jesus) went on to become the rock of the Church. "Such are our Watchtower logicians," Cholmeley sighed. A different sort than David Gareta, Shadrach Sinkala accepted his imprisonment at Mazabuka for the same offense with resignation and without agreeing to obey the law in the future.[20] The "honest fanatic" Justice Macdonnell confronted in 1919, Shadrach went in and out of the regime's fiery furnaces more than once.

The second phase of Shadrach Sinkala's round trips between pulpit and jail occurred as the deportees of 1919 were being permitted to return to their homes. The action of the mid-1920s spread along well-traveled routes: Livingstone, Pemba, Mazabuka, Broken

Hill, Mkushi, Serenje, and from there either northward or eastward. Shadrach elected to stay in Mazabuka, but he taught converts later arrested as far away as Fort Jameson District in the Eastern Province. As the veterans made new converts and the converts in turn taught others, they wired the colony in preparations for the again-imminent Watchtower Millennium. Revival broke out in new areas—now upon a settler farm, now in a remote hamlet. It spread like an electrical fire.

The content of the revival was the same as it had been in other episodes, except that the American myth received more elaboration than before. The African detective Thomas Luenje reported J. B. Manda's preaching thus:

> America will be the chief of this country with the black people: the whites will go back to England. Let us return to Nyasaland to teach our brothers. . . . We must not stop, we of the Watchtower Church. . . . Though we have no white leader, only black. . . . These white people—the country is not theirs; when America comes you will see that America and we will own the country.[21]

One local messenger, Chikombi, reported on these preachings in detail. His report was substantiated by villagers. Chikombi convinced the native commissioner (NC) that the religious teaching was a cover for seditious intentions. "If we had a few more Chikombi's, . . . we should discover that the teachings of these pseudo-evangelists regarding adultery, wife-beating and the like are inextricably mixed up with subversive or at least mischievous propaganda."[22]

The effect of the new revival was not the same everywhere. In general, Fife/Abercorn, the scene of extensive repression after 1919, was inhospitable to the new prophesying. Some parents went directly to officials to demand protection for their children from the renewed danger. Other people anxious to avoid trouble made overtures to the local missions. The secretary for native affairs, R.S.B. Tagart, could even report that some Watchtower converts were backsliding: "From Abercorn district the news is that many perverts to Watchtower are anxious to return to the missions to which they formerly belonged."[23] Elsewhere the brush was dry and ready for a spark. In East Luangwa District, "only the more reliable chiefs managed to stand up and prosecute preachers for insolence"; only some chiefs "used their common law right to turn nuisances out of the villages."[24] It was soon obvious that heavy-handed but ineffectual repression might further the extension of a rapidly expanding movement and drive its more resourceful elements underground.

In these circumstances, Justice Macdonnell's policy of selective toleration evolved into "compassionate toleration." Tagart told the beleaguered NC at Serenje that "an attitude of compassionate toleration does more to bring the mischievous vanity of those self-styled pastors who pose as prophets and saviors of souls into contempt among natives than direct orders forbidding them to preach."[25] A circular duly went out from the secretary's office instructing local officials to "give rope" to the preachers. They should only make arrests if they had "definite proof of seditious propaganda likely to lead to civil disturbance or defiance of constituted authority." Otherwise, it was better to ridicule the preachers publicly than to prosecute them, to "humor" them as persons "mentally deficient."[26] Ordinary villagers would lose interest in the movement, the secretary was sure, as soon as the preachers' extravagant prophecies failed. When Malcolm Moffat, of the Free Church mission at Chitambo, signaled his alarm, Tagart told him that this policy was "the wisest line to take at present and those, like yourself, with a long and intimate experience of local natives, would know best how to 'point the moral and adorn the tale' among the people around you."[27] He reassured Moffat that the local NC would be able to handle "any contingency" and expressed pleasure that "mission and Boma [were] alive to the necessity of combating the movement and [were] working in cordial cooperation to this end."

When, on the same day, Tagart wrote to Moffat's not-very-distant neighbor, the NC at Serenje, the picture was somewhat different. The NC had written to complain that his paltry bush prison was overloaded with Watchtowerites inside and out. Worse, he found it impossible to enforce a rule prohibiting intercourse with prisoners. Supporters of those arrested assembled outside the prison, singing hymns, shouting encouragement to the prisoners, and sweeping the prison yards as if they themselves were inmates. Fearing trouble, the NC was requesting reinforcements. Tagart reiterated the new policy of compassionate toleration—the NC "shouldn't miss an opportunity to ridicule the preachers' pretensions . . . to powers of prophecy and promises of salvation"[28]—declaring it to be superior to a policy of arrest and direct repression. But, in case the worried official had not grasped the real reason for toleration, Tagart went on to spell it out. The NC was not to attempt the removal of Watchtower prisoners to the stronger jail at Broken

Hill "in view of the possibility of their inciting others to resist authority and possibly to aid in their escape." Tagart spoke vaguely of "trying to find additional warders" for Serenje jail, but it was "at present inadvisable" to transfer the prisoners; direct confrontation had to be avoided unless it was absolutely certain that the regime would prevail.

If Tagart's compassionate toleration did not appeal to whites on the line-of-rail, it appealed still less to those in remoter areas. The DC Stokes, in Luapula Province, wrote that revival had broken out there, and that it seemed to be taking its old form: baptism without preparation; few restrictions after baptism other than a prohibition against adultery; the usual attacks upon mission methods; no evident sedition. When Stokes discovered that the preachers were being wined and dined in many villages, he "thought that this was getting a bit thick and that the whole thing might develop into a religious revival if left alone." He summoned the headmen and warned them against giving the preachers any support and then sent out messengers to "warn" the villagers. Compassionate toleration might be practical along the line-of-rail, Stokes observed, but upcountry, where villages were visited infrequently, a bad situation might be well advanced before Europeans knew anything about it.

> It is not "sedition" that I am afraid of with these people. What I do fear is that given enough rope they will work themselves and the people into such a state of religious frenzy by continuous praying, shouting, drumming, sleepless nights, etc., that all [preachers and converts] will get out of hand and then only harsh methods will bring them back to their senses.[29]

Thus, to protect the villagers from themselves—not, like the panicky settlers, to protect himself—Stokes called for strict repression, hence for reinforcements. Unfortunately, that solution was impractical. To have resorted to strong police action then not only would have been costly in itself, but it would have set a costly precedent. Thenceforth, anything short of it would not suffice as "repression." This the regime's slender resources would not permit. Stokes got no reinforcements.

Settlers' discomfiture was understandable. Even where they were not physically endangered, Watchtower revival frequently attacked their economic interests. One planter fumed that a certain "Good Heart" was preaching workers away from their jobs, and that the Labour Ordinance was not protecting him. Under its provisions, he was required to file formal complaints, incident by incident.

Well, in planting season who had time for this? A general sweep was overdue.[30] J. E. Stephenson complained not that laborers deserted him, but that he found it impossible to recruit any new ones.[31] His apprehension grew when he learned from loyal workers that Watchtower adherents had been discussing the division of his property after the Millennium. Thus, what people knew increased their apprehension about what they did not know. I imagine that settlers and their wives busied themselves chasing down rumors—and that their anxious inquiries must have led informants to "adorn the tale." Some settlers lost even their trusted employees to the movement, although not all left their jobs. A farmer near Broken Hill reported in February 1925 that the prime movers turned out to be his "most intelligent boys who both speak and write English." Their decision to stay may well have been as disconcerting as the decision of others to depart, for no one knew what was next. The movement was "of a Religious Political character," the farmer declared, "and amongst the subjects discussed is a Native government at an early date."[32]

As if it were not serious enough that trusted clerks and foremen were being baptized, chiefs and headmen joined their better-educated countrymen in the rush to Watchtower baptism. One old headman was summoned by the preacher Mutale and asked if he had destroyed his spirit hut. When questioned by an official, the old man "seemed highly amused that he should be expected to irritate his ancestral spirits at the insistence of a Muwemba [Bemba] houseboy."[33] But he nevertheless had accepted baptism like everyone else. Chief Mukanya stood firm in opposition, but he turned out to be unable to control his headmen, who went all out in the general excitement. As one of them put it, "We see baptism here today." Chief Kabwata explained his baptism, perhaps disingenuously, by saying that he had merely wanted to be "in fashion."[34] The real reason for the enormous success of the call to baptism was the same here as elsewhere. When Chief Chanuka admitted that he would have been called a wizard if he had not consented to be baptized with his people, Cadet Sandford drew the correct inference: "Chief Chanuka's comment emphasizes the point that anyone refusing to be baptized ran the risk of being accused of witchcraft or of adultery the next time anyone died or any woman came to childbirth."[35] (The two preachers arrested at Chanuka's each had sacks of charms in his possession.) Even in villages near Lusaka, the capital, headmen and chiefs were converted "together with all their friends."

Officials reassured one another in varying ways. Cadet Sandford converted settlers' fantasies about bloodthirsty nighttime rituals into commonplaces about the African mind.

> I can see nothing very strange in the wholesale success of the movement. It is undoubtedly a very strong religious revival, the tenets of which appeal more nearly than any other to the comfort and happiness of a very superstitious people.

J. Moffat Thompson, who followed R.S.B. Tagart as secretary for native affairs, thought that people were baptized as a kind of "free insurance." Besides, the movement would never amount to much in political terms:

> No doubt the more enlightened leaders wish to start an independent African National Church, but I can see no great harm in that, it need not be a political movement and owing to the lack of cooperation among the various tribes, I doubt if it could ever develop into one.[36]

According to another observer, the movement's own tactics would hasten its downfall. In view of the tactics—destroying spirit shrines, baptizing wives first in order to pressure husbands—the movement would surely fall into disrepute. "The natives resent any interference with their superstitions and their women; the teachers soon will not be tolerated in the villages."[37]

Still more encouraging, the preachers seemed to be learning the conditions under which they would be tolerated by the government. After mid-1924, there were no more calls to leave places of work en masse,[38] and "seditious" utterance of other kinds became infrequent. The revival seemed to be turning into what officials took to be a purely religious revival. As such it would founder on its false predictions and its aggressive tactics. Opposition would only create martyrs, Sandford said, and martyrs might turn to "more direct politics." Official policy ran the same gamut it would run again with the advent of the Bamucapi, and for the same reason: scant resources, the thinness of the "thin white line."

Appearances mattered in both cases. As hired hands and servants, Watchtower adherents were well placed to look upon the settlers' initial panic and take heart. Unable to remove the source of the panic, officials attempted the next best thing, urging the white community to get hold of itself. J. W. Hinds, the magistrate at Lusaka, made precisely this point. By raising a furor over preaching and baptizing, whites were making themselves ridiculous in the eyes of the Africans all around them.

> The Dutch raise yearly the native rising bogey. . . . They talk a lot. In this way rumors are spread, fancies become fact, a refractory farm hand a rebel, and so on *ad lib*. Last year we had an example in the native with the gold teeth scare who thoroughly scared the whole subdistrict. All this I know is extremely childish and silly, but the worst of it is that the natives know the white men's weakness and undoubtedly laugh at us.[39]

To resort to force, as many demanded, would have amounted to taking seriously a superstitious movement that the regime hoped to crush with ridicule. The regime would show itself to be lacking in a sense of humor and proportion, as one official said later.[40] Despite their sense of the proper proportion of things (or perhaps because of it), officials often went to great lengths not to reveal the depth of their worry, for sometimes the redoubted African observers were uncomfortably near at hand. When, in the aftermath of the 1919 events, the DC at Fife was struggling over the translation of some Watchtower documents composed in Namwanga, the secretary for native affairs advised him not to seek the aid of an African clerk. Even a trusted employee, as Donald Siwale (later the Reverend Donald Siwale) was at Fife, should only be asked the meanings of "isolated words"; the whole should be pieced together in private.[41]

Although Zambia's colonial administrators nearly always counted upon manipulating the nonviolent presence of the regime, all dreamed no doubt, at one time or other, of something less intricate. Even Tagart, author of "compassionate toleration," protested to the governor early on that failure to prosecute under the Native Schools Ordinance was being "invariably taken as a sign of weakness."[42] Even he apparently indulged for a time the fantasy of riding against Watchtower crowds, conquering and to conquer. The belief that they could always choose to employ force probably helped officials maintain the forgetful arrogance that Anthony Kirk-Greene identified as virtually a professional qualification. Lewis Gann and Peter Duignan have described the sometimes hilarious eccentricities that went with the cultivation of forgetfulness.[43] However accomplished, the seasoned officer's job was to cover every sign of apprehension. In this largely ungarrisoned and unpoliced colony, he had to present a self-confident professional countenance to blacks and whites equally.

Tagart was sensible enough in the end not to be stampeded into dependence upon a degree of force that was not practical. His compassionate toleration was a way of protecting the regime's prestige by disengaging it from the active enforcement of its own law. But, while the policy protected the regime's prestige, it put that of missionaries and customary rulers to severe test. For if officials could choose to fight or not to fight the Watchtower fire, chiefs and missionaries worked and lived in the fire's path.

USING THE MISSIONS TO REPRESS THE WATCHTOWER

Like the settlers, the missionaries wished for stern repression but did not get it. They argued their case by charging sedition, the charge to which the regime responded best. But the words and deeds that the missions branded as sedition went even further beyond conventional definitions than the regime was prepared to go. To verbal attack upon the regime and the exercise of a non-existent African right to strike, they added blasphemy, obscenity, and plain disrespect. African mission teachers near Fort Jameson made the following report in 1924:

> They say they will cast down the Europeans because they are rich. They sit on chairs and despise "us poor people." They say America is coming to remove the white men and give us our freedom.[44]

The teachers emphasized that preachers were careful not to say these things in public, but only did so at night, in private homes. "Also they say that in 1925 the world will come to an end, and the authority of the dragon will cease; the dragon is King George." The established authorities were alleged to be the kingdoms of Gog and Magog, continued the shocked teachers. In the same breath they reported the story that Queen Victoria had been an adulteress and a bigamist and therefore, obviously, there was no punishment for these things; and they cited Jesus' refusal to punish an adulteress as additional evidence. They asserted that Paul and Lydia (Acts 16) had lived in adultery. They went on with the outrageous assertation that there was no hell and no paradise.[45] The fact that evangelists and missionaries retailed such stories as seditious indicates the way in which disrespect for missions' religious teaching was taken at grass-roots level. Given the actual structure of rule, they could be taken in no other way. Blasphemy was indeed tantamount to sedition.

But, for officials, blasphemy was not sedition. Some were undoubtedly amused by missionaries' quaint, sometimes antique, sensitivities—in the twentieth century, the hordes of Gog and Magog had lost any general power to terrify. Besides, it was present policy to ridicule the Watchtower and not to worry seriously. Officials instructed missionaries to hold their flocks by persuasion and not to depend upon the regime's police power. The same Sylvester who had argued against the Native Schools Ordinance on the grounds that it was unenforceable also argued that nongovernmental groups must not depend upon the administration to repress the Watchtower.

> If the N.C.'s can be trusted to watch the movement intelligently, and with sympathy, to keep a weather eye open for more alarming developments and if missionaries could be asked to rely more on their own powers of persuasion and argument than upon the *vis et arma* of the government, if settlers could from time to time be reassured as to their safety and the more intelligent taken a little into the confidence of the authorities, then, I think, the teachers and evangelists might be left to run their course.[46]

Following this bit of advice, the Reverend Mr. Ranger of the Universities Mission produced a pamphlet refuting the Watchtower attack upon the missions and challenging the foremost preachers to an open debate on the Scriptures.[47]

Even though the administration did not take blasphemy as seriously as the missions did, it was not indifferent to their fate. As early as 1923, the secretary for native affairs noted the importance of the missions' schools as a barrier against the Watchtower:

> Unless something is done in the way of education on sound lines to counteract the propaganda of this sect they will cause more trouble later on, but the fact that all chiefs and headmen are against the movement is some guarantee that the government will have ample warning of any revival.[48]

The function of mission schools was not merely the ideological one of delivering the benefits of colonial rule. The school networks provided informal policing. One DC in a largely unevangelized area missed this support, calling mission teachers invaluable "liaison officers" of the regime.[49] Not only could they provide detailed information on events in the villages, but they could also give early warning of danger. It was usually they who provided whatever detailed reports of Watchtower preaching the regime got.

Where networks of schools existed, the Watchtower was much less successful than where there were none. In Lundazi District, for example, mission schools were credited with forestalling the emergence of any revival whatever through 1924 and 1925. The first signs appeared only in 1926, upon the arrival of Isaac Nyasulo, a resolute veteran of 1919. The administration welcomed the move when the White Fathers decided in 1924 to expand into Petauke District. It was no less pleased when the Dutch Reformed and Universities Missions finally settled the longstanding dispute that had prevented the establishment of any schools in the portion of the Eastern Province inhabited by the Kunda people and moved in simultaneously. According to one of the Kunda chiefs, the Watchtower had been successful in his area because the "children [had been] missing their education."[50] The coming of schools could make the difference between widespread disaffection and relative quiet.

Knowing their importance, missionaries naturally expected direct help from the administration. Thus we find Father Siemienski insisting upon the arrest of a Headman Riumbika and his son.[51] The reason: After having requested schools himself, Riumbika turned the teacher away as soon as he arrived. In the interval between the request and the teacher's arrival, the headman's son had become a preacher and had baptized his father. Riumbika now infuriated the priest by claiming that although he himself was in favor of the Catholic school, his people had turned against the idea and he could do nothing. Siemienski's head teacher, Petrol, was told that he would only preach "to sticks and empty houses"; and he would be starved out if he bothered to return. Another teacher was threatened with a beating if he did not leave the village forthwith. Thus missionaries themselves had to contend sometimes with terrifying opposition. Less fortunate than Siemienski, whose African staff bore the brunt of what Siemienski called the chiefs' "two-facedness," the Reverend Mr. Pauw himself was chased out of Kunda country altogether.[52] Especially in newly opened, remote fields, where they could not count upon the speedy arrival of the vis et arma of the administration, missionaries could not be certain not to fall victim to sudden popular violence. Small wonder that they demanded at least that the regime enforce its own ordinance against unauthorized preaching. The policy of compassionate toleration had left them high and dry.

The injustice of compassionate toleration was aggravated by the requirement that established missions comply with the ordinance. Not only did they regularly certify their preachers, but they also obeyed the provision that prohibited them from entering a new village unless requested to do so by a chief or headman. But Watchtower preachers entered at will. Siemienski stated his predicament forthrightly in his teetering English:

> When Watchtower preachers tell that they are teaching "pure" Christianity; there are all right, and I remain without any argument. I am very sorry, Sir, to disturb you with this stupid thing, but when I shall leave this movement in peace, all my district becomes Watchtower and the mission is finished.[53]

Siemienski's predicament was inevitable under the loose and ambiguous compact the administration had with the missions and their liaison officers.

Still, the arrangements were not so self-defeating as would appear at first sight. The prominent role former Mwenzo evangelists had played in the events of 1919 had escaped no one's notice. Although a large network of schools might offer protection, it might do the opposite unless white missionaries constantly supervised their black coreligionists. But, after the outbreak of 1919, when administrative officers were being prodded to visit their areas and "get in touch with their people," Livingstonia kept working in the old way: The black teachers traveled; the white missionaries remained at the station. A district official warned that Mwenzo's overextended network of schools might result once again in the transformation of mission teachers into Watchtower militants and the network of mission schools into a ready-made Watchtower network.[54] Thus, although the amended Native Schools Ordinance was ostensibly directed against unauthorized Watchtower preachers, it was also calculated to force missions to tighten their organizations.

The need to control preachers and teachers sometimes conflicted with missionaries' Christian priorities. In the early 1920s, the Reverend Dr. Chisholm was still struggling to rebuild Mwenzo's devastated network. In one of many urgent requests for more money and new manpower, he reminded his superior in Scotland that "it is through [the schools] that we keep in touch with our members and their children and gain new members."[55] The matter was clearcut. If there were no schools, there would be no church. In 1921, only 250 new Christians out of 1,000 applicants were baptized. As he strove to carry on with limited means, Chisholm had no choice but to depend upon his African preachers and teachers in Zambia. Most of Mwenzo's schools were "poor bush schools," in Chisholm's own words, whose "best boys" worked as school inspectors and evangelists. Chisholm's concession to the administration's anxiety about these largely unsupervised workers was to offer to give certificates to his "reliable" teachers, so that it would be easy to distinguish between apostates and loyal employees.

When the amended ordinance was adopted, with Justice Macdonnell's strictures on both preachers and teachers, Chisholm got more than he had bargained for. Not only were the missions required to use certified teachers, not mere preachers, in their schools and to increase the ratio of white to black personnel, at dramatically increased cost, but they were also required to await the direct request of a chief or village headmen for a school. If the requirement of teachers' certification was taken at all seriously, Chisholm said, forty-eight "bush schools" would have to be closed forthwith.[56] The requirement of a headman's request was more burdensome still. As Chisholm saw it, many headmen were too lethargic to make official requests at the *boma* and, to a certain extent, fearful of trouble whose nature they could not possibly foresee. The amended law's provisions meant that the Free Church's effort to get back into touch with its former constituents could be blocked by lazy traditionalists: altogether unacceptable from the mission's standpoint. Worst of all, the new provisions regulated preaching, too. The Reverend Mr. Elmslie declared this part of the new measure "intolerable": "The spread of the Gospel has been by the life and testimony of those whose hearts have been changed and we cannot admit any rule which would shut the mouth of a Christian who desires to lead others to Christ."[57] Furious, Elmslie devised a scheme according to which all adherents of Livingstonia Mission, from catechumens to baptized members, would be given printed certificates. Two years later, in exactly the same spirit, Watchtower preachers would be forging their own. When it came to resisting civil constraint upon religion, by circumventing one law in order to obey a higher law, the Watchtower did not stand alone.

Chisholm believed that headmen might hold up the reconstruction of the Free Church's schools out of "lethargy" and "fear." Probably they had other reasons as well. The revised ordinance gave headmen an opportunity to recoup some of the influence they had been losing to mission teachers—it was not, after all, the Watchtower but the Free Church that had initially taught contempt for heathen observances and for unconverted village headmen and elders. But whatever headmen's reasons for moving slowly or not at all to bring back Mwenzo teachers, the administration intended to safeguard customary authority against sudden disruption by Christian teaching. It saw little to choose between disruption by Watchtower preachers and the same by mission evangelists. If Mwenzo's school network had seemed fully dependable as a hedge against disorder, the administration would probably have found a way to exempt it from the new rules. The administration did not do so.

The administration's policies appear to crisscross and cancel each other out, but in fact they made sense. If the missions were to buffer the regime, it was only reasonable that officials leave them to settle their relations with their constituencies more or less on their own. To have protected them with police force each time they requested it would have removed the buffer and set officials in the missionaries' assigned front-line position. Further, the use of police on behalf of one mission would have opened the field to all the rest. Evangelical Protestants would not have taken kindly to exclusive aid to Catholics ("Romanists," as they usually said), and vice versa. From there it would have been only a short step into missionaries' interdenominational rivalries. Anyone could see that Siemienski, Moffat, Pauw, Ranger, and the rest were best left to use whatever resources they could muster from their separate Catholic, Free Church, Anglican, and other Christianities.

Censorship of Watchtower publications was the only form of police assistance that the administration offered missions. Even this they did far from consistently. In February 1925, the Criminal Investigation Division examined a package addressed to one Reynald Sanje, which contained a copy of the Watchtower Society's pamphlet, "The Golden Age," published during the time of Rutherford's editorship. This pamphlet described the established missions as "Satan's emissaries, desperately endeavoring to withhold the truth from the people."[58] Their preachers were "tares and goats who profess to represent God but who are servants of the present order of things, and opponents of the kingdom of heaven." The pamphlet castigated the activities of the Church Missionary Society in Nigeria, calling it "the greatest commercial and trading association in Africa." It reiterated the traditional charge of money madness:

Taking advantage of the credulity of the natives all kinds of taxes and dues are imposed upon the people. Should these not be paid up to the church periodically, so that one is financially in balance with the church at the time of death, his corpse will not be brought into the church, which the people believe to be the gateway to heaven.

The CID official who read the pamphlet forwarded it to Sanje, "as there [was] nothing of a seditious nature contained therein." On the strict view that the regime was indifferent to religion, there was none.

British readers achieved no meeting of the minds on the literature's seriousness. Mrs. Fraser, a firm Free Church woman, thought that the pamphlet "Enemies" contained "nothing particularly seditious, immoral, or subversive to government in the book which is almost entirely an attack on the Roman Catholic Church." More sensitive than Mrs. Fraser to the implications of anti-Catholic propaganda, the DC Sandford felt that "these attacks on the Roman Catholic religion are likely to create suspicion and disunity," but that there was "nothing subversive in the ordinary sense." Except during World War II, when the society's pacifism was unacceptable, complete censorship was never attempted. Even then one analyst declared that

> the book ["Government"] would be better boosted than banned. There is some good war propaganda in it. . . . Hitler Satan Incarnate, etc. . . . As the Minister of Supply said the other day, "That's the stuff to give 'em." If it were not for the unfortunate mix-up with the Roman Catholic religion, the book would almost be worth issuing free with every *chitupa* [pay slip].[59]

Sandford who took the attack on missions seriously, reported that the pamphlets "Government and Peace" and "Religion" appeared to be "primarily attacks on institutional religion . . . [and] to emphasize the hypocrisy and repressiveness of Governments"; in the renewed revival of the early 1930s, "much of the literature . . . [was] openly antagonistic to the recognized churches in general, and their missionaries in particular. From this brief description will be realized the unsettling and harmful effect of such doctrines not only on the minds of natives, but even on Europeans of a certain class." The Magistrate Goodall was blunt: The literature was obviously "undesirable reading for half-baked natives."[60] Thus, attitudes toward the society's literature varied over time, according to individual taste, religious choice, and status in the structure of the colony. The policy with respect to Watchtower literature went back and forth from toleration to censorship.

It was not only the apparently seditious content of the Watchtower pamphlets or its attacks upon established churches that caused some observers to worry. As is usual where political and religious authorities work in symbiotic relationship, Bible-reading itself came into question: If people could read on their own, what conclusions would they reach? A report on the 1935 revival in Petauke District contended that

> the allegorical nature of the Bible can assume disconcerting and undesirable meanings when discoursed upon by persons without the education or intelligence (and possibly the desire) to interpret it correctly.[61]

Another reporter extolled the virtue of a purely catechetical teaching of religion, in preference to free interpretation. In Lovale, Bible-reading had led to millenarian rumors. The DC wrote his supervisor:

> I have often wondered what these phrases . . . "Black Sheep," "Resurrection," "Tree of Life," etc. . . . convey to natives when translated literally, as they are, into the native languages in gospels and hymns. . . . I am not a Roman Catholic myself, but was . . . brought up in a Catholic country, the West of Ireland. I believe that the Church discourages the reading of the Bible amongst its ill-educated adherents in numerous countries to prevent these very misunderstandings.[62]

It was not only that Watchtower preachers misinterpreted "allegorical" passages. Their very pride in a new conversion and in a new book knowledge could also upset the religious inequality on which many missionaries had become dependent. Like followers of the Watchtower elsewhere—and indeed, like new Protestants everywhere—Zambian members delighted in argument based on Scripture citations. Attempting to lecture L. C. Mwambulah on his obligation to obtain a chief's permission before preaching, a DC told Mwambulah, "Render unto Caesar that which is Caesar's." The preacher topped him by finishing the quote: "And unto God what is God's."[63] The preacher Samson, who was active in Fort Jameson District, floored in debate a local Dutch Reformed missionary. In the mission-based literate culture of the time, this was bound to be effective. The DC reported that Samson's performance had made even the *boma* messengers "shaky."[64] Catechetically trained evangelists for the White Fathers, who had learned their Christianity by rote, were no match for Protestant-educated Watchtower converts and were on the retreat by the mid-1930s.[65]

Even if the regime had made up its mind to censor consistently, it could not have managed the task. The ponderous legal machinery required publications to be examined individually and banned title by title. The society joined the widespread evasion of this ban by giving old publications new titles or new covers, and by republishing banned English-language publications in local languages.[66] And if publications were stopped in the mail, itinerant preachers simply carried them up the labor routes. During World War II, when the regime took the unprecedented step of making the mere possession of a Watchtower pamphlet a criminal offense, the enforcement of the law was shifted to chiefs and headmen. This presented other problems.

USING CUSTOMARY RULERS AGAINST THE WATCHTOWER

In a letter to the governor in early 1924, Tagart showed how the missions and customary rulers fit into the strategy of compassionate toleration.

> In order to combat further the undesirable element in the movement, it is suggested that the heads of the various recognized missions in the territory be circularized with a view to inducing them to start counterpropaganda and that the Native Commissioners of those subdistircts where the sect still flourishes be directed to explain on all possible occasions to chiefs and headmen that *we object to the movement in so far as it attacks their authority and is subversive to law and order.*[67]

In other words, reliable mission teachers were to be the regime's vanguard and chiefs its rear guard, while local officials protected the regime's prestige by standing above the fray. But this strategy had a major disadvantage: It embarrassed customary rulers as much as it did missionaries.

Paradoxically, the very breadth of their powers under the Native Schools Ordinance constituted the main embarrassment. Chiefs were free to go further than officials could in suppressing religious practice that attacked their authority or that was, in their eyes, subversive to law and order. But this sword cut two ways. Every unauthorized meeting held in the teeth of orders not to do so could discredit a chief in the eyes of his own people. Equally, it could lower a chief's esteem in the eyes of a local official, whose esteem in the eyes of his own superiors depended in turn upon the impression he made as a keeper of order in his district. If the chief failed, the official looked bad. At the same time, chiefs were reluctant to show themselves to be unreliable proxies of the administration. Both stood to suffer in the event of serious local disorder. As the German proverb has it, "Caught together, hung together."

It appears that DCs did not leave chiefs to reach the desired conclusions on their own. Tagart reported that the chiefs of Isoka District were informed of the administration's tolerance for law-abiding preachers, but were "warned against encouraging the movement in any way"; their superiors gave them a word to the wise. When chiefs and headmen accepted baptism, together with their people, as a kind of "free insurance," J. Moffat Thompson urged local administrators to identify and back chiefs who opposed the movement.[68] Chiefs who took no side received urgent "suggestions." A DC reported to Tagart the encouraging news that certain chiefs had moved against Watchtower preaching even before it was suggested to them.[69] Tagart reported (in Macdonnell's jargon) that they had used "their common law right" to turn nuisances out of their villages as soon as this right was explained to them.[70] The "right" to turn out nuisances became the duty to stamp out the Watchtower. Still others were given material incentives to greater vigilance in the future.

Despite all this, the policy was not a simple matter of pushing customary rulers forward to do what the administration could not do directly. The administration continued to have scruples against religious persecution. Still and all, it was realized, chiefs were often better placed than administrators to say what behavior threatened their authority. As time passed, few officials would turn a deaf ear to complaints about the noise of *chongo*. Nevertheless, the theoretical difficulty of repressing religion per se remained. The administration did not hesitate to back its African agents insofar as Watchtower activity attacked their authority, but it continued to restrain them from engaging in "purely religious persecution."[71] Since the chiefs quickly understood that they were expected to stamp out the Watchtower, they found this stipulation as puzzling as the administration's seemingly casual attitude toward violations of the Native Schools Ordinance. A group of chiefs in Fort Jameson District complained as soon as this equivocal policy was presented to them. When the DC Cholmeley explained that the administration had no objection to adherents' praying quietly at home, Chief Kakumbi replied on behalf of his colleagues:

> We do not agree with what the Native Commissioner told the Watchtower leaders yesterday that he didn't mind them praying privately as long as their actions were confined to prayer. ... We do not want the Watchtower to think that it is only we chiefs who disapprove of them and that the Boma does not care. We find it very hard to satisfy the Boma that these Watchtowers are opposed to the Government. All of us know this for certain. *We think that the sect should be stamped out. We do not wish the Boma to leave us to stamp it out.*[72]

The events in Fort Jameson illustrate the pressure compassionate toleration placed upon customary rulers. At the beginning of the revival, Cholmeley gave out the usual assurances that the excitement would simmer down when the prophecies failed.[73] In August 1924, he "ridiculed" David Gareta, telling him that people would soon see the difference between genuine baptism and that given by preachers with "a few months' training at a coal mine."[74,a] He showed the missionaries the way by disputing religious questions with the Watchtowerites himself. In September, Cholmeley could report that the mission teachers were deliberately overstating Watchtower sedition in order to place the movement in ill repute. Apart from their criticism of mission methods, he wrote, the Watchtower's basic teachings were like the missions'. Baptism excepted— the main attraction of the movement seemed to be "sure salvation for the asking of any of half a dozen natives from a Southern Rhodesian coal mine." Moreover, the policy against arrests seemed to be working. It deprived preachers of martyrdom and its attendant propaganda advantage. Cholmeley was confident that the movement need not be taken seriously, thanks to Tagart's policy of compassionate toleration.

Two months later, Cholmeley could not condemn compassionate toleration strongly enough. The regime had become "too lax" about corporal punishment. Leniency had led to an erosion of respect and to dangerous disillusionment on the part of ordinary people. "The natives of this country are accustomed to discipline," Cholmeley declared. "They prefer it to disorder. I believe the restoration

---

[a] In fact, however, Gareta had studied for two years at Watchtower headquarters in South Africa. He had apparently been sent back to Zambia by the society as its official representative. In this capacity, he went to the DC requesting the exclusive right to preach and select preachers.

of it in this respect would be welcomed with an almost universal sigh of relief." He even hinted that Watchtower propaganda had sinister alien origins.

> They are aiming at freedom from control, absence of govern- ment discipline. It is unnecessary, though it might be inter- esting, to trace it to its source. In its tendencies it is sheer bolshevism. . . . The whole thing, in my humble opinion, is a symptom of the dangerous disease that results from "a little learning" with possibly some innoculation from those countries where anything in the shape of discipline is anathema and a campaign against it regarded as the highest stage of human development.[75]

In the meantime, Watchtower adherents had correctly seen the new toleration as evidence of the regime's weakness. Cholmeley reported that preachers were telling "raw natives" that the gov- ernment could do nothing to stop them.

Chiefs protested the regime's policy with increasing insistence. They also learned to protest with greater skill. After establishing that they were not taken in by the preachers' grandiose claims— said one, "They cannot even pay their tax and where are they going to get books to teach the children and young people?"[76]—they made it clear that they at least did not doubt the administration's ability to stamp out the movement. Why, then, did it not do so? Cholmeley quoted them in his urgent demand for a change of policy.

> Chiefs and headmen, shocked by the unwholesome and unor- thodox propaganda, ask what the Boma thinks of these people. "Does the Boma know what they are doing and saying? Does the Boma approve of them?" "Are these people," Kapatamoya has just written to ask, "to defile the country?"

In contrast to his earlier observation, that the basic teaching of the Watchtower was the same as that of the missions, Cholmeley now said, "There can no longer be any pretense that it is a purely religious or educational movement. . . . As far as religion enters into it at all, it is a crude distortion, a peg on which they hang their real motives." Still, Cholmeley could find no peg on which to hang his demand for reinforcements.

> Even though evidence may be lacking that there is preaching of sedition, etc., it is subversive in its tendencies. It is disturbing the minds of the people. It is bringing the government into

discredit. And these effects are produced by propagandists who have all been implicitly warned and have incontinently disregarded their warning.[77]

The cold reaction of the new secretary for native affairs was that "it is possible that the reason why [Cholmeley found] it difficult to obtain evidence of seditious preaching is that there [was] in fact very little of it."[78] As in the 1919 events, the chiefs and the line officers were not at first able to make men farther away hear the seditious voice of Watchtower revival.

Chief Kakumbi eventually found a remarkable new definition of sedition: the new confidence and independence of Watchtower deaconnesses. He argued that continued toleration of the Watchtower's meetings would lead to an upsurge in crime, and especially murder. Taken by itself, this argument would have amounted to no more than a commonplace of conservative politics everywhere: that innovation of any kind inevitably leads to the most hideous lawlessness. But Kakumbi was able to found his arguments upon attitudes he shared with British officials. Once he had done this, it only remained to draw out the implications in terms of African custom. Kakumbi's British interlocutors had already noticed that the wives of migrant laborers were almost always the first to join. They had seen Watchtower deaconnesses in villages along the road from Fort Jameson to Broken Hill holding classes for children. Well, now, the rest was obvious: Quiet prayer meetings were perfect settings for adultery by Watchtower deaconnesses. Cuckolded husbands would reappear, murder the lovers, and then turn against the chiefs they had trusted to guard the wives' virtue.

At last, the chiefs had found an argument grounded in "native law and custom" that suited the British. Cholmeley took it up with a will: "The system of deaconnesses appeals to female vanity, but it is liable to lead to immorality and suspicion of immorality which may in turn lead to disorder."[79] For good measure, he added that although the husbands of one or two of the most notorious deaconnesses had long been absent, the women were "visibly pregnant." He then restored to the integrity of couples what the colonial economy had taken away: Kakumbi and his colleagues had his blessing when they made rules to permit the punishment of women attending prayer meetings, even peaceful ones, without the express permission of their "guardians." According to Cholmeley, who warmed to his task of protecting African marriages, such an order "may not be in keeping with modern ideas, but native women have not attained modern standards of independence." Thus, by a roundabout path through immemorial custom, the colony's legal imagination came to encompass meanings of sedition previously unimagined. First something old, then something new.

Avory-Jones,[b] a veteran of 1919 who replaced Cholmeley, argued that local conditions must be taken into account in determining "what words and conduct do tend to disturbance." Avory-Jones's new formulation broadened the idea of "government" to that of "social order," and the idea of "revolt" to that of anything which "might make the work of administration more difficult." There would still be no punishment for religious teaching or preaching as such.

> If however that preaching and teaching contains in it words or conduct which tend to *disturbance of the government or of social order, or to "discontent and dissatisfaction," or even to obstruct or make more difficult the work of administration,* then such words or conduct plainly come under the head of sedition and are punishable as such.[80]

The relevant local conditions in this were conventional rules about women's place, as set forth by beleaguered chiefs. These conditions included the fact, evident to all, that Watchtower revival was undermining chiefs' control over previously docile subjects. Kakumbi declared that women converts' immorality, or their suspected immorality, might lead to his demise as a ruler to be taken seriously by his subjects. As he put it, "We are responsible to the Boma and our brothers who are in Southern Rhodesia to look after our people."[81] If Kakumbi and his colleagues were unable to uphold their responsibility to their "brothers," they could not uphold their responsibility "to the Boma." In the face of an expanding revival, a chief was trapped whatever he did—if he made common cause with the forces of revival, or if he opposed it and lost control of his people. In either case, his stock with the administration could not but decline. "The Boma must help us," Kakumbi concluded.

The *boma* finally helped by carrying out massive arrests, in some areas taking in as many as three hundred villagers at a time. The police constable Sergeant Stubbs reported in late 1925 that many villages in the vicinity of Fort Jameson were denuded, so massive

---

[b] Avory-Jones was a veteran of the post–World War I outbreak in the northern districts. Macdonnell declared him "quicker on the uptake" in matters of formal legality than either Dewhurst or Draper had been (NAZ, ZA 1/10, P. J. Macdonnell to Admin., 5/5/1919).

had been the arrests.[82] Even so, Fort Jameson town and the villages surrounding it continued to seed remoter villages with Watchtower propaganda, and the revival continued through 1926 and into 1927. But patrolling and police swoops remained impractical most of the time. Chiefs still bore major responsibility for repression. The chiefs who had succeeded in repressing the movement at the beginning continued to succeed: chiefs Jumbe and Kawaza received public commendation and conspicuous gifts in return for their vigorous co-operation. Other chiefs, like Chuaula and Mkanya, were urged to view these gifts, in which they did not share, as "incentives" to greater enterprise.[83] But the incentive of greed had drawbacks.

In Fife, we recall, Chief Kafwimbe confiscated property belonging to certain Watchtower converts who offended him. Here, Chief Kavimba was awarded cash damages from Watchtower converts who offended him. But, when it was discovered a year later that Kavimba had raided a Watchtower village and converted property of the residents to his own and his loyal followers' use, the tables were turned, and Kavimba had to be prosecuted.[84] In this case, it was a chief who had not received a reward who eventually exposed Kavimba's wrongdoing at the *boma*. The fact that the regime only learned of the excesses a year after they occurred, from a disgruntled subordinate, reveals once again how thin the regime's presence was. Official reports convey a lingering notion that once "sedition" received adequate definition, men could unleash vast forces hitherto kept in check by ill-founded liberal inhibitions against religious persecution. Nothing of the sort was the case. The regime had no vast reserve of unused power. The officials who eventually prosecuted Kavimba were fully aware that customary rulers who were in theory servants of the state might easily become its enemies—not by opposing it but by defending it in ways that created new local discontent.

DOMESTICATING THE WATCHTOWER

As we saw, one part of the regime's strategy rested upon the reform of Christian missionary bodies to assure that recognized mission societies maintained adequate control over their African adherents. Eventually, it applied this reasoning to the Watchtower Bible and Tract Society. But the Watchtower did not begin as the other missions had, with missionaries-in-charge hiring African assistants to work in the villages. For many years it depended exclusively on

African leadership. When the revival of the mid-1920s moved into high gear, the Big Two of the Zambian Watchtower were Gabriel Phiri and Rabison (a deportee from Fife).[85] No white missionary was in sight.

To some officials, the mere absence of white leadership made the movement unsavory. "Uncontrolled missionary effort is worse than Rabies," said the secretary for native affairs.[86] To others, it had still more sinister meaning. Isaac Nyasulo's judge was convinced that the Watchtower was being "fanned from outside": "If it were possible to trace the whole thing to its source, we should feel better in case of emergency."[87] The regime concluded that the time had come to make the acquaintance of the society's white millenarians and, if possible, join hands with them.

But the regime moved cautiously. It already had a presumption against the society, and there were two key questions. Was the Watchtower a legitimate religious society? And would it supervise its African followers in a spirit of fraternal collaboration? The first was answered when inquiries by the CID established that the Watchtower had no ties with the Third International and that its white leaders in South Africa were reputable citizens.[88] The question of supervision was more difficult, since the Watchtower had never even attempted to become a recognized missionary society. Explaining to the governor the arrests of Watchtower preachers under the Native Schools Ordinance, Tagart said:

> We have always insisted on the principle that native teachers of recognised religions require constant and direct supervision by their European supervisors, a fortiori teachers of unrecognised religions. Since the Watchtower makes no effort at supervision, and until it alters its policy in this respect we must, to be consistent, oppose it in every possible way.[89]

Nevertheless, the administration made acquaintance. It found the society's attitude reassuring. When Brother Ankethill wrote to inquire about his followers' complaints of persecution, he declared that "the society I represent has no sympathy with law-breakers and we always inculcate obedience to the government."[90] And Thomas Walder, who appeared in Livingstone in late 1924, publicly criticized the misdeeds of certain preachers.[91] He went on to explain that although he had as yet no certificates to distribute, African preachers must stop forging them and stop preaching without them. Moreover, they were not to break the law or interfere with other Christians. They must forswear adultery, drink, and other bad habits, set an example, and above all, avoid trouble with the regime. In the meantime, they were to stop preaching and baptizing but merely "confirm the faithful." He sent a message to all Watchtower preachers informing them that he was the society's "manager" in Zambia. Shortly he would send a "white brother who will assist you and teach you." (I. B. Malenga conveyed this message to Tomo Nyirenda early in 1925.) All this seemed promising.

At Abercorn, where the Watchtower was conscientiously law-abiding except on the issue of certification, the local magistrate favored informal recognition. Walder, who seemed "anxious to guide the movement along lines which avoid trouble with the government," would be useful since he seemed to have the respect of important local preachers. Still, the CID took the view that an open accord between Walder and the regime would be a mistake. The basis of the movement's "appeal to a certain class of native mind, is the fact that it is a purely native movement, controlled and guided entirely by natives in what they conceive to be entirely native interests."[92] Order would be better served by not making the Watchtower a recognized missionary society.

William Dawson took up Walder's work the following year. Dawson's task was to submit a list of preachers he could recommend for official certification under the liberalized Native Schools Ordinance. They would then be certified by a local DC or magistrate, rather than by a recognized European missionary. In this way, officials reasoned, the more respectable element in the movement would be brought within range of friendly advice.[93] The plan immediately ran into a snag. Dawson's list included Watchtower lawbreakers already notorious in the eyes of the regime. For example, John Dauti Tembo, whom Dawson highly recommended, had been prosecuted for witchcraft violations. It was dangerous, Tagart lectured Dawson, to give "authority to the semi-educated native until one [was] thoroughly satisfied as to his moral character. . . . Clever natives who have lost the confidence of their employers . . . have joined the 'Watchtower' Society and become accepted leaders therein."[94] While Tagart vented his annoyance with the African Watchtower upon the unfortunate Dawson, baptizing continued despite the order to stop. It did not matter whether a European headed the movement or not. African preachers remained free to do as they liked.

A heavy blow to the new policy came when officials realized the full extent of Tomo Nyirenda's activities. In the midst of the general panic, the society abruptly retreated. There was no one, Dawson declared, who understood the doctrines, no one who was a member of the society, no one he could authorize to preach or teach. Even the simpler conceptions eluded the African mind, he continued, the society's "most advanced followers [Malawians in Zimbabwe] just grasp that they must live a good life."95 But, impervious to the irony of his view, Dawson insisted, "We go further than that—we delve into society, political organizations, etc. Our teaching is beyond their conceptions."

Tagart was not displeased by the prospect of losing the society as an "ally" of the administration.

> So for Dawson and his ramification I would like to see the whole lot out of Northern Rhodesia. THEY ARE DOING NO GOOD. Uncontrolled missionary effort is worse than Rabies. There are some beauties hanging about I would like to see safely put away for a long time. . . . I hope Dawson does drop everything in Northern Rhodesia. (He has dropped enough as it is.)96

It soon became clear that African resistance to white control was by no means the only obstacle to using the society as a tool of the administration. Although Dawson and Tagart concurred in their estimate of the African preachers, they did so for different reasons. Tagart saw them as nuisances and criminals. Dawson saw their doctrinal errors, above all with respect to baptism. "[To us] any fit individual can do the immersing. *They* only allow a pastor or elder to do it," he complained. And still more serious: "Baptism is to us a consecration and not a washing of sins."97 Dawson insisted upon these theological niceties in his conversations with Tagart. Tagart's worries about baptism were quite other than these. The two men failed to communicate.

> I have had talks with Dawson. He has been holding meetings and talking all sorts of stuff. (1) that the government of Northern Rhodesia do not blame his Society for the Mwana Lesa murders . . . (2) the churches could have prevented the Great War; (3) things like the Mwana Lesa murders are permitted by God *with some object in view, etc. etc.*98

More perhaps than other mission societies, the interest of Dawson's "ramification" in propagating the Gospel was out of phase with the interests of the administration.

No less than other mission societies, the Watchtower derived its authority from God when it could not agree with the administration. Sometimes, as in late 1924, the Watchtower Society appeared to share the administration's interest in law and order. But this shared interest did not bind it eternally to Satan's worldly organization in Zambia. Trouble came almost immediately. When the society agreed to stop its activities in Zambia, it did not mean to stop conveying the Word of God to those in Zambia who desired to hear it. The office in South Africa kept sending Bibles and pamphlets to interested Africans (which included both Watchtower adherents and loyal mission teachers for whom publications in English were hard to come by). The administration regarded these continued indirect contacts as a breach of good faith. When the question of admitting white members of the society arose again, it was argued that the society's word was not its bond.

The question arose again in the mid-1930s, when the Watchtower entered its next big expansion. From their experience with Walder and Dawson, officials had learned that if white representatives of the society were admitted, they would have two movements to domesticate instead of one: The African adherents would have to learn to avoid trouble; the white missionaries would have to learn to behave like other missionaries. Before 1936, seeing no reason to compound their troubles, the administration concentrated upon the task of controlling African preachers and their followers. After the excitement of the 1920s cooled, the administration tightened its rural organization. The Native Authorities Ordinance of 1930 formalized the powers of customary leaders under indirect rule. The new native courts were popular. With the incentive of grants-in-aid from public funds for the improvement of schools, the missions were stabilizing themselves.

At first the new arrangements seemed adequate. When Watchtower-led witch finding broke out on a large scale in Lovale in 1931, it was suppressed under the Witchcraft Ordinance.[99] In 1934, an outbreak of arson associated with witchcraft was punished under the Collective Punishment Ordinance.[100] When disrespect to chiefs recurred in the Mumbwa, Namwala, and Ndola districts, and throughout the Luapula region, the newly reinforced chiefs moved effectively and with official backing. Luapula chiefs were authorized to burn down the houses of the Watchtowerites who had moved to the outskirts of their villages.[101]

Nevertheless, some of the old difficulties remained. Some chiefs were still unreliable. Sudden excitement still posed a threat in remote areas. Most of all, the Depression presented new difficulties. As it deepened, the tone of Watchtower preaching caused official anxiety. Still there was no revolt. Men struggled patiently to pay their taxes, even though there was little opportunity for wage employment and no policy allowing for the payment of taxes in kind. In view of the relative calm, official attitudes toward the Watchtower relaxed, and "selective toleration" enjoyed new life. Indeed, the director of African education went so far as to suggest that the Watchtower actually served a useful purpose.

> With reasonable treatment the better class leader will, I think, of his own choice avoid political agitation which might get him into trouble. They and their like talk a great deal about the probable near departure of the Europeans from the country and God's preferential treatment of the Africans in the future, but this talk is no more dangerous than the nonsense which is often talked at the Welfare Association's meetings. It provides a safety valve. Most natives are sensible enough to take the talk at its real value and enjoy it in the same way some Europeans enjoy hearing an exaggerated political speech.[102]

This "safety valve" theory did not call for "some sort of European control." It seemed preferable to encourage the development of law-abiding separatist churches. The director thought that DOs would be well placed to moderate this development, and that only chiefs and missionaries objected to the policy, for parochial reasons:

> the missionaries because they are afraid that their adherents may be seduced into the movement and the chiefs because they resent the authority gained by some of the leaders and also to some extent because they imagine that it is their duty to Government to be hostile.

At the same time, there was less talk of ridiculing Watchtower ideas than before. Selective toleration meant giving potential new allies the impression that they were being taken seriously and taken into the regime's confidence. These tactical considerations outweighed the stringent objections of the Lunda chiefs who saw their own authority being whittled away, despite their success in burning Watchtower homes.

In the new liberalized circumstances, harmful elements of former times now resurfaced, transformed. A preacher identified as Zerubbabel, veteran of four arrests in Fort Jameson in 1924–1926, now changed his stripes. He and his followers engaged in eccentric behavior: They wore black-and-white uniforms, carried long black-and-white staves, and refused to cut or wash their hair. But they adhered to the new rules. Whenever they wished to hold an open meeting, they obediently told the headman concerned in advance, so that an observer could be sent. They kept their meetings within the limit of thirty people at a time. They even found a new method of baptism. They now baptized by laying on hands. Most promising of all, Zerubbabel actively sought advice from white officials. "It would seem," the DO reported, "that the best prophylactic to the movement is firm rule combined with the display in a visible form of the benefits of British dominion—Jembe [the local chief] contemplates building a Court House."[103] The attitudes of new Watchtower preachers, many with no records of arrest, also showed wholesome change. One group wrote to the *boma* at Mazabuka to request permission to preach. "We are not like those of the past, who were preaching to the people bad things, in the years 1924 and 1925," they said.

> We do not hide ourselves from the Boma, but we like the Boma to know that we are Watchtower preachers for this country of Northern Rhodesia because we know that the Boma rules us. . . . We also say that everyone must hoe and work and not to despise Chiefs and the Boma and other people.[104]

Although conciliatory requests seemed to support the new theory, in practice, administrators refused most of the applicants permission to preach, while reminding them that it was illegal to preach without. In most areas the chiefs were left to suppress the movement as they saw fit, while the government "neither countenanced nor suppressed it."[105] Ambiguous by design, the policy was calculated to maximize preachers' insecurity, thus increasing the likelihood that they would try very hard to convince a local administrator that they deserved certification.

> This combination of economic and political discussion and religious views of an extreme nature, which in their essence have not a great deal in common, undoubtedly contains elements of a very grave potential political danger. This . . . it is very tentatively suggested, might be to a great extent arrested by a strictly conditional recognition of the Watchtower "Church" . . . I am inclined to think that such recognition would . . . make its leaders extremely anxious to keep it free from anything that might bring it into disfavor with the government and so lead to the withdrawal of recognition.[106]

Thus, eventual approval would be a hard-won reward. In any case, I imagine, an administrator would be reluctant to have been responsible for the "go-ahead" if at some time in the future "selective toleration" backfired. It had in the past.

Moreover, not all conciliatory preachers co-operated fully. Joseph Sibakwe capitalized on the administration's weak points. He preached "harmlessly" in Lusaka but changed his tone in the surrounding rural areas. More worrisome, Sibakwe appeared to be part of a well-organized network. When in town, he received hospitality in the ironing room of the Lusaka Hotel. When he held meetings in the workers' compounds, he drew large crowds—even though announcements could be passed only by word-of-mouth. Worst of all, he disrupted the regime's plans by emptying the ranks of the Lusaka Welfare Association, whose activities the regime was trying to guide into "wholesome" channels. Sibakwe's success upstaged Isaac Muwamba, the association's Anglophile head. Muwamba was then recruited to an expanded function as the regime's ally against Sibakwe.[107] But even though undercover activities were set in motion against Sibakwe and people like him, toleration remained the regime's policy. There was no alternative.

While espionage went on under cover of toleration, officials debated the next step. Since they could not silence Watchtower preaching, three choices remained: de jure toleration; repeal of the Native Schools Ordinance; or doing nothing, which meant de facto toleration. De jure toleration would mean once again taking the chance of allowing the Watchtower Bible and Tract Society to send a white missionary to Zambia and then determining whether to declare it a recognized missionary society. The DC Goodall, who had been sent to mop up Abercorn after the 1919 events, argued forcefully against even conditional recognition, which would constitute "a public confession of apprehension, impotence, defeat."[108] The de facto permission that many preachers daily exercised was no solution either. It was keeping the Native Schools Ordinance in limbo; and that embarrassed everyone while satisfying no one. Chiefs, missionaries, officials, and Watchtower preachers all hung suspended in the twilight of the ordinance so long as it was not enforced across the board. Repeal of the ordinance would have removed the embarrassment, but it was out of the question. The ordinance had been written to solve a broader religious problem than the Watchtower's alone. Finally the regime decided to do nothing, that is, to continue in de facto toleration of black Watchtower preachers. When, in 1932, Petrus de Jaeger and Robert Nisbet applied for visas to represent the Watchtower Bible and Tract Society in Zambia, the request was denied.[109]

But the regime did not long retain the option of doing nothing. The boom descended upon selective toleration in 1935, when black miners struck and rioted on the Copperbelt. The details of the strike are beyond the scope of this study.[110] Suffice it to say that the regime again "saw the abyss opening" to swallow up customary respect. It promptly attributed the strike to Watchtower propaganda. This view is remarkable, given the social context of the new copper towns. From within that extraordinary implantation of white frontiersmen swaggering among black "tribesmen," beer halls, dynamite, and workingmen's dormitories, the most powerful social corrosive visible to some observers was the Christian Millennium of Watchtower preaching. In the search for a public explanation of the events, Watchtower prophesying even dwarfed the economic cataclysm of the Great Depression. Thus, the Watchtower was duly indicted as a "predisposing cause" of the unprecedented "lawlessness" of an African strike. The strike forced a reconsideration of many aspects of the regime's organization. This reconsideration inevitably affected the missions' and the administration's attitude toward Christian enterprise generally, but the Watchtower received much of the blame.

The society responded in the prevailing currency. It claimed that the Bembas, many of whom had come to the Copperbelt from Catholic (WF) areas, were Catholics; ergo, the strike was a Catholic plot.[111] Other Christian groups applied the same currency to their own account. Anxious to seize back the towns from "eccentric" religion and the abyss, Protestant groups determined to work together more closely than they had in the past. They formed the United Copperbelt Mission in 1937. In the same year, they launched *Mutende*, an English-language newspaper: It was time to compete with *Watchtower Magazine* by producing "wholesome" reading matter for Africans.[112] The regime decided that the time had come to give the society a second chance to found a white-controlled mission in Zambia. The society had reached the same conclusion independently.

Even before the commission that investigated the strike set to work, the Watchtower Society requested and received permission to dispatch a European representative, the same Petrus de Jaeger who had been refused a visa three years earlier. The governor presented the about-face in terms of selective toleration:

> I trust that the establishment of European representation will
> at least serve to distinguish the one type from the other [that
> is, the harmful from the harmless elements] and place one in

a position to deal with the genuine Watchtower movement as an organized society.[113]

Although the society still had not been formally recognized thirteen years later, despite the presence of white Watchtower representation, a new governor was able to recommend this policy to his counterpart in Zaire:

> There can be no doubt that their activities had much to do with the disturbances in the Copperbelt in 1935. As a result of the findings of the Commission of Enquiry into those disturbances that Watchtower activities had much to do with the disturbed state of mind of the Africans, the Society was prevailed upon to station in Lusaka a European to supervise the activities of its African adherents. There can, I think, be little doubt that this innovation has greatly improved the attitude of the members of the Society.[114]

Those who decided to admit a Watchtower representative were taking a calculated risk. The difficulties that had dogged earlier attempts to remake the Watchtower Society in the image of other missions had not disappeared in the interim. Whether or not a European representative could establish effective control over far-flung African Watchtower cells was still unknown. And whether the white representative would help was still open to question: No one knew for certain that people who agreed with the society's literature were within the regime's intellectual reach—for the literature was still generally regarded as "unwholesome." All missions that were formally recognized acknowledged a duty not only to avoid interference with the regime but also to support it actively. They signed the following pledge:

> I hereby undertake to give all due obedience and respect to the lawfully constituted government, and while carefully abstaining from participation in political affairs, it is my desire and purpose that my influence, in so far as it may be properly exerted in such matters, should be so exerted in loyal cooperation with the Government; and, in particular, if engaged in educational work, I undertake to do all in my power to promote good-will and understanding between the people and the Government of the country, and to make those under my care law-abiding and good citizens.[115]

Since it was not known whether white members of the society would adhere to these norms, the society did not receive formal recognition, and its representative was not asked to sign the pledge. Caution seemed called for.

When de Jaeger arrived, the administration gave him the peculiar task of compiling a report to show that his society's literature was not calculated to undermine established authority.[116] Possibly the administration's real purpose was to allow time to study de Jaeger's character and conduct. In any case, it did observe him, and on a twenty-four-hour basis. De Jaeger complained that spies lingered even on the porch of his house.[117] The surveillance yielded many reports, for the most part critical ones. He simply did not conduct himself as recognized missionaries did. For his part, de Jaeger seems to have accepted his task in the spirit in which it was given him. He prepared the report with all deliberate speed—no faster. Within weeks, he had broken all the informal rules of missionary etiquette. But he did nothing that violated the letter of the missionary pledge. Its spirit was another matter.

The surveillance reports bring out the spirit of the norms that were supposed to govern missionary behavior. The DC at Ndola found de Jaeger's behavior "extraordinary" in his "making of extensive enquiries amongst Africans."[118] If inquiries were to be made, it seems, they were to be made among white men. This alone would have made de Jaeger "a dangerous man to have on the Copperbelt in these abnormal times." But there was worse. De Jaeger made no move not calculated to defeat the regime's plan to minimize the Watchtower's status and visibility. He took the unheard of step of obtaining authority from the commission to hire legal counsel to represent the interests of the society and those of adherents who gave testimony.[119] Hiring counsel for Africans implied a quite unacceptable recognition that Africans and Europeans could have opposite interests of equal validity before the commission. The administration forced the commission to withdraw the authority it had given. Resorting to the next best thing, de Jaeger helped witnesses to prepare and coordinate their testimony himself. As this could not be done without discussing at least some white officials in an unfavorable light, de Jaeger broke another unwritten rule. Said the DC at Ndola, "I particularly object to his use of His Excellency's [the Governor's] name and the Commission in his conversations with natives."[120] A proper missionary would have known enough to express his indignation about a particular abuse to its perpetrator, not to its victim.[c]

---

[c] In fairness, it should be said that missionaries sometimes violated this norm as well and were rebuked by the administration. Reacting to missionaries' criticism of

De Jaeger bought a full page of the *Northern Rhodesian Advertiser* in order to reprint an article originally published in Paris, "Jehovah's Witnesses and Watch Tower No More Subversive than the Bible." Then, to add insult to injury, he bought up the whole edition of 3,000 copies and personally distributed it free. Within two weeks of his arrival, the chief secretary concluded that it was "advisable to get someone more senior."[121] Unfortunately, however, the report was not yet ready. The missionary and the governor played cat and mouse about the report for weeks, then months. At length, de Jaeger was removed from the Copperbelt to Lusaka, where he was assigned space in a building opposite police headquarters.

Still, no one could say that he had violated the missionary pledge, even though he had not signed it. But he did violate outrageously the unwritten norms that joined missionaries with their white kith and kin. He did nothing that was, strictly speaking, "political" and, still less, politically radical. At the same time, his every move was both political and radical in its consequences, even though conservative and apolitical in intent. So far as de Jaeger and the society were concerned, the first order of business was to fight against religious slander. The second was to show Africans and Europeans that genuine members of the society would have nothing to do with strikes or any other kind of civil disorder. In the context of colonial Zambia in 1935, however, these conservative aims appeared as the opposite. The administration finally obtained his recall.[122]

De Jaeger's successor, L. V. Phillips, took up promptly where his colleague had left off. But he added new elements to the subversive role that the Watchtower Society was to play. Those who had opposed the acceptance of a white representative had correctly foreseen that this move would enhance the prestige of the Watchtower among Africans. But no one foresaw that such a leader could also be an effective advocate of religious toleration. Before long, African members were streaming into Phillips' headquarters from remote areas to complain about chiefs' bad and sometimes illegal treatment of members. In this way, Phillips became the keeper of Justice Macdonnell's liberal conscience. He battled daily against religious

---

the violence with which the strike was put down, Governor Young told the General Missionary Conference: "Standing here as Saul among the prophets I venture to suggest . . . a way in which the mission can help the government . . . and that is by prayer. It would be a great support to know that your prayers were joined with mine in this, but I beg that if for any reason you feel that your prayer is not being answered you will let me know privately, and give me a chance of mending my ways before you proclaim the fact in public" (NAZ, HM 4/cc/1/4/1, "General Missionary Conference," Ndola, July 1935).

persecution per se. Shortly after Phillips arrived, the provincial commissioner at Mkushi complained about his conduct:

> It is unfortunate that Mr. Phillips cannot be persuaded to desist from so lightly accepting reports by natives on the behavior of Europeans in general and the Provincial Administration Officer in particular. It is an action which cannot conduce to necessary respect for the sole representative of the Government at a station such as Mkushi.[123]

For many years, Phillips belabored the regime with its own rule of religious toleration. More than that, he belabored local officials with apocalyptic threats. On the Day of Judgment, those who had opposed Christ's Kingdom on earth would be destroyed. Satan and his worldly allies were in their death throes. He said these things in the hearing of Africans. He wrote them in the letters he sent to DCs in their lonely outposts. Finally the secretary for native affairs stepped in to shield his men from Phillips' endless stream of correspondence. One of them gratefully commented that Phillips' rhetoric had begun "to have a depressing effect" on him.[124]

BUT whatever its troubles with the Watchtower's unquiet mission, the regime achieved part of its purpose. After the mid-1930s, no more spectacular outbursts of Watchtower enthusiasm occurred, and the Watchtower dropped out of the picture as the sole political threat of any importance. Some writers have concluded that the Watchtower's political influence ceased at this time, giving way to movements that were specifically political in a modern sense. This is not true. Although secular militants took a growing share of official attention, Watchtower adherents continued into the 1950s to attack their old targets—missions and customary authorities. They continued as before to hammer and chisel away at the pillars of empire in Zambia. But they were joined by fresh crews of undoers.

7

SPIRITUAL POLITY AND ITS ENEMIES: THE PATTERN OF MILLENARIAN REVIVAL

> Before all, [religion] is a system of ideas with which individuals represent to themselves the society of which they are members, and the obscure but intimate relations they have with it.
>
> EMILE DURKHEIM

HAVING SOUGHT RECOGNI-tion on the grounds that his society was law-abiding, L. V. Phillips did all in his power to make good the claim. He set out to build a unified organization from the disparate local cells black preachers had established, and to impose doctrinal unity upon his brethren. Those who acquiesced became Jehovah's Witnesses proper (after 1931, the society's name for its members), the "orthodox" branch of the Watchtower family. Not all acquiesced. Preachers in Zambia had for twenty years worked independent of any white supervision closer than Cape Town; and they had plenty of room in a vast territory to keep doing so. Phillips was seldom close by enough to stifle the inspiration of a Manasse Nkhoma to speak against farm work. And the now-heretical "baptism of fire," established in some congregations long before anyone had heard of him, continued long after he had been heard from on the subject. Phillips battled against this rite into the 1940s.

Still, despite differences, the orthodox and unorthodox branches of the Watchtower[a] shared many points of theology. Moreover, they recognized neither the territorial pretensions of the estab-

[a] Finding it impossible to distinguish with assurance between "Watchtower" groups and "Witnesses" proper before the late 1940s, I have continued for most part to use the former term.

lished missions nor the demands of chiefs and headmen, if these comported idolatry. And, while thus sabotaging the machinery of indirect rule, they both took care to avoid direct confrontation with white officialdom, except in matters of religious liberty. But since colonial arrangements left little room for the quiet exercise of this liberty, they jointly offended religious opponents of political importance.

THE STRUGGLE AGAINST FALSE RELIGION

Upon learning of the regime's intention to admit a Watchtower representative, the Methodist missionary G. E. Greenfield blasted this "right about face," in the pages of the *Bulawayo Chronicle*. He regaled the *Chronicle*'s readers with a detailed account of the society's false religion: According to the Watchtower, nobody possessed an immortal soul; eternal punishment and reward did not begin at the hour of death but awaited Jesus' return to earth; there were no such places as heaven and hell but only states of life and death; and at the end there would be either permanent life on an earth made new or permanent bodily death. Such teachings amounted to "ecclesiastical bolshevism."[1] Greenfield's curious joining of antagonists—"ecclesiastical" and "bolshevism"—suggests the "obscure but intimate relations" theology had with polity in his mind.

Theology consorted with polity on the ground as well. When L. V. Phillips and his brethren took the offensive against false religion, mission schools stood in their path, side by side with mission churches. Schools became a political battlefield. Widespread during the 1930s and 1940s, this fight took various forms. Watchtower parents often refused to send their children to school at all or else withdrew them as soon as they had learned to read. Sometimes their opposition to missionary education took the form of a more radical demand, that schools be detached from churches altogether. This demand reverberated in Fife (where Mwenzo controlled education, without serious competition, until the late 1930s) as early as 1922. Since Mwenzo's schools were vulnerable to criticism on other than religious grounds, Watchtower adherents did not make this demand alone.[2] But their outlook about mission schools became associated with their disdain for authorities of "the world." Thus, in 1935, when the DC at nearby Isoka proposed to halt Watchtower baptizing and thereby prevent disorder, the disorder he specifically mentioned was the disruption of school attendance.[3] So closely were order and school attendance associated that, where Watchtower parents decided to send their children to school, DCs took the decision as evidence in itself that they had finally settled down to become law-abiding subjects.[4] It is remarkable that boycotting schools indicated lawlessness: School attendance by African children was neither compulsory nor free. (It did not become so until after Zambia's independence.)

To seem law-abiding in the DC's sense, Watchtower parents had no choice but to expose their children to false religious teaching. Wherever children studied, they acquired vivid information about heaven and hell; and they were very likely to sing the words "my soul" often in their classrooms. At the very least, some parents thought, a few Watchtower hymns might be added. Others went further. The preacher Norris Cres Gondwe denied that tax money should support mission schools at all. As he put it,

> Whoever says that the school belongs exclusively to himself causes the British rule amiss because Government does not take tax money for nothing, but it repays to the enjoyment of the people. So the duty of Jehovah's Witnesses is to glorify the Name of GOD and His Kingdom on earth under Christ, to warn the people about the forthcoming fearful thing which shall bring them destruction. It is coming, to destroy evil people who refuse God and his Kingdom.[5]

If there was theology to be taught, then Watchtower believers had their own. It extended to other activities of the schools. The scout troops (popular adjuncts of the churches, hence of the schools) had an objectionable militaristic flavor. Drill formations and marching as part of school exercises were objectionable for the same reason, as were flag saluting and the singing of "God Save the King."[6]

In wartime, the boycott of schools threatened strategic interests. A rumor attributed to Watchtowerites held that groups of boys who gathered in the Free Church and Dutch Reformed schools, supposedly to learn the three Rs, were being shanghaied into the military instead.[7] It may not be true that school buildings actually served as recruitment depots for the armed forces. And even if this had occurred, the Dutch Reformed schools probably would not have been involved.[b] But the rumor nevertheless conveys the

[b] Although the Dutch Reformed Church was officially pacifist during World War II, we need not dismiss the rumor a priori. Conceivably, given the presence in the Eastern Province of South African settlers—who required British protection against African unrest—local DCs may have found ways to make quiet forms of collaboration

flavor of a time in which nearly all missions found their way around the Sixth Commandment and took care to inform their adherents of the reasons. Only the Seventh-Day Adventists and the Dutch Reformed missions joined the Watchtower in taking an official position against the war. (L. V. Phillips actually went to jail in 1944 rather than obey a call-up order.)[8]

During lesser emergencies as well, schools occupied sensitive political territory. In 1932, as the Depression ravaged African livelihoods, any node of group disaffection spelled trouble. In that difficult year, a certain Mulemwa started preaching in Mongu. He accosted pupils on the byways leading to the schools of the Paris Evangelical Mission and lectured unemployed workers in their gathering places. Mulemwa exploited the Depression effectively: When proclaiming that the end of the world was near and whites would soon leave, he pointed to known whites actually leaving, businesses failed. According to the DC, Mulemwa preached "charity toward all men and the worthlessness of all worldly goods." This preaching caused the chief "great offense."[9]

Just then the Mongu native authority was producing a new worldly good. In response to popular demand, the chief was helping to erect a school building and actively encouraging attendance. Mulemwa's preaching daily contradicted him. Worse, Mulemwa was collecting most of his followers among a group of recent immigrants from Angola. There was "already a little feeling" between these immigrants and the indigenous majority. To add religious difference to an already troubled mixture was to heat up a local politics that was simmering on its own.

The situation at Mongu was one variety of a larger species, conflict between those who desired to send their children to a school and those who sought to close it down. This sort of conflict, which simmers below the surface of strikes and boycotts everywhere, raises the threat of sniping among factions that permanently disagree. From the standpoint of local authority at Mongu, an irreducible factional division was quite as disruptive as unanimous defection to Watchtower ideas. Secular education would have closed off this source of trouble. But the colonial regime in this part of Africa spent little of its subjects' tax money on African education. It con-

in the war effort attractive to neighboring local missionaries. Only detailed research in the area can establish whether principle bent in accord with local circumstances there, as commonly happened on a variety of issues elsewhere in the colony.

tinued to depend upon missions, whose outlays it supplemented by grants-in-aid.

Trouble over schools arose again in the Southern Province, at the end of World War II. The NA headed by Chief Kayingu joined forces with the Methodist Missionary Society and the administration to build a school.[10] In response, the Watchtower group asked permission to establish their own school and to build it in a prominent place—next to that of the NA. Kayingu held that arguments and fighting would inevitably result. He spoke from experience. Thirteen years previously, when he had been only a native authority councilor, a large revival had swept the area. During the excitement, his predecessor had narrowly escaped being deposed by the British for inability to control his subjects. Norris Cres Gondwe alluded to the incident in his written appeal of the NA's original veto:

> Chief Kayingu does not understand properly about the Watchtower Bible and Tract Society. His advisors, Ephraim, the Native Court Clerk, and [the] teacher Jeremiah, are telling him lies that if you allow Watchtower Government will take away your chieftainship.[11]

No doubt remembering the close call of Kayingu's antecedent, the DC and his superior concurred in upholding Kayingu's decision—although not without soul-searching about the principle of religious toleration. They concluded at length that the NA would have to be upheld if indirect rule was to work at all.

Thus, religious liberty was not consistent with indirect rule as it evolved in the 1930s and 1940s. The regime hoped to strengthen the NAs as agencies of local government and development by involving them in education. But, given the historical pattern, education meant co-operation with the established missions. In turn, this co-operation made the site fought for by Gondwe and his followers the territory of a petty "state church." Thus, the old pattern of Watchtower activism persisted, but in a somewhat changed form. Whereas customary rulers and missionaries had often been rivals in the past, colonial progress tended to make them allies. Both, therefore, continued to be natural targets of militant revival—but together rather than separately. In sum, rival schools were cut from the same cloth as rival baptisms. Both were means of propagating the Watchtower version of the truth in a polity built upon other true versions of the Christian Millennium. In colonial Zambia, religion engaged much more than individual consciences.

The institutional groundwork of peaceful toleration had not been laid.

Watchtower adherents pressed their theological fight in vigorous local actions. In Mporokoso District, for example, they loudly proclaimed their beliefs in the vicinity of the local Protestant church while services were being held inside. One member of this group (led, according to the official report, by "a particularly insolent woman") tied a hoe to a tree and banged it in accompaniment to Watchtower hymns.[12] In the country of the Bemba chief Mukwikile, Watchtower adherents upset Catholic and Protestant evangelists alike by holding rival services in the same villages, at the same times.[13] One incident of this sort illustrates once again the practical continuity between the territory of the missions and the regime. The group at Mporokoso forced the cancellation of a speech the DC planned to give one Sunday morning. By the time he arrived, their noisy worship had scattered the mission congregation the DC was expecting to find still gathered in church at the conclusion of the service.[14]

Thus, although the coming of L. V. Phillips put an end to the Watchtower as a movement openly committed to shaking colonial law and order, it did not put an end to open commitments that had the same result. Songs insulting missionaries and African evangelists continued to be composed and performed. The old practices of calling loyal mission members snakes and goats continued. In some cases the injunction against contact with them went so far as a prohibition against even shaking hands.[15] The old tendency toward separatism persisted likewise. The congregation Hanoc Sindano founded in 1918 survived into the 1950s as a separate settlement called Jerusalem.[16] Jeremiah Gondwe's Jerusalem, established in the 1930s, still exists.[17] Countless family-sized Watchtower settlements flourish in the vicinity of Broken Hill.[18] Finally, the tendency to undermine black authorities, while avoiding confrontation with white ones, remained an outstanding feature of Watchtower activism.

WAR BETWEEN THE WATCHTOWER AND CUSTOMARY RULERS

Typically, war between Watchtowerites and chiefs grew directly out of the British peace, as a letter of 1940 from the chief's court at Kalimankonde illustrates:

I do not like you Watchtowerites to preach in my country because your preaching is preventing people to do government work. I do not want you at all. When I sent you to go and do road work you refused to obey and said you would not do government work. You spoke before me that you could not work for Government, why have you now said that you do not know the reason I have put you in prison for?[19]

In this scene we catch the chief pivoting midway of the two-way communication that was his burden under indirect rule. The "bwana" has assigned the chief a quota of road work. The chief has turned first to his people for the required volunteers and then back to the "bwana" to explain his action against those who said no. At Kalimankonde, Watchtowerites said *no* to the chief as mouthpiece for colonial priorities in his district. Elsewhere they said *no* to the chief as chief. Or they did both, since the chief's two faces were often indistinguishable.

Chiefs waged the British peace by causing the voice of the *boma* to be heard in the vernacular. Therefore, much of the fighting occurred at the pivot point where an order that had originated in English, from a square office adorned with forms, files, and a typewriter, was heard again in a grass- or clay-walled enclosure, in one's mother tongue, from a person whose right to respect one at first found hard to deny. At this pivot point, old-fashioned piety carried modern commandments, but it slumped under the unaccustomed weight.

Concerted Impiety

The regime was frequently called upon to repair the instruments of its bicultural ventriloquism. It took up the tools of this repair where it could find them. When a Watchtower group at Senanga refused to make the *shoelela* salute to the Mulena Mukwae (the Paramount Chieftainess) and the *kandelela* salute to her subchiefs, the DC cast about for means of reinforcing customary pieties. A new tool was just then on the drawing board. The incident occurred at the time when the central administration was calculating whether to admit Petrus de Jaeger, Phillips' predecessor, into Zambia. Unlike the Reverend Mr. Greenfield, who anathematized all Watchtowerites as "ecclesiastical bolsheviks," regardless of color, the DC was ready to make distinctions. Giving the principle of selective toleration hearty support, he hoped that the white missionary would soon arrive to help "weed out [the] undesirables" and, generally, "help us who have the duty of preserving Public Order and the King's peace in these outlying regions."[20]

The DC's public order had already suffered, first in certain villages, then in court. British prosecutors charged members of the Senangan group with "sedition"—no doubt because the local aristocracy had their ear and had made them understand the augustness of royal personage: Where anyone can say, "L'état c'est moi," failure to make ritual obeisance does indeed constitute sedition. But the local prosecutors went down in defeat when the charge failed in court. As usual, away from the sunlight of African royalty, and away from the quotidian practicalities of ruling, what counted were British definitions of the crime. A memorandum from the attorney general's office recommended that, in future, all such cases should be tried as a breach of customary etiquette "likely to lead to a breach of the peace."[21] Small wonder that the DC hoped for the speedy arrival of a missionary who might be prevailed upon to collaborate—and thus make trials a last resort.

While it is remarkable that the king's peace in Senanga implied the performance of the *shoelela* and *kandelela* salutes, the situation was not unique. A chief in Mporokoso District fined Watchtower adherents for their refusal to greet him politely upon his arrival in their presence. Instead of shouting, as custom required, they greeted him with an insolent silence.[22] The silent group was fined for "disorderly conduct," an exotic Central African form of this misdemeanor. Resistance to chiefs' work as agents of the regime underlay both incidents. The Senangan group combined disrespect to their rulers with refusal to co-operate in the taking of the census (implicitly, defiance of the tax law) and intimidation of the enumerators, who saw the census lists they placed in villages go up in smoke. Nor did the affair stop at disrespect and threat of physical violence. By the time it had run its course, many villages had passed out of control by the headmen whom the Mulena Mukwae and her subordinates (hence the regime) recognized, and were being run instead by Watchtower pastors.[23] At Mporokoso the Watchtower group did not go so far. They agreed to do their quota of road work, as the chief commanded, but contemptuously ignored him when he arrived to inspect the work site. The local administration upheld the chief's decision to punish his subjects' disrespect because it was felt that even silent discourtesy injured the chief.

The connection between ritual disrespect and political dissent was at some times very obvious and at others less so. It was obvious during the war, when ritual disrespect to the chiefs of Barotseland usually punctuated their visits to promote the buying of war bonds.[24] Events in the Luangwa Valley at about the same time bring out a less obvious connection between customary etiquette and colonial policy. There Chief Mulendema and his colleagues complained that the Watchtower was "agitating our sons."

> We do not like [the Watchtower] sir, together with all our headmen who replied the same word, "we do not like it." . . .
> The reasons why we do not like it are these—1) they have no help to government, they do not offer themselves or recruit for war work; 2) they do not respect their country and their chiefs; 3) they send women on long journeys to go to preach without the consent of their husbands; 4) they do not keep well their dead relatives.[25]

Mulendema's letter sets forth the double orientation of chiefs' work. On the one hand they worked as executive agents of the regime and, on the other, as defenders of customary piety. From Mulendema's practical standpoint, refusal to do war work and failure to "keep . . . dead relatives" were both manifestations of a single problem of authority. If he did not preside over respect for the ancestors, he did not preside over respect for the Crown. The regime could no more be indifferent to the dead than it could be to the prosecution of the war.

Buttressing Piety

When, in 1940 and 1941, the question arose whether to ban the Watchtower movement altogether, one argument in favor was that "the spirit being bred among the younger generation [by the Watchtower] is detrimental to tribal authority, which it is the policy of the government to support."[26] The Watchtower represented a "trend to personal emancipation from existing forms of authority," offering "a prospect of widespread lawlessness instead."[27] Long before the war imposed its special burdens upon customary rulers, the DC at Ndola was already castigating the Watchtower for its "vile attack upon native social life" and quoting Chief Shibuchinga to the effect that the Watchtower "had killed real respect for government and chiefs and now is to kill what remains of old native custom."[28] Shibuchinga had gotten the ear of the DC on the subject of the notorious "baptism of fire" practiced in certain Watchtower conventicles. This rite involved the performance of sexual intercourse with persons forbidden by customary law, and it was said to convey extraordinary benefits. According to Chief Mujmanzone, "[The preachers] cheat them by saying that they have a spirit if they do [these things]."[29] When, by means of incest and adultery, they got their spirit, a "gibbering, shivering . . . fit" carried them yet further beyond worldly good and evil; the same transport left the worldly rulers exposed to contempt. The antinomianism of the baptism of fire therefore stood condemned by administrators, missionaries, and chiefs alike. It derailed the regime's civilizing mission, as borne by Mujmanzone and his colleagues. And it seemed detestable in itself.

But, in a broader sense, antinomianism was the heart of the civilizing mission. The churches battled for lawlessness wherever a heathen lawfulness blocked their propagation of the Gospel. The colonial economy propagated lawlessness by so reorienting social life that individuals found it more and more impractical to be law-abiding in customary terms. Such novelties as work for a wage, residence in a town, and acceptance of Christ as one's personal savior did the same antinomian work as the baptism of fire. All attacked the old-fashioned kinship organization as a mode of integrating lives and livelihoods. All transformed its logic into an illogic, and an imposition. In short, "the vile attack upon native social life" that so disconcerted, when shouted by an ecstatic convert, actually began in the quiet of mission and *boma*.

Not surprisingly, we sometimes find the two institutions proclaiming it together. A DC at Mumbwa once marveled at the achievement of his local Watchtowerites. Not only had they ceased drumming and dancing, he observed, but they had also abandoned the practice of wailing at funerals. They had even built European-style graveyards. The DC found it "remarkable" that the congregation had achieved "overnight" changes that the administration and the churches had failed for decades to effect.[30] Thus, at Mumbwa, civilization comported disrespect for the dead. But at Mulendema's, Watchtower disrespect for the dead threatened civilization. Such contrasts were commonplace. The British regime traveled down the years in self-contradiction. Its normal locomotion called for one foot constantly on the accelerator and the other constantly on the brake.

No one experienced a rougher ride in consequence than did customary rulers. It was not simply that these rulers had to enforce an established tradition. Their assignment was to coerce a new generation into respect for rules that corresponded less and less, as time passed, to anyone's routine mode of life. In some instances, they invented new "traditional" rules. In others, they themselves were the novelty. For example, the late 1930s saw the birth of a contradiction in terms: the urban chief. Generally of aristocratic lineage, the urban chief left his family's rural seat to preside in town over courts that supposedly administered an already extant "native law and custom." Of course, he could actually do nothing of the kind.[31] But even then—perhaps especially then—the terms of discourse in which he had to proceed rang more and more hollowly as the substance to which they corresponded melted away. In the long run, his assignment was impossible to fulfill. In the short run, it made a "politics of custom" the terrain of formidable activism, by a chief and by his opponents.

The activism of chiefs enforced the demand for change, when it came from above. But, when the demand came from below, to advocate change was to enter what the regime called "politics." As "civil servants" of a kind, chiefs were enjoined to stand above it. Thus, when a Native Welfare Association was formed at Mwenzo in 1925, the administration patronized it as a useful outlet for educated Africans (provided, of course, they did nothing of substance), but swiftly warned the chiefs who had attended its early meetings to stay away.[32] According to theory, chiefs had no need to join the agenda of commoners; they had their own. And they certainly had no need to take part in petition writing, letters to the editor of local newspapers, and similar "political" activities engaged in by the Welfare Association. Chiefs had a direct route to the administration. Moreover, their regular meetings with administrators provided for the harmonious airing of grievances and suggestions. And a lively *ndaba*, well attended by the people, did the work of a parliament. In this abundance of two-way communication, the people had all the representation they needed. When postindependence writers set out to formalize the theory of single-party government in Africa, they had the colonial example not far behind them.

Colonial theory notwithstanding, chiefs were expected to amplify only the British voices from above. The meeting held at Kasempa in 1937 illustrates their role. Since the governor himself attended, all present must have beheld the full regalia of the empire: chiefs resplendent in their best outfits set off with beads and furs; *boma* messengers and police impressive in heavily starched shorts and crimson fezzes; DCs marvelous in white pith helmets and dress uniforms; the governor distinguished in sashes, fringes, and plumed headdress; an enormous Union Jack flapping over a meeting ground swept and pounded by a village corvée. The regime periodically made arrangements to amplify its own voice.[33] Preparation, long expectation, and grand spectacle served a purpose.

When Kasonso stood up to accuse the Watchtower young people of "spoiling the land," he got a sympathetic hearing. Someone even took notes as he listed the degrees of kinship within which custom prohibited sexual relations and marriage. But when his brother chief rose, on behalf of respectable subjects, to request schooling in English, the governor intoned "His Majesty's policy": to educate in the vernacular during the first four years[34] (all the schooling the majority of children then had access to). His Majesty's policy originated in a concern for the preservation of indigenous culture. Colonial educators were convinced that the too-rapid spread of an alien education would create a class of misfits. But the popular demand originated in a concern for advancement in the world the aliens were making. From that point of view, the vernacular policy seemed a way to designate another generation as untutored Africans, aliens in this new world. The people listened as their representative in the halls of power made his case—and got his succinct answer. No agitator could have discredited the chiefs as mouthpieces from below more thoroughly than the governor did in this encounter. Some latter-day aristocrats are born to irrelevance. These had irrelevance thrust upon them.

But if chiefs were irrelevant when people searched the horizon, they had to be reckoned with from day to ,day. Chiefs had the authority to give or withhold permission to establish a homestead. They administered marriage, divorce, and the property transactions related thereto. They took on the role of guardianship when men left their families to find work. They apprehended criminals and reported troublemakers to the *boma*. They gathered the workers to maintain roads. They presided in court, collecting fees and fines as they went. In wartime, they translated Britain's call for sacrifice. At all times they collected taxes—taxes on hunting and fishing; taxes on guns, radios, fishnets, and bicycles; and above all, the poll tax, the tax on reaching male adulthood in the colony. In the regime's peculiar lexicon, all of these were the nonpolitical tasks of orderly administration. But their accomplishment was hardly nonpolitical at grass-roots level. Chiefs often had to proceed in the teeth of strong local opposition, from both Watchtower and non-Watchtower subjects. Since everything had to be accomplished through the evolutionary conservatism of the customary order, it is no wonder that militant politics often spoke in the language of custom.

Militant Administration

When battles spilled beyond the territory of native law and custom, officials stepped in to hand the chiefs other tools. P. J. Macdonnell had taught that Watchtowerites should be selectively tolerated, but that colonial laws could be selectively enforced against them. In the mid-1930s and again during World War II, local officials rediscovered this principle. Since opposition extended beyond Watchtower groups, but was not easily targetable, "selection" acquired fresh meaning. Trumpeting conversion, and doing all that followed from it, the Watchtower provided a conspicuous target. Administrators armed their African colleagues with Macdonnell's weaponry against it.

Following a salvo from the administrative weapon in Luapula, a certain Mwendaifya found himself suddenly reentered on the tax roll, despite the lifetime exemption he had obtained on grounds of poverty and old age. L. V. Phillips promptly forwarded an angry protest to the chief secretary: The DC, W. F. Stubbs, was guilty of religious persecution, pure and simple. When queried, Stubbs denied the charge. In the first place, he said, Mwendaifya had obtained his exemption under false pretenses: He had appeared at the *boma* wearing ashes in his hair and tattered clothes, whereas in fact he was a prosperous potato trader, owner of a substantial modern house, and father of several children all of whom were attending school. In the second place, it was the chief who had acted, not the DC; after the chief exposed Mwendaifya, the DC only applied the tax regulations. In any case, Stubbs went on, "I think it even more important than formerly that the chief should have the last say in whatever exemptions are given." Furthermore, Mwendaifya had brought the trouble upon himself. Had he "not been badly involved in the Watchtower he might possibly have his exemption still as he would have kept out of sight. This is the only connection there is between the cancellation of his exemption and his religion."[35] Stubbs conceded that he had a reputation for persecution, but hoped that his superior would believe that he had only enforced existing provisions "with a sense of fair play." He did not claim, and had no reason to claim, that the tax law was enforced uniformly, across the board. His superior knew better.[36] The giving (and withholding) of tax exemptions provided chiefs with a kind of patronage for distribution among co-operative subjects.

Like the tax law, the law that regulated settlement could not be enforced uniformly. The old rules setting the minimum size of a settlement and requiring a chief's authorization were more often broken than obeyed. By the 1930s, it was commonplace for men returning from work in town to establish themselves in well-built houses outside established villages, in order to escape the constraints and obligations of village life. But while the regime had to ignore many instances in which the builders did not obtain their chief's permission, it did not have to ignore all. In 1920, Leviticus Kanjele was jailed for building a house without authorization.[37] In 1935, several chiefs in the Luapula Valley received authorization (by Stubbs) to burn down illegal Watchtower settlements.[38] In 1936, when a Watchtower preacher living in a village near the Copperbelt built a house at the edge of his village, the chief stepped in to tear it down.[39] The DC, who described the house as "enormous," large enough to accommodate Watchtower study meetings, concurred with the chief's view that the owner of the house was "too proud." Similar incidents occurred in the Petauke and Kawambwa districts, and no doubt elsewhere as well.

The increasing independence of women provides another example of norms widely breached on the quiet, but loudly breached by Watchtower converts. The DC at Senanga turned his spotlight on the women in remarks about subversive preaching: "By that I do not mean that I think they openly preach sedition, but that they tend to make the people depise the law and flout authority, especially the women."[40] From there he went on to rediscover the same link with murder that his colleague had discovered at Fort Jameson a decade earlier. The chiefs told him that women used their Watchtower itinerating as cover for adultery. The DC passed on to his superiors the chiefs' forecast of mayhem when the husbands returned home. But the chiefs', and the DC's, own argument unmasked the migratory labor system as the real destroyer of family-life in its time-honored forms.[41] The administration implicitly recognized this by supporting chiefs in their effort to prevent women from following the men to the towns.[42] (Only in the 1940s did the regime decide to make the Copperbelt a place where a stabilized male labor force could move out of barracks and into compounds where their families could join them.)[43]

During the mobilization for World War II, the Watchtower again stood out in the selective perception of the regime. A police report of late 1940 observed that, although the religious teaching was not seditious in the ordinary sense, it was hindering the war effort. In the words of the report, "All teaching [was], however, assuming a

more important role than the purely religious."[44] The odd phrasing
derives from a special definition of "religious," which accommo-
dated patriotic sermons in mission churches but not their rebuttals.
Watchtower adherents did not, however, limit themselves to
worldly talk. In 1941, a group near Mumbwa held a prayer meeting.
They chose to pray at exactly the hour when the regimental band
was to offer a recruitment parade and concert—such performances
being calculated to dazzle villagers into patriotic enthusiasm by
means of fancy uniforms and stirring music.[45] Most people chose
the prayer meeting over the concert. Actions of this sort earned
the Watchtower its reputation.

But, in fact, unwillingness to make wartime sacrifices was widespread. It was reported in the Eastern Province that, the day after
the regimental recruiter appeared, the *boma* was flooded with ap-
plications for passports to leave the territory in search of employment, despite men's extreme reluctance to leave their homes for
any reason.[46] There military recruitment was hindered by the fear
that more land would be sold to white settlers in the men's absence.
One frank official admitted that the fear was justified.[47] Another
frankly admitted that some chiefs were not performing up to stand-
ard: The *khotla* in Barotseland "failed to set an example" by joining
up themselves or encouraging their families to do so. Moreover,
they were "lazy and grasping," and people listening to their ex-
hortations took that into account.[48] Elsewhere villagers resisted
pressure to cultivate increased acreages of crops specified by the
administration, and evaded recruitment for other tasks dictated by
the emergency.

The administration itself betrayed the fact that resistance to mobilization was not restricted to Watchtower agitation. A minute from
the chief legal officer to the chief secretary proposed new measures
for the enforcement of what were technically called "reasonable
instructions" by the DCs. (This brought into existence the crime of
disobedience to reasonable instructions of the DCs, to be added to
the already-existing crime of disobedience to "reasonable orders"
of the native authorities.) The new powers, the minute said, would
"cramp the style of Watchtower adherents, and of the many natives
who, having no connection with the Watchtower, or Phillips, or
their literature whatsoever, are beginning to realize that they can
flout the administration simply by saying, 'I cannot do this, I am a
Watchtower man.'"[49] And from the Eastern Province came the
revealing observation that so many people were claiming to be
conscientious objectors that it was becoming difficult "to distinguish

the real from the pseudo adherents of the Watchtower."[50] In this context, Alex Muwamba, free-lance booster of official policies, made his classic judgment, which I quote again: "I do not think they join the movement to become Christians but to avoid death by being killed."[51] Administrators rarely managed to demonstrate, even to their own satisfaction, that Watchtower preaching accounted for the lack of popular enthusiasm for the military effort. Indeed, they had in hand an uncharacteristic promise of cooperation from L. V. Phillips, who instructed local preachers to stop referring to the war at all in their work.

Nevertheless, in the view of most DCs polled in mid-1942, the Watchtower was seriously hindering the war effort, and strong action should be taken against it.[52] The result was a proposal to ban the movement altogether. Practically speaking, such a policy would have required the incarceration of an unknown but rapidly growing number of people. Legally speaking, it would have required an extraordinary suspension of civil liberties. In any event, the administration settled on a less drastic course: banning the books instead.[c] The publication, printing, distribution, and possession of Watchtower literature were made punishable by imprisonment. Since even the lesser course involved an assault upon civil liberties, it required explanation. The governor's letter to the secretary of state for the colonies was a far cry from what it would have taken to justify a policy of jailing all Watchtower members.

The pamphlets "Fascism or Freedom," "War or Peace" . . . [and others] contained some pacifist propaganda, and in varying degrees some passages apparently attacked all recognized au-

---

[c] I was unable to determine what settled the administration's final decision to take the less drastic course. The view of the chief secretary, that "as a people we are not good at being ruthless," is surely only part of the truth, although some officials certainly objected on principle. For example, two DCs argued that the incarceration of Watchtowerites would resemble Nazi practice (see NAZ, Sec/Nat 312 [vol. 7], memo, 20/3/1941). Another important obstacle may have been the difficulty of determining whom to arrest and of calculating beforehand the effect of large-scale arrests upon the general population. Conceivably, also, the literature ban may have constituted a preliminary step. The law read that those possessing literature were required to surrender it at their local *bomas*, and officials may have envisaged the possibility of collecting at that time, for possible future use, the names of subscribers, routes of importation, modes of distribution, and the like. The DC at Kasempa did indeed use people's compliance with the law in this way (see NAZ, Sec/Nat 312 [vol. 7], DC [Kasempa] to CS, 15/3/1941). The records do not show that Watchtowerites throughout the colony made this easy method of intelligence gathering available to all DCs.

thority in the form of secular governments, and also recognized religions, in particular the Roman Catholic Church. It was considered that this propaganda and these attacks were likely to have a deleterious effect upon the untutored minds of Africans, and result in the spread of subversive doctrines.[53]

The governor's letter to Britain groped for intangibles of outlook and attitude. In the colony, these matters were tangible. Customary rulers struggled to execute wartime policies with little more to aid them than their moral influence. Their burden increased in step with the regime's exactions from the population. The exactions generated a war within the war. During 1940, events reached such a pass in Mkushi District that the regime reinforced the beleaguered chief by sending out a detective. Ten days' plainclothes surveillance of the preacher Isaac Mwape revealed the swaggering owner of a gold-headed walking stick, "an educated man," the DC said, "with a supercilious manner, which in itself must be very galling to an old chief."[54] The investigation uncovered nothing the governor could have cited in a letter telling the secretary why large-scale arrests of Watchtower adherents were needed. Yet Mwape and his followers effectively obstructed the chief in the performance of his job.

Chiefs on the Copperbelt reported obstruction when they toured to collect subscriptions to the War Fund.[55] And Alex Muwamba wrote to report Watchtower opposition to the "Food for Britain" appeal, a war-era charity.[56] The provincial commissioner observed, in reaction, that there was "no question of compulsory subscription and the chiefs have been told this clearly," but that the Watchtower's lack of enthusiasm for the food appeal was "a potential source of trouble between the NA's and [Watchtower] adherents."[57] It may or may not be the case that chiefs clearly distinguished between orders to administer programs like the War Fund and Food for Britain, supposedly free will, and others that were compulsory. It would not seem extravagant speculation to suppose that chiefs' good reputations as "progressive" leaders were contingent upon their performance in both kinds of activity. In this way, chiefs' attitudes were forged and honed as they went about their tasks. By 1948, the governor could report, with some justice, that chiefs were "almost uniformly hostile to the Watchtower."[58] But the governor was reporting the outcome of a long, and by no means spontaneous, evolution.

PEACE BETWEEN THE WATCHTOWER AND CUSTOMARY RULERS

During the outbreak of 1932 in the Eastern Province, a touring official complained that many chiefs' aversion to the Watchtower consisted only in the fear that it would "get them into trouble with the *boma*."[59] Many of his contemporaries condemned "hypocrisy" and "two-facedness" on the part of chiefs who only pretended dislike. At Mkushi, chiefs and headmen arrested Watchtower adherents, or even reported their activities, only when they "deem[ed] it politic."[60] Around Lusaka, the chiefs "affected a vigorous dislike" for the movement, when talking to an official or a missionary, but accepted baptism themselves and encouraged others to do so.[61] Again, many village headmen near the Copperbelt (including many old men, from whom conservative views would normally be expected) became "avowed ringleaders" of Watchtower activity.[62] They seem to have defied their chiefs in order to join a "baptism of fire" that they could not beat. One of the Mwinilunga chiefs actually tried to compel his people to join. The DC caught him threatening to fine anyone who refused to be baptized.

Local administrators met the challenge in various ways. DCs constantly "reminded" chiefs and headmen of their considerable authority under the Native Authority Ordinance. They supplemented the reminders with various inducements. The offer of gifts and cash bounties noted earlier in the case of Chief Kavimba probably continued in order, as the DC said, "to encourage others."[63] To discourage noncooperation, DCs imposed fines. A letter to L. V. Phillips from the chief secretary admitted that a headman who failed to report unauthorized meetings was liable to a fine of one pound.[64] Since interpretations of long standing acknowledged their right punish subjects holding or participating in unauthorized meetings, it appears that the administration moved to the odd position of compelling the exercise of a right. It is difficult to say how prevalent this sort of measure became. Given the formal principle of religious toleration, it probably occurred more often than was formally acknowledged. Phillips' incessant querying brought this particular measure to light. But the many cases in which chiefs and headmen defended their actions by saying in effect that they were "only doing their jobs" suggest that they were under constant informal pressure to take various sorts of action against Watchtower groups.

Accused of disrupting an orderly Watchtower study meeting, Chief Mumbwa replied that he had only acted on instructions. As a result of a complaint by Phillips, the provincial commissioner finally questioned his subordinate, one Sharpe. The reply was roundabout. Sharpe explained that, when Mumbwa had come to the *boma* to request instructions, he had been away. Mumbwa spoke to Mrs. Sharpe instead. Speaking vintage "Macdonnellese," she told Mumbwa something

> to the effect that it was within his powers to refuse to allow such meetings (under orders made by the Kaonde-Ila N.A.'s) if he felt they would cause offence or annoyance to headmen and people not of the Watchtower sect, or if he feared that they would cause unrest in this area.[65]

According to the DC, Mumbwa did not find his way through the rambling formula and apparently "translated this advice into the direct statement." To avoid trouble, many chiefs sought explicit instructions from the local administration before making any move at all.

Thus, in addition to the "almost uniform hostility" the governor noted, the historical reality includes many varieties of "peace" between customary rulers and the Watchtower. Some chiefs took the path of collaboration, as Shaiwila did, although without Shaiwila's excess; others took the war path, but with varied results. Some took a middle ground of toleration; others swung from one extreme to the other. A coherent pattern emerges only when we set the issue within the context of the doubly articulated colonial state, in which forces above had a different vector than forces below, and in which chiefs were, by definition, two-faced.

The Forces Above

The British administration stood ready to remove a chief or headman if he proved "unsatisfactory." But, in dealings with the Watchtower, the road to satisfaction was not obvious. A ruler could suffer either by joining the movement or by trying to beat it. As we saw, at Mwenzo in 1919, Watchtower baptizing isolated the establishment from the people, thereby rendering the establishment ineffective. In the Mwana Lesa episode, by contrast, baptizing united the establishment and the people, but at the expense of the British regime. Other episodes approximated these patterns.

During 1935, in the villages near Lusaka, various chiefs said they had been baptized even though the prophecies seemed silly. If they had not accepted baptism, they said, they would have suffered denunciation as witches and thereby lost the confidence of their subjects.[66] During the excitement of 1932 in the vicinity of Fort Jameson, chiefs who "stood firm" (as the DC approvingly said) lost the allegiance of their headmen, who went over to the Watchtower.[67] Battling obediently, they lost control of their chiefdoms. A chief who could not control his headmen (and through them the villagers) could not offer the regime his chiefdom. Once this became apparent, he struggled on the slippery slope to deposition. Such was the fate of Subchief Litungi, who failed to stop Watchtower pastors from displacing the recognized headmen under his jurisdiction. Charging "weakness," Litungi's immediate superior, Ngambela, removed him from office.[68]

One can readily see that customary rulers confronted unattractive choices. There was no genuine middle position between the extremes of opposing the movement and co-operating with it. A chief could only hope to succeed by judiciously shifting ground—avoiding the fate of the chiefs at Mwenzo by tolerating the movement, and even co-operating when this was indicated; making arrests when arrests were unavoidable, when his personal strength was overwhelming, or when it was in every sense "politic" to do so. Where it seemed wise to give way before public opinion, chiefs and headmen often did so, braving the threat of fine because they feared their people more. So long as serious crime was avoided, co-operation need not trap a chief into the fate of Shaiwila. By bending to local political reality, however, a chief ran the risk of losing the confidene of the *boma*. But by not bending to local reality, he ran the same risk. Thus, as Lugard saw so clearly, indirect rule was not hospitable to the inflexible application of principles. Given his circumstances, equivocation and a certain duplicity were a chief's most practical choices. In order to get by, many a sharp-witted chief must have cultivated a reputation for absent-mindedness.

The Forces Below

An intelligence report of 1944 identified baptizing as the active ingredient of the Watchtower's mobilization from below.

> [The Watchtower] is moving farther and farther away from any organized connection with a church under European control. Its teachings are equally well adapted to advanced or primitive mentalities. To the latter, whose ancestral terror of magic they exploit, they promise liberation from the witch

doctors through baptism, and, at the same time, the means of holding out against the orders of established authority. To the advanced native they preach not only racial equality but the overthrow of established power, the submission of the European to the African and the seizure of wealth held by the foreign occupants of the country. An early arrival of the Messiah, announced from time to time, will bring paradise on earth, and whilst awaiting this event, the orders of the whites should no longer be obeyed as those who do so will be pitilessly massacred.[69]

Where popular opinion held Wachtower baptism in high esteem, a chief or headman faced strong pressure to permit it and often to be baptized himself. (Recall that many of Shaiwila's subjects preceded him to the rite; their enthusiastic reports led him to inquire about Tomo Nyirenda and then to arrange a meeting.) Baptism that promised not only salvation but also deliverance from witchcraft easily converted an affair of individual choice into one of compulsion: Choose salvation or be exposed as a public menace. Not a few chiefs chose salvation. The minimum step of accepting baptism led logically to the establishment of some definite relationship with the baptizer. Thus the rite of baptism marked terrain on which accommodation could be worked out. But since the regime demanded that chiefs oppose the rite, it also marked the terrain of conflict. On the subject of the Watchtower, no less than on the subject of witchcraft eradication, the demands of the customary and the colonial polities pushed in opposite directions. This seems to have occurred near Lusaka during the revival of 1935.[70]

T. F. Sandford, who arrested two Watchtower preachers, reported that the two had in their possession sacks of charms that people had surrendered before their baptisms. One of them called the chiefs liars for claiming that baptism had been forced upon them. Quite the contrary, he said, several had invited them to baptize. This suggests that the preachers had been recruited in the same way that Tomo Nyirenda had been—to serve as a ritual official working on behalf of constituted authority. Like Nyirenda's, his popularity would then redound to the chief as well. (Let us note, however, that Sandford's observation does not necessarily disprove the chiefs' plea of coercion. As we saw in the case of the *mucapi* revival, many rulers were forced into taking the lead of a movement that they could not quash. By skillfully managing the cure of witchcraft, a Watchtower preacher, like a *mucapi*, could use his own popularity as leverage against a reluctant chief. Most likely, both preachers and chiefs made calculations that varied from case to case depending upon local circumstance.)

Official sources sometimes imply that crafty medicine men exploited villagers' credulity for their own purposes. One DC described the rites of confession and surrendering charms that preceded Watchtower baptism as "the strongest and first-played card of the local Watchtower"[71]—that is, as a technique cynically applied to manipulate public fear. Of course there was an element of manipulation. Salesmen often increase and even transform demand by the very act of meeting it. But this should not be taken to mean that either the preachers or the chiefs conspired against their people across a cultural gulf between different mentalities. Both the chiefs and the Watchtower preachers operated within existing assumptions about witchcraft and existing modes of political practice. Both customary rulers and preachers functioning as ritual specialists applied a technique that they knew conformed to the expectations of the populace and that met a widely felt need. In short, they operated according to an established pattern.

Reports from Mwinilunga in 1933 exhibit this pattern. The DC described withcraft as "concealed but rampant" in the villages. In the atmosphere of the time, even the *boma* was recruited to the service of cure. On various occasions, the DC said, old women adopted him as a kind of *mucapi*. Confessing the most astounding acts of murder and necrophagy, they asked to be punished at the *boma*. Probably the old women calculated that the DC could preempt any witch finder who turned up in their villages to meet the public's demand for cure. At the same time, various chiefs adopted the Watchtower openly. Some of them organized mass public burnings of medicines. When questioned by the DC about their open violations of the Witchcraft Ordinance, they explained that they had only meant "to help the people."[72]

Chiefs in Namwala District made similar use of Watchtower baptism. One chief went so far as to tell the DC that it had been necessary to take away witchcraft "so that people [would] depend on government, not on witchcraft."[73] The DC quoted the remark as evidence of the "native" illogic that was his lot to contend with. But the chief was making a claim that a DC like F. H. Melland would have respected. According to Melland, we recall, the Witchcraft Ordinance hobbled indirect rule by prohibiting the open, ceremonious trial of witches by the regime's own establishment. Indeed, he "knew of cases" in which the ruler and the witch doctor were one and the same. Meanwhile, since the machinations of witches continued, the demand for cure remained. The ordinance pushed the provision of cure into the twilight of public usage, as Prohibition in the United States pushed the sale of alcohol, and with analogous consequences: "Bootleg" witch doctors swept into the vacuum created by the law. The Namwala chief was only attempting to do his part, by bringing the cure of witchcraft back into the pale of legality. He proceeded according to logic that both he and his people understood.

On the Logic of the Pax Africana

From the standpoint of those who administered the *pax Britannica*, a headman or chief was only such by virtue of "recognition" in his post and thereafter by performance in the tasks assigned to him. If his two-way communication between villages and *boma* produced satisfactory results, then his "recognition" was likely to continue. But from within the first articulation, recognition presupposed tasks and results of a different kind.

According to an account by the DC W. V. Brelsford, a certain headman, Sileti, suffered abandonment by his subjects.[74] In the hard times of the mid-1930s, his village dwindled until only a very few houses remained. One day Sileti decided to make a trip. On the way he had a piece of luck. While passing through the bush he encountered a famous hunter, Rumbola, who was sick and in distress. Sileti rescued the hunter and returned him home, to the great jubilation of Rumbola's neighbors and kinsmen. The news spread rapidly but changed as it spread. The rescue became a resurrection: Sileti had brought back Rumbola from the dead. Villagers began to come from miles around seeking cure and advice from Sileti. They also brought him presents and helped him cultivate his field, thus taking the initial steps toward joining Sileti's renascent village. Sileti's quickly became a large and flourishing community. A few months later, Sileti's son Kampola arrived home from the Copperbelt. Together with a friend, Kampola began to distribute *chimbuku*, a new medicine. At that point, Sileti's village began to attract a new stream of visitors, followed by a stream of invitations to export the *chimbuku*. Brelsford then stepped in to call a halt: "Witch doctors who suddenly rise to fame are liable to become dangerous men. . . . One usually suspects something more than success with medicine when one hears of the sudden rise to fame of a doctor."

Brelsford intervened at one pole of a movement from ritual protection and cure offered routinely by constituted authority to the same things offered by new personnel, or by the old personnel with renewed reputation and power. Sileti no doubt continued to adjudicate, to report the census, to transmit orders from higher up in the administrative chain of command, to produce men for communal labor, and so on. (And Kampola might have, if he had eventually succeeded or overthrown his father.) The observations of both Melland and Brelsford illustrate my contention that Watchtower baptizing, understood as both salvation and cure, had definite political meaning within the customary order. This meaning would not have escaped rulers anointed by the regime but dependent for whatever power they had upon the confidence of the villagers subject to them.

These observations about co-operation between ritual healers and customary rulers point to a kind of deep structure of customary authority, a grid across which Watchtower revival passed repeatedly and from which it took comprehensible form. The control of witchcraft was built into the norms and expectations surrounding public authority and cannot be divorced from the complex of ritual duties that defined it. If leadership was both conceived of and practiced in ritual terms, it is because daily life took shape by now resisting, now accommodating the unseen forces that defined human existence. Once embodied in the ordinary, the unseen forces became seen facts: beauty, good manners, hard work for conventional rewards, conventional reactions to everyday events, guilt and outrage, duty and entitlement, scandal, decency, sane judgment, and so on through the catalog of any society's tangible inheritance of intangibles. Ritual, then, was one use of the "language" in which all activity, including rule, was experienced, described, and legitimated. It provided one medium through which the thousand novelties of each day's coming and going instantly acquired the semblance of any day's unremarkable routine. It did not merely symbolize something other than itself. As in all social orders, the metaphysical and the physical came to rest, or went into motion, in the plain midst of the humdrum. If we look closely at attempts to widen the scope of a particular *pax Africana*, we notice this same deep structure: the salience of the ritual expert, either established or upstart; and the expansion of ritual functions that had other, routine uses.

Terence Ranger's seminal book, *Revolt in Southern Rhodesia*, describes the means by which the Shona and Ndebele peoples jointly resisted the imposition of British rule.[75] Ranger shows how well-known mediums, working from established spirit shrines, made possible the widened *pax Africana* that such a military project required. The shrines provided a "national" network, which gathered the restricted and largely kinship-based organization into a territorial unit. In ordinary times, the shrines were used in the transmission of cures and advice. During the war, they no doubt continued to do this but, in addition, they provided a ready-made agency for the wide transmission of military intelligence and instructions, and for co-ordination not only between competing Shona subgroups but also between the Shonas as a whole and their erstwhile military opponents, the Ndebeles. As the fighting continued, they transmitted extraordinary new cures, such as a medicine designed to set streams aflame and singe the hoofs of pursuing cavalry.

The use of medicine also sustained the Maji Maji guerrilla resistance in southern Tanzania.[76] The medicine was designed to make the fighters invulnerable to bullets and is said to have inspired very great daring. According to research by Gilbert Gwassa and John Iliffe, however, the leader, Kinjikitile, did more than create a powerful warrior's mystique. By anointing local leaders with the *maji* ("water") at a central shrine, he was able to achieve a remarkable expansion in the scale of joint action: Some twenty different ethnic groups became allies. The movement began with the distribution of a new cure, and pilgrims streamed to the shrine to get it. Then Kinjikitile exhorted the people to obey the high god, recognized by all groups, who had commanded the war. Kinjikitile also became posessed by the spirit Lilungu, whose cult was shared in most details by all the groups who joined the fighting. Thus, the distributor of the medicine proceeded in terms of a known metaphysics.

Kinjikitile's possession gave him extraordinary powers, among them the ability to detect witches in his presence. As one witness said, pure from sin himself the man possessed by Lilungu could not tolerate their presence; "witches stank before him." It is not difficult to imagine that, as the groups embarked on the dangerous path of resistance, those reluctant to go forward risked exposure as witches. From his possession, Kinjikitile also acquired the power to set aside peacetime legality. Freedom from sin and the ability to detect witches seem to have been connected to antinomianism within the *lilungu* cults. Adherents were permitted to do things forbidden to ordinary mortals, and indeed, to do things contrary to norms whose violation was conventionally attributed to witches or to the bewitched.[d] According to an informant questioned by Gwassa,

> People who have Lilungu were feared very much since the days of old. They can do anything. . . . And if a man with Lilungu killed a person where could you go to charge [him]? The Lukumbi [interclan court]? Never at all! His affairs are god-like. A man with Lilungu does not fear anything. He can even go naked. Those things that are forbidden or are too dangerous to eat, he eats.[77]

Again, it is not difficult to imagine the military uses of such liberties. The destruction of barriers based on food prohibitions would enhance interclan and interethnic co-operation. The removal of the fear and possible social condemnation attached to walking in the bush at night would facilitate nighttime movements. The fact that killing could not be authoritatively handled by existing institutions suggests that war leaders who were at the same time cult adherents may have displaced some or all of the peacetime establishment, and that internal dissidents might be summarily dispatched. Above all, the antinomianism built into the *lilungu* cult could legitimate abrupt changes in collective life.

To take a precolonial example, I. N. Kimambo and C. K. Omari have shown how a leader in Upare (Tanzania) manipulated key rituals and their functionaries.[78] By lengthening the period of male initiation and placing the initiation schools under central control, he acquired an army and the beginning of a state composed of all Pare-speaking villages. By creating a "national" rite through which men passed into adulthood, he undercut the power of the lineage elders who had previously controlled separate rites. In this example, as in the others, ritual put markers around political territory, and vice versa.

Although insufficient to display the full logic of the *pax Africana*, these examples suggest that Watchtower baptizers followed its terms—as did the Bamucapi and the chiefs who patronized them, the old women at Mwinilunga, the chiefs at Namwala, Melland at Mkushi, and Sileti and his son. The ritual function of leadership, including the eradication of witchcraft, belonged to a deeply rooted and well-known political pattern. This point requires emphasis, for

[d] Cf. the comment of Chief Kasonso, in 1937: "The preachers fool them and say they will get a spirit if they do these things."

a widely held view conceives of modern antiwitchcraft movements merely as anomic responses to the pressure of modern conditions and attributes to Watchtower millenarianism the same psychological roots. This simplified view takes no account of the social patterning that is observable in widely separate places and times.

Nor does it predict the matter-of-factness with which at least some Watchtowerites went about the business of suppressing witchcraft. A group of preachers who wrote to the DC at Mazabuka proceeded with the quiet rectitude of Sunday school teachers. "Please with honor, we, your servants, report to you, Sirs," they began. "We are the Watchtower Bible and Tract Society preachers and the reason for which we ask from you, Sir, is that we wish to preach." After dissociating themselves from the American apocalypse of 1924, which they knew the DC would object to, they spelled out their beliefs:

> And, we are not like those of the past, who were preaching to people bad things, in the years 1924 and 1925. But we, have started in 1923 up to the year 1931 and please, Sirs, we let you know about our preachings, we say every Christian should not steal or commit adultery or use by means of witchcraft any medicine or poison to kill people—it is a bad thing. Or to keep a killing medicine—such things are not wanted. And accuse somebody being a wizard—this is not wanted to a Christian. Also that Christians should not drink beer to be drunk or make quarrels or to marry two wives—such things are bad. Every Christian must live in peace with all people.[79]

Notice that the authors evidently regard the conquest of witchcraft as a normal function of the congregations they hope to form, one about which they address the DC without hesitation. Notice, also, that they pose the issue of conquering witchcraft matter-of-factly, side by side with other social issues and in the same tone of voice.

I underline this point, for nothing is more elusive to a Western observer than a conception of witchcraft as a commonplace feature of daily life. Misleading terms like *supernatural* come easily to mind. But the writers of the letter are concerned about ordinary, not extraordinary events and, above all, about right behavior. By stating that as Christians they preach against witchcraft, they refer to nothing more or less than the maintenance of good order. They apparently take it for granted that the DC, as an agent of law and order, will be sympathetic to their aims.

In contending that Watchtower baptizing was grafted onto routine expectations about the control of withcraft, I am guided by the works of Douglas, Schoffeleers, Parkin, Park, and others who draw attention to the political dynamics of witchcraft within the customary order.[80] Watchtower baptizing took shape from these existing dynamics, and its relationship to existing rulers followed logically: Anyone exercising authority would be automatically assumed to offer ritual protection and healing; and, conversely, anyone offering protection and healing would automatically be understood to claim leadership or association with leadership. In short, discourse about witchcraft and its control was ipso facto discourse about power and authority. In former times, the administration of the poison ordeal to detect witches was a function of power constituted as legitimate authority, and it followed an established legitimate procedure. When exercised in the context of a well-developed consensus,[81] the execution of witches by means of the ordeal represented the collectivity itself. The chief, or the doctor working under the chief's aegis, was merely the agent of the collectivity, and it was the collectivity that gave the witch-finding medicine moral power. Where colonial law prevented the collectivity from asserting itself in this way, we see power being assembled and focused in the manipulation of new cures, often under new leadership and in the interest of new collectivities. Douglas, who observed the passage of a modern medicine movement among the Leles (Zaire), concluded that it is hard not to recognize the gap in collective life that opened with the demise of the poison ordeal.

Baptism as Political Mobilization

From the standpoint of colonial order, the capacity of Watchtower baptizing to assemble large groups quickly constituted a threat to order that loomed independent of the movement's specific teachings. Repeatedly during the 1920s, 1930s, and 1940s, baptism combined with prophecy, possession, and healing showed a remarkable capacity to generate new collectivities—or, as in the case of the Mwana Lesa revival, to regenerate old ones. Either way, baptism itself made for the rapid amalgamation of a following under forceful leaders. Official observers often calmed themselves during high phases of revival and prophecy with the thought that preachers would lose influence as soon as their prophecies did not materialize. In fact, the failure of a supernatural Armageddon to begin did not hinder preachers' itinerating through the same areas again and again, achieving each time a degree of success. Baptism associated with healing created a dynamism toward mass participation independent of Watchtower prophecies. Universal or near-universal baptism could and did occur in the absence of universal belief. And where mass baptizing fell short of universality, potentially dangerous new divisions came into play. It may indeed have been a vision of this possibility that led the Mwinilunga chief referred to earlier to compel universal baptism by the threat of fine. He could reasonably have decided to use his authority in order to impose baptism universally and thereby keep the king's peace.

In the wake of the Copperbelt strike, the Committee on Race Relations saw the relation of Watchtower baptism to the king's peace otherwise. After surveying the scene, they concluded that "one of the most subversive influences militating against the maintenance of amicable social relations that came to our notice is that of the Watchtower movement." They went on to construct a terrifying scenario of a violently constructed new *pax Africana* that could throw itself against the *pax Britannica*. Although almost certainly mistaken in claiming that a territory-wide program existed, their picture of how one might evolve was not fundamentally wrong. Quite likely, their vividly drawn sequence of possible events contributed to the regime's decision to admit Petrus de Jaeger. Any white influence must have seemed preferable to none.

> It looks as if the program is to enlist all natives in a movement, which, having gathered sufficient strength, will one day arise en masse to rid the entire land of all white people, by any method whatsoever. To realise this program there are a large number of men called "preachers." From the information we have received we conclude, and deplore the fact, that these "preachers" are largely former members of the Protestant missions who have been disciplined. . . .
>
> The movement battens on fear. An African native is a creature of fears and very particularly of the fear that even unknown to himself he may become possessed of a demon, which will cause him to bring sickness or bad luck to his village. This may eventually mean death at the hands of the villagers, if suspicion falls upon him. Now, the exploitation of this fear on the part of the "preachers" constitutes the most prolific avenue of convert-making. By "confession" and "baptism" the "preachers" promise cleaning from all magical influences and evil spirits, and furthermore, a thing of paramount value, immunity to the possibility of being bewitched by others.

With satanic malignity the "preachers" pick out certain people in the village whom they declare have magic medicine in their houses, medicine to kill or injure others, or they declare that these people are witches and are practicing witchcraft. The promise of cleansing, on the part of the "preachers," is therefore extremely alluring. "Confession" is made, "baptism" is given and the people are now members. But, of the few, who absolutely refuse to confess something which they know they do not possess, examples must be made. Usually old women are picked out by the "preachers" and cruelly treated in order to extort confessions. As many people as possible are collected to witness the proceeding, so that fear strikes through the heart of everybody. Converts are made by the score from now on through the whole countryside, as the news goes everywhere.[82]

Although intended to discredit Watchtower preachers, the committee's point about coercion is not fundamentally wrong. Their scenario is a useful corrective to another mode of argument, in which the problem of order in African villages was solved by faith alone.

It became a commonplace of anthropological thinking that order arose from the operation of shared belief in myths, rituals, and supernatural sanctions. With the white regime in sole possession of the right to use force lawfully, scientists found a novel solution to the political problem of order: Among African peoples, belief took over virtually all the space force occupies in the equation elsewhere. This theory committed Westerners, in effect, to the concrete efficacy of the supernatural; and the scientist came near to regarding beliefs in the same way a fetishist regards an idol that commands with its lips of wood and smites from its painted pedestal. In the words of Fortes and Evans-Pritchard, "Members of an African society feel their unity and perceive their common interests in symbols, and it is their attachment to these symbols which more than anything else gives their society cohesion and persistence."[83]

Some DCs absorbed this scientific sophistication and made it supersede the crude early judgments of heedless civilizers. W. V. Brelsford wrote in this vein that African villagers' fear of witchcraft did not deserve condemnation: "It is the belief in the supernatural, especially the belief in the power of spirits to punish evil deeds, which has done more than anything else to maintain the moral order of the tribes."[84] DCs like Brelsford learned to pause on the byways of colonial Africa to reerect the shrines they found scattered by unbelievers. Science confirmed them in the task of protecting belief. Paradoxically, science committed Westerners more profoundly to belief in the efficacy of the supernatural than would ever be required of an ordinary villager, whose daily experience of the supernatural invoked nothing different in kind from anything else in the here and now. Whereas Brelsford, through the fog of science, only "suspect[ed] something more than success with medicine when one hear[d] of the sudden rise to fame of a witch-doctor," the people of Sileti's took it for granted. They proceeded to give Sileti and his son their due, benefiting from their power to cure, all the while knowing how closely the power to cure and the power to kill neighbor one another in the real world.

The order described by subjects in terms of spirits and witches never worked by means of mere belief in the supernatural. Like all ideologies, this one worked not only because of belief but also despite unbelief. As the Swahili proverb says, "The devil you know will eat you but will not devour you completely" (*Zimwi likujualo halikuli likakwisha*). The belief that it is right and one's duty to obey supports every system of legitimate authority; but provision for the use of force everywhere supplements the belief. Force provides a weapon in reserve for the liquidation of those parts the "devil" does not finish off. But the spirit-dominated anthropological theory of order within the customary order envisaged complete devourment.

It followed from this theory that the customary order was law-abiding and legitimate only when it talked about, believed in, or kowtowed before invisible spirits. The very same order was altogether unrecognizable when the spirits materialized physically, in ways the *pax Britannica* did not provide. They could, and did, materialize in the form of new groups, with new leaders, each time Watchtower preachers launched a campaign of baptizing. Since these new groups and leaders emerged as potent forces in the midst of established polities, it is no wonder that chiefs and headmen so often attempted to make them allies.

ALTHOUGH the political capacity of Watchtower baptizing grew out of its use as a technique of witchcraft eradication, the movement must not be assimilated to the technique. The legacy of baptizing was the formation of new groups legitimated on new bases. These groups went on to pursue new purposes. Thus, for example, Norris Cres Gondwe's groups went on to press the constitutional case for secular schools. Gondwe referred obliquely to his group's prehistory in a letter to the DC.

> They used to say long ago that Watchtower members are not respecting the chiefs, they are doing bad things; they are gathering in the bush and other such lies. Now they say that because there is a school.[85]

This group undoubtedly came together at first amid collective practice that involved the cure of witchcraft, but by thirteen years later, it had jettisoned its first stage.[e] The same seems to have occurred in Mwinilunga District. Watchtower groups formed in 1933 amid the enthusiasm of witchcraft eradication offered strong collective resistance to their chiefs' efforts to mobilize war work during World War II.

Watchtower baptizing differed from older methods of witchcraft eradication in another important respect. A baptism that involved the renunciation of medicines altogether rather than the introduction of new, supposedly more powerful ones, probably accentuated the need for protection from the malign influences of the unregenerate. Converts who thus decided to live apart added point to the Biblical injunction to "get out from among them and be clean." Although groups were formed using the language and techniques of possession, healing, and witchcraft eradication, they were not forever bound to these activities alone. To say, therefore, that Watchtower baptizing employed the political tool of witchcraft eradication is not to assimilate baptism to witchcraft eradication without remainder.

Most writers on the Watchtower movement have not noticed the effectiveness of antiwitchcraft baptism in galvanizing politically effective groups. Cultural interpretations of the movement have ignored its political importance. Political interpretations generally ignore this aspect of the Watchtower as a mere background detail of local culture, while regarding the Mwana Lesa episode as a

[e] The official position of later Jehovah's Witnesses is that the groups that "prayed in the bush" never legitimately belonged to the movement. Representatives of the society in Zambia from the mid-1920s to the late 1940s regularly "disfellowshipped," or suspended for periods of time, members who engaged in excesses likely to cause the society trouble with the colonial authorities. But the fact remains that John Dauti Tembo, a well-trained preacher dispatched from the society's headquarters in South Africa, was successfully prosecuted for violating the provision of the Witchcraft Ordinance against "the use of subtle craft" (see NAZ, ZA 1/10, Legal Department of all Magistrates, 1924).

deviation from the Watchtower's mainstream. I have shown, however, that Watchtower baptizing, with its connotation of deliverance
from witchcraft, administered shock after shock to the fundamental
relationships of indirect rule. If the antiwitchcraft action of the
Watchtower is allowed to recede, while its anticolonial talk is left
center stage, the mass mobilization that took place remains unex-
plained. If my interpretation is right, then witchcraft eradication
stands center stage, and no political analysis that fails to take account of it can claim to have done its work. To assert the importance
of this mechanism is not to deny the Watchtower's anticolonial
thrust but to clarify it.

Groups are mobilized on the basis of the known. Mobilization
begins on the basis of existing features of collective life—the attributes of leadership, its functions, its language, its symbolic panoply,
the attributes of groups and their members, provision for main-
taining group coherence, and of course a practical program with
alternative suggestions about what comes after what. These things
cannot all be invented by each new group or for each new task.
Nor need they be—social models with which to begin are always
available. Hobsbawm makes this point when he speaks of the
"drill" modern revolutionaries have followed since the French Revolution.

> The sort of things revolutionaries do is, let us say, to organize
> a mass demonstration, throw up barricades, march on the town
> hall, run up the tricouleur, proclaim the republic one and
> indivisible, appoint a provisional government, and issue a call
> for a Constituent Assembly. (This, roughly, is the "drill" which
> so many of them learned from the French Revolution. It is
> not, of course, the only possible procedure.)[86]

Hobsbawm's last observation, that the procedure taken is not the
only possible one, is important. The procedures that activists follow
originate in a given group's history. They are not the same at all
times and places. Revolutions have no "natural" targets. The "drill"
of the Anabaptists targeted universal baptizing by the Universal
Church. Since the same procedure today would not hit a recog-
nizable political target, it is not easy to comprehend the ferocity
with which the Church struggled against their "second baptism."
The "drill" of Central African revivalists called for universal baptism, but not all such calls resound politically. It is hard to imagine
conditions in which contemporary evangelists' daily struggle for

universal baptism would arouse political consternation in the United States.

But in Central Africa, mass baptism and the chain of events it set in motion threatened the two key articulations of the colonial state. It disturbed the relations of customary rulers with their superiors and with the population at large. Because the political interpretation of millennial revival operates within the frame of reference of the urban-based colonial state, it has led many writers to doubt, or even ignore, the reactions of those who manned the state's front lines. For their part, the revivalists appear in a fog of merely symbolic and displaced protest. But as Marx wrote, "Mankind begins no *new* work, but consciously accomplishes its old work."[87]

The ritual of witchcraft eradication could shift from one set of players to another—from Bamucapi to old-fashioned medicine men to prophets to village headmen. It could shift from one form to another—from internal washing with medicine to external washing in a baptismal stream to symbolic washing by the use of incised medicines to laying on of hands. It could shift from locale to locale, from time to time, and from purpose to purpose. Throughout, it maintained similarities of form. These similarities point to an underlying structure in the phenomenon of revival, not political or emotional contingencies, and not mere details of culture. The cure of witchcraft met known problems in familiar terms, while at the same time providing for innovation and the adoption of entirely novel purposes. Above all, it provided the means of making collectivity authoritative. Along with prophecy, possession, and healing, it was the foundation on which Watchtower revival built.

But for the peculiar structure of the colonial order, the men who became Watchtower leaders might have functioned as itinerant witch finders had in the past, creating local convulsions of no wider import. Under colonial rule, however, villages and chiefdoms were enveloped by a territorial state, ruled from white islets whose alien population was in turn reenveloped by the vast countryside and its people. These islets of rule were connected to the rural masses by mission churches and customary polities. Each in its own way extended the reach of a regime too thinly spread to rule directly.

But these institutions, while alien to the regime, were akin to the Watchtower. Both shared with the Watchtower, and with revival movements generally, the ambition to define right conduct according to a higher law than that of the state they imperfectly served. Thus, the Watchtower could challenge both on their own ground. Under such conditions, conflict over right conduct led to political conflict. Or, more precisely, the two amounted to one and the same thing. Colonial Central Africa illustrates Hobsbawm's suggestion that in some kinds of community, the line between religion and politics cannot be drawn, that millenarian movements will "automatically and always be both in some manner." In our case, they were both in a quite specific manner.

What Hobsbawm says of European peasants' slowness to adopt secular ideologies can equally be applied here. "The peasantry remained totally beyond the range of any ideological language which did not speak with the tongues of the Virgin, the Saints, and Holy Writ, not to mention the more ancient gods and spirits which still hid behind a slightly christianized facade."[88] African villagers spoke and acted in a language similar to the one Hobsbawm describes. Their doing so is an artifact of the institutions that exercised routine direction of everyday life in the countryside. As we have abundantly seen, crucial political fights turned on theology—on the uselessness (or uses) of ancestral rites, and on the falsity (or truth) of established meanings of the Gospel. Though the Central African scene was complicated by the presence of more than one theology, associated with more than one kind of religious institution, the principle was the same with respect to both missions and customary polities. Religious fights were political and social struggles.

Throughout, I have criticized an assumption that pervades writing about millennial revival—that activists were speaking a garbled language that represented fantastically what could have been expressed "realistically." It has been my contention that millennial activists spoke the language of the institutions that ruled them directly. The political order that colonialism introduced had a language of its own, a language its upholders spoke as their native tongue. Since social scientists usually speak the same language, they hear millenarians speaking it badly. Thus have African millenarians become aliens in their own land. I have tried to show that, even if millenarians were doomed in the long run, they were of their land and their historical time—and that, as rational actors, they lived in it.

CONCLUSION

AND YET, ARGUMENT FOR the rationality of millenarians can hardly convince moderns. We deal offhandedly with the success of prediction not arrived at by methods we accept. And we seldom resist the temptation of safe prediction at millenarians' expense: "The millennium will not come," as Bryan Wilson announced, having studied believers who said the colonizer would not stay.[1] We cannot doubt Wilson's rationality on the grounds that his prediction will likely be proved wrong.

But being proved right or wrong cannot be the point. If failed prediction established irrationality, millenarians would be quickly joined in that estate by their unbelieving opponents. First would come Lord Lugard, who wrote in 1922 that political independence was "not yet visible on the horizon of time."[2] He would be joined by Margery Perham and the other experts who, she says, imagined right up to the eleventh hour and beyond that many years' colonial tutoring remained. In 1939, "a senior man from the Colonial Office" said, "Well, at any rate in Africa we can be sure that we have unlimited time in which to work."[3] And the Britons would be joined by those African politicians who were overtaken by events, along with their would-be tutors.

Still, for moderns, if failure to predict correctly does not necessarily stigmatize, correct prediction does not necessarily exalt. While Lugard sat satisfied with his vision of many years' British presence in Africa, Shadrach Sinkala thundered at about the same time, to everyone who would hear him, that the British would leave soon. Lugard was wrong; Shadrach was right. Yet wrong—for as moderns and as social scientists, we do not seek knowledge through reflection upon truth and error of this kind. To us, a false prediction reached by a recognized method is not comparable with a true prediction reached by faith. Faith promises us nothing certain. Correct method promises us salvation from error—certainly, if not immediately. Shadrach's method held out no hope of correct prediction, correctly arrived at. He therefore fails the test of rationality.

But if Shadrach fails this test, does anyone among his contem-

porary opponents of British domination pass it? Consider the petition writers and protoconstitutionalists, of whom there were always a certain number in the Western-educated strata. Do they?
At first glance, it would appear that they do: They speak a here-
and-now language, which makes them sound like the men who
ultimately negotiated independence. But does apparent resemblance to the winners of the 1960s equal rational method? I propose
not. If anything amounted to stereotyped ritual and empty incantation, pathetic in its inability to move anything, it was appeal to
democratic principle in the 1920s and 1930s, the heyday of empire.
Upholding natural rights and liberal values against empire was so
much incomprehensible "talking in the unknown tongue," at a time
when natural rights and liberal values argued for it. The "palladium
of democracy" (which Perham tells us the literate displayed, often
eloquently) offered protection only to the superstitious—or the
visionary. In towns, where the protoconstitutionalists shared their
dreams, the regime glared at these detribalized upstarts, these politicians without legitimate function, these "boys" without wholesome leisure occupation. It threatened with dismissal the employees
among them. It saw need for more football fields, tearooms, "suitable" reading matter—and other measures, some harsher. But in
the 1920s and 1930s, the regime was never moved to deploy force
against groups of constitutionalist talkers.

It did so move against the inarticulate talkers of 1918 and their
successors. Whereas officials might seek the simple advantage of a
football field in a town, or perhaps an exemplary firing here or
there, they confronted a picture in the countryside that was much
larger and much darker. Speaking comprehensibly in the jargon
of the Prophets, or speaking incomprehensibly in the unknown
tongue, millenarians repeatedly taxed the regime's ability to keep
order. In the 1920s, they launched what amounted to strikes among
farm workers. In 1935, they were taxed with major responsibility
for the first strike by African miners. In 1942, they so complicated
military recruitment that the regime talked of suspending even
those liberal freedoms which applied to imperial subjects. Thus,
whatever we might say about the mental methods of men like Shadrach, we are not entitled to disparage their political method.

Or are we? After all, an irrational talker might hit upon a correct
prediction by accident—conceivably, for example, I could predict
whether it will rain next Thursday, without making a single observation, without even thinking hard. In similar fashion, could
not an irrational actor achieve results by coincidence, without know-

ing why, indeed, without specifically intending them? I suggest not. Whereas nothing I do visibly affects the weather, what millenarians did visibly affected the colonial state. If Jesus' immediate return to earth was the centerpiece of a grand and abstract theory, his servants' activism here on earth produced visible and tangible facts. British witnesses worried about these facts and about the African witnesses to them, who stood nearby. Since we have no means of consulting Shadrach and his colleagues, we cannot know how, or how far, they calculated their results in advance of experience; but I think we can be certain that, after experience, few could have missed those results or have failed to take them into account. Anyone wishing to deny these millenarians their method must explain the results in some other way. My own proposal is simply this: The Shadrachs knew how the colonial machinery worked. They knew because it worked upon them. But this point is neither self-evidently true nor unanimously upheld by scientific researchers. Let us see for the moment what it would mean, if true, and then return to ways in which it might be disputed.

If true, it would mean that the machinery of the colonial state is revealed by the actions of millenarians. What is revealed in this way is not what habit has taught us to see: that the colonial state was a "modern" specimen. Quite the contrary, it calls to mind medieval forerunners, in which the Church was civically empowered or worked hand in glove with the state, bearing part of the cost, and in which law and administration formed a crazy quilt of local particularity. In short, as it functioned in the Central African countryside, the colonial state was a throwback. We found it exploiting not only the ideological resources of Christian churches but also their organizational means, as its European ancestors did. We found it upholding the principle of unfree labor, something alien in the twentieth century to Britain's own evolving modern mentality. We found it championing old-fashioned forms of local authority as well, to which custom accorded symbolic and practical obedience. For example, we could compare the requirement that African villagers shout their respect to arriving chiefs with the requirement that English villagers doff their hats to arriving nobility. Quakers who refused "hat honor" were subversives, as were Watchtowerites who kept quiet.

We found a motley assemblage of such etiquettes supported ultimately (in official theory) upon the authority of the British Crown, although they usually had no wider application than a given locality. Again, we found magistrates on the bench engaged in theological disputation with the accused, clerics engaged in civil arrest or demanding earthly punishment for blasphemy, civil servants scrutinizing the way ordinary subjects interpreted the Bible. The colonial state simply did not hold the territory in its grip with a uniform law, a rational hierarchy, or an uncompromisingly "modern" vision. Perhaps the dream of doing so was there, but it was fulfilled on the blueprint only, not on the ground. Far from being modern, our colonial state resembled the cheaper governmental systems of Europe's past. We can accept Hobsbawm's judgment that millenarianism is an "archaic" form of social movement only if we add this: In our case, an archaic form of movement threw itself against an archaic form of state.

Two predictions would follow. First, the natural trajectory of such a state is nondemocratic. The cheap governmental systems of Europe's past did not conceive of democracy as a good owed to a hoi polloi of rude rural subjects; they did not aspire to it, and were not fitted for it. Fitted instead for "natural" inequality, they were authoritarian by instinct and by reflex, in principle and in practice. Having chosen to rule cheaply and in consequence archaically, our British administrators and magistrates did not plant democratic seeds. Given their method of ruling, they would have been incapable of such planting—even if it had been their goal, and it was not. Thus, postcolonial regimes did not receive from them a respectable inheritance of democratic institutions, as is sometimes said, and then fritter it away. Where riches of democracy exist in Africa, they are self-made, or they are new wealth.

The second prediction is that cheap rule disappears as an option for the postcolonial state. The postcolonial state cannot retain its colonial progenitor's functionally diffuse building blocks—the mission evangelist who is also a kind of policeman; the ancestral priest who also keeps the census; the DC who is also a magistrate, a *mucapi* to calculating old women, and a builder of roads—and yet be. For a simple reason: So long as these stand, so does the colonial state; the new state comes into being precisely by knocking them down. With the collapse of such building blocks, we would expect to witness the reverse of Lugard's economical telescoping of state functions, and we in fact do. We witness massive growth in the cost of government, a growth that occurs for reasons independent of patronage or corruption and of the need for technically trained individuals and the infrastructure on which their effectiveness depends. The postcolonial regime that wills its society modern must pay the price of overthrowing and then replacing the institutions that made its predecessor archaic.

I have come this far by assuming the correctness of my proposal that millenarians could attack strategically, because they could see how the colonial machinery worked. Now is the time to examine this proposal more closely. I start from the view that ordinary actors possess a knowledge of social structure; that, in other words, the actors' "If I do so-and-so, such-and-such will happen" is not simply there to be quickly transcended in favor of higher-order general-izations; and, finally, that the actors with whom we are concerned appreciated better than we moderns can what will happen in reality if a spirit speaks through someone's mouth or if Jesus sends a sign. Not everyone starts from such a view. In the introduction to their classic *African Political Systems*, Meyer Fortes and E. E. Evans-Prit-chard say, "Africans have no objective knowledge of the forces determining their social behavior." Again, "The African does not see beyond the symbols; it might well be said that if he understood their meaning [that is, their social function], they would lose the power they have over him."[4] (The anthropologists' present tense dates from 1940.) They picture the African as subject to myths, rites, dogmas, and symbols that give his society order by guiding his behavior round and round deeply pounded tracks, and that allow him to think within that order, not about it.

In one sense they are right, if not in their parochial terms of the African, certainly in more general terms of the human subject. Max Weber put this point in terms of an awareness (and an affect) experienced from within the horizon of any given "legitimate or-der": that it is "right" and one's "duty" to obey (or to command). Marxists labeled this human reality "false consciousness" and "ide-ology," and they set off on a career of exposing as what they are the quieting spirits of acceptance that hover in any society's "su-perstructure." If this social function of such spirits were always visible to the naked eye, the unmasking would be unnecessary. We would have to make more skeptical still the Swahilis' skeptical wis-dom, that "the devil you know will eat you but will not devour you completely." In this case, the devil everyone knew would never get even the smallest piece of anyone. But ideology does do its work; the devil does feed, early and often. The anthropologists are right to this extent. But the Swahilis are right to urge that the devil never quite finishes off the meal. Marx kept enough out of the devil's maw to go over to an offensive of unmasking and unmaking, as he insisted in the *Theses on Feuerbach*.

If Marx, a native in his own social world, could see beyond the symbols, what would stop a Shadrach from doing so? If we follow Weber and Marx, the answer is certainly not that social mystification is at work in his society but idle in theirs. And, if we wish to answer that such a step requires genius, we cannot presume in the abstract that our subject lacked this quality. Fortunately, however, we need not search even a minute more for an abstract answer. We know for a fact that in 1919, Shadrach saw beyond the symbols far enough to desecrate an ancestor shrine, watch the political order of the northern districts unravel, and draw from the experience a vocation to preach the ultimate unraveling of the whole political order.[a] Shadrach learned to see the machinery "through struggle," as Marx would have said, if in no other way. If we still doubt that he could have grasped the machinery of his own society, we float in our doubt until we try to answer the question, Compared to whom and to what? Two possible candidates are his opponents, the local DC and Margery Perham's "colonial expert."[5]

However if A.H.M. Kirk-Greene is right about the DC's "theory," the DC drops immediately out of the competition. "Essentially," he writes, "the DC administered with an authority erected upon his own self-confidence," and a sense of "superiority" that was "at once unquestioned and unquestioning." He goes on:

And if the administration of the empire may, after all be looked on as one great confidence-trick, a huge game of white man's bluff, it was one the colonial administrator played, wittingly and unwittingly, upon himself as well as upon the subject races.[6]

If, indeed, such is the theory that a real DC could assent to, once freed from occupational pressure, it is more like Shadrach's than unlike it. Kirk-Greene's DC stepped out on faith. To all that was not of the faith, he was blindfolded. If he saw beyond the symbols, they would lose their power over him. Thus we are back to the anthropologists' African without objective knowledge, and to Weber's legitimate ruler encased in the consciousness that it is "right" and his "duty" to command. But this is not a theory that known facts let us entertain for very long. Recall, for example, the DC who pleaded in the 1920s against the passage of unenforceable laws—on the grounds that "the native" was "altering" and no longer

---

[a] I trust it is obvious to the reader that the possibility of Shadrach's having acquired his daring as a mission proselyte is not a telling counterargument.

respected the white man simply because he was white. This particular man saw beyond the symbols. In this objective knowledge he was not alone.

As we saw, F. H. Melland argued systematically what was visible beyond. Melland realized the necessity of upholding his subordinates' superiority in order to promote his own. By so doing, he arrived at a different theory than the one Kirk-Greene proposes. And this one, although again more like Shadrach's than unlike it, did not depend upon faith. Melland's theory disclosed the mirror image of Shadrach's. He and his opponent approached the old idols along the same road, but from opposite directions: intended order from the north, intended disorder from the south. At their meeting point, having arrived at the same practical theory, and method, both reached for the same practical levers. The millenarian on the ground and the official he met there shared the same world in common. Accordingly, each turned to the chiefs, with what results we have abundantly seen.

Our second candidate for possession of a theory superior to Shadrach's (although, again, not superior prediction) is Margery Perham's "colonial expert." This candidate is really two: first, the person administratively interested in the colonial society as a whole; second, the person anthropologically interested in its African segment. Although sometimes the two are one and the same individual, as in Perham's case, it is important to distinguish them analytically. As an anthropologist, Perham enjoyed the freedom to set and solve problems not set by mundane administrative practicality. Unlike the theorist of colonial administration, she had a scientific purpose, to address questions of general import about the working of society, and she was bound by rules of scientific method as understood within the discipline. Still, and here the two personages merge again, both had the operating theory of indirect rule in common. According to Perham, Britons unconverted to this theory condemned it roundly in the 1930s and denounced anthropology as its "evil genius."[7]

In tune with a nonscientific trial-and-error practicality, the theorist of colonial administration more often posed the question, How can we keep the machinery running? than the question, How does it work? The machinery came to him ready-made, as the computer does to the keypunch operator; but its insides were complex. The anthropologist studied the complex circuits inside. The administrator hunted and pecked in the search for the most useful keys, from time to time aided in this search by the research under way.

The two thus took their separate places in a mental division of labor. This division had large ramifications for the power of the "experts' " theory. For if one part focused upon the keyboard, while the other focused upon individual circuits, no third part theorized the computer as a whole. Knowledge about the whole had either the one slant or the other.

Accustomed to pushing the familiar keys, the administrative theorist kept on pushing them, controlling whatever those keys controlled. But the keyboard was, after all, an inheritance from the precolonial past. The keyboard ignored the groups coming into existence in the colonial present, except perhaps to send the detribalized denunciatory messages: For some intents and purposes it would be better if they did not exist. Margery Perham did not remove herself from the error when she asked, looking back, "In Nyasaland and Northern Rhodesia, was it wise almost at the eleventh hour to try to set chiefs in the forefront of the battle against nationalists, since nationalists, after all, had the future in their hands?"[8] By a historical irony, the chiefs, whom official theory never recognized as the State as such, over the decades when they were no less, dramatically gained this recognition in the eleventh hour, at the precise moment when their state was no more.

The view from the computer's inside, although more refined in many ways than the view from the keyboard, was no more comprehensive. According to T. O. Beidelman, who meticulously described the Kaguru "circuit" in colonial Tanzania, but who walked back and forth past mission and *boma* barely noticing them except, perhaps, to deplore their existence, "it is as though anthropological curiosity stopped at the color bar and that European colonialists were just like us." Like his colleagues, he thought of his Ukaguru "as existing outside any immediate colonial experience, which is ironic, since anthropology's best practitioners have advocated the study of a society in its totality."[9] Thus stated, Beidelman's charge is not so serious as might appear. It is not at all evident that we would know today as much as we do, about the inner working of societies differently constituted than the modern West's, if anthropologists had not minutely studied the smaller "totalities" they chose to. Their science simply picked up certain problems and left others aside. And, as to their approach to the color bar, we must note this: The guiding outlook of their work, which combined a passion for detail with a humane aspiration, does not suffer in comparison with its ethnocentric competitors.

The substantial charge is that anthropology's part in the mental division of labor respected boundaries established by administrative practicality, not by science. Perham shows us rather poignantly how, once British domination (and therefore *some* method of ruling) seemed the large given, the passion for detail and the humane aspiration confounded themselves with it in the mind:

> In the thirties I sat at the feet of Professor Malinowski, alongside some brilliant anthropologists, who went on to bury themselves for a year or two within a single African tribe, learning its language and customs and emerging finally to report what a wonderfully integrated but brittle social mechanism they had been observing. It would surely, so we then thought, be arrogant roughly to impose upon these societies our own culture, our own forms of government.[10]

Posing its questions within the framework of British ruling reduced the analytical scope of a science that aspired to ask general questions about how societies work. As a result, at least one area of inquiry could not develop normally. A deformation occurred. Administrative thought recognized no African politics: none that organized relations among Africans; none that organized the relations of Africans to Britons; and none that organized the relations of the African "circuits" to the "computer" as a whole. Anthropology fit itself into this scheme. Its way of thinking about politics and power suited the bureaucratic mode round about it. While the nonscientists transformed problems of politics into problems of administration, the scientists transformed problems of politics into problems of culture. They found in culture a substitute for politics.

Even so, however, further qualification of the charge is necessary. For in one sense, we can consider even a deformity functional. Like the acrobat's hyperextended joints or the ballerina's bunions, the deformity was a condition that attended the performance of certain feats. Substituting culture for politics, anthropology has provided means of insight into the connections between civil society and the state. Elaborating culture's "power" to constrain individual action, anthropology has provided tools with which to spell out in detail, as concrete observables, what Marxists and Weberians sketch in shorthand as "legitimation" or as "false consciousness." Such tools help us to explore the vast inner horizon of political order. Properly extended, they can help us incorporate theoretically a phenomenon we repeatedly observe but resist theorizing: the "cultural" or "symbolic" part of any social movement, not only the one studied here.

For example, we might begin to see why, in the American 1960s, the violation of sexual conventions tended to join with the violation of the draft law, why free love and rumors of it attended the "real" political issue of peace—and why counterdemonstrations by the forces of "law and order" responded in the same currency, with odd epithets like "Commie-fag!" And, if we were looking at the Iranian revolution, we might do better than we have thus far in theorizing how the mullahs succeeded with strikes, in the oil fields where the comrades failed; and how anti-imperialism has joined with such things as public punishment of adultery to form a new political compound. We might also find out how it happens that military strength abroad becomes inseparable, in some American minds, from Christian strength within families; or why Maoism and its political opponents keep crossing and recrossing the territory of familial piety and the error (or truth) of the long-dead Confucius. Examples showing the recombination of seemingly "real" political issues with seemingly "mere symbolic" expressions can easily be multiplied at great historical and contemporary length. It is quite clear that when ordinary people move politically, whether to conserve or to rupture, they move culturally at the same time. So, too, do rulers and would-be rulers.

Thus, developing within limits first set nonscientifically, anthropology went on to create a new scientific possibility: means of exploring in a coherent way the cultural terrain on which political power is everywhere made real; means of doing better than the psychological makeshifts with which we often make do when confronted by the "symbolic" outriders of "real" political movements. But it did not exploit this possibility. In this respect, anthropology developed the bunions but did not perform the ballerina's leaps. It discovered the power of symbols in one arena and then lost it in another. When anthropology turned to the study of millenarianism in the societies where it had previously clarified ancestor worship, the powerful symbols of before became mere symbols after. Thus, a Lucy Mair who had managed to see how a chief's ancestor cult upheld his power could still see in millenarian cults "not a reinforcement of political action but a substitute for it."[11] Functionalism created the possibility of higher leaps than that. Its practitioners thudded instead across the restricted space of its part in the colonial division of mental labor. Nevertheless, Lucy Mair consistently called millenarianism only "a substitute" for politics, because so, in official presumption, was the faith of the ancestors; but this state of affairs existed only as official presumption.

The presumption could only appear to be reality because anthropologists did not have to ask of the computer as a whole, How does it work? They did not have to answer scientifically a question that had already been answered, as far as it would be, bureaucratically and by law. Colonial law recognized chiefs, blocked all independent movement toward the deposition of chiefs, and closed off rebellion against bad government, except as notarized by itself. In these circumstances, Fortes and Evans-Pritchard could exhibit for calm viewing the conservative trajectory even of African rebellion: "The social system is, as it were, removed to a mystical plane, where it figures as a system of sacred values beyond criticism or revision. Hence people will overthrow a bad king, but the kingship is never questioned."[12] Max Gluckman is often quoted for having said much the same thing years later.[13] Given what was legally established and bureaucratically upheld, they did not have to ask what such conservatism might mean practically speaking—if acted upon in fact—to their compatriots seated before the colonial keyboard. For a simple reason: It could not be acted upon in fact. British rule precluded it.

But it was acted upon in fact, and with effect, by millenarian activists: Hanoc Sindano, we recall, was "treated like a chief." Such occurrences confronted functionalist theory of the preexisting order with definite limits. Millenarians operated beyond. Millenarians were not blindered subjects within the magical kingdom of African culture; and they were something more than weaponless talkers against the British one. Confronted with them, functionalist theory made the heaviest possible thud—tautology. Millenarians were victims of "anomie," that is, they no longer felt bound by an established law and order, neither in the magical kingdom without the sanction of force nor in the unmagical one with it. A Shadrach fit nowhere in the anthropological scheme. He was an abomination that fit no category. Thus, his own and the rationality of those who followed him became fair game—as evil is to good in a religious order, irrationality is to its opposite in a scientific one. Thence followed millenarians' confusion and hysteria, which provided an account of why they reached for symbolic weapons as a substitute for real ones. To Lucy Mair they stood comparison with Western depth psychology's Western patients. I submit that the hypothesis of millenarians' irrationality has stood in the stead of a comprehensive and self-consistent theory of the order in which they lived.

A scientific vision of order can include the most mobile and volatile observed reality; thus, an overarching order links the hurricane with the sunshiny day. A ruler's vision of order is otherwise.

Colonial rulers understood as order the quiet they wished to impose upon a mobile and volatile colonial reality. Functionalist anthropology tended to accept as a given the colonial ruler's understanding. It did so largely by default, I would say, rather than by positive intent, for its own intellectual focus required no systematically constructed alternative to it. Functionalist theory produced no theory of the colonial whole, period. It only reposed from time to time upon a fuzzy consensus based upon kinship with the rulers, one made fuzzier by the sort of ill-defined difference that makes one ignore a kinsman with whom one is not always on cordial terms. So a Beidelman averted his eyes from the *boma* he had to pass by in his research; a Fortes and an Evans-Pritchard said their word about the colonial monopoly of force and said no more. I submit that this fuzzy consensus made anthropologists fail to see in millenarianism the order they had previously seen in immense, meticulously drawn detail. Instead they tended to see disorder where officials did. By theoretical default, different weather seemed to have different causes.

Thus, anthropological thought about the colonial order could not surpass a Shadrach's. In a fundamental sense, it could not even compete with a Shadrach's, for it did not organize the facts of the whole society that he confronted with mind and body. He had no scientific theory that abstracted away from the colonial reality. Anthropologists had. He lived within the colonial present, they within the ethnographic one. From his standpoint—of the whole, in the colonial present—the discoveries that organized anthropologists' passion for detail and their humane aspiration about ruling were neither here nor there. He did not need to have described for him the languages and customs of "a single African tribe." "Buried" for a lifetime in such details—and, besides, often a polyglot visitor during the colonial period among the different customs of his own land—he had an insider's familiarity with much that was reportable news to the anthropologist. (Indeed, when he spoke English, as was not uncommon, it was not uncommonly he who reported the news.) Nor did he need to have his society's coherence made visible to him. Societies always present themselves to their insiders as coherent, even though from day to day it is the insiders who make and remake the coherence. What he did need to theorize, as a practical matter, was a coherent view of the colonial computer's two parts. And this need, as a practical matter, the anthropologist did not share.

Shadrach and the administrative theorist stood alone on the frontier between the two worlds of colonial society. They stood there as practical people following daily routines, not as scientists. They stood there unaccompanied by the scientifically disciplined. They drew their analyses and predictions by means of rough-and-ready empirical method. Based upon his own analysis, the administrator predicted a long-lived British hegemony in Africa, and he did his best to make his prediction so. In retrospect, it is clear that Shadrach did better in prediction.

Or did he? He said, Soon, the reader will say; and "soon" is vague. Or is it? When people finally ask themselves, How long? and answer back, Not long! they are already in motion. And they, too, are doing their best to make the prediction so. They go forward with their empirical analysis, whatever its potential, whatever its limits. But in so doing they are not at all dumb objects of the unreachable, as we all are when we ask, How long will the drought continue? or When will the torrent cease?

ABBREVIATIONS

Admin.	Administrator
Atty. Gen.	Attorney General
BSAC	British South Africa Company
CID	Criminal Investigation Division
CS	Chief Secretary
DC	District Commissioner
KAR	King's African Rifles
LMR	*Livingstonia Mission Report*
LN	*Livingstonia News*
Mag.	Magistrate
MR	*Missionary Record*
NA	Native Authority
NAZ	National Archives of Zambia
NC	Native Commissioner
NLS	National Library of Scotland
OIC	Officer in Charge
PC	Provincial Commissioner
RFM	*Review of Foreign Mission Committee of the Church of Scotland*
SNA	Secretary for Native Affairs
UE	University of Edinburgh
UFCFMC	*Report of the United Free Church Foreign Mission Committee*

NOTES

Introduction

1. NAZ, BS1/149, Tanguy before David Mackenzie-Kennedy, JP, 13/11/1918. For an excellent general discussion of the order, see Joseph Bouniol, ed., *The White Fathers and Their Missions*, London, 1929.

2. In his classic paper "An Analysis of Sect Development," *American Sociological Review* 24 (Feb. 1959), 3–15, Bryan Wilson postulated that millenarians are typically passive. But outstanding exceptions have been described by Norman Cohn, *The Pursuit of the Millennium: Revolutionary Millenarians and Mystical Anarchists of the Middle Ages*, New York, 1970 (following the classic account of Ernst Troeltsch, *The Social Teachings of the Christian Churches*, London, 1931); Vincent Shih, *The Taipeng Revolutionary Ideology*, Seattle, 1972; and Michael Adas, *Prophets of Rebellion: Millenarian Protest Movements against the European Colonial Order*, Chapel Hill, N.C., 1979.

3. NAZ, ZA 1/10, Moffat to Tagart, 26/5/1924.

4. NAZ, ZA 1/10, unsigned letter to Mag. (Mazabuka), 25/3/1924.

5. NAZ, ZA 1/10 (1925), J. E. Stephenson to Mag. (Broken Hill), 5/3/1925; ZA 1/10, "Watchtower 1919–1926," J. E. Stephenson to Acting SNA, 13/2/1926, J. E. Stephenson to Atty. Gen., 13/2/1926; ZA 1/10 (vol. 3), Sidney Cooke to NC (Chilanga), 28/11/1924; ZA 1/10 (1925), Macpherson to DC (Broken Hill), 27/2/1925.

6. NAZ, ZA 1/10, J. E. Stephenson to Atty. Gen., 13/2/1926.

7. NAZ, ZA 1/10, J. E. Stephenson to SNA, 16/3/1926.

8. This process began immediately following the Boer War, became the object of detailed planning in 1913, gained momentum after World War I, but was enacted into law only in 1928–1929 (see Robert I. Rotberg, *The Rise of Nationalism in Central Africa: The Making of Malawi and Zambia, 1873–1964*, Cambridge, Mass., 1965), pp. 29–39.

9. NAZ, ZA 1/10, vol. 3, J. W. Hinds, Esq. (Lusaka), to D. Mackenzie-Kennedy (Chilanga), 5/3/1925.

10. NAZ, ZA 1/10 (1924), *Rex* vs. *Isaac Nyasulo* and *Rex* vs. *J. B. Manda*, 18/3/1924.

11. NAZ, Sec/Nat 312, vol. 1, Directeur d'Administration to Gouverneur, Northern Rhodesia, 18/7/1929; Vice-Governor-General, Elizabethville, to Governor, Northern Rhodesia, 9/9/1929.

12. George Shepperson, "Nyasaland and the Millennium," in Sylvia L. Thrupp, ed., *Millennial Dreams in Action: Studies in Revolutionary Religious Movements*, New York, 1970, p. 145.

13. NAZ, ZA 1/10 (vol. 3), J. Moffat Thompson to J. W. Hinds, 13/3/1925.

14. NAZ, ZA 1/10, J. E. Stephenson to SNA, 16/3/1926.

15. NAZ, ZA 1/10 (1925), P. J. Macdonnell, memorandum, n.d.

16. Eric J. Hobsbawm, *Primitive Rebels: Studies in Archaic Forms of Social Movement in the Nineteenth and Twentieth Centuries*, New York, 1965, p. 65. Some authors have contested the sociological analysis of millennial movements in Africa, contending that scholars must understand revivals as religion, so to speak, "as such." See, for example, Michael Banton, "African Prophets," *Race* 5 (1963), 42–55. One methodology for studying religion as such has been proposed by H. W. Turner, "Methodology for the Study of Modern African Religious Movements," *Comparative Studies in Society and History* 8 (Apr. 1966). Turner's methodology includes the assumption that God is at work in history.

17. Hobsbawm, *Primitive Rebels*, p. 66.

18. Ibid., p. 2.

19. Peter Worsley, *The Trumpet Shall Sound: A Study of Cargo Cults in Melanesia*, New York, 1968, pp. 243ff.

20. Sholto J. Cross, "The Watchtower Movement in South Central Africa, 1908–1945," Ph.D. diss., Oxford University, 1973, p. 29.

21. Cf. Neil J. Smelser, *A Theory of Collective Behavior*, New York, 1962, p. 47, whose synthesis of the approach I am discussing includes a long list of conceptions that are often used interchangeably: anomie, strain, pressure, malintegration, disequilibrium, disintegration, imbalance, disorganization, inconsistency, conflict, and deprivation.

22. Anthony F. C. Wallace, "Revitalization Movements," in Seymour M. Lipset and Neil J. Smelser, eds., *Sociology: A Decade of Progress*, Englewood Cliffs, N.J., 1961.

23. Bryan R. Wilson, *Magic and the Millennium: A Sociological Study of Religious Movements among Tribal and Third-World Peoples*, London, 1973.

24. Daniel Biebuyck, "La Société kumu face au Kitawala," *Belgian African Review* (Jan. 1957), p. 38, my translation.

25. Specialists may find it of interest to reflect that Max Weber was never so fascinated by prophets' miraculous penumbra as his intellectual successors have been. He thought that "ethical *rationalization*" derived from the work of charismatic prophets and their disciples (see Talcott Parsons' valuable introduction to Max Weber, *The Sociology of Religion*, Boston, 1964, pp. xxxiiff., and Weber's own discussion, pp. 46–59 and elsewhere in the volume).

26. Worsley, *Trumpet Shall Sound*, p. lvi.

27. Lucy P. Mair, "Independent Religious Movements in Three Continents," in John Middleton, ed., *Gods and Rituals*, London, 1968, p. 333.

28. Worsley, *Trumpet Shall Sound*, pp. ix–xxi, 32–48, 266–272.

29. For a clear discussion of the problem of rationality as it has been related to cargo cults, see I. C. Jarvie, "Explaining Cargo Cults," in Bryan

R. Wilson, ed., *Rationality*, New York, 1971, pp. 50–61. The essays of Alasdair MacIntyre, Stephen Lukes, Robin Horton, Martin Hollis, and I. C. Jarvie and Joseph Agassiz are also of interest in this connection.

30. Wilson, *Magic and the Millennium*, p. 500.

31. A.J.F. Købben, "Prophetic Movements as an Expression of Social Protest," *Internationales Archiv für Ethnographie* 49 (1960), 125, my italics. Cf. Robert Kaufmann, *Millénarisme et acculturation*, Brussels, 1964, pp. 67–68.

32. See Karen E. Fields, "Charismatic Religion as Popular Protest: The Ordinary and the Extraordinary in Social Movements," *Theory and Society* 11 (1982), 326–328.

33. Christopher Hill, *The World Turned Upside Down: Radical Ideas during the English Revolution*, New York, 1972, pp. 21–22.

34. Karen E. Fields, "Revival and Rebellion in Colonial Central Africa: Social and Political Consequences of Missionary Enterprise," Ph.D. diss., Brandeis University, 1977.

PART 1: THE PROBLEM OF POLITICAL ORDER

1. J. E. Stephenson, *Chirupula's Tale*, London, 1937, p. 63.

2. Lugard was in touch with Johnston, Sharpe, and Rhodes, as well as with the Reverend Dr. Robert Laws of Livingstonia Mission and agents of its sister organization, the African Lakes Company (see Lewis H. Gann, *A History of Northern Rhodesia: Early Days to 1953*, London, 1964, pp. 37, 61; Kenneth John McCracken, *Politics and Christianity in Malawi, 1875–1940: The Impact of Livingstonia Mission in the Northern Province*, Cambridge, 1977, p. 83).

3. Andrew D. Roberts, *A History of the Bemba: Political Growth and Change in North-eastern Zambia before 1900*, London, 1973, pp. 251ff.; Robert I. Rotberg, *Christian Missionaries and the Creation of Northern Rhodesia, 1880–1924*, Princeton, 1965, pp. 19–26.

4. On the commercial aims of Livingstonia and Blantyre, see McCracken, *Politics and Christianity*, pp. 17–33, 42–47, 55–59.

5. Donald Fraser, *Winning a Primitive People*, London, 1922, p. 8; W. P. Livingstone, *Laws of Livingstonia: A Narrative of Missionary Adventure and Achievement*, London, 1921, p. 242; Rotberg, *Christian Missionaries*, pp. 23, 61–66, 100–101.

6. See Gann, *History of Northern Rhodesia*, pp. 24–94.

7. Martin L. Kilson, *Political Change in a West African State: A Study in the Modernization Process*, Cambridge, Mass., 1966, p. 24.

1. INDIRECT RULE

1. Lucy P. Mair, "Chieftainship in Modern Africa," *Africa* 9 (July 1936), 313; J. Van Velsen, ed., *The Life of a Zambian Evangelist: The Reminiscences of the Reverend Paul Bwembya Mushindo*, Lusaka, 1973, pp. 46, 49.

2. Cf. the formulations of these classic works: K. A. Busia, *The Position of the Chief in the Modern Political System*, London, 1951, p. 117; J. A. Barnes, *Politics in a Changing Society: A Political History of the Fort Jameson Ngoni*, London, 1954, pp. 136, 162; Lloyd Fallers, "The Predicament of the Modern African Chief: An Instance from Uganda," *American Anthropologist* 57 (Apr. 1955), 298. However, Joan Vincent, "Colonial Chiefs and the Making of Class: A Case Study from Teso, Eastern Uganda," *Africa* 47 (1977), 146ff., and Mahmood Mamdani, *Politics and Class Formation in Uganda*, New York, 1976, have looked into the dynamics of chiefs' ability to compel.

3. A.H.M. Kirk-Greene, "The Thin White Line: The Size of the British Colonial Service in Africa," *Journal of the Royal African Society* 79 (Jan. 1980), 42–44.

4. Placing white officials in the foreground, Kirk-Greene says that the system rested on "coercion, collaboration, confidence, and competence," mainly on the latter two. See also Terence O. Ranger, "Making Northern Rhodesia Imperial: Variations on a Royal Theme, 1924–1938," *African Affairs* 79 (July 1980); D. A. Low, *Lion Rampant: Essays in the Study of British Imperialism*, London, 1973; H. F. Morris and James S. Read, *Indirect Rule and the Search for Justice: Essays in East African Legal History*, London, 1972, in all of which the actions of Britons alone come into clear focus.

5. Margery Perham, *The Colonial Reckoning*, London, 1963, p. 87.

6. Margery Perham, introduction to Frederick John Dealtry Lugard, *The Dual Mandate in British Tropical Africa*, 5th ed., London, 1965, p. xlii.

7. NAZ, ZA 7/1/14/1, "Annual Report upon Native Affairs, 1930–1931," gives the date in Zambia as 1929. Robert I. Rotberg, *The Rise of Nationalism in Central Africa: The Making of Malawi and Zambia*, Cambridge, Mass., 1965, p. 50, gives 1930. According to a personal communication from Terence O. Ranger, Kasum Datta, "The Policy of Indirect Rule in Northern Rhodesia, 1920–1958," Ph.D. diss., University of London, 1976, gives it as 1924. These discrepancies may arise from the fact that Indirect Rule involved a series of enactments, some of which derived from older arrangements for devolving tasks upon African rulers.

8. See Robin J. Short, *African Sunset*, London, 1973, pp. 184ff., for tart commentary on this evolution by an old-style DC.

9. Kirk-Greene, "Thin White Line," table 9, p. 36.

10. NAZ, ZA 7/1/14/1, "Annual Report upon Native Affairs, 1930–1931."

11. NAZ, KDH 1/1.

12. See Rotberg, *Rise of Nationalism*, pp. 22–24, 48–50.

13. Ibid., p. 27.

14. Lewis H. Gann, *The Birth of a Plural Society: The Development of Northern Rhodesia under the British South Africa Company, 1894–1914*, Manchester, 1958, p. 75; NLS, Free Church of Scotland, *Aurora* 2 (1 Dec. 1898).

15. NAZ, ZA 1/10, Macdonnell to Admin., 5/5/1919.

16. NAZ, BS1/129–133, Administrator's Report for the Year Ending 31/3/1905.

17. NLS, 7884, Chisholm to Smith, 3/4/1901; Edinburgh University, Africa Papers (Livingstonia), George Shepperson, NUG 26, Report of A. Dewar to Foreign Mission Committee, Free Church, 1897–1898.

18. George Kay, "Social Aspects of Village Regrouping in Zambia," University of Hull, 1967, pp. 9–15.

19. Louis Oger, "Spirit Possession among the Bemba: A Linguistic Approach," presented at the Conference on the History of Central African Religions, Lusaka, 30 August–8 September 1972, mimeographed.

20. Kay, "Social Aspects of Regrouping," pp. 14–15, 44–46. On the difficulty of implementing the same policy in the neighboring Lunda area, see Ian Cunnison, "Headmanship and the Ritual of Luapula Villagers," *Africa* 26 (1956), 4–8.

21. Kay, "Social Aspects of Regrouping," p. 14.

22. Lewis H. Gann and Peter Duignan, *The Rulers of British Africa, 1870–1914*, Stanford, Calif., 1978, pp. 198, 214.

23. Perham, introduction to Lugard, *Dual Mandate*, p. xl.

24. Lugard, *Dual Mandate*, p. 618.

25. Margery Perham, "A Re-statement of Indirect Rule," *Africa* 7 (1934), 321–334 rebuts this ever-hardy idea.

26. Leo Marquard, "The Problem of Government," in J. Merle Davis, ed., *Modern Industry and the African*, London, 1933, p. 251.

27. Cf. John E. Flint, "Frederick Lugard: The Making of an Autocrat (1858–1943)," in Lewis H. Gann and Peter Duignan, eds., *African Proconsuls: European Governors in Africa*, New York, 1978, pp. 308–310, a contrary view.

28. Lugard, *Dual Mandate*, p. 58.

29. Max Weber, *The Sociology of Religion*, with an introduction by Talcott Parsons, Boston, 1963, p. 107.

30. NLS, 7884, Elmslie to Smith, 14/2/1901; W. P. Livingstone, *Laws of Livingstonia: A Narrative of Missionary Adventure and Achievement*, London, 1923, p. 275.

31. Livingstone, *Laws of Livingstonia*, p. 176.

32. Brian Garvey, "The Development of the White Fathers Mission among the Bemba-speaking Peoples, 1891–1964," Ph.D. diss., University of London, 1974, pp. 57–59; NLS, 8982, Vellum, Report on Missionary Conference, 1925.

33. NAZ, ZA 7/1/7/1, "Annual Report upon Native Affairs, 1923–1924" and frequently in other reports; Garvey, "Development of the White Fathers Mission," p. 139.

34. NAZ, ZA 7/1/5/1 and ZA 7/1/15/1, "Annual Report upon Native Affairs," 1920–1921 and 1931–1932, respectively.

35. Garvey, "Development of the White Fathers Mission," pp. 129–161.

36. NAZ, ZA 1/9/158/2, "Memo re the Closing of Schools in Petauke District," 25/3/1930, where the original ordinance is cited; also NAZ, BS1/113, Prentice to Wallace, 4/4/1908, and Wallace to Prentice, 10/4/1908.

37. NLS, *Livingstonia Mission Report*, hereafter LMR (1901), 6.

38. NAZ, BS1/115, E. Schaeffer to NC (Chinsali), 28/4/1907 and 2/9/1908, Kaunda to NC 9/9/1908, Young to Wallace, 9/9/1908, Young to Admin., 11/6/1909, Peuth to Leyer, 18/7/1910.

39. Livingstone, *Laws of Livingstonia*, p. 378; Elizabeth G. K. Hewat, *Vision and Achievement, 1796–1956: A History of the Foreign Missions of the Churches United in the Church of Scotland*, London, 1960, pp. 215–216.

40. Lugard, *Dual Mandate*, p. 78.

41. See note 36, above; for the reaction of the Livingstonia missionaries, see United Free Church Foreign Mission Committee, *Review of Foreign Missions* (1915), 43.

42. Audrey I. Richards, *Land, Labour and Diet: An Economic Survey of the Bemba Tribe*, London, 1939, p. 258n.

43. Lugard, *Dual Mandate*, pp. 590–591. Cf. Busia, *Position of the Chief*, pp. 133ff.

44. Monica Wilson, "An African Christian Morality," *Africa* 10 (1937), 288ff.

45. Hewat, *Vision and Achievement*, p. 217.

46. Gann, *Birth of a Plural Society*, p. 50; NAZ, ZA 7/1/17/1, "Annual Report upon Native Affairs, 1934," p. 37, shows 399 schools run by 15 different mission societies receiving aid.

47. Lugard, *Dual Mandate*, p. 616.

48. Richards, *Land, Labour and Diet*, pp. 27–28.

49. Lugard, *Dual Mandate*, p. 589.

50. Rotberg, *Rise of Nationalism*, pp. 120–121. Nuances of etiquette, such as an African's obligation to doff his hat and walk modestly, are nicely brought out in this account.

51. Max Gluckman, J. A. Barnes, and J. C. Mitchell, "The Village Headman in British Central Africa," *Africa* 19 (1949), 89.

52. Kirk-Greene, "Thin White Line," p. 44.

53. This concept was developed by Georges Balandier, *Sociologie actuelle de l'Afrique noire: Dynamique sociale en Afrique centrale*, 2d ed., Paris, 1963.

54. This explanation of the system appears in Martin Kilson, *Political Change in a West African State: A Study in the Modernization Process*, Cambridge, Mass., 1966, p. 215. One variant holds that the post–World War I disillusionment with "civilization," widespread in Britain's ruling strata, fostered a philosophical attraction to nobly "savage" institutions (see Morris and Read, *Indirect Rule*, pp. 12–16). Another explanation holds indirect rule to have been a natural extension of Britain's culture and past history (see Perham, "Re-statement of Indirect Rule," pp. 332–333).

55. Lugard, *Dual Mandate*, p. 197.

56. Ibid., p. 617.

57. Ibid., p. 594.

58. Ibid., pp. 197, 409.

59. Ibid., pp. 577–585.

60. Ibid., p. 197.

61. Cf. Kilson, *Political Change in a West African State*, and Mamdani, *Politics and Class Formation in Uganda*, on the creation of a community of material interest between chiefs and administrations.

62. Lugard, *Dual Mandate*, p. 135.

63. See note 4, above.

64. NAZ, ZA 7/1/16/2, "Annual Report upon Native Affairs, 1933"; Richards, *Land, Labour and Diet*, p. 27.

65. Frank H. Melland, "Ethical and Political Aspects of African Witchcraft," *Africa* 8 (Jan. 1936), 498.

66. Lugard, *Dual Mandate*, p. 135.

67. Ibid., pp. 113, 193.

68. Ibid., p. 194.

69. See the general critique by T. O. Beidelman, *Colonial Evangelism: A Socio-historical Study of an East African Mission at the Grassroots*, Bloomington, Ind., 1982, p. 2.

70. M. Fortes and E. E. Evans-Pritchard, eds., *African Political Systems*, London, 1958, p. 16.

71. Talcott Parsons, ed., *Max Weber: The Theory of Social and Economic Organization*, Boston, 1969, pp. 115–118; see also Alfred Schutz, "Common-sense and Scientific Interpretation of Human Action," in Maurice Natanson, ed., *Collected Papers I*, The Hague, 1971; and Harold Garfinkel, *Studies in Ethnomethodology*, Englewood Cliffs, N.J., 1967, upon which this analysis draws.

72. See Karen E. Fields, "Political Contingencies of Witchcraft in Colonial Central Africa: Culture and the State in Marxist Theory," *Canadian Journal of African Studies* 16 (1982), 567–593.

2. THE POLITICS OF CUSTOM

1. One example of the genre by an American professor (University of Pennsylvania) is Daniel F. Brinton, *Races and Peoples: Lectures on the Science of Ethnography*, New York, 1890. See also the discussion of Michael Banton, *The Idea of Race*, Boulder, Colo., 1977.

2. Malcolm Hailey, *An African Survey: A Study of the Problems Arising in Africa South of the Sahara*, London, 1957, pp. 206–207, my translation from Lyautey's French. Cf. Robert Delavignette, *Les Vrais chefs de l'empire*, Paris, 1939, p. 125.

3. Brian Weinstein, "Félix Eboué (1844–1944)," in L. H. Gann and Peter Duignan, eds., *African Proconsuls: European Governors in Africa*, New York, 1978, p. 163.

4. See pertinent observations of H. F. Morris, "The Framework of Indirect Rule in East Africa," in H. F. Morris and James S. Read, eds., *Indirect Rule and the Search for Justice: Essays in East African Legal History*, London, 1972, pp. 21–36.

5. Quoted by Frederick John Dealtry Lugard, *The Dual Mandate in British Tropical Africa*, London, 1965, p. 216.

6. Karl Mannheim, *Ideology and Utopia: An Introduction to the Sociology of Knowledge*, New York, 1936, p. 118.

7. NAZ, KTO 2/1 (vol. 2), p. 155. More recent research (Andrew Roberts, *A History of the Bemba: Political Growth and Change in Northeastern Zambia before 1900*, London, 1973, p. 16) suggests that the headmen of Chinsali District were tributaries of the Shimwalule, although not in a sense that would have made him a reasonable choice for native authority.

8. Audrey I. Richards, "Tribal Government in Transition: The Babemba of North-eastern Rhodesia," Supplement to the *Journal of the Royal African Society* 34 (Oct. 1935), 11.

9. Thus, Max Gluckman wrote about "rituals of rebellion," not the real thing (see his *Order and Rebellion in Tropical Africa*, New York, 1963, and his *Custom and Conflict in Africa*, New York, 1964). My tone of impatience notwithstanding, I do not wish to minimize our intellectual debt to the work that was accomplished using the theoretical apparatus of functionalist anthropology.

10. Audrey I. Richards, *Land, Labour and Diet: An Economic Survey of the Bemba Tribe*, London, 1939, p. 25.

11. L. H. Gann, *The Birth of a Plural Society: The Development of Northern Rhodesia under the British South Africa Company, 1894–1914*, Manchester, 1958, p. 25.

12. E. H. Lane-Poole, *Native Tribes of the Eastern Province of Northern Rhodesia: Notes on Their Origin and History*, Lusaka, 1949, pp. 11, 53–54.

13. W. P. Livingstone, *Laws of Livingstonia: A Narrative of Missionary Adventure and Achievement*, London, 1921, p. 176.

14. Cf. J. E. Stephenson, *Chirupula's Tale*, London, 1937, pp. 187–188.

15. NAZ, ZA 7/1/3/1, Annual Report (Northern Province), 1915.

16. On this point, see Richards, *Land, Labour and Diet*, pp. 256ff.; also Morris, "Framework of Indirect Rule," pp. 31, 33, on the importance of tribute in Uganda's arrangements for indirect rule.

17. Richards, *Land, Labour and Diet*, pp. 358–359.

18. Richards, "Tribal Government," p. 19.

19. Lugard, *Dual Mandate*, p. 616; Richards, "Tribal Government," p. 18.

20. NAZ, ZA 7/1/3/1, Annual Report (Northern Province), 1933.

21. Richards, "Tribal Government," p. 19.

22. NAZ, ZA 7/1/17/1, Annual Report (Northern Province, Isoka District), 1934.

23. NAZ, ZA 7/1/3/1, Annual Report (Northern Province), 1915.

24. Sholto J. Cross, "The Watchtower Movement in South Central Africa, 1908–1945," Ph.D. diss., Oxford University, 1973, p. 173.

25. See the series of correspondence in NAZ, Sec/Nat 312 (vol. 7): C. G. Fane-Smith to PC (Kasama), 23/7/1942; DC (Kawambwa) to L. V.

Phillips, 10/8/1942; Minutes CGS to Acting CS, 28/9/1942; "Sanction for N. A. Orders," 8/10/1942.

26. Griffith Quick, "Some Aspects of the African Watchtower Movement in Northern Rhodesia," *International Review of Missions* 29 (1940), 216–226.

27. NAZ, Sec/Nat 312 (vol. 6), "Extracts of Letters," Alex Muwamba to T. F. Sandford, 3/10/1940.

28. NAZ, Sec/Nat 312 (vol. 5), "Meeting of Kasempa Chiefs, Minutes," 1/8/1937.

29. James M. Ault, "Making 'Modern' Marriage 'Traditional,'" *Theory and Society* 12 (1983).

30. NAZ, Sec/Nat 312 (vol. 2), "Memo No. 7, Watchtower and Mucapi," n.d.

31. NAZ, Sec/Nat 312 (vol. 7), L. V. Phillips to G. R. Phillips, 18/7/1944.

32. Claude Lévi-Strauss, *Les Formes élémentaires de la parenté*, Paris, 1949.

33. NAZ, BS/149, J. Moffat Thompson to Ass't. Mag. (Fife), 23/1/1920.

34. NAZ, KSZ 7/1/1, Annual Report (Northern Province), 1912–1913. I am indebted to James M. Ault for this reference.

35. Christopher Hill, *The World Turned Upside Down: Radical Ideas during the English Revolution*, New York, 1972, pp. 32ff.

36. Examples: Kenneth Bradley, *The Diary of a District Officer*, New York, 1966; and Robin J. Short, *African Sunset*, London, 1973.

37. John C. Nottingham, "Sorcery among the Akamba in Kenya," *Journal of African Administration* 11 (1959), 3–4.

38. F. H. Melland, "Ethical and Political Aspects of African Witchcraft," *Africa* 8 (Jan. 1935), 503, my italics. Cf. Geoffrey St. J. Orde-Browne, "Witchcraft and British Colonial Law," *Africa* 8 (Jan. 1935); and NAZ, ZA 1/15/M/2, in which W. F. Stubbs, DC (Chinsali), counseled toleration of the Bamucapi. Stubbs tasted the medicine and pronounced it "harmless."

39. Melland, "Ethical and Political Aspects of African Witchcraft," p. 499, my italics.

40. Gann, *Birth of a Plural Society*, pp. 97–98; Orde-Browne, "Witchcraft."

41. See Mary Douglas, "Techniques of Sorcery Control," in John Middleton and E. H. Winter, eds., *Witchcraft and Sorcery in East Africa*, London, 1963, as well as other papers in this useful volume. The same point is made by Max Marwick, "Another Modern Anti-Witchcraft Movement in East Central Africa," *Africa* 20 (1950).

42. Quoted in Keith V. Thomas, *Religion and the Decline of Magic*, New York, 1971, p. 523.

43. Melland, "Ethical and Political Aspects of African Witchcraft," p. 496, my italics.

44. Lucy P. Mair, *Witchcraft*, New York, 1969; J. R. Crawford, *Witchcraft and Sorcery in Rhodesia*, London, 1967.

45. See NAZ, ZA 7/1/14/1, ZA 7/1/16/5, and ZA 7/1/8/1.

46. NAZ, ZA 1/15/M/2, J. Moffat Thompson to CS, 30/10/1933. The folio ZA 1/15/M/2 contains most references to the Mucapi movement.

Unless otherwise indicated, all references to the movement cited hereafter come from this source.

47. DC (Chinsali) to PC (Isoka), 29/11/1933.

48. Terence O. Ranger, "Mucapi and the Study of Witchcraft Eradication," presented to the Conference on Central African Religions, Lusaka, 1973. I am indebted to Dr. John Higginson for the information that the Bamucapi spread into Mozambique.

49. Audrey I. Richards, "A Modern Movement of Witchcraft," *Africa* 8 (1935), 451, 455.

50. Chisholm to DC (Isoka), 2/1/1934.

51. Testimony of Gideon and Simon in *Rex* vs. *Longwani*, Lundazi.

52. DC (Chinsali) to PC (Isoka), 29/11/1933.

53. Ranger, "Mucapi," p. 5.

54. Ibid., p. 4.

55. Ibid.

56. Ibid., p. 6.

57. NAZ, ZA 7/1/15/1, Annual Report (Northern Province), 1931–1932, ZA 7/1/16/5, Annual Report (Northern Province), 1933.

58. Extract from *East Africa*, 20/7/1933.

59. Edward Shaba, quoted by Ranger, "Mucapi," p. 2. This example is drawn from the Tanzanian side of the movement.

60. DC (Chinsali) to PC (Isoka), 29/11/1933.

61. Richard Stuart, "The Mucapi on Likoma Island," presented to the Conference on Central African Religions, Lusaka, 1973, mimeographed, p. 15.

62. Ibid., p. 14.

63. Brian Garvey, "The Development of the White Fathers Mission among the Bemba-speaking Peoples, 1891–1964," Ph.D. diss., University of London, 1974, p. 174.

64. DC (Chinsali) to PC (Isoka), 29/11/1933.

65. Griffin to DC (Lundazi), 27/7/1933.

66. Colcutt to PC (Northern Province), 13/6/1933.

67. Griffin to DC (Lundazi), 27/7/1933.

68. Native Commissioner's Court (Lundazi), 18/9/1933.

69. DC (Chinsali) to PC (Isoka), 29/11/1933. Their attitude toward the Bamucapi differed markedly from their attitude toward the Watchtower apostles in 1919. Then, all but the Shimwalule vigorously opposed the revival.

70. "Extracts from Minutes of the Provincial Commissioners' Conference," 1934.

71. J. Moffat Thompson to DC, 14/8/1933.

72. H. C. Hill to DC, 24/4/1934; Chisholm to DC, 2/1/1934.

73. PC (Isoka) to DC, 22/1/1934.

74. DC (Isoka), Minute, 8/1/1934.

75. Griffin to CS, 26/7/1933.

76. DC (Chinsali) to PC (Isoka), 29/11/1933.
77. DC (Kawambwa) to PC (Kasama), 1/9/1934.
78. Hill to CS, 6/9/1934.
79. PC (Kasama) to DC (Kawambwa), 5/9/1934.
80. Hill to CS, 24/4/1934.
81. Ibid.
82. "Extracts from Tour Report No. 3" (Abercorn), 16/6/1934.
83. *Rex* vs. *Longwani.*
84. Griffin to DC (Lundazi), 27/7/1933.
85. DC (Kawambwa) to PC (Kasama), 1/9/1934.
86. Ibid.
87. DC (Chinsali) to PC (Isoka), 29/11/1933.
88. Quoted by DC (Isoka), Minute, 8/1/1934.
89. Provincial Commissioners' Conference, 14–15 May 1934.
90. PC (Ft. Jameson) to CS, 19/10/1933.
91. *Rex* vs. *Longwani.*
92. Marwick, "Another Modern Anti-Witchcraft Movement," p. 85.
93. DC (Chinsali) to PC (Isoka), 29/11/1933.
94. NAZ, ZA 7/1/16/4, Annual Report (Kaonde-Ila Province, Mwinilunga District), 1933.
95. Peter Bolink, *Towards Church Union in Zambia: A Study of Missionary Cooperation and Church Union Efforts in Central Africa,* Sneek, 1967, p. 108.
96. Elizabeth Hopkins, "The Politics of Crime: Aggression and Control in a Colonial Context," *American Anthropologist* 75 (June 1973).

PART 2: THE POLITICAL PROBLEM OF EVIL

1. George Shepperson, "Trends and Prospects in African Christianity," in C. G. Baeta, ed., *Christianity in Tropical Africa: Studies Presented and Discussed at the Seventh International African Seminar, University of Ghana,* Apr. 1965, London, 1968, p. 354.

2. James Davison Hunter, *American Evangelicalism: Conservative Religion and the Quandary of Modernity,* New Brunswick, N.J., 1983, p. 26.

3. This account of the early Watchtower is drawn mainly from Herbert Hewitt Stroup, *The Jehovah's Witnesses,* New York, 1945, and David Marley Cole, *Jehovah's Witnesses: The New World Society,* New York, 1955.

4. NAZ, Sec/Nat (vol. 7), "Analysis of Publications," 14/10/1947.

5. This discussion is based upon field work I conducted at Kingdom Halls in the Boston area during the spring of 1973 and at a regional Assembly in Milan, Italy, in August 1978.

6. Personal communication by Mr. Mutale Chanda, formerly a resident of Kitwe.

7. Stroup, *Jehovah's Witnesses,* pp. 106–107. It appears that some early conversions involved miraculous healing. What survives today is the prohibition against consuming animal blood, a prohibition that is applied to

blood transfusions as well as to everyday diet. This teaching, now a central one, appears in the primer *Truth*.

8. Cole, *Jehovah's Witnesses*, p. 90.

9. Ibid., p. 149; see also Barbara Grizzuti Harrison, *Visions of Glory: A History and a Memory of Jehovah's Witnesses*, New York, 1978, pp. 185–212.

10. NAZ, Sec/Nat 312 (vol. 7), *Times* (London), 17/9/1942, 18/9/1942.

11. NAZ, Sec/Nat 312 (vol. 7), CID to Admin., 14/6/1942.

12. NAZ, Sec/Nat 312 (vol. 5), Quarterly Report (Kawambwa), 31/12/1931.

13. Stroup, *Jehovah's Witnesses*, p. 147.

14. Bruno Bettelheim, *The Informed Heart: Autonomy in a Mass Age*, Glencoe, Ill., 1960, pp. 20–21, 122–123, 182.

15. Stroup, *Jehovah's Witnesses*, p. 15.

16. Watchtower Bible and Tract Society of Pennsylvania, *The Truth That Leads to Eternal Life*, New York, 1968, pp. 55–64; Stroup, *Jehovah's Witnesses*, pp. 128–129.

17. Stroup, *Jehovah's Witnesses*, p. 129; NAZ, ZA 1/10, CID to SNA, 5/2/1925.

18. Watchtower, *Truth*, p. 146.

19. Robert I. Rotberg, *The Rise of Nationalism in Central Africa: The Making of Malawi and Zambia, 1873–1964*, Cambridge, Mass., 1965, p. 143.

20. See the examples drawn by Harrison, *Visions of Glory*, pp. 213–218.

3. PROPHETIC THUNDER

1. Robert I. Rotberg, *The Rise of Nationalism in Central Africa: The Making of Malawi and Zambia, 1873–1964*, Cambridge, Mass., 1965, pp. 55–93 et passim; Sholto J. Cross, "The Watchtower Movement in South Central Africa, 1908–1945," Ph.D. diss., Oxford University, 1973; Kenneth John McCracken, "Livingstonia Mission and the Evolution of Malawi, 1875–1939," Ph.D. diss., University of Cambridge, 1967; George Shepperson and Thomas Price, *Independent African: John Chilembwe and the Origins, Setting and Significance of the Nyasaland Native Rising of 1915*, Edinburgh, 1958, pp. 153–160, 182–185.

2. This analysis of Livingstonia's policies and their consequences is greatly indebted to the work of Kenneth John McCracken, cited above. See also his *Politics and Christianity in Malawi, 1875–1940: The Impact of the Livingstonia Mission in the Northern Province*, Cambridge, 1977.

3. Joseph Bouniol, ed., *The White Fathers and Their Missions*, London, 1929, p. 80; NLS, 7904, "Instructions to the Lake Nyassa Party from the Foreign Mission Committee of the Free Church with the Concurrence of the Committee of the Reformed Presbyterian Church," May 1875.

4. W. P. Livingstone, *Laws of Livingstonia: A Narrative of Missionary Adventure and Achievement*, London, 1923, pp. 170–176; Donald Fraser, *Winning a Primitive People*, London, 1922, p. 8; Roland Oliver, *The Missionary Factor in East Africa*, London, 1952, pp. 94–162.

5. However, part of Livingstonia's role was formal. In 1912, the Reverend Dr. Robert Laws accepted responsibility for representing African interests on the Nyasaland Legislative Council.

6. Livingstone, *Laws of Livingstonia*, pp. 266, 275.

7. NAZ, BS1/113, Codrington to Prentice, 15/7/1904, and Beaufort to Laws, 3/6/1905.

8. George Shepperson has treated Booth's career in detail; see *Independent African* and "Joseph Booth and the Africanist Diaspora," Herskovits Lecture, 6 March 1972. According to Barbara Grizzuti Harrison, *Visions of Glory: A History and a Memory of Jehovah's Witnesses*, New York, 1978, p. 315, Jehovah's Witnesses now disparage him as a "religious hitchhiker."

9. Cf. T. O. Beidelman, *Colonial Evangelism: A Socio-Historical Study of an East African Mission at the Grassroots*, Bloomington, Ind., 1982, pp. 99–126, 211.

10. McCracken, "Livingstonia Mission," p. 333; Shepperson, *Independent African*, p. 160.

11. Hans Gerth and C. Wright Mills, eds., *From Max Weber: Essays in Sociology*, New York, 1958, p. 306.

12. Shepperson, *Independent African*, p. 135.

13. NAZ, ZA 1/9/158/2, CS to SNA, 20/4/1933, but the incident referred to had occurred many years previously. The chief secretary was outlining the administrative headache of Christian proliferation.

14. A. G. Blood, *The History of the Universities Mission to Central Africa*, 3 vols., London, 1957, 2:134.

15. NLS, *Livingstonia Mission Report*, 1912, p. 38 (hereafter LMR); Shepperson, "Joseph Booth," p. 2.

16. Rotberg, *Rise of Nationalism*, pp. 63–66.

17. Shepperson, *Independent African*, p. 86, photographs facing pp. 167, 183.

18. Ibid., pp. 152–153.

19. NLS, *Aurora* (June 1901), p. 24.

20. McCracken, "Livingstonia Mission," p. 311.

21. Shepperson, *Independent African*, p. 154; Harry W. Langworthy, "Elliot Kamwana," unpublished manuscript, 1984.

22. NLS, "The First Wave of Ethiopianism in Central Africa," *Livingstonia News* 7 (Aug. 1909), 57 (hereafter LN).

23. Rotberg, *Rise of Nationalism*, p. 67.

24. Bengt Sundkler's classic *Bantu Prophets in South Africa*, London, 1961, ignores this aspect of the South African religious scene; but John Sherrill, *They Speak with Other Tongues: The Story of a Reporter on the Trail of a Miracle*, New York, 1964, has shown that when Pentecostalist missionaries reached South Africa early in this century, they found a highly diverse and effervescent white Protestant environment.

25. LMR (1909), p. 33.

26. NLS, *Missionary Record* (1909), p. 7 (hereafter MR).

27. NLS, LMR (1900), p. 5.

28. NLS, *Report of the United Free Church Foreign Mission Committee* (1907), p. 40 (hereafter UFCFMC).

29. NLS, LN 2 (Apr. 1909).

30. Rotberg, *Rise of Nationalism*, p. 75.

31. J. E. Stephenson, *Chirupula's Tale*, London, 1937, pp. 63, 226.

32. McCracken, "Livingstonia Mission," p. 250; NLS, *Aurora* (Aug. 1902), p. 65.

33. NLS, *Aurora* (Oct. 1898), p. 33.

34. NLS, LMR (1902), p. vii.

35. NLS, *Aurora* (Apr. 1902), pp. 65–66.

36. Kenneth John McCracken, "Underdevelopment in Malawi: The Missionary Contribution," presented to the Institute for Commonwealth Studies Postgraduate Seminar: Colonial Rule and Local Response in the Nineteenth and Twentieth Centuries, London, Spring 1974, p. 10.

37. NLS, LN 2 (Feb. 1909), 3, and 2 (June 1909), 43.

38. Cf. Beidelman, *Colonial Evangelism*, pp. 166–171.

39. NLS, *Aurora* 2, 41–42.

40. NLS, LN 3 (Feb. 1910), 14.

41. NLS, LN 2 (1909), statistical tables.

42. McCracken, "Livingstonia Mission," p. 311.

43. Monica Wilson, "An African Christian Morality," *Africa* 10 (1936), 281. The Moravian and the Berlin Mission Societies enjoyed close ties of cooperation with Livingstonia. On the corresponding Catholic theology, see Brian Garvey, "The Development of the White Fathers Mission among the Bemba-speaking Peoples, 1891–1964," Ph.D. diss., University of London, 1974, pp. 149–200.

44. Edward P. Thompson, *The Making of the English Working Class*, New York, 1963.

45. NLS, LN 2 (Oct. 1909), 77.

46. NLS, *Aurora* 2 (Oct. 1898).

47. McCracken, "Livingstonia Mission," p. 315.

48. NLS, LMR (1900), pp. 4–5.

49. McCracken, "Livingstonia Mission," p. 312.

50. NLS, LN 3 (Feb. 1910), 14.

51. NLS, LMR (1901), p. 7, (1907), p. 24, and (1909), p. 50.

52. NLS, LMR (1902), p. 30.

53. NLS (1909), p. 20.

54. *Report of the Foreign Mission Committee of the Church of Scotland*, Edinburgh, 1929, p. 205 (hereafter RFM).

55. McCracken, *Politics and Christianity in Malawi*, pp. 57–109.

56. W. Vernon Stone, "Livingstonia Mission and the Bemba," *Bulletin of the Society for African Church History* 2 (1968), 3.

57. NLS, LN 2 (Aug. 1909), 85.

58. NLS, UFCFMC (1907), p. 28.

59. McCracken, "Livingstonia Mission," p. 148.

60. NLS, MR (1916), p. 147.

61. Ibid., pp. 317, 358–365.

62. NLS, LN 3 (Feb. 1910), 10.

63. NLS, "Annual Report of the Livingstonia Mission Committee of the Free Church," Edinburgh, 1911, p. 23 (hereafter "Annual Report").

64. NAZ, ZA 1/10 (vol. 3), I. C. Muwamba to D. MacKenzie-Kennedy, 22/6/1924.

65. Rotberg, *Rise of Nationalism*, p. 68.

66. NLS, LN 2 (Aug. 1909), 52.

67. NLS, "Annual Report," Edinburgh, 1909, p. 36.

68. NLS, LN 2 (Apr. 1909).

69. UFCFMC (1909), p. 34.

70. Blood, *History of the Universities Mission*, p. 196.

71. NLS, LN 2 (Aug. 1909), 52.

72. NLS, LMR (1919), p. 32.

73. George Shepperson, "Nyasaland and the Millennium," in Sylvia L. Thrupp, ed., *Millennial Dreams in Action: Essays in Comparative Study*, The Hague, 1962, pp. 15–151.

74. NLS, LMR (1910), p. xi.

75. Bengt Gustaf Malcolm Sundkler, *Zulu Zion and Some Swazi Zionists*, London, 1976.

76. NLS, LN 2 (Aug. 1909), 57.

77. NLS, LN 2 (Apr. 1909), 23.

78. Ibid., and 2 (Aug. 1909), 57.

79. NLS, LN 2 (Jan. 1909), 24.

80. NLS, LN 3 (Feb. 1910), 5.

81. See, for example, Bengt Sundkler, *Bantu Prophets*, London, 1961; John V. Taylor and Dorothea Lehmann, *Christians of the Copperbelt: Growth of the Church in Northern Rhodesia*, London, 1961; and H. M. Turner, *African Independent Church: The Life and Faith of the Church of the Lord (Aladura)*, 2 vols., London, 1967.

82. UE, Gen 766, Macalpine Papers, "Summary of Marambo Reports," typescript, n.d. (ca. 1900).

83. NAZ, ZA 1/10 (vol. 3), I. C. Muwamba to D. MacKenzie-Kennedy, 22/4/1924.

84. Peter Bolink, *Towards Church Union in Zambia*, Sneek, 1967, p. 108.

85. NLS, LN 2 (Aug. 1909), 57.

86. NLS, UFCFMC (1909), p. 4.

87. NLS, LN 2 (Aug. 1909), 57.

88. NLS, UFCFMC (1909), p. 4.

89. Ibid., p. 37.

90. NLS, LN 2 (Apr. 1909), 24.

91. NLS, "Annual Report," Edinburgh, 1911, p. ix.

92. NLS, LN 2 (Aug. 1909), 86; LMR (1909), p. 15.

93. McCracken, "Livingstonia Mission," p. 339; NLS, LMR (1912), p. 28.

94. McCracken, "Livingstonia Mission," p. 338.

95. Rotberg, *Rise of Nationalism*, p. 84.

96. Ian Linden, with Jane Linden, *Catholics, Peasants and Cewa Resistance in Nyasaland, 1889–1939*, Los Angeles, 1974.

4. CHARISMATIC FIRE

1. NAZ, ZA 1/10, Admin. to High Commissioner for South Africa, 16/4/1923, my italics.

2. Robert I. Rotberg, *The Rise of Nationalism in Central Africa: The Making of Malawi and Zambia, 1873–1964*, Cambridge, Mass., 1965, p. 142.

3. NAZ, BS1/113, BS1/115, BS1/118; ZA 1/9/158/2; NLS, *Livingstonia Mission Report* (1900–1910), passim (hereafter LMR).

4. Quoted in Kenneth John McCracken, "Livingstonia Mission and the Evolution of Malawi, 1875–1939," Ph.D. diss., University of Cambridge, 1967, p. 282.

5. NLS, LMR (1901), p. v.

6. NLS, LMR (1902), p. 31.

7. NLS, *Livingstonia News* 2 (Apr. 1902). Hereafter LN.

8. L. H. Gann, *The Birth of a Plural Society: The Development of Northern Rhodesia under the British South Africa Company, 1894–1914*, Manchester, 1967, pp. 29–31; Brian Garvey, "The Development of the White Fathers Mission among the Bemba-speaking Peoples, 1891–1964," Ph.D. diss., University of London, 1973, p. 154.

9. NAZ, BS1/115, Peuth to Leyer, 18/7/1910.

10. NAZ, HM4/cc/1/4, Fell to McMinn, 4/10/1924.

11. NAZ, Sec/Nat 313/1, Jalland to CS, 19/2/1935.

12. I am indebted to Dr. Jaap Van Velsen for directing my attention to the competitive aspect of missionary enterprise. Cf. Georges Balandier, *Sociologie actuelle de l'Afrique noire*, Paris, 1955, p. 419.

13. Sholto J. Cross, "The Watchtower Movement in South Central Africa, 1908–1945," Ph.D. diss., Oxford University, 1973, p. 202.

14. NAZ, ZA 1/10 Peuth to Commanding Officer, Northern Rhodesia Police, 19/2/1920.

15. NAZ, Sec/Nat 312 (vol. 7), Phillips to SNA, 13/7/1942.

16. NAZ, BS1/115, Memo, Magistrate's Office, 20/9/1910.

17. NAZ, ZA 1/9/158/2, J. Moffat Thompson to CS, 24/3/1934.

18. NAZ, HM4/cc/1/4, Fell to Wareham, 2/1/1925.

19. Joseph Bouniol, ed., *The White Fathers and Their Missions*, London, 1929, p. 111.

20. Brian Garvey, "The Northern Districts of Zambia during the First World War, 1914–1918," Lusaka, 1973–1974, pp. 7–8.

21. NLS, Free Church of Scotland, *Review of Foreign Missions*, Edinburgh (1915), pp. 43–45 (hereafter RFM).

22. Bouniol, *White Fathers*, p. 269.

23. Garvey, "Development of White Fathers Mission," p. 207.

24. Garvey, "Northern Districts," p. 9.

25. Henry S. Meebelo, *Reaction to Colonialism: A Prelude to the Politics of Independence in Northern Zambia, 1893–1939*, Manchester, 1971, p. 137.

26. Ibid., p. 135.

27. Garvey, "Northern Districts," pp. 9–10.

28. Cross, "Watchtower Movement," pp. 192–193.

29. Meebelo, *Reaction to Colonialism*, p. 135.

30. Garvey, "Northern Districts," p. 14; idem, "Development of White Fathers Mission," p. 216.

31. NAZ, ZA 1/10 (1924), Coxhead to Mag. (Abercorn), 27/5/1919.

32. NAZ, ZA 1/10, Draper to Secretary, 11/7/1919.

33. Quoted in Rotberg, *Rise of Nationalism*, p. 135.

34. Garvey, "Northern Districts," pp. 7, 8, 14.

35. Garvey, "Development of White Fathers Mission," p. 204.

36. NAZ, ZA 1/10, Draper to Secretary, 11/7/1919.

37. NAZ, ZA 7/1/3/1, Annual Report (Northern Province), 1915.

38. Garvey, "Northern Districts," p. 10.

39. NAZ, ZA 1/10, Draper to Secretary, 11/7/1919.

40. Cross, "Watchtower Movement," p. 163.

41. NAZ, ZA 1/10 (3290), Dewhurst to DC (Kasama), 5/13/1919.

42. NAZ, ZA 1/10 (1924), Coxhead to Mag. (Abercorn), 27/5/1919, quoting from a report by P. J. Macdonnell, which is no longer in the archives.

43. NLS, RFM (1915), pp. 43, 45.

44. Ibid.

45. Ibid.

46. NAZ, BS3/445, Report of the Visiting Commissioner, H. C. Marshall, 25/8/1919.

47. F. H. Melland, *In Witchbound Africa*, London, 1923, p. 26.

48. Garvey, "Northern Districts," p. 17.

49. NAZ, ZA 1/10, CID (Bulawayo) to Commandant, Northern Rhodesia Police, 13/3/1919.

50. Cross, "Watchtower Movement," p. 194.

51. NAZ, ZA 1/10, Macdonnell to Admin., 5/5/1919.

52. Meebelo, *Reaction to Colonialism*, p. 136; Cross, "Watchtower Movement," p. 194.

53. NAZ, ZA 1/10, Peuth to Officer Commanding, NR Police, 19/2/1920.

54. NAZ, ZA 1/10 (3290), Macdonnell, Confidential Memo, 17/4/1919; ZA 1/10 (1919–1926), Stokes to Goodall, 31/2/1922.

55. NAZ, ZA 1/10/1, "The Watchtower Movement in Tanganyika District," 6/2/1919.

56. Cross, "Watchtower Movement," p. 208; ZA 1/10 (1919–1926), Report of Robert Simpelwe, 26/4/1920.

57. George Shepperson, "Nyasaland and the Millennium," in Sylvia L.

Thrupp, ed., *Millennial Dreams in Action: Essays in Comparative Study*, The Hague, 1962, p. 150.

58. NAZ, ZA 1/10, Macdonnell to Admin., 5/5/1919.

59. Meebelo, *Reaction to Colonialism*, p. 142.

60. See Ian Cunnison, "Headmanship and the Luapula Village," *Africa* 26 (1956), 2–16.

61. NAZ, ZA 1/10 (to 12/1/1919), Draper to Admin., 19/1/1919.

62. Ibid.

63. Ibid.

64. NAZ, ZA 1/10 (1925), Macdonnell, Memo, 1925.

65. Meebelo, *Reaction to Colonialism*, p. 155.

66. Cross, "Watchtower Movement," pp. 194–201.

67. NAZ, BS1/149, Tanguy before D. MacKenzie-Kennedy, JP, 13/11/1918.

68. Garvey, "Northern Districts," pp. 15–16.

69. NAZ, ZA 1/10 (3290), Dewhurst to DC (Kasama), 17/3/1919.

70. NAZ, ZA 1/10 (1919–1926), Macdonnell to Admin., 5/5/1919.

71. NAZ, ZA 1/10 (3290), Dewhurst to DC (Kasama), 17/3/1919.

72. NAZ, ZA 1/10 (3290), Dewhurst to DC (Kasama), 5/3/1919 and 17/3/1919.

73. NAZ, ZA 1/10 (1919–1926), Macdonnell to Admin., 5/5/1919; Cross, "Watchtower Movement," pp. 208, 284.

74. NAZ, ZA 1/10, Commandant's Report, KAR to HQ, 6/1/1919.

75. NAZ, ZA 1/10 (3290), Dewhurst to DC (Kasama), 17/3/1919.

76. NAZ, ZA 1/10 (3290), Dewhurst to DC (Kasama), 5/3/1919.

77. NAZ, ZA 1/10 (vol. 3), J. Moffat Thompson to DC (Abercorn), 14/9/1920.

78. NAZ, ZA 1/10 (3290), Dewhurst to DC (Kasama), 17/3/1919.

79. Quoted in NAZ, ZA 1/10/1, Draper to Admin., 6/2/1919.

80. NAZ, ZA 1/10, Macdonnell to Admin., 5/5/1919.

81. NAZ, ZA 1/10 (3290), Draper to DC, 17/3/1919.

82. NAZ, ZA 1/10/1, Minutes of Ndaba at Chunga Village.

83. NAZ, ZA 1/10 (3290), Dewhurst to DC, 17/3/1919, my italics.

84. NAZ, ZA 1/10, Draper to Admin., 19/1/1919.

85. Gann, *Birth of a Plural Society*, p. 99.

86. Cross, "Watchtower Movement," p. 206; NAZ, ZA 1/10, Dewhurst to DC, 21/9/1919.

87. NAZ, ZA 1/10 (to 12/2/1919), Dewhurst to DC, 21/11/1918.

88. NAZ, ZA 1/10/1, E. Peuth to Acting DC, 22/12/1918.

89. NAZ, ZA 1/10, Draper to Admin., 19/1/1919.

90. NAZ, ZA 1/10, Draper to Admin., 19/1/1919.

91. Talcott Parsons and A. M. Henderson, eds., *Max Weber: The Theory of Social and Economic Organization*, New York, 1969, pp. 71, 361–363; Hans Gerth and C. Wright Mills, eds., *From Max Weber: Essays in Sociology*, New York, 1975, p. 295.

92. See, for example, Louis Oger, "Spirit Possession among the Bemba: A Linguistic Approach," presented to the Conference on the History of Central African Religions, Lusaka, 1973, which describes a technical vocabulary and formal procedures for the treatment of possessed individuals.

93. See, for example, Mary Douglas, "Techniques of Sorcery Control," in John Middleton and E. H. Winter, eds., *Witchcraft and Sorcery in East Africa*, New York, 1963, p. 125.

94. See John Iliffe and Gilbert Gwassa, "Kinjikitile and the Ideology of Maji Maji," in Terence O. Ranger and John A. Weller, eds., *Themes in the Christian History of Central Africa*, Berkeley, Calif., 1975.

95. Ioan Lewis, *Ecstatic Religion: An Anthropological Study of Possession and Shamanism*, London, 1971.

96. In Max Gluckman, ed., *Order and Rebellion in Tribal Africa*, New York, 1963.

97. Christopher Hill, *The World Turned Upside Down: Radical Ideas during the English Revolution*, New York, 1972.

98. NAZ, ZA 1/10 (1919–1926), Macdonnell to Admin., 5/5/1919.

99. Cross, "Watchtower Movement," pp. 208, 284.

100. NAZ, BS3/445, Report of H.C. Marshall, Visiting Commissioner.

101. NAZ, ZA 1/10, Macdonnell to Admin., 5/5/1919.

102. NAZ, ZA 1/10 (3290), DC (Kasama) to Admin., 26/2/1919, telegram.

103. NAZ, BS1/149, Chisholm to Draper, 1/3/1919.

104. NAZ, ZA 7/1/4/1, Annual Report (Northern Province, Chinsali District), 1919–1920.

105. NAZ, BS1/149, Chisholm to Draper, 1/3/1919.

106. NAZ, BS3/445, Report of H. C. Marshall, Visiting Commissioner; ZA 1/10, Dewhurst to DC, 25/6/1919.

107. NAZ, ZA 1/10, Dewhurst to DC, 25/6/1919.

108. NAZ, ZA 1/10 (1919–1926), SNA to Secretary, 4/4/1923, quoting a report made by Father Peuth in 1920.

5. THE WATER NEXT TIME

1. NAZ, ZA 1/10 (1919–1926), NC (Ft. Jameson) to Mag., 21/7/1925; Terence Ranger, "The Mwana Lesa Movement of 1925," in Terence O. Ranger and John Weller, eds., *Themes in the Christian History of Central Africa*, Berkeley, Calif. 1975, p. 66; A. G. Blood, *The History of the Universities Mission to Central Africa*, 3 vols., London, 1957, 2:40, 285.

2. Robert I. Rotberg, *The Rise of Nationalism in Central Africa: The Making of Malawi and Zambia, 1873–1964*, Cambridge, Mass., 1965, pp. 36–39.

3. Sholto J. Cross, "The Watchtower Movement in South Central Africa, 1908–1945," Ph.D. diss., Oxford University, 1973, p. 49.

4. Watchtower Bible and Tract Society of Pennsylvania, *Yearbook of Jehovah's Witnesses, 1972*, pp. 234–235.

5. NAZ, KSM 3/1/1, "Summary of the Events, 1926." The source of all archival references cited in this chapter is the National Archives of Zambia.

6. KSM 3/1/2, testimony of Mulakasa and Kalungaka.

7. KSM 3/1/1, exhibit 22, Mulakasa, Chungwe.

8. Ibid., ex. 3, Kunda.

9. Ranger, "Mwana Lesa Movement," p. 55.

10. KSM 3/1/1, ex. 5, Sukuta.

11. Ibid., ex. 2, Chinye Makaika.

12. Ibid., ex. 1, Chipulilo.

13. Ibid., ex. 3, Kunda.

14. KSM 3/1/2, Ntembelwa Chondoka.

15. Ibid., ex. 10, Ndakawila.

16. Ranger, "Mwana Lesa Movement," pp. 49–50.

17. KSM 3/1/1, ex. 22, Mulakasa, my italics.

18. Ibid.

19. Ibid., "Summary"; cf. J. R. Crawford, *Witchcraft and Sorcery in Rhodesia*, London, 1967, pp. 248–255.

20. Many such letters are to be found in KSM 3/1/1.

21. KSM 3/1/1, ex. 23, Elyakuka Busi to Tomo Yedwa, n.d.

22. Ibid., ex. 10, Sukuta.

23. Ibid., ex. 22, Chawala.

24. Ibid., ex. 4, Kunda; ex. 3, Nkufye, Kunda.

25. KSM, 3/1/2, Mwewa.

26. KSM 3/1/1, ex. 3, Chifwalo.

27. Ibid., ex. 22.

28. KSM 3/1/2, ex. 10, Sukuta.

29. KSM 3/1/1, "Summary"; KSM 3/1/2, ex. 10, Chisenga.

30. KSM 3/1/1, ex. 10, Sukuta.

31. Ibid., ex. 22, Kunda Chinilankwa.

32. KSM 3/1/2, ex. 22, Chapamwanda.

33. Ibid., ex. 22, Msonka.

34. Ibid., ex. 22, Chigwalo.

35. Ranger, "Mwana Lesa Movement," p. 48; ZA 1/10 (1925), *Rex* vs. *Tomo Nyirenda et al.*, "Address to Prisoners."

36. Ranger, "Mwana Lesa Movement," p. 72; KSM 3/1/2, Chitina and Mwashe.

37. KSM 3/1/2, Mukalwe.

38. Ibid., Chibansa.

39. KSM 3/1/1, ex. 10, Sukuta.

40. Cross, "Watchtower Movement," p. 253.

41. KSM 3/1/1, ex. 10, Sukuta.

42. Cross, "Watchtower Movement," p. 259; ZA 1/10 (1925), P. J. Macdonnell, "Address to Prisoners."

43. Ranger, "Mwana Lesa Movement," p. 48.

44. KSM 3/1/1, ex. 10, Sukuta.

45. Ibid.

46. Ibid., "Summary."

47. Ibid., ex. 5, Muswalo.

48. Ibid., "Summary."

49. ZA 1/10 (1925), quoted by Macdonnell, "Address."

50. KSM 3/1/1, ex. 19, Wanga (of Mwaluka's).

51. Ibid., ex. 11, Stanley William Cooper, Clerk of Magistrate.

52. Frederick John Dealtry Lugard, *The Dual Mandate in British Tropical Africa*, 5th ed., London, 1965, pp. 581–582.

53. ZA 1/10 (1925), J. E. Stephenson to Mag. (Broken Hill), 15/11/1925.

54. Cross, "Watchtower Movement," p. 245.

55. Ranger, "Mwana Lesa Movement," pp. 62–63.

56. Ibid., p. 63.

57. Ibid., p. 61; J. E. Stephenson, *Chirupula's Tale*, London, 1929, pp. 141, 156–158.

58. Stephenson, *Chirupula's Tale*, pp. 187–188.

59. Robin J. Short, *African Sunset*, London, 1973.

60. L. H. Gann, *The Birth of a Plural Society: The Development of Northern Rhodesia under the British Africa Company, 1894–1914*, Manchester, 1958, pp. 95, 100.

61. Ranger, "Mwana Lesa Movement," p. 74.

62. Ibid., pp. 59–60.

63. KSM 3/1/1, "Summary."

64. Ranger, "Mwana Lesa Movement," p. 74.

65. On the connection between adultery and sorcery see, for example, E. E. Evans-Pritchard, *Witchcraft, Magic and Oracles among the Azande*, London, 1937, pp. 406–407.

66. Ranger, "Mwana Lesa Movement," p. 47; KSM 3/1/1, "Summary."

67. KSM 3/1/1, ex. 5, Muswalo.

68. Ibid.

69. Ibid., ex. 1, Sukuta.

70. Ibid., ex. 10, Sukuta.

71. Ibid., ex. 5, Muswalo.

72. Ibid., ex. 6, Kawamba.

73. Ibid., ex. 5, Sukuta.

74. Ibid., ex. 3, Sukuta; ex. 6, Kawamba.

75. Ibid., ex. 5, Verdict.

76. Ibid., ex. 6, Musanla, Mwelwa.

77. Ibid., ex. 10, Sukuta.

78. Ibid., ex. 6, Kawamba.

79. Ibid.

80. Ibid., ex. 1, penciled notation.

81. Ibid., Chipulilo, Koni.

82. Ibid., ex. 5, Muswalo.

83. Ibid., ex. 10, Sukuta.

84. Ibid., ex. 6, Kawamba.

85. Ibid., ex. 3, Chifwalo.

86. Ibid., ex. 10, Musanla.
87. Ibid., ex. 6, Kawamba; ex. 3.
88. Ibid., ex. 5, Verdict of F. L. Brown, JP.
89. Ibid., ex. 5, Muswalo.
90. Ibid., ex. 2, Musakanya.
91. Ibid., ex. 22, Mulakasa.
92. Ibid., ex. 1, Kabwela.
93. Ibid., ex. 1, Kabwela; ex. 22, Makani, Kunda Chinilankwa.
94. Ranger, "Mwana Lesa Movement," p. 51.
95. KSM 3/1/1, ex. 22, Kunda.
96. Ibid., ex. 5, Mulonda.
97. Ibid., ex. 22, Mulakasa.
98. Ibid., ex. 22, Chungwe.
99. Ibid., ex. 22, Mulakasa.
100. Ibid., ex. 22, Kunda Chinilankwa.
101. Ibid., ex. 1, Mulalika.
102. Ibid., ex. 1, Mwelwa.
103. Ibid., ex. 1, Chisenga.
104. Ibid., T. J. Chicken.
105. Ibid., ex. 1, Koni.
106. Ibid., ex. 22.
107. Ibid., ex. 1, Chisenga.
108. Ibid., ex. 7, Mwaluka.
109. Ibid., ex. 7, Mwape.
110. Ibid., ex. 7, Mwaluka.
111. Ibid., ex. 23, Kalunga.
112. KSM 3/1/2, ex. 22, Chungwe, Mulakasa.
113. KSM 3/1/1, "Summary."
114. Ranger, "Mwana Lesa Movement," p. 63.
115. Cf. David Parkin, "Medicines and Men of Influence," *Man* 3 (1968), 424–440.
116. KSM 3/1/1, ex. 6, Kunda Sawongo.
117. KSM 3/1/2, ex. 10, Chindalupako.
118. KSM 3/1/1, ex. 6, Kunda Sawongo.
119. KSM 3/1/2, Mwewa.
120. Ibid., ex. 22, Kabwela.
121. KSM 3/1/1, ex. 22, Mulakasa.
122. Ibid., ex. 5, Mulonda.
123. Ibid., ex. 5, Mulonda, Letele.
124. Ibid., ex. 1, Kalunga.
125. Ibid., ex. 2, Chinye Makaika.
126. KSM 3/1/2, Mushiri.
127. KSM 3/1/1, ex. 2, Kabwela.
128. KSM 3/1/2, Loloma.
129. KSM 3/1/1, ex. 11, Ntembelwa.

130. Ibid., ex. 7, Finding.

131. ZA 1/10 (1925), J. E. Stephenson to Mag. (Broken Hill), 15/11/1925, emphasis in the original.

132. ZA 1/10, J. E. Stephenson to Atty. Gen., 13/2/1926.

133. KSM 3/1/1, "Summary."

PART 3: ELEMENTARY NORMS OF THE RELIGIOUS LIFE

1. Sholto J. Cross, "The Watchtower Movement in South Central Africa, 1908–1945," Ph.D. diss., Oxford University, 1973, p. 225.

2. Dr. George Bond, personal communication, September 1983.

3. NAZ, ZA 1/10 (1925), "Watchtower Natives—Prosecutions of, Comment and Review."

4. NAZ, Sec/Nat 312 (vol. 7), L. V. Phillips to G. R. Phillips, 23/9/1944. Manasse Nkhoma is remembered today as a founder of Jehovah's Witnesses in Zambia (Watchtower Bible and Tract Society, *Yearbook of Jehovah's Witnesses, 1972*, p. 236).

5. Talcott Parsons, ed., *Max Weber: Theory of Social and Economic Organization*, New York, 1969, pp. 124–126.

6. Emile Durkheim, *The Elementary Forms of the Religious Life*, New York, 1965, p. 257.

6. COERCIVE TOLERANCE

1. NAZ, ZA 1/10 (1925), "Watchtower Natives—Prosecutions of, Comment and Review."

2. NAZ, ZA 1/10 (1924), Mag.'s Ofc. (Mazabuka) to DC (Livingstone), 3/3/1924.

3. Copies of various warrants appear in ZA 1/10 (vol. 3).

4. NAZ, ZA 1/10 (1924–1925), P. J. Macdonnell to Admin., 5/5/1919, my italics.

5. NAZ, ZA 1/10 , Acting SNA Tagart to Gov., 15/4/1924.

6. NAZ, ZA 1/10 (1924), P. J. Macdonnell to Admin., 5/5/1919; ZA 1/10 (vol. 3), Mag. (Abercorn), 23/2/1922; ZA 1/10 (vol. 3), SNA to Mag. (Abercorn), 3/5/1922.

7. NAZ, ZA 1/10 (vol. 3), Superintendent CID, 12/12/1923.

8. NAZ, ZA 1/10 (vol. 3), "Report on Meschech Simwanza," NC (Fife), 12/8/1924.

9. NAZ, ZA 1/10 (1924), *Rex vs. Isaac Nyasulo et al.*, 18/3/1924.

10. NAZ, ZA 1/10 (1924), Governor (Northern Rhodesia) to Governor (Nyasaland), 11/4/1924; Governor (Nyasaland) to Governor (Northern Rhodesia), 16/4/1924.

11. NAZ, ZA 1/10 (vol. 4), Venning to NC, 17/4/1925.

12. NAZ, ZA 1/10 (vol. 3), NC (Chilanga) to DC (Broken Hill), 26/3/1925.

13. NAZ, ZA 1/10 (vol. 3) Report by SNA, "Pan-Africanism and the

Possession of Firearms among the Natives of Northern Rhodesia," High
Commissioner's Dispatch, 26/2/1923.

14. NAZ, ZA 1/10 (1924), CID to SNA, 30/7/1924.

15. NAZ, ZA 1/10, NC (Chilanga) to SNA, 4/12/1926.

16. NAZ, HM 4/cc/1/4, General Missionary Conference, 1924; ZA 1/10,
Acting SNA to Tagart to Gov., 15/4/1924.

17. NAZ, ZA 1/10, P. J. Macdonnell to Registrar, 28/8/1924.

18. NAZ, ZA 1/10, *Rex* vs. *Isaac Nyasulo et al.*, 18/3/1924.

19. NAZ, ZA 1/10 (1924), Mag. (Ft. Jameson) to SNA, 26/9/1924.

20. NAZ, ZA 1/10 (1924), Mag.'s Ofc. (Mazabuka) to DC (Livingstone),
3/3/1924.

21. NAZ, ZA 1/10 (1924), *Rex* vs. *Isaac Nyasulo et al.*, 18/3/1924.

22. NAZ, ZA 1/10 (vol. 3), NC (Chilanga) to DC (Broken Hill), 26/3/
1925.

23. NAZ, ZA 1/10, SNA to Mag. (Broken Hill), 11/2/1925.

24. NAZ, ZA 1/10, Tagart to Ass't. Mag. (Serenje), 14/4/1925.

25. NAZ, ZA 1/10 (1924), Tagart to Ass't. NC (Serenje), 12/6/1924.

26. NAZ, ZA 1/10 (1924), SNA circular, 5/6/1924.

27. NAZ, ZA 1/10, Tagart to Moffat, 12/6/1924.

28. NAZ, ZA 1/10 (1924), Tagart to Ass't. NC (Serenje), 12/6/1924.

29. NAZ, ZA 1/10, Stokes to Tagart, 13/6/1926.

30. NAZ, ZA 1/10 (vol. 3), Sidney Cooke to NC (Chilanga), 28/11/1924.

31. NAZ, ZA 1/10, J. E. Stephenson to SNA, 16/3/1924.

32. NAZ, ZA 1/10 (1925), Macfarlane to DC (Broken Hill), 27/2/1925.

33. NAZ, ZA 1/10 (vol. 3), NC (Chilanga) to DC (Broken HIll), 27/2/
1925.

34. NAZ, ZA 1/10 (vol. 3), Cholmeley to SNA, 22/7/1924 and NC (Chilanga) to DC (Broken Hill), 26/3/1925.

35. NAZ, ZA 1/10 (vol. 3), NC (Chilanga) to DC (Broken Hill), 26/3/
1925.

36. NAZ, ZA 1/10 (vol. 3), J. Moffat Thompson to Hinds, 13/3/1925.

37. NAZ, ZA 1/10 (vol. 4), Venning to NC (Chilanga), 17/4/1925.

38. NAZ, ZA 1/10 (vol. 3), Hinds to DC (Broken Hill), 5/2/1925.

39. NAZ, ZA 1/10 (vol. 3), Hinds to NC (Chilanga), 5/3/1925.

40. NAZ, Sec/Nat 312 (vol. 1), Director of Native Education to CS, 15/
8/1931.

41. NAZ, ZA 1/10 (vol. 3), NC (Abercorn) to SNA, 15/7/1921.

42. NAZ, ZA 1/10 (1924), Acting SNA Tagart to Gov., 15/4/1924.

43. Lewis H. Gann and Peter Duignan, *The Rulers of British Africa, 1870–
1914*, Palo Alto, Calif., 1978, pp. 214ff.

44. NAZ, ZA 1/10 (vol. 3), "Report on Watchtower by UMCA Teachers,"
1924.

45. Cf. Christopher Hill, *The World Turned Upside Down: Radical Ideas
during the English Revolution*, New York, 1972.

46. NAZ, ZA 1/10 (vol. 3), NC (Chilanga) to DC (Broken Hill), 26/3/ 1925.

47. NAZ, ZA 1/10, Bishop of Northern Rhodesia (Anglican) to SNA, 19/10/1924.

48. NAZ, ZA 1/10 (1923), Report of SNA Latham, 2/1923.

49. NAZ, ZA 1/10 (1926–1927), DC to SNA, 3/5/1925.

50. NAZ, ZA 1/10, DC (Ft. Jameson) to Acting SNA, 22/4/1924.

51. NAZ, ZA 1/10 (vol. 3), Siemienski to DC, 17/2/1925, Siemienski to Officer Commanding, CID, 19/10/1924.

52. NAZ, ZA 1/10, Bishop of Northern Rhodesia (Anglican) to SNA, 19/10/1924.

53. NAZ, ZA 1/10 (vol. 3), Siemienski to DC, 17/2/1925.

54. NAZ, ZA 7/1/4/1, Annual Report (Northern Province), 1919–1920.

55. NLS, 7885/1, Chisholm to Ashcroft, 11/1/1920; *Review of Foreign Missions*, 1921, p. 40.

56. NLS, 7886/1, Chisholm to Ashcroft, 11/9/1923.

57. NLS, 7885/1, Elmslie to Ashcroft, 8/5/1922.

58. NAZ, ZA 1/10 (1924–1925), CID, "Report on Watchtower Publications," 1925; CID to SNA, 5/2/1925.

59. NAZ, Sec/Nat 312 (vol. 8), "Analysis of Publications," 14/10/1947.

60. NAZ, Sec/Nat 312 (vol. 1), CID to CS, 11/6/1932 and Director of Native Education to CS, 11/6/1932.

61. NAZ, Sec/Nat 312 (vol. 2), "Petauke Tour Report No. 1, 1935."

62. NAZ, Sec/Nat 312 (vol. 1), DC (Kasempa) to CS, 19/4/1932.

63. NAZ, Sec/Nat 312 (vol. 5), L. C. Mwambulah to L. V. Phillips, 25/4/ 1937.

64. NAZ, ZA 1/10 (vol. 3), DC (Ft. Jameson) to SNA, 12/11/1924.

65. Brian Garvey, "The Development of the White Fathers Mission among the Bemba-speaking Peoples, 1891–1964," Ph.D. diss., University of London, 1974, p. 254.

66. NAZ, Sec/Nat 312 (vol. 7), extract from Hansard, 17/7/1941.

67. NAZ, ZA 1/10 (1924), Tagart to Gov., 15/4/1924, my italics.

68. NAZ, ZA 1/10 (vol. 3), J. Moffat Thompson to Hinds, 13/3/1925.

69. NAZ, ZA 1/10 (vol. 3), DC (Ft. Jameson) to SNA, 12/11/1924.

70. NAZ, ZA 1/10, Tagart to Ass't. Mag. (Serenje), 14/4/1925.

71. NAZ, Sec/Nat 312 (vol. 1), SNA to CS, 21/2/1930.

72. NAZ, ZA 1/10, NC to Mag. (Ft. Jameson), 21/7/1925. Letter dated 20/7/1925 is forwarded with this communication, my italics.

73. NAZ, ZA 1/10, DC (Ft. Jameson) to Acting SNA, 22/9/1924, from paraphrased extract of E. Jordan, 16/9/1924.

74. NAZ, ZA 1/10 (1924), Mag. (Ft. Jameson) to SNA, 14/8/1924.

75. NAZ, ZA 1/10 (1924), DC (Ft. Jameson) to SNA 12/11/1924.

76. NAZ, ZA 1/10, NC to Mag. (Ft. Jameson), 21/7/1925.

77. NAZ, ZA 1/10 (1924), DC (Ft. Jameson) to SNA, 12/11/1924.

78. NAZ, ZA 1/10, SNA Tagart to Mag. (Ft. Jameson), 12/9/1924.

79. NAZ, ZA 1/10 (1919–1926), NC (Ft. Jameson) to Mag., 21/7/1925.

80. NAZ, ZA 1/10 (1924), DC (Ft. Jameson) to SNA, 20/11/1924, my italics.

81. NAZ, ZA 1/10 (1919–1926), NC (Ft. Jameson) to Mag., 21/7/1925, my italics.

82. NAZ, ZA 1/10 (1926–1927), "Patrol Report, Fort Jameson," 10/6/1926.

83. NAZ, ZA 1/10 (1926–1927), Acting SNA to DC (Ft. Jameson), 3/7/1926.

84. NAZ, ZA 1/10 (1926–1927), "Patrol Report, Fort Jameson," 10/6/1926.

85. NAZ, ZA 1/10 (vol. 3), Ass't. Mag. to DC (Broken Hill), 30/3/1925.

86. NAZ, ZA 1/10, DC (Broken Hill) to D. MacKenzie-Kennedy, 31/10/1925.

87. NAZ, ZA 1/10 (1924), *Rex* vs. *Isaac Nyasulo et al.*, 18/3/1924.

88. NAZ, ZA 1/10 (1924), CID to SNA, 4/11/1924.

89. NAZ, ZA 1/10 (1924), Acting SNA to Gov., 15/4/1924.

90. NAZ, ZA 1/10 (1924), "Enquiry re Harry Anckethill (WTBTS), 20/12/1921 by CID, Cape Town"; Anckethill to NC (Mazabuka), 26/3/1924.

91. NAZ, ZA 1/10 (1919–1926), Walder (WTBTS) to Gov., 10/9/1924; Goodall (Abercorn) to SNA 23/12/1924.

92. NAZ, ZA 1/10 (vol. 3), Goodall (Abercorn) to SNA, 20/2/1925.

93. NAZ, Sec/Nat 312 (vol. 1), Acting Director of Native Education to CS, 15/8/1931.

94. NAZ, ZA 1/10 (vol. 3), Tagart to Dawson, 28/8/1925.

95. NAZ, ZA 1/10, Dawson to CS, 21/11/1925.

96. NAZ, ZA 1/10, DC (Broken Hill) to D. MacKenzie-Kennedy, 31/10/1925.

97. NAZ, ZA 1/10, Dawson to CS, 21/11/1925.

98. NAZ, ZA 1/10, DC (Broken Hill) to D. MacKenzie-Kennedy, 31/10/1925.

99. Sholto J. Cross, "The Watchtower Movement in South Central Africa, 1908–1945," Ph.D. diss., Oxford University, 1973, pp. 178, 339–350.

100. NAZ, Sec/Nat 312 (vol. 2), Comm'r. of Police to SNA, 20/6/1934.

101. Griffith Quick, "Some Aspects of the African Watchtower Movement in Northern Rhodesia," *International Review of Missions* 29 (1940), 220.

102. NAZ, Sec/Nat 312 (vol. 1), J. R. Keith to CS, 15/8/1931.

103. NAZ, Sec/Nat 312 (vol. 1), DC (Ft. Jameson) to PC, 5/2/1930.

104. NAZ, Sec/Nat 312 (vol. 1), "Ex-local men" to DC (Mazabuka).

105. NAZ, Sec/Nat 312 (vol. 1), SNA to CS, 9/5/1932.

106. NAZ, Sec/Nat 312 (vol. 1), "Mweru-Luapula Quarterly Report," 30/6/1931.

107. NAZ, Sec/Nat 312 (vol. 1), Det. Inspect. CID to Ass't. Comm'r., Northern Rhodesia Police, 20/4/1932.

108. NAZ, Sec/Nat 312 (vol. 1), Goodall to SNA, 16/2/1932.

109. NAZ, Sec/Nat 312 (vol. 1), Immigration Officer to CS, 11/6/1932.

110. See the detailed account in the *Report of the Commission Appointed to enquire into the Disturbances in the Copperbelt, Northern Rhodesia, October, 1935*, London, 1935.

111. NAZ, Sec/Nat 312 (vol. 2), G. R. Phillips (WTBTS) to CS, 1/7/1935; (vol. 3), Petrus de Jaeger to CS, 27/8/1935; and (vol. 7), L. V. Phillips to SNA, 6/1/1943.

112. A. G. Blood, *The History of the Universities Mission to Central Africa*, 3 vols., London, 1957, 3:54.

113. NAZ, Sec/Nat 312 (vol. 2), Gov. to Malcolm Macdonald, MP, 20/7/1935.

114. NAZ, Sec/Nat 312 (vol. 8), Gov. (Northern Rhodesia) to Gov. (Belgian Congo), 21/5/1948.

115. NAZ, Sec/Nat 312 (vol. 5), Acting CS, Circular, 7/11/1936.

116. NAZ, Sec/Nat 312 (vol. 2), Executive Council Minutes, "Watchtower Literature: The Crisis," 6/8/1935.

117. NAZ, Sec/Nat 312 (vol. 3), Petrus de Jaeger to CS, 27/8/1935.

118. NAZ, Sec/Nat 312 (vol. 3), DC (Ndola) to PC, 16/9/1935.

119. NAZ, Sec/Nat 312 (vol. 3), DC (Ndola) to PC, 23/8/1935.

120. NAZ, Sec/Nat 312 (vol. 3), DC (Ndola) to PC, 16/9/1935.

121. NAZ, Sec/Nat 312 (vol. 3), DC (Ndola) to PC, 7/9/1935.

122. NAZ, Sec/Nat 312 (vol. 5), G. R. Phillips to CS, 27/3/1936.

123. NAZ, Sec/Nat 312 (vol. 5), PC to CS, 19/5/1937.

124. NAZ, Sec/Nat 312 (vol. 7), DC (Mumbwa) to PC Southern Province, 19/9/1944.

7. SPIRITUAL POLITY AND ITS ENEMIES

1. NAZ, Sec/Nat 312 (vol. 5), *Bulawayo Chronicle*, "Right About-Face," 22/4/1936.

2. NAZ, ZA 1/10 (1919–1926), Ass't. Mag. (Fife), 31/3/1922.

3. NAZ, Sec/Nat 312 (vol. 1), Tour Report (Isoka), 27/5/1932.

4. NAZ, Sec/Nat 312 (vol. 1), Annual Report (Northern Province, Mweru-Luapula-Kawambwa), 14–31/12/1932; (vol. 7), PC (Serenje) to CS, 14/7/1943.

5. NAZ, Sec/Nat 312 (vol. 8), Gondwe to DC (Namwala), 29/6/1946, emphasis in original.

6. NAZ, Sec/Nat 312 (vol. 6), A. E. Muwamba to T. F. Sandford, 31/8/1940; Sec/Nat 312 (vol. 7), extract from Central Province Newsletter, 11/2/1941.

7. NAZ, ZA 1/10 (vol. 7), extract from Central Province Newsletter, 11/12/1949, extract from Hansard, 16/7/1941.

8. NAZ, Sec/Nat 312 (vol. 7), PC (Southern Province) to Acting CS, 14/7/1944.

9. NAZ, Sec/Nat 312 (vol. 1), Tour Report No. 1, Mongu, 1932.

10. NAZ, Sec/Nat 312 (vol. 8), PC (Southern Province) to CS, 17/9/1946.

11. NAZ, Sec/Nat 312 (vol. 8), Gondwe to DC (Namwala), 29/6/1946.

12. NAZ, KSU 1/10, Barnes to Phillips, 23/10/1938.

13. NAZ, Sec/Nat 312 (vol. 9), DC (Chinsali) to DC (Kasama), 23/2/1948.

14. NAZ, KSU 1/10, DC (Mporokoso) to PC (Northern Province), 2/11/1945.

15. NAZ, ZA 1/10, Statement of D. Bulaya to CID (Broken Hill), 2/3/1925.

16. Sholto J. Cross, "The Watchtower Movement in South Central Africa, 1908–1945," Ph.D. diss., Oxford University, 1973, p. 208; NAZ, Sec/Nat 312 (vol. 4), Report on Native Opinion (Eastern Province), 8/1940.

17. Cross, "Watchtower Movement," pp. 280–281. I am indebted to John Higginson for the information that this settlement still existed as late as 1976.

18. Norman Long, "Religion and Socio-Economic Action among the Serenje-Lala of Zambia," in C. G. Baeta, ed., *Christianity in Tropical Africa*, London, 1968; A. G. Blood, *The History of the Universities Mission to Central Africa*, 3 vols., London, 1957, 3:406–407.

19. NAZ, Sec/Nat 312 (vol. 7), Northern Province Newsletter, 13/1/1940.

20. NAZ, Sec/Nat 312 (vol. 5), DC (Senanga) to PC (Mongu), 5/8/1936.

21. NAZ, Sec/Nat 312 (vol. 5), Atty. Gen., Minute, 8/1936.

22. NAZ, KSU 1/10, "Complaints of Jehovah's Witnesses by Chief Mporokoso," 13/3/1946; PC (Northern Province) to L. V. Phillips, 5/11/1938.

23. NAZ, Sec/Nat 312 (vol. 3), DC (Mongu-Lealui) to PC (Mongu), 25/8/1935.

24. NAZ, Sec/Nat 312 (vol. 7), Public Opinion (Barotseland), 5/1941. Senanga was part of Barotseland, but the revolt there affected the Lovales, a tributary people living under the overlordship of the Lozis. The resistance to the sale of war bonds was not limited to this group or even to the Watchtower.

25. NAZ, Sec/Nat 312 (vol. 7), Mulendema to DC (Luangwa), 2/8/1942.

26. NAZ, Sec/Nat 312 (vol. 7), DC (Mwinilunga) to OIC (Kaonde-Lunda Province), 1940.

27. NAZ, Sec/Nat 312 (vol. 7), Tour Report No. 9 (Kaonde-Lunda Province), 1940.

28. NAZ, Sec/Nat 312 (vol. 2), Tour Report No. 1 (Ndola District), 1935.

29. NAZ, Sec/Nat 312 (vol. 5), Meeting of Kasempa Chiefs, 8/1937.

30. NAZ, Sec/Nat 312 (vol. 3), DC (Livingstone) to CS, 10/9/1935; also (vol. 2), Tour Report No. 3 (Mumbwa), 1934.

31. See James M. Ault, "Making 'Modern' Marriage 'Traditional,' " *Theory and Society* 12 (1983).

32. Robert I. Rotberg, *The Rise of Nationalism in Central Africa: The Making of Malawi and Zambia, 1873–1964*, Cambridge, Mass., 1965, pp. 130, 132.

33. See the vivid description of the empire's portable fanfare by Lewis

H. Gann and Peter Duignan, *The Rulers of British Africa, 1870–1914*, Palo Alto, Calif., 1978, p. 223.

34. NAZ, Sec/Nat 312 (vol. 5), Meeting of Kasempa Chiefs, 8/1937.

35. NAZ, Sec/Nat 312 (vol. 5), PC (Northern Province) to CS, 8/12/1936 and DC to PC (Northern Province), 23/11/1936.

36. James Ault has reported, based on research in the administrative files of Barotseland, that officials speak of "acceptable levels" of tax exemption. It appears that tax exemption evolved into a significant form of political patronage distributable by chiefs (personal communication, March, 1983).

37. NAZ, ZA 1/10 (3290), Acting Mag. (J. Moffat Thompson) to SNA, 5/2/1920.

38. Griffith Quick, "Some Aspects of the African Watchtower Movement in Northern Rhodesia," *International Review of Missions* 29 (1940), 220.

39. NAZ, Sec/Nat 312 (vol. 5), Case Record No. 28, PC (Central Province) to CS, 9/6/1936 and de Jaeger to Commissioner of Police, 1/7/1936.

40. NAZ, Sec/Nat 312 (vol. 3), DC (Mongu-Lealui) to PC, 25/8/1935.

41. New forms of marriage arose in adaptation to the new conditions. See Margaret Read, "Migrant Labor in Africa and its Effect on Tribal Life," *International Labour Review* 45 (June 1942), 20; and idem, "People, Land and Livelihood: The Social Ecology of Three Malawi Villages," unpublished typescript, n.d., pp. 52–55.

42. Leo Marquard, "The Problem of Government," in J. Merle Davis, ed., *Modern Industry and the African*, London, 1933, p. 239.

43. Michael Burawoy, "The Color of Class on the Copper Mines: From African Advancement to Zambianization," Lusaka, University of Zambia, 1972, pp. 14–15; Hortense Powdermaker, *Copper Town: Changing Africa*, New York, 1962, pp. 112, 153.

44. NAZ, Sec/Nat 312 (vol. 4), Tour Report (Ft. Jameson), 12/1940.

45. NAZ, Sec/Nat 312 (vol. 7), DC (Mumbwa) to PC (Southern Province), 13/2/1941.

46. NAZ, Sec/Nat 312 (vol. 4), Tour Report (Ft. Jameson), 12/1940.

47. NAZ, Sec/Nat 312 (vol. 4), Report on Public Opinion, PC (Eastern Province), 8/1940.

48. NAZ, Sec/Nat 312 (vol. 7), Public Opinion (Barotseland), 5/1941.

49. NAZ, Sec/Nat 312 (vol. 7), Minute CGS to Acting CS, 28/9/1942.

50. NAZ, Sec/Nat 312 (vol. 5), Note to Executive Council, 4/4/1941.

51. NAZ, Sec/Nat 312 (vol. 6), extracts from letters to the Hon. T. F. Sandford, from Alex Muwamba, 3/10/1940.

52. NAZ, Sec/Nat 312 (vol. 9), Note for Executive Council re. Sect. 43 of Penal Code, n.d.

53. NAZ, Sec/Nat 312 (vol. 7), Acting Gov. (Northern Rhodesia) to Secretary of State for the Colonies, 28/4/1941.

54. NAZ, Sec/Nat 312 (vol. 6), Central Province Tour Report No. 3, 1940.

55. NAZ, Sec/Nat 312 (vol. 7), Tour Report by SNA (Copperbelt), 7/ 1942.

56. NAZ, Sec/Nat 312 (vol. 6), A. Muwamba to T. F. Sandford, 31/8/ 1940. In connection with this, a particularly offensive rumor attributed to the Watchtower after the war claimed that the territory would be ceded to the Americans for payment of war debts (see NAZ, Sec/Nat 312 [vol. 9], Report by Labour Officer, Lusaka, 17/12/1947).

57. NAZ, Sec/Nat 312 (vol. 8), Acting PC to CS, 26/3/1946.

58. NAZ, Sec/Nat 312 (vol. 8), Gov. (Northern Rhodesia) to Gov. (Belgian Congo), 21/5/1948.

59. NAZ, Sec/Nat 312 (vol. 1), Tour Report (Ft. Jameson), 19/7/1932.

60. NAZ, ZA 7/1/16/2, Annual Report (Western Province, Mkushi District), 1933.

61. NAZ, Sec/Nat 312 (vol. 1), Tour Report No. 3, Lusaka, 1932.

62. NAZ, Sec/Nat 312 (vol. 2), Ndola Tour Report No. 1, 1935.

63. NAZ, ZA 1/10 (1926–1927), Patrol Report (Ft. Jameson), 10/6/1926.

64. NAZ, Sec/Nat 312 (vol. 7), CS to L. V. Phillips, 28/7/1942.

65. NAZ, Sec/Nat 312 (vol. 7), DC (Mumbwa) to PC, 8/7/1944.

66. NAZ, ZA 1/10, Tour Report Chisamba Farms, 12/3/1935.

67. NAZ, Sec/Nat 312 (vol. 1), Tour Report (Ft. Jameson), 1932.

68. NAZ, Sec/Nat 312 (vol. 3), DC (Mongu-Lealui) to PC, 25/8/1935.

69. NAZ, Sec/Nat 312 (vol. 7), GSI HQ E. Afr., "Weekly Intelligence Review No. 14," week ending 20/10/1944.

70. NAZ, ZA 1/10, Tour Report Chisamba Farms, 12/3/1935.

71. Terence O. Ranger, "Mucape and the Study of Witchcraft Eradication," presented at the Conference on the History of Central African Religions, Lusaka, 1973, p. 37.

72. NAZ, ZA 7/1/16/2, Annual Report (Western Province, Mwinilunga District), 1933.

73. NAZ, Sec/Nat 312 (vol. 2), Case No. 17, before J. Gordon Reade, Namwala, 1935.

74. NAZ, HM/38, Brelsford Papers, W. V. Brelsford, "Chimbuku," unpublished typescript, n.d. (ca. 1950).

75. Terence O. Ranger, *Revolt in Southern Rhodesia, 1896–1897: A Study in African Resistance*, Evanston, Ill., 1967.

76. John Iliffe and Gilbert Gwassa, "Kinjikitile and the Ideology of Maji Maji," in Terence O. Ranger and I. N. Kimambo, eds., *The Historical Study of African Religion*, Berkeley, Calif., 1972, esp. pp. 202–206. But cf. the somewhat contrasting views of Michael Adas, *Prophets of Rebellion: Millenarian Protest Movements against the European Colonial Order*, Chapel Hill, N.C., 1979.

77. Iliffe and Gwassa, "Kinjikitile," p. 205.

78. I. N. Kimambo and C. K. Omari, "The Development of Religious Thought and Centers among the Pare," in Ranger and Kimambo, eds., *Historical Study of African Religion*, pp. 118–119. A similar step, in the

creation of the Zulu state, has been brilliantly described by Eugene V. Walter, *Terror and Resistance: A Study of Political Violence*, New York, 1972.

79. NAZ, Sec/Nat 312 (vol. 1), "Ex-local men" to DC (Mazabuka), 10/8/1931.

80. Mary Douglas, "Techniques of Sorcery Control," in John Middleton and E. H. Winter, eds., *Witchcraft and Sorcery in East Africa*, New York, 1964; Matthew Schoffeleers, "The History and Political Role of the Mbona Cult among the Manganja," Ranger and Weller, eds., *Themes in Christian History of Central Africa*; David J. Parkin, "Medicines and Men of Influence," *Man* 3 (1968); George Park, "Divination and Its Social Contexts," in John Middleton, ed., *Magic, Witchcraft, and Curing*, New York, 1967.

81. George Park has illustrated the formal and substantive ingredients in the production of such consensus in his paper, "Divination and its Social Contexts." Matthew Schoffeleers, "The History and Political Role of the Mbona Cult among the Manganja," in Ranger and Weller, eds., *Themes in Christian History of Central Africa*, quotes an oral tradition to the effect that a revival movement designed to overthrow a leader accused of misusing the poison ordeal was the origin of the Kaphwiti chiefdom in Malawi.

82. NAZ, Sec/Nat 312 (vol. 3), Report on Race Relations, n.d. (ca. 1935).

83. Meyer Fortes and E. E. Evans-Pritchard, eds., *African Political Systems*, London, 1958, p. 17.

84. NAZ, Brelsford Papers, "Chimbuku," n.d. (ca. 1950?).

85. NAZ, Sec/Nat 312 (vol. 8), Gondwe to DC (Namwala), 29/6/1946.

86. Eric J. Hobsbawm, *Primitive Rebels: Studies in Archaic Forms of Social Movement in the Nineteenth and Twentieth Centuries*, New York, 1959, p. 58.

87. Robert C. Tucker, ed., *The Marx-Engels Reader*, Princeton, 1972, p. 10.

88. Eric J. Hobsbawm, *The Age of Revolution, 1789–1848*, New York, 1962, p. 259.

CONCLUSION

1. Bryan Wilson, *Magic and the Millennium: A Sociological Study of Religious Movements among Tribal and Third-World Peoples*, London, 1973, p. 500.

2. Frederick John Dealtry Lugard, *The Dual Mandate in British Tropical Africa*, London, 5th ed., 1965, p. 198, on which point he cites several "students of history and sociology."

3. Margery Perham, *The Colonial Reckoning: The End of Imperial Rule in Africa in the Light of British Experience*, New York, 1962, p. 141.

4. Meyer Fortes and E. E. Evans-Pritchard, eds., *African Political Systems*, London, 1958, pp. 17, 18.

5. In her introduction to the 1965 edition of Lugard's *Dual Mandate*, p. xlvii, she says: "What [Lugard] did not foresee was that a small minority of Westernized Africans would appeal successfully to the masses and lead them to independence across the ruins of chieftainship. But then most colonial experts failed to foresee this right up to the eve of the event."

6. A.H.M. Kirk-Greene, "The Thin White Line: The Size of the British Colonial Service in Africa," *African Affairs: Journal of the Royal African Society* 79 (Jan. 1980), 43–44.

7. Margery Perham, "A Re-Statement of Indirect Rule," *Africa* 7 (1943), 323.

8. Perham, *Colonial Reckoning*, p. 145.

9. T. O. Beidelman, *Colonial Evangelism: A Socio-historical Study of an East African Mission at the Grassroots*, Bloomington, Ind., 1982, p. 2.

10. Perham, *Colonial Reckoning*, p. 143.

11. Lucy P. Mair, "Independent Religious Movements in Three Continents," in John Middleton and E. H. Winter, eds., *Gods and Rituals*, London, 1968, p. 315.

12. Fortes and Evans-Pritchard, *African Political Systems*, p. 18.

13. Max Gluckman, *Custom and Conflict in Africa*, New York, 1964; and idem, *Order and Conflict in Tribal Africa*, New York, 1963.

INDEX

administration, size of, 33-34
Aggrey, James Kwegyir, 11, 12, 194
Alien Natives Ordinance, 200
America: images of, 10-12, 165, 204
Anabaptists, 21, 123, 147
anthropology: and indirect rule, 61, 64-66
Antinomianism, 71, 106-107, 118, 237, 246, 261

Bamucapi. *See* mucapi
Banda, Yohane Afwenge, 134
Bemba people, 37-38, 64-67 *passim*, 79-84 *passim*, 88, 134, 232, 242
Berlin Conference (1884-85), 26
Bisa people, 72
Booth, Joseph, 102, 104, 105, 125
Branch, Thomas, 104
Brelsford, W. V., 259-60, 266-67
British South Africa Company (BSAC), 25, 36, 165, 176, 193; and missions, 43, 44, 45, 101, 130, 161; political methods of, 37-38, 66, 113, 175; and Watchtower movement, 128, 154, 161
Bulawayo *Chronicle*, 238

Cargo cults, 17-18
censorship: and the Watchtower movement, 215-18, 252-53
Central Africa: conquest of, 25-32
Cewa people, 28
charisma, 16, 17, 129, 156, 159; and healing, 4; and politics, 129; and prophesying, 6-7; and talking in tongues, 4; and Watchtower movement, 117, 128, 129, 154-58; Weberian theory of, 156
chiefs. *See* customary rulers
Chilembwe, John, 104-105, 125-26
Chisholm, James, 150; on amalgama-

tion of villages, 37; on effects of World War I, 134, 137, 213-14; on mucapi movement, 80, 85, 87; on Watchtower movement, 160-61
Christian Native Marriage Ordinance, 110
Church of Scotland, 27. *See also* Livingstonia mission
Citimukulu (paramount chief of Bemba people), 134
Collective Punishment Ordinance, 172, 228
color bar, 48-50
Copperbelt: Watchtower movement on, 70; strike of 1935, 232, 265
Cross Sholto, 16, 132, 174
culture, defined, 59
customary rulers: accommodation with Watchtower movement, 179-85, 191, 207, 254, 256-59; and colonial economy, 72, 78-79; key role of in indirect rule, 30-32, 36-40; legitimacy of, 63-68, 157, 259, 260-64; loss of authority, 152-54, 157, 174-77, 259, 270, 274; and mucapi movement, 82-84, 87-88; opposition to Watchtower movement, 204, 218-24, 228, 240-48; undermined by Watchtower adherents, 69-70, 139-41, 145, 149-52, 160-61, 170, 253; and World War I, 136-37

Dawson, William, 226-27
democracy: and colonial state, 247, 275
Domingo, Charles, 125
Draper, Charles, 141-43, 144, 149-55 *passim*, 199
Dupont, Joseph, 26, 66
Durkheim, Emile, 196-97, 237
Dutch Reformed Church mission, 164,

Missionaries.

writing tools of colonialism.

3 ~~two~~ ways in which they are viewed -pg 15

cultural - grasp of vision of a new world

pre political.

fantastical.